Uncertainty, Risk and Information

An Economic Analysis

Kindle Direct Publishing; 1st edition (December 2019)

Copyright © 2019 Giacomo Bonanno
All rights reserved.

ISBN: 9781708284817

Giacomo Bonanno is Professor of Economics at the
University of California, Davis
http://faculty.econ.ucdavis.edu/faculty/bonanno/

Preface

In the last three years I wrote three open access textbooks: one on *Game Theory* (http://faculty.econ.ucdavis.edu/faculty/bonanno/GT_Book.html), one on *Decision Making* (http://faculty.econ.ucdavis.edu/faculty/bonanno/DM_Book.html) and the third on *The Economics of Uncertainty and Insurance* (http://faculty.econ.ucdavis.edu/faculty/bonanno/EUI_Book.html). This book is an extension of the last one: it incorporates it and augments it with the addition of several new chapters on risk sharing, asymmetric information, adverse selection, signaling and moral hazard. It provides a comprehensive introduction to the analysis of economic decisions under uncertainty and to the role of asymmetric information in contractual relationships. I have been teaching an upper-division undergraduate class on this topic at the University of California, Davis for 25 years and was not able to find a suitable textbook. Hopefully this book will fill this gap.

I intend to add, some time in the future, a further collection of exercises with detailed solutions. Details will appear on my web page.

I am very grateful to Elise Tidrick for teaching me how to use spacing and formatting in a (perhaps unconventional) way that makes it easier for the reader to learn the material.

I would like to thank Mathias Legrand for making the latex template used for this book available for free (the template was downloaded from http://www.latextemplates.com/template/the-legrand-orange-book).

Contents

1 Introduction ... 9

Insurance

2 Insurance: basic notions ... 15

2.1	**Uncertainty and lotteries**	**15**
2.2	**Money lotteries and attitudes to risk**	**16**
2.3	**Certainty equivalent and the risk premium**	**19**
2.4	**Insurance: basic concepts**	**21**
2.5	**Isoprofit lines**	**25**
2.6	**Profitable insurance requires risk aversion**	**30**
2.6.1	Insuring a risk-neutral individual	30
2.6.2	Insuring a risk-averse individual	31
2.6.3	The profit-maximizing contract for a monopolist	32
2.6.4	Perfectly competitive industry with free entry	34
2.7	**Exercises**	**36**
2.7.1	Exercises for Section 2.2: Money lotteries and attitudes to risk	36
2.7.2	Exercises for Section 2.3: Certainty equivalent and risk premium	38
2.7.3	Exercises for Section 2.4: Insurance: basic concepts	39
2.7.4	Exercises for Section 2.5: Isoprofit lines	40
2.7.5	Exercises for Section 2.6: Profitable insurance requires risk aversion	42
2.8	**Solutions to Exercises**	**42**

3 Expected Utility Theory ... 55
3.1 Expected utility: theorems — 55
3.2 Expected utility: the axioms — 63
3.3 Exercises — 71
3.3.1 Exercises for Section 3.1: Expected utility: theorems ... 71
3.3.2 Exercises for Section 3.2: Expected utility: the axioms ... 73
3.4 Solutions to Exercises — 74

4 Money lotteries revisited ... 79
4.1 von Neumann Morgenstern preferences over money lotteries — 79
4.1.1 The vNM utility-of-money function of a risk-neutral agent ... 79
4.1.2 Concavity and risk aversion ... 80
4.1.3 Convexity and risk loving ... 83
4.1.4 Mixtures of risk attitudes ... 84
4.1.5 Attitude to risk and the second derivative of the utility function ... 85
4.2 Measures of risk aversion — 86
4.3 Some noteworthy utility functions — 92
4.4 Higher risk — 93
4.4.1 First-order stochastic dominance ... 94
4.4.2 Mean preserving spread and second-order stochastic dominance ... 95
4.5 Exercises — 99
4.5.1 Exercises for Section 4.1: vNM preferences over money lotteries ... 99
4.5.2 Exercises for Section 4.2: Measures of risk aversion ... 100
4.5.3 Exercises for Section 4.3: Some noteworthy utility functions ... 102
4.5.4 Exercises for Section 4.4: Higher risk ... 103
4.6 Solutions to Exercises — 104

5 Insurance: Part 2 ... 113
5.1 Binary lotteries and indifference curves — 113
5.1.1 Case 1: risk neutrality ... 114
5.1.2 Case 2: risk aversion ... 115
5.1.3 Case 3: risk love ... 117
5.1.4 The slope of an indifference curve ... 118
5.2 Back to insurance — 121
5.2.1 The profit-maximizing contract for a monopolist ... 124
5.2.2 Perfectly competitive industry with free entry ... 125
5.3 Choosing from a menu of contracts — 127
5.3.1 Choosing from a finite menu ... 127
5.3.2 Choosing from a continuum of options ... 128

5.4	**Mutual insurance**	**138**
5.5	**Exercises**	**140**
5.5.1	Exercises for Section 5.1: Binary lotteries and indifference curves	140
5.5.2	Exercises for Section 5.2: Back to insurance	141
5.5.3	Exercises for Section 5.3: Choosing from a menu of contracts	143
5.5.4	Exercises for Section 5.4: Mutual insurance	146
5.6	**Solutions to Exercises**	**147**

II Risk Sharing

6 Risk Sharing and Efficiency 165

6.1	**Sharing an uncertain surplus**	**165**
6.2	**The Edgeworth box**	**167**
6.3	**Points of tangency**	**175**
6.3.1	Risk averse Principal and risk neutral Agent	175
6.3.2	Risk neutral Principal and risk averse Agent	176
6.3.3	A general principle	178
6.3.4	Both parties risk averse	178
6.3.5	Both parties risk neutral	181
6.3.6	Pareto efficiency for contracts in the interior of the Edgeworth box	182
6.4	**Pareto efficient contracts on the sides of the Edgeworth box**	**183**
6.4.1	Risk averse Principal and risk neutral Agent	183
6.4.2	Risk neutral Principal and risk averse Agent	184
6.4.3	Both parties risk averse	186
6.5	**The Edgeworth box when the parties have positive initial wealth**	**187**
6.6	**More than two outcomes**	**193**
6.6.1	Risk-neutral Principal and risk-averse Agent	194
6.6.2	Risk-averse Principal and risk-neutral Agent	197
6.6.3	Both parties risk neutral	197
6.6.4	Both parties risk averse	198
6.7	**Exercises**	**199**
6.7.1	Exercises for Section 6.1: Sharing an uncertain surplus	199
6.7.2	Exercises for Section 6.2: The Edgeworth box	199
6.7.3	Exercises for Section 6.3: Points of tangency	201
6.7.4	Exercises for Section 6.4: Pareto efficient contracts on the sides of the Edgeworth box	204
6.7.5	Exercises for Section 6.5: The Edgeworth box when the parties have positive initial wealth	206
6.7.6	Exercises for Section 6.6: More than two outcomes	207
6.8	**Solutions to Exercises**	**209**

III Asymmetric Information: Adverse Selection

7 Adverse Selection — 227

7.1 Adverse selection or hidden type — 227
7.2 Conditional probability and belief updating — 229
7.2.1 Conditional probability — 230
7.2.2 Belief updating — 231
7.3 The market for used cars — 234
7.3.1 Possible remedies — 241
7.3.2 Further remarks — 241
7.4 Exercises — 243
7.4.1 Exercises for Section 7.2.2: Conditional probability and belief updating — 243
7.4.2 Exercises for Section 7.3: The market for used cars — 245
7.5 Solutions to Exercises — 247

8 Adverse Selection in Insurance — 253

8.1 Adverse selection in insurance markets — 253
8.2 Two types of customers — 254
8.2.1 The contracts offered by a monopolist who can tell individuals apart — 256
8.3 The monopolist under asymmetric information — 257
8.3.1 The monopolist's profit under Option 1 — 258
8.3.2 The monopolist's profit under Option 2 — 259
8.3.3 The monopolist's profit under Option 3 — 263
8.3.4 Option 2 revisited — 274
8.4 A perfectly competitive insurance industry — 276
8.5 Exercises — 283
8.5.1 Exercises for Section 8.2: Two types of customers — 283
8.5.2 Exercises for Section 8.3: The monopolist under asymmetric information — 284
8.5.3 Exercises for Section 8.4: A perfectly competitive insurance industry — 286
8.6 Solutions to Exercises — 287

IV Asymmetric Information: Signaling

9 Signaling — 297

9.1 Earnings and education — 297
9.2 Signaling in the job market — 299
9.2.1 Signaling equilibrium — 299
9.2.2 Pareto inefficiency — 301
9.2.3 Alternative interpretation of a signaling equilibrium — 302

9.3	**Indices versus signals**	**305**
9.4	**More than two types**	**309**
9.5	**A more general analysis**	**311**
9.6	**Signaling in other markets**	**322**
9.6.1	Market for used cars	322
9.6.2	Advertising as a signal of quality	323
9.6.3	Other markets	324
9.7	**Exercises**	**325**
9.7.1	Exercises for Section 9.2: Signaling in the job market	325
9.7.2	Exercises for Section 9.3: Indices versus signals	328
9.7.3	Exercises for Section 9.4: More than two types	329
9.7.4	Exercises for Section 9.5: A more general analysis	330
9.7.5	Exercises for Section 9.6: Signaling in other markets	330
9.8	**Solutions to Exercises**	**331**

V Moral Hazard

10 Moral Hazard in Insurance ... 343

10.1	**Moral hazard or hidden action**	**343**
10.2	**Moral hazard and insurance**	**344**
10.2.1	Two levels of unobserved effort	345
10.2.2	The reservation utility locus	348
10.2.3	The profit-maximizing contract for a monopolist	354
10.3	**Exercises**	**359**
10.3.1	Exercises for Section 10.2.1: Two levels of unobserved effort	359
10.3.2	Exercises for Section 10.2.2: The reservation utility locus	361
10.3.3	Exercises for Section 10.2.3: The profit-maximizing contract	362
10.4	**Solutions to Exercises**	**363**

11 Moral Hazard in Principal-Agent ... 369

11.1	**Moral hazard in Principal-Agent relationships**	**369**
11.2	**Risk sharing under moral hazard**	**370**
11.3	**The case with two outcomes and two levels of effort**	**374**
11.4	**The case with more than two outcomes**	**388**
11.5	**Exercises**	**393**
11.5.1	Exercises for Section 11.2: Risk sharing under moral hazard	393
11.5.2	Exercises for Section 11.3: Two outcomes and two levels of effort	394
11.5.3	Exercises for Section 11.4: The case with more than two outcomes	398
11.6	**Solutions to Exercises**	**400**

12	Glossary	409
	Index	413

1. Introduction

This book offers an introduction to the economic analysis of uncertainty and information.

Life is made up of a never-ending sequence of decisions. Many decisions – such as what to watch on television or what to eat for breakfast – do not have major consequences. Other decisions – such as whether or not to invest all of one's savings in the purchase of a house, or whether to purchase earthquake insurance – can have a significant impact on one's life. We will concern ourselves with decisions that potentially have a considerable impact on the wealth of the individual in question.

Most of the time the outcome of a decision is influenced by external factors that are outside the decision maker's control, such as the side effects of a new drug, or the future price of real estate, or the occurrence of a natural phenomenon (such as a flood, or a fire, or an earthquake). While one is typically aware of the existence of such external factors, as the saying goes "It is difficult to make predictions, especially about the future".[1] Most decisions are shrouded in uncertainty and this book is about how uncertainty affects the actions and decisions of economic agents.

We begin by examining, in **Chapter 2**, what explains the existence and profitability of insurance markets. For this we simply appeal to the definition of risk aversion, without the need for the full power of expected utility theory.

Chapter 3 develops the Theory of Expected Utility, which is central to the rest of the book.

In **Chapter 4** we use the theory of expected utility to re-examine the notion of attitude to risk (risk aversion, risk neutrality and risk love), discuss how to measure the degree of risk aversion of an individual and develop a test for determining when, of two alternative risky prospects, one can unambiguously be labeled as being more risky than the other.

---

[1] This saying is often attributed to the physicist Niels Bohr, but apparently it is an old Danish proverb.

With the help of expected utility theory, in **Chapter 5** we study the demand side of insurance markets. We then put together the analysis of the supply side of insurance, developed in Chapter 2, with the analysis of the demand side, to determine the equilibrium of an insurance industry under two opposite scenarios: the case where the industry is a monopoly and the case where there is perfect competition with free entry.

In **Chapter 6** we address the issue of efficient risk sharing. We consider the case of an individual, referred to as "the Principal", who is contemplating hiring another individual, referred to as "the Agent", to perform a task, whose outcome is uncertain (because it is affected by external factors). We consider all the possible forms of payment to the Agent (e.g. a fixed wage or a payment contingent on the outcome) and ask what contracts are Pareto efficient, in the sense that there is no other contract that they both prefer. We study how Pareto efficiency relates to the optimal way of allocating risk between the two parties to the contract.

In Chapters 7-9 we turn to the issue of asymmetric information. It is often the case that one of the two parties to a contract has more information than the other party about aspects of the transaction that are relevant to both parties. For example, the seller of a used car has knowledge about the quality of the car that the potential buyer cannot easily acquire before the purchase, or a job applicant knows more about herself than the potential employer can find out from an interview. Asymmetric information can manifest itself in different forms. One type of asymmetric information gives rise to the phenomenon of "adverse selection", which is studied in Chapters 7 and 8. **Chapter 7** deals with the general phenomenon of adverse selection, with particular focus on the market for used durable goods, while **Chapter 8** is devoted to the analysis of adverse selection in insurance markets. This is the situation where there are different types of individuals, with different propensities to incur losses, and – while each individual knows his or her own type – the insurance company does not. We study how the asymmetry of information affects the decisions of the suppliers of insurance and re-examine the conditions for an equilibrium in the two types of industry structure examined in Chapter 5, namely monopoly and perfect competition.

In **Chapter 9** we study another phenomenon that arises in the context of asymmetric information, namely the phenomenon of "signaling". Signaling refers to the attempt by the informed party to credibly convey information to the uninformed party. When the latter is uncertain about the characteristics, or "type", of individual he/she is about to sign a contract with, he/she might offer contractual terms that are unappealing to some individuals, thereby creating an incentive for the "better" types to engage in costly activities that allow them to "separate themselves" from the worse types and to credibly convey information about themselves.

While the asymmetric information studied in Chapters 7-9 is also referred to as "hidden type", the informational asymmetry studied in Chapters 10 and 11 is called "hidden action" or "moral hazard". It refers to situations where what cannot be observed by one of the two parties to a contract is not the type of the other party, but his/her behavior. When such behavior has an effect on the outcome, it becomes important for the uninformed party to design the contract in such a way that it creates an incentive for the other party to act in a "desirable" way. For example, in the case of insurance, the probability that the insured individual will face a loss – and thus apply for a reimbursement from the insurance company – may be affected by the behavior of the individual, in particular by the effort and care exerted in loss prevention. In such a situation the insurance company might want to offer only insurance contracts that will create an incentive for the insured to exert appropriate effort towards reducing the probability of loss. **Chapter 10** deals with the phenomenon of moral hazard in insurance, while **Chapter 11** revisits the Principal-Agent relationships studied in Chapter 6 and analyses the effect of moral hazard in that context.

Whenever possible, throughout the book we have tried to illustrate the relevant concepts graphically in two-dimensional diagrams. The book is richly illustrated with approximately 150 figures and tables.

At the end of each section of each chapter the reader is invited to test his/her understanding of the concepts introduced in that section by attempting several exercises. In order not to break the flow of the exposition, the exercises are collected in a section at the end of the chapter. Complete and detailed answers for each exercise are given in the last section of each chapter. In total, the book contains more than 150 fully solved exercises. Attempting to solve the exercises is an integral part of learning the material covered in this book.

The book was written in a way that should be accessible to anyone with minimum knowledge of calculus, in particular the ability to calculate the (partial) derivative of a function of one or two variables.

This book does not necessarily follow conventional formatting standards. Rather, the intention was to break each argument into clearly outlined steps, highlighted by appropriate spacing.

Insurance

2 Insurance: basic notions 15
- 2.1 Uncertainty and lotteries
- 2.2 Money lotteries and attitudes to risk
- 2.3 Certainty equivalent and the risk premium
- 2.4 Insurance: basic concepts
- 2.5 Isoprofit lines
- 2.6 Profitable insurance requires risk aversion
- 2.7 Exercises
- 2.8 Solutions to Exercises

3 Expected Utility Theory 55
- 3.1 Expected utility: theorems
- 3.2 Expected utility: the axioms
- 3.3 Exercises
- 3.4 Solutions to Exercises

4 Money lotteries revisited 79
- 4.1 von Neumann Morgenstern preferences over money lotteries
- 4.2 Measures of risk aversion
- 4.3 Some noteworthy utility functions
- 4.4 Higher risk
- 4.5 Exercises
- 4.6 Solutions to Exercises

5 Insurance: Part 2 113
- 5.1 Binary lotteries and indifference curves
- 5.2 Back to insurance
- 5.3 Choosing from a menu of contracts
- 5.4 Mutual insurance
- 5.5 Exercises
- 5.6 Solutions to Exercises

2. Insurance: basic notions

2.1 Uncertainty and lotteries

Most of the important decisions that we make in life are made difficult by the presence of uncertainty: the final outcome is influenced by external factors that we cannot control and we cannot predict with certainty. Because of such external factors, any given decision will typically be associated with different outcomes, depending on what "state of the world" will actually occur. If the decision-maker is able to assign probabilities to these external factors – and thus to the associated outcomes – then one can represent the uncertainty that the decision maker faces as a list of possible outcomes, each with a corresponding probability. We call such lists *lotteries*.

For example, suppose that Ann and Bob are planning their wedding reception. They have a large number of guests and face the choice between two venues: a spacious outdoor area where the guests will be able to roam around or a small indoor area where the guests will feel rather crammed. Ann and Bob want their reception to be a success and their guests to feel comfortable. It seems that the large outdoor area is a better choice; however, there is also an external factor that needs to be taken into account, namely the weather. If it does not rain, then the outdoor area will yield the best outcome (success: denote this outcome by o_1) but if it does rain then the outdoor area will give rise to the worst outcome (failure: denote this outcome by o_3). On the other hand, if Ann and Bob choose the indoor venue, then the corresponding outcome will be a less successful reception but not a failure (call this outcome o_2). Let us denote the possible outcomes as follows:

o_1 : successful reception
o_2 : mediocre reception
o_3 : failed reception.

Clearly they prefer o_1 to o_2 and o_2 to o_3. At the time of deciding which venue to pay for, Ann and Bob do not know what the weather will be like on their wedding day. The most they can do is consult a weather forecast service and obtain probabilistic estimates. Suppose that the forecast service predicts a 30% chance of rain on the day in question. Then we can represent the decision to book the outdoor venue as the following lottery

$$\begin{pmatrix} \text{outcome:} & o_1 & o_3 \\ \text{probability:} & 0.7 & 0.3 \end{pmatrix}$$

On the other hand, the decision to book the indoor venue corresponds to the following degenerate lottery:

$$\begin{pmatrix} \text{outcome:} & o_2 \\ \text{probability:} & 1 \end{pmatrix}$$

Throughout this book we will represent the uncertainty facing a decision-maker in terms of lotteries.[1] This assumes that the decision-maker is always able to assign probabilities to the possible outcomes. We interpret these probabilities either as "objective" probabilities, obtained from relevant past data, or as "subjective" estimates by the individual. For example, an individual who is considering whether or not to insure her bicycle against theft, knows that there are two relevant basic outcomes: either the bicycle will be stolen or it will not be stolen. Furthermore, she can look up data on past bicycle thefts in her area and use the proportion of bicycles that were stolen as an objective estimate of the probability that her bicycle will be stolen; alternatively, she can use a more subjective estimate: for example she might use a lower probability of theft than suggested by the data, because she knows herself to be very conscientious and – unlike other people – to always lock her bicycle when left unattended.

In this chapter we will focus on lotteries where the outcomes are sums of money. More general lotteries will be considered in Chapter 3.

2.2 Money lotteries and attitudes to risk

Definition 2.2.1 A *money lottery* is a probability distribution over a list of outcomes, where each outcome consists of a sum of money. Thus, it is an object of the form
$\begin{pmatrix} \$x_1 & \$x_2 & ... & \$x_n \\ p_1 & p_2 & ... & p_n \end{pmatrix}$ with $0 \leq p_i \leq 1$ for all $i = 1, 2, ..., n$, and $p_1 + p_2 + ... + p_n = 1$.

We assume that the individual in question is able to rank any two money lotteries. For example, if asked to choose between getting $400 for sure, which can be viewed as the degenerate lottery $\begin{pmatrix} \$400 \\ 1 \end{pmatrix}$, and the lottery[2] $\begin{pmatrix} \$900 & \$0 \\ \frac{1}{2} & \frac{1}{2} \end{pmatrix}$, she will be able to tell us if she prefers one lottery to the other or is indifferent between the two. In general, there is no "right answer" to this question, as there is no right answer to the question "do you prefer coffee or tea?": it is a matter of individual taste.

---

[1] For some analysis of decision-making in situations where the individual is *not* able to assign probabilities to the outcomes see my book *Decision Making* (http://faculty.econ.ucdavis.edu/faculty/bonanno/DM_Book.html).

[2] We can think of this lottery as tossing a fair coin and then giving the individual $900 if it comes up Heads and nothing if it comes up Tails.

2.2 Money lotteries and attitudes to risk

Definition 2.2.2 Given a money lottery $L = \begin{pmatrix} \$x_1 & \$x_2 & ... & \$x_n \\ p_1 & p_2 & ... & p_n \end{pmatrix}$, its *expected value* is the number $\mathbb{E}[L] = x_1 p_1 + x_2 p_2 + ... + x_n p_n$.

For example, the expected value of the money lottery

$$\begin{pmatrix} \$600 & \$180 & \$120 & \$30 \\ \frac{1}{12} & \frac{1}{3} & \frac{5}{12} & \frac{1}{6} \end{pmatrix}$$

is $\frac{1}{12}600 + \frac{1}{3}180 + \frac{5}{12}120 + \frac{1}{6}30 = 165$.

Definition 2.2.3 Let L be a non-degenerate money lottery (that is, a money lottery where at least two different outcomes are assigned positive probability)[a] and consider the choice between L and the degenerate lottery

$$\begin{pmatrix} \$\mathbb{E}[L] \\ 1 \end{pmatrix}$$

(that is, the choice between facing the lottery L or getting the expected value of L with certainty).

Then

- An individual who prefers $\$\mathbb{E}[L]$ for certain to L is said to be *risk averse* (relative to L).

- An individual who is indifferent between $\$\mathbb{E}[L]$ for certain and L is said to be *risk neutral* (relative to L).

- An individual who prefers L to $\$\mathbb{E}[L]$ for certain is said to be *risk loving* or *risk seeking* (relative to L).

---
[a] A money lottery $\begin{pmatrix} \$x_1 & \$x_2 & ... & \$x_n \\ p_1 & p_2 & ... & p_n \end{pmatrix}$ is non-degenerate if, for all $i = 1, 2, ..., n$, $p_i < 1$.

Note that, if an individual

(1) is **risk neutral** relative to *every* money lottery,

(2) has transitive preferences[3] over money lotteries and

(3) prefers more money to less,

then we can tell how that individual ranks any two money lotteries.

---
[3] That is, if she considers lottery A to be at least as good as lottery B and she considers lottery B to be at least as good as lottery C then she considers A to be at least as good as C.

For example, how would a risk-neutral individual rank the two lotteries $L_1 = \begin{pmatrix} \$30 & \$45 & \$90 \\ \frac{1}{3} & \frac{5}{9} & \frac{1}{9} \end{pmatrix}$ and $L_2 = \begin{pmatrix} \$5 & \$100 \\ \frac{3}{5} & \frac{2}{5} \end{pmatrix}$? We shall use the symbol $\succ$ to denote strict preference and the symbol $\sim$ to denote indifference.[4] Since $\mathbb{E}[L_1] = 45$ and the individual is risk neutral, $L_1 \sim \$45$; since $\mathbb{E}[L_2] = 43$ and the individual is risk neutral, $\$43 \sim L_2$; since the individual prefers more money to less, $\$45 \succ \$43$:

$$L_1 \sim \$45 \succ \$43 \sim L_2.$$

Thus, by transitivity, $L_1 \succ L_2$ (see Exercises 2.10-2.13).

On the other hand, knowing that an individual is *risk averse* relative to *every* money lottery, has transitive preferences over money lotteries and prefers more money to less, is not sufficient to predict how she will choose between two arbitrary money lotteries. For example, as we will see in Chapter 3, it is possible that one risk-averse individual will prefer $L_3 = \begin{pmatrix} \$28 \\ 1 \end{pmatrix}$ (whose expected value is 28) to $L_4 = \begin{pmatrix} \$10 & \$50 \\ \frac{1}{2} & \frac{1}{2} \end{pmatrix}$ (whose expected value is 30), while another risk-averse individual will prefer L_4 to L_3.

Similarly, knowing that an individual is *risk loving* relative to *every* money lottery, has transitive preferences over money lotteries and prefers more money to less, is not sufficient to predict how she will choose between two arbitrary money lotteries.

> (R) Note that "rationality" does not, and should not, dictate whether an individual should be risk neutral, risk averse or risk loving: an individual's attitude to risk is merely a reflection of that individual's **preferences**. It is a generally accepted principle that *de gustibus non est disputandum* (in matters of taste, there can be no disputes). According to this principle, there is no such thing as an irrational preference and thus there is no such thing as an irrational attitude to risk.
>
> From an empirical point of view, however, most people reveal through their choices (e.g. the decision to buy insurance) that they are risk averse, at least when the stakes are sufficiently high. It is also possible (as we will see in Chapter 4) for an individual to have different attitudes to risk, depending on how high the stakes are (e.g. an individual might display risk aversion, by purchasing home insurance, as well as risk love, by purchasing a lottery ticket).

> Test your understanding of the concepts introduced in this section, by going through the exercises in Section 2.7.1 at the end of this chapter.

---

[4] Thus $A \succ B$ means that the individual prefers A to B and $A \sim B$ means that the individual is indifferent between A and B.

2.3 Certainty equivalent and the risk premium

Given a set of money lotteries $\mathscr{L}$, we will assume that the individual under consideration has well-defined preferences over the elements of $\mathscr{L}$. As before, we shall use the symbol $\succ$ to denote *strict preference* ($L_1 \succ L_2$ means that the individual prefers lottery L_1 to lottery L_2) and the symbol $\sim$ to denote *indifference* ($L_1 \sim L_2$ means that the individual is indifferent between L_1 and L_2, that is, she considers L_1 to be just as good as L_2). Finally, we use the symbol $\succsim$ to signify "at least as good as": $L_1 \succsim L_2$ means that the individual considers L_1 to be at least as good as L_2, that is, either she prefers L_1 to L_2 or she is indifferent between L_1 and L_2. The following table summarizes the notation:

notation:	interpretation:
$L_1 \succ L_2$	the individual prefers L_1 to L_2
$L_1 \sim L_2$	the individual is indifferent between L_1 and L_2
$L_1 \succsim L_2$	the individual considers L_1 to be at least as good as L_2, that is, either $L_1 \succ L_2$ or $L_1 \sim L_2$.

We shall assume that the individual is able to rank any two lotteries (her preferences are complete) and her ranking is transitive:

- (completeness) for every L_1 and L_2, either $L_1 \succsim L_2$ or $L_2 \succsim L_1$ or both,

- (transitivity) if $L_1 \succsim L_2$ and $L_2 \succsim L_3$ then $L_1 \succsim L_3$.[5]

We shall also assume throughout that the individual prefers more money to less, that is,

$$\begin{pmatrix} \$x \\ 1 \end{pmatrix} \succ \begin{pmatrix} \$y \\ 1 \end{pmatrix} \text{ if and only if } x > y. \tag{2.1}$$

Suppose that, for every money lottery L there is a sum of money, denoted by C_L, that the individual considers to be just as good as the lottery L; then we call C_L the *certainty equivalent of lottery L* for that individual.

Definition 2.3.1 The *certainty equivalent of a money lottery L* is that sum of money C_L such that

$$L = \begin{pmatrix} \$x_1 & \dots & \$x_n \\ p_1 & \dots & p_n \end{pmatrix} \sim \begin{pmatrix} \$C_L \\ 1 \end{pmatrix}$$

Typically, the certainty equivalent of a given money lottery will be different for different individuals. However, all risk-neutral individuals will share the same certainty equivalent; in fact, it follows from the definition of risk neutrality (Definition 2.2.3) that

- for a **risk-neutral** individual, the certainty equivalent of a money lottery L coincides with the expected value of L:

$$C_L = \mathbb{E}[L].$$

---

[5] In Exercises 2.10-2.13 the reader is asked to prove that transitivity of the "at least as good" relation implies transitivity of strict preference and of indifference.

On the other hand, for a risk-averse individual (who, furthermore, prefers more money to less and whose preferences are complete and transitive) the certainty equivalent of a money lottery will be *less* than the expected value:

- for a **risk-averse** individual, for every money lottery L,

$$C_L < \mathbb{E}[L].$$

In fact, by definition of risk aversion, $\begin{pmatrix} \$\mathbb{E}[L] \\ 1 \end{pmatrix} \succ L$ and, by definition of certainty equivalent, $L \sim \begin{pmatrix} \$C_L \\ 1 \end{pmatrix}$. Thus, by transitivity, $\begin{pmatrix} \$\mathbb{E}[L] \\ 1 \end{pmatrix} \succ \begin{pmatrix} \$C_L \\ 1 \end{pmatrix}$; hence, by (2.1), $\mathbb{E}[L] > C_L$. Similarly,

- for a **risk-loving** individual, for every money lottery L,

$$C_L > \mathbb{E}[L].$$

From the notion of certainty equivalent we derive another notion which can be used to compare the degree of risk aversion across individuals.

Definition 2.3.2 The *risk premium of a money lottery L*, denoted by R_L, is the amount by which the expected value of L can be reduced to induce indifference between the lottery itself and the reduced amount for certain:

$$L = \begin{pmatrix} \$x_1 & \ldots & \$x_n \\ p_1 & \ldots & p_n \end{pmatrix} \sim \begin{pmatrix} \$(\mathbb{E}[L] - R_L) \\ 1 \end{pmatrix}$$

It follows from Definitions 2.3.1 and 2.3.2 that $C_L = \mathbb{E}[L] - R_L$ or, equivalently,

$$R_L = \mathbb{E}[L] - C_L.$$

Thus, for a risk-neutral individual the risk premium is zero, while for a risk-averse individual the risk premium is positive (and for a risk-loving individual the risk premium is negative). Furthermore, we can label a risk-averse individual as **more risk-averse** (relative to lottery L) than another risk-averse individual if the risk premium for the former is larger than the risk premium for the latter. In fact, the risk premium can be interpreted as the price (relative to the expected value) that the individual is willing to pay to avoid facing lottery L. For example, consider three individuals: Ann, Bob and Carla. They all have the same initial wealth $\$6,000$ and they are facing the lottery L where with probability 50% their wealth is wiped out and with probability 50% their wealth is doubled: $L = \begin{pmatrix} \$0 & \$12,000 \\ \frac{1}{2} & \frac{1}{2} \end{pmatrix}$.

Suppose that Ann's risk premium for this lottery is $R_L^{Ann} = 900$, Bob's is $R_L^{Bob} = 500$ and Carla's is $R_L^{Carla} = 0$. Then Ann and Bob are risk averse and Ann is more risk averse than Bob, while Carla is risk neutral. Ann would be willing to pay up to $900 (thus reducing her wealth from $6,000 to $5,100) in order to avoid the lottery L, while Bob would only be willing to pay up to $500 (thus reducing his wealth from $6,000 to $5,500) in order to avoid the lottery L; on the other hand, Carla would not be willing to pay any amount of money to avoid L, since she is indifferent between keeping her initial wealth of $6,000 and playing lottery L.

> Test your understanding of the concepts introduced in this section, by going through the exercises in Section 2.7.2 at the end of this chapter.

2.4 Insurance: basic concepts

Insurance markets are a good example of situations where uncertainty can be represented by means of money lotteries.

Consider an individual who has an initial wealth of $\$W_0 > 0$ and faces the possibility of a loss in the amount of $\$\ell$ ($0 < \ell \leq W_0$) with probability p ($0 < p < 1$). For example, it could be an individual who owns a plot of land worth $80,000 and a house built on it worth $220,000 (so that $W_0 = 80,000 + 220,000 = 300,000$). She is worried about the possibility of a fire destroying the house (thus $\ell = 220,000$) and, according to publicly available data, the probability of this happening in her area is 2% (thus $p = 0.02$). An insurance company offers her a contract and she has to decide whether or not to purchase that contract. An insurance contract is typically expressed in terms of two numbers: the *premium*, which we will denote by h, and the *deductible*, which we will denote by d. The premium can be thought of as the price of the contract: it is paid no matter whether the loss is incurred or not. The deductible is the portion of the loss that is *not* covered. If $d = 0$ we say that the contract offers *full insurance*, while if $d > 0$ then we say that the contract offers *partial insurance*:

$$\begin{aligned} d &= 0 \quad \text{full insurance} \\ d &> 0 \quad \text{partial insurance.} \end{aligned}$$

In the above example, if the deductible is $40,000 then, if the loss occurs, the insurance company makes a payment to the insured in the amount of $\$(\ell - d) = \$(220,000 - 40,000) = \$180,000$ (and, of course, if the loss in *not* incurred then the insurance company does not make any payments to the insured).

The following table summarizes the notation used in this book in the context of insurance:

W_0	initial wealth
ℓ	potential loss
p	probability of loss
h	premium
d	deductible
$\ell - d$	insured amount
(h, d)	insurance contract.

It will be useful to represent the initial situation and possible insurance contracts graphically. We shall do so by using *wealth diagrams* where, on the horizontal axis, we represent the individual's wealth if a loss occurs, denoted by W_1, and, on the vertical axis, the individual's wealth if there is no loss, denoted by W_2; we shall also refer to the former as *wealth in the bad state* and to the latter as *wealth in the good state*. The no-insurance situation can be represented in the wealth diagram as the point $NI = (W_0 - \ell, W_0)$, as shown in Figure 2.1.

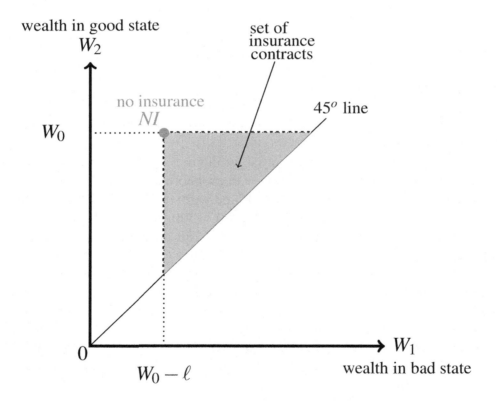

Figure 2.1: The no-insurance point (*NI*) and the set of possible insurance contracts (the shaded triangle).

The purpose of an insurance contract is to protect the individual in case she experiences a loss: thus an insurance contract can be thought of as a point in the diagram where the horizontal coordinate is larger than $W_0 - \ell$ (which is the individual's wealth in the bad state if she does not insure), while the vertical coordinate is smaller than W_0 because of the

2.4 Insurance: basic concepts

premium. The set of possible insurance contracts (encoded in terms of the corresponding wealth levels for the individual, in the bad state and in the good state), is shown in Figures 2.1 and 2.2 as a shaded triangle. The "45° line"– which is the line out of the origin with an angle of 45° – is the set of points (W_1, W_2) such that $W_1 = W_2$. As we will see below, the points on the 45° line represent full-insurance contracts.[6]

How do we translate an insurance contract (h,d), expressed in terms of premium h and deductible d, into a point in the (W_1, W_2) diagram? If the individual purchases contract (h,d) then she pays the premium h in any case (that is, whether or not she incurs a loss) and thus her wealth in the good state is equal to $W_2 = W_0 - h$; the premium reduces her wealth also in the bad state, but in this state there is a further reduction due to the deductible, so that $W_1 = W_0 - h - d = W_2 - d$. Conversely, given a contract expressed as a point (W_1, W_2) we can recover the premium and deductible as follows: $h = W_0 - W_2$ and $d = W_2 - W_1$. It is clear from this that $d = 0$ if and only if $W_1 = W_2$, that is, if and only if the point lies on the 45° line.

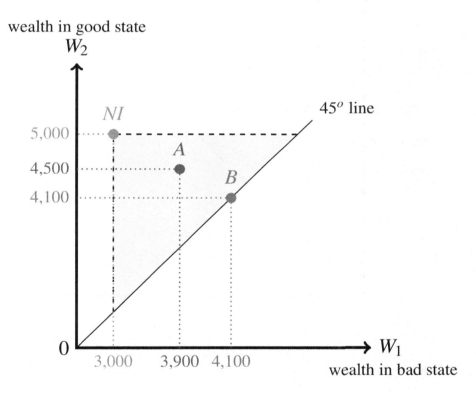

Figure 2.2: The no-insurance point and two insurance contracts.

In Figure 2.2 three points are shown: the no-insurance point $NI = (3,000, 5,000)$ and two possible insurance contracts: $A = (W_1^A = 3,900, W_2^A = 4,500)$ and $B = (W_1^B = 4,100, W_2^B = 4,100)$. From NI we deduce that

$$W_0 = 5,000 \quad \text{and} \quad \ell = 5,000 - 3,000 = 2,000.$$

---

[6]Expressed in terms of premium and deductible, the set of insurance contracts is $\{(h,d) : h > 0, d \geq 0, h + d < \ell\} \cup \{(0, \ell)\}$. We have added the trivial contract with $h = 0$ and $d = \ell$ for convenience: it is equivalent to no insurance. Expressed in terms of wealth levels, the set of insurance contracts is $\{(W_1, W_2) : W_0 - \ell < W_1 \leq W_2 < W_0\} \cup \{(W_0 - \ell, W_0)\}$.

Let h_A denote the premium of contract A and d_A the deductible; then

$$h_A = W_0 - W_2^A = 5,000 - 4,500 = 500 \quad \text{and} \quad d_A = W_2^A - W_1^A = 4,500 - 3,900 = 600.$$

Similarly, let h_B denote the premium of contract B and d_B the deductible; then

$$h_B = W_0 - W_2^B = 5,000 - 4,100 = 900 \quad \text{and} \quad d_B = W_2^B - W_1^B = 4,100 - 4,100 = 0.$$

Hence A is a partial-insurance contract, while B is a full-insurance contract.

Figure 2.3 shows how to view the premium and deductible corresponding to a contract $A = (W_1^A, W_2^A)$.

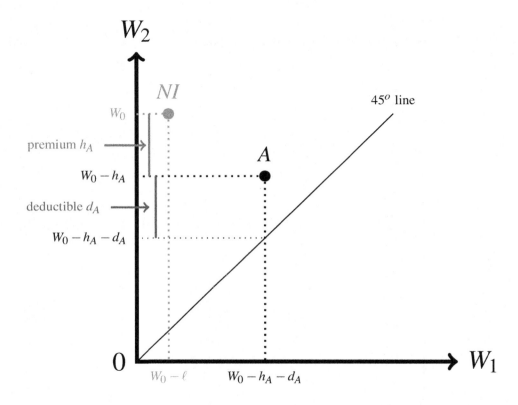

Figure 2.3: The graphical representation of the premium h_A and the deductible d_A corresponding to a contract $A = (W_1^A, W_2^A)$.

As shown in Figure 2.1, there are many potential insurance contracts (the points in the shaded triangle). Will an insurance company be willing to offer any of them? Would an individual be willing to accept any of them? The first question has to do with the incentives of the supplier of contracts (the insurer), while the second question has to do with the incentives of the potential customer (the insured).

We will address the first question in the next sections and postpone a full analysis of the second question to Chapter 4.

> Test your understanding of the concepts introduced in this section, by going through the exercises in Section 2.7.3 at the end of this chapter.

2.5 Isoprofit lines

Throughout this book we shall assume that insurance companies are *risk neutral* and that their objective is to *maximize expected profits*.[7] Selling a contract (h,d) to a customer corresponds to the following money lottery (in terms of profits) for the insurer:

$$\begin{pmatrix} \$h & \$[h-(\ell-d)] \\ 1-p & p \end{pmatrix}. \qquad (\blacktriangle)$$

Given an insurance contract (h,d), we denote by $\pi(h,d)$ the expected value of the corresponding profit lottery ($\blacktriangle$), that is, the expected profit from the contract:

$$\pi(h,d) = (1-p)h + p[h-(\ell-d)] = h - p\ell + pd. \qquad (\blacktriangle\blacktriangle)$$

By the assumption of risk neutrality, the insurance company will be indifferent between any two contracts that yield the same expected profit. For example, if $\ell = 4,000$ and $p = \frac{5}{100}$, the two contracts $A = (h_A = 800, d_A = 1,000)$ and $B = (h_B = 825, d_B = 500)$ yield the same expected profit:

$$\pi(A) = 800 - \tfrac{5}{100} 3{,}000 = 650 \qquad \text{and} \qquad \pi(B) = 825 - \tfrac{5}{100} 3{,}500 = 650.$$

> **Definition 2.5.1** A line in the (W_1, W_2) plane joining all the contracts that give rise to the same expected profit is called an *isoprofit line*.

We want to show that an isoprofit line is a downward-sloping straight line with slope $-\frac{p}{1-p}$. Let $A = (W_1^A, W_2^A)$ and $B = (W_1^B, W_2^B)$ be two contracts that yield the same expected profit, that is,

$$\underbrace{W_0 - W_2^A}_{=h_A} - p\ell + p \underbrace{(W_2^A - W_1^A)}_{=d_A} = \underbrace{W_0 - W_2^B}_{=h_B} - p\ell + p \underbrace{(W_2^B - W_1^B)}_{=d_B}.$$

Deleting $W_0 - p\ell$ from both sides of the equation and rearranging the terms we get

$$-(1-p)W_2^A - pW_1^A = -(1-p)W_2^B - pW_1^B$$

or, equivalently,

$$\frac{\text{rise}}{\text{run}} = \frac{W_2^A - W_2^B}{W_1^A - W_1^B} = -\frac{p}{1-p}$$

which gives the slope of the line segment joining points A and B. Note that the slope is a constant, that is, it does not vary with the points A and B that are chosen.

---

[7] The assumption of risk neutrality is not needed if the insurance company sells the same contract to a large number of individuals. Let n be a large number of customers insured by the insurance company with contract (h,d). Let n_0 be the number of customers who do not suffer a loss and n_1 be the number of customers who suffer a loss (thus $n_0 + n_1 = n$). Then the insurer's *total* profits will be $(n_0 + n_1)h - n_1(\ell - d)$, so that profit *per customer*, or profit *per contract*, is $\frac{nh - n_1(\ell-d)}{n} = h - \frac{n_1}{n}(\ell-d)$. By the Law of Large Numbers in probability theory, $\frac{n_1}{n}$ will be approximately equal to p (the probability of loss), so that the profit per customer will be approximately equal to $\pi(h,d) = h - p\ell + pd$ as defined above.

Figure 2.4 shows an isoprofit line and two contracts, A and B, on this line.

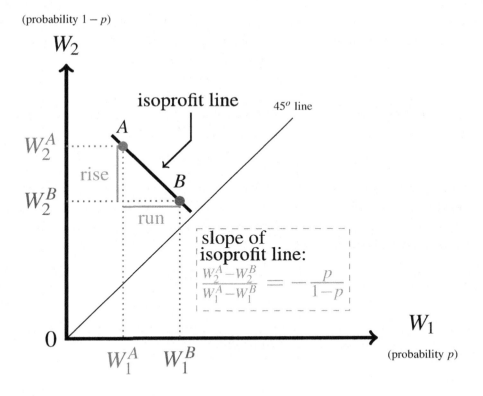

Figure 2.4: The slope of an isoprofit line.

Thus

- isoprofit lines are straight lines,

- isoprofit lines are downward-sloping or decreasing, since the slope is negative: $-\frac{p}{1-p} < 0$ because $0 < p < 1$.

Consider two insurance contracts $A = \left(W_1^A, W_2^A\right)$ and $B = \left(W_1^B, W_2^B\right)$. From the point of view of the potential buyer, these two contracts correspond to the wealth lotteries

$$A = \begin{pmatrix} W_0 - h_A - d_A & W_0 - h_A \\ p & 1 - p \end{pmatrix} \quad \text{and} \quad B = \begin{pmatrix} W_0 - h_B - d_B & W_0 - h_B \\ p & 1 - p \end{pmatrix}$$

where $h_A = W_0 - W_2^A$ is the premium of contract A and $d_A = W_2^A - W_1^A$ is the deductible of contract A and, similarly, $h_B = W_0 - W_2^B$ and $d_B = W_2^B - W_1^B$. Let

$$\pi(A) = h_A - p\ell + pd_A \quad \text{and} \quad \pi(B) = h_B - p\ell + pd_B$$

be the expected profits from contracts A and B, respectively. We want to show that

$$\pi(A) = \pi(B) \quad \text{if and only if} \quad \mathbb{E}[A] = \mathbb{E}[B], \tag{2.2}$$

2.5 Isoprofit lines

that is, A and B lie on the same isoprofit line if and only if the two wealth lotteries A and B have the expected value. In fact,

$$\mathbb{E}[A] = p(W_0 - h_A - d_A) + (1-p)(W_0 - h_A) = W_0 - h_A - pd_A = W_0 - (h_A + pd_A)$$

$$\mathbb{E}[B] = p(W_0 - h_B - d_B) + (1-p)(W_0 - h_B) = W_0 - h_B - pd_B = W_0 - (h_B + pd_B)$$

Thus $\mathbb{E}[A] = \mathbb{E}[B]$ if and only if $h_A + pd_A = h_B + pd_B$ if and only if (subtracting $p\ell$ from both sides)

$$\underbrace{h_A + pd_A - p\ell}_{=\pi(A)} = \underbrace{h_B + pd_B - p\ell}_{=\pi(B)}$$

For each point in the (W_1, W_2) plane there is an isoprofit line that goes through that point. Hence the plane is filled with parallel isoprofit lines (each with slope $-\frac{p}{1-p}$).

Let $A = (W_1^A, W_2^A)$ and $B = (W_1^B, W_2^B)$ be two insurance contracts and suppose that B lies *below* the isoprofit line that goes through A, as shown in Figure 2.5, so that $\pi(B) \neq \pi(A)$. Does B represent a contract that yields higher or lower profits than A? In other words, if the isoprofit line through one contract is below the isoprofit line through another contract, which of the two lines corresponds to a higher level of profit?

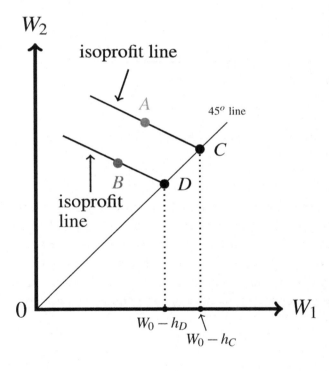

Figure 2.5: A lower isoprofit line corresponds to a higher level of profit.

As shown in Figure 2.5, let C be the full-insurance contract that lies on the isoprofit line through A and D the full-insurance contract that lies on the isoprofit line through B. Then $\pi(A) = \pi(C)$ and $\pi(B) = \pi(D)$. Thus, if we show that $\pi(D) > \pi(C)$ then it follows that $\pi(B) > \pi(A)$. The proof that $\pi(D) > \pi(C)$ is straightforward: contract D

guarantees a wealth of $W_0 - h_D$ to the consumer (where h_D is the premium of contract D) and contract C guarantees a wealth of $W_0 - h_C$ to the consumer (where h_C is the premium of contract C); since $W_0 - h_D < W_0 - h_C$, it follows that $h_D > h_C$ which implies that $\pi(D) = h_D - p\ell > \pi(C) = h_C - p\ell$.[8]

Thus we have shown that moving from an isoprofit line to a lower one corresponds to moving from lower profits to higher profits. This is illustrated in Figure 2.6.

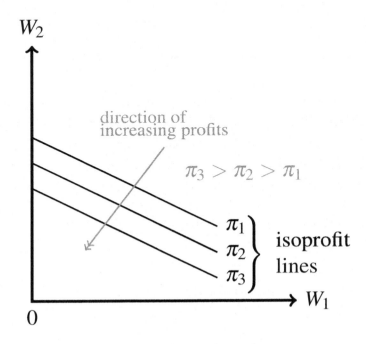

Figure 2.6: The direction of increasing profits.

Among the isoprofit lines there is one which is of particular interest, namely the *zero-profit line*, that is, the line that joins all the contracts that yield zero profits. Like all the other isoprofit lines, this is a straight line with slope $-\frac{p}{1-p}$. Furthermore, it goes through the no-insurance point NI; in fact, NI can be thought of as a trivial contract with zero premium and full deductible: such a contract obviously involves zero profits because the insurance company receives no payment ($h_{NI} = 0$) and makes no payment ($d_{NI} = \ell$ so that $\ell - d_{NI} = 0$).

(R) The zero-profit line is also called the *fair odds line*.

---

[8]In Exercise 2.21 the reader is asked to give an alternative proof of the fact that, if contract B lies below the isoprofit line through contract A, then $\pi(B) > \pi(A)$.

2.5 Isoprofit lines

The zero-profit line is shown in Figure 2.7. Points above the line represent contracts that yield negative profits and points below the line represent contracts that yield positive profits.

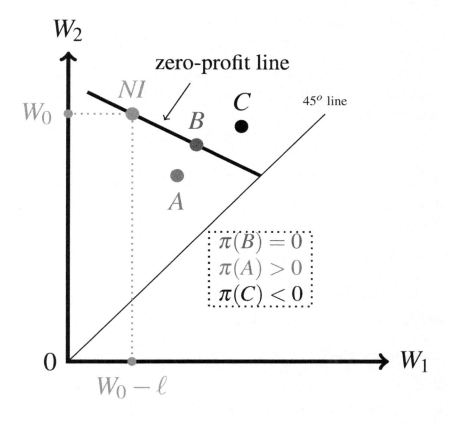

Figure 2.7: The zero-profit line.

Test your understanding of the concepts introduced in this section, by going through the exercises in Section 2.7.4 at the end of this chapter.

2.6 Profitable insurance requires risk aversion

2.6.1 Insuring a risk-neutral individual

Recall that the no-insurance option corresponds to the wealth lottery

$$NI = \begin{pmatrix} W_0 & W_0 - \ell \\ 1-p & p \end{pmatrix} \quad \text{whose expected value is} \quad \mathbb{E}[NI] = W_0 - p\ell \tag{2.3}$$

where, as usual, W_0 is the initial wealth, ℓ the potential loss and p the probability of loss. Now suppose that the individual is **risk neutral** and is offered an insurance contract (h,d) that yields positive profits, that is,

$$h - p\ell + pd > 0 \quad \text{or, equivalently} \quad h + pd > p\ell. \tag{2.4}$$

For the potential customer, such a contract corresponds to the wealth lottery

$$A = \begin{pmatrix} W_0 - h & W_0 - h - d \\ 1-p & p \end{pmatrix}$$

whose expected value is

$$\mathbb{E}[A] = W_0 - h - pd = W_0 - (h + pd) \tag{2.5}$$

Using the fact that, by (2.4), $h + pd > p\ell$, we get that

$$\mathbb{E}[A] < W_0 - p\ell = \mathbb{E}[NI]. \tag{2.6}$$

By risk neutrality, the individual is indifferent between NI and $\mathbb{E}[NI]$ for sure and is also indifferent between A and $\mathbb{E}[A]$ for sure. Assuming that the individual prefers more money to less, by (2.6) she prefers $\mathbb{E}[NI]$ for sure to $\mathbb{E}[A]$ for sure: denoting, as before, indifference by $\sim$ and strict preference by $\succ$, we can write this as

$$NI \sim \mathbb{E}[NI] \succ \mathbb{E}[A] \sim A.$$

Assuming that the individual's preferences are transitive, it follows that

$$NI \succ A,$$

that is, the individual strictly prefers not insuring to purchasing contract A. Hence *it is not possible for an insurance company to make positive profits by selling insurance contracts to risk-neutral individuals*: the individuals will simply not buy the offered insurance contracts.

Although it is intuitively clear that also a risk-loving individual would reject any insurance contract that would yield non-negative profits to the insurer, the proof requires more tools than we have developed so far.[9]

Thus we are left with the case of a risk-averse individual, to which we now turn.

---

[9] In Exercise 2.22 (at the end of this chapter) the reader is asked to show that a risk-loving individual would reject a full-insurance contract that yields zero profits to the insurance company.

2.6.2 Insuring a risk-averse individual

In this section we show that, if an individual is risk averse, it is possible for an insurance company to make positive profits by offering a contract that will be accepted by the individual.

The argument assumes that the individual's preferences are **continuous**, in the sense that if she prefers contract B to contract A then contracts that are sufficiently close to B are still better than A. This is shown in Figure 2.8. Suppose that contract B is preferred to contract A; then continuity of preferences says that, if we take some other contract C in a "sufficiently small disk" around B, then it will be true also for C that it is better than A.[10]

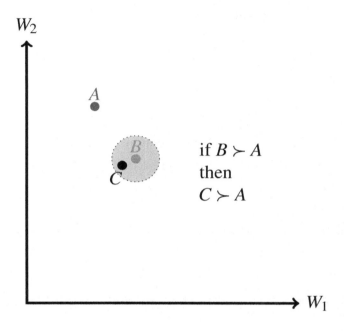

Figure 2.8: Continuity of preferences.

Now consider a risk-averse individual. By definition of risk aversion, she will strictly prefer the full-insurance contract B with premium $h = p\ell$ to not insuring, since such contract leaves her with a wealth of $W_0 - p\ell$ for sure and $W_0 - p\ell$ is the expected value of the no-insurance lottery NI:

$$B \succ NI. \tag{2.7}$$

Contract B yields zero profits for the insurer:[11]

$$\pi(B) = 0. \tag{2.8}$$

By continuity of preferences and (2.7), any contract C sufficiently close to B will also be such that

$$C \succ NI. \tag{2.9}$$

---

[10] This is similar to the property of real numbers that, if $b > a$ then any number c in a sufficiently small interval around b will also be greater than a.

[11] In fact, contract B lies at the intersection of the zero-profit line and the 45° line.

If we choose such a contract C which is *below* the zero-profit line, then – as we saw in Section 2.5 – $\pi(C) > \pi(B)$ and thus, by (2.8), $\pi(C) > 0$ and, by (2.9), the individual will purchase contract C, since it makes her better off relative to not insuring. Hence it is possible to sell a profitable contract to a risk-averse individual.

The above argument is illustrated graphically in Figure 2.9.

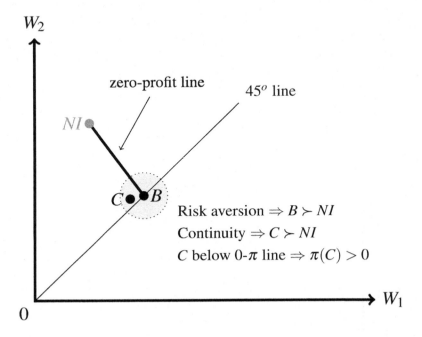

Figure 2.9: Contract C yields positive profits and is better than no insurance.

2.6.3 The profit-maximizing contract for a monopolist

Suppose that the insurance industry is a monopoly, that is, there is only one firm in the industry. Would a profit-maximizing monopolist want to offer a full insurance contract or a partial insurance contract to a risk-averse individual? Extending the argument of the previous section, we can show that for the monopolist *the profit-maximizing choice is to offer full insurance*.

Consider any *partial* insurance contract $B = (h_B, d_B)$ (thus $d_B > 0$) that the potential customer is willing to purchase (thus $B \succ NI$); note that the monopolist's profit from this contract is

$$\pi(B) = h_B - p\ell + pd_B.$$

We want to show that there is a full-insurance contract $C = (h_C, 0)$ which the potential customer is willing to purchase ($C \succ NI$) and is such that $\pi(C) > \pi(B)$, so that it cannot be profit-maximizing to offer contract B.

Let A be the following full-insurance contract: $A = (h_B + pd_B, 0)$. The monopolist's profit from this contract would be

$$\pi(A) = h_B + pd_B - p\ell = \pi(B),$$

2.6 Profitable insurance requires risk aversion

that is, A and B lie on the same isoprofit line and hence the monopolist is indifferent between these two contracts. The customer, however, would strictly prefer contract A to contract B: $A \succ B$. In fact, purchasing contract $B = (h_B, d_B)$ can be viewed as playing the lottery $\begin{pmatrix} W_0 - h_B & W_0 - h_B - d_B \\ 1 - p & p \end{pmatrix}$ whose expected value is $W_0 - h_B - pd_B$ and the full-insurance contract A guarantees this amount with certainty; thus, by the assumed risk-aversion of the customer, $A \succ B$. By continuity of preferences, any contract C sufficiently close to A would still be such that $C \succ B$ and thus, by transitivity (since, by hypothesis, $B \succ NI$) $C \succ NI$. Choosing such a contract below the isoprofit line going through contracts A and B ensures that $\pi(C) > \pi(B)$. Hence if the monopolist were to switch from contract B to contract C the customer would still purchase insurance and the monopolist's profits would increase. The argument is illustrated in Figure 2.10.

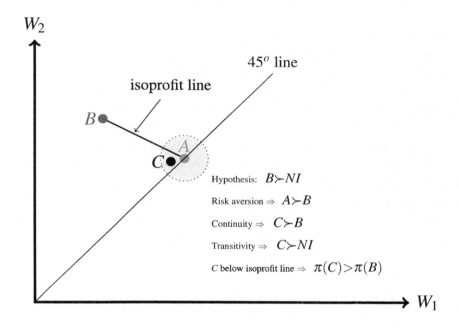

Figure 2.10: Contract C yields higher profits than contract B and is still better than NI.

Thus a monopolist would offer a full-insurance contract to the potential customer. What is the maximum premium that the monopolist would be able to charge for full-insurance without turning the customer away? We can answer this question by appealing to the notion of risk premium (Definition 2.3.2): the monopolist can set the premium up to the amount

$$h_{max} = p\ell + R_{NI}$$

where R_{NI} is the customer's risk premium for the no-insurance lottery $NI = \begin{pmatrix} W_0 & W_0 - \ell \\ 1 - p & p \end{pmatrix}$; that is, the maximum premium the customer would be willing to pay for full insurance is equal to the expected loss, $p\ell$, augmented by the risk premium, R_{NI}. In fact, $\mathbb{E}[NI] = W_0 - p\ell$ and thus, by definition of risk premium,

$$NI \sim \begin{pmatrix} W_0 - p\ell - R_{NI} \\ 1 \end{pmatrix}.$$

In other words, if the customer purchases insurance at premium $h_{max} = p\ell + R_{NI}$ then she is guaranteed the certainty equivalent of the no-insurance lottery. If offered full insurance at this premium, the potential customer would be indifferent between insuring and not insuring; thus the monopolist might want to offer full insurance at a slightly lower premium in order to provide the customer with an incentive to purchase insurance.

2.6.4 Perfectly competitive industry with free entry

In the previous section we considered the extreme case of complete absence of competition, that is, the case where the insurance industry is a monopoly. In this section we consider the opposite extreme, namely an insurance industry where competition is so intense that profits are driven down to zero. The story that is often told for such a mythical industry is that there is free entry into the industry and thus, if firms in the industry are making positive profits, then some new entrepreneur will enter seeking to share in these profits; entry of new firms intensifies competition and drives profits down. We shall assume that all the potential customers in the industry are identical, in the sense that they have the same preferences, the same initial wealth and face the same potential loss with the same probability (the case where potential customers are not identical will be analysed in Chapter 8). Furthermore, we assume that if a new contract is introduced that the insured customers prefer to their current contract, then they will switch to the new contract.

Define a *free-entry competitive equilibrium* as a situation where

1. each firm in the industry makes zero profits, and

2. there is no unexploited profit opportunity in the industry, that is, there is no currently not offered contract that would yield positive profits to a (existing or new) firm that offered that contract.

By adopting a simple extension of the argument used in the previous section, we now show that at a competitive free-entry equilibrium all the active firms, that is, all the firms that are actually selling insurance,[12] offer the same contract, namely the "fair" full-insurance contract with premium $h = p\ell$.

---

[12] There could be inactive firms whose contracts nobody purchases: these firms are also trivially making zero profits.

2.6 Profitable insurance requires risk aversion

The first step in the argument is that – by the zero-profit condition – any actually purchased contract must lie on the zero-profit line. Suppose that there is a contract, call it A, that is currently being purchased by some customers (thus $A \succsim NI$) and is different from the "fair" full-insurance contract with premium $h = p\ell$; call the latter contract B: see Figure 2.11. By definition of risk aversion, it must be that $B \succ A$ and, by continuity of preferences, any contract sufficiently close to B must also be better than A (thus, since $A \succsim NI$, by transitivity of preferences such a contract B is better than no insurance). Pick a contract C sufficiently close to B (so that $C \succ A$) and below the zero-profit line (see Figure 2.11). Then $\pi(C) > 0$ and thus a firm that offered this contract would attract all the customers who are currently purchasing contract A and would make positive profit, so that the initial situation cannot be a free-entry competitive equilibrium.

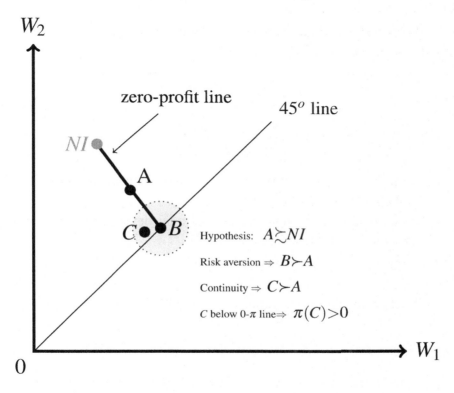

Figure 2.11: Contract C yields positive profits and is better than A (and NI).

We have seen that, no matter whether the insurance industry is a monopoly or a perfectly competitive industry, the outcome is qualitatively the same, namely that potential customers are offered full insurance (and only full insurance). There is an important difference, however: in a perfectly competitive industry the premium of the full-insurance contract is the "fair" premium $h = p\ell$, while the premium that the monopolist charges for full insurance is higher, namely $h = p\ell + R_{NI}$ (recall that R_{NI} is the risk premium of the no-insurance lottery).

> Test your understanding of the concepts introduced in this section, by going through the exercises in Section 2.7.5 at the end of this chapter.

2.7 Exercises

The solutions to the following exercises are given in Section 2.8 at the end of this chapter.

2.7.1 Exercises for Section 2.2: Money lotteries and attitudes to risk

Exercise 2.1 Consider the following money lottery:

$$\begin{pmatrix} \$10 & \$15 & \$18 & \$20 & \$25 & \$30 & \$36 \\ \frac{3}{12} & \frac{1}{12} & 0 & \frac{3}{12} & \frac{2}{12} & 0 & \frac{3}{12} \end{pmatrix}$$

(a) What is its expected value?

(b) If a risk-neutral individual is given a choice between the above lottery and $23 for sure, what will she choose?

Exercise 2.2 Consider the lottery $\begin{pmatrix} o_1 & o_2 & o_3 \\ \frac{3}{10} & \frac{5}{10} & \frac{2}{10} \end{pmatrix}$ where

- o_1 is the outcome where you get $100 and an A in the class on the Economics of Uncertainty and Information,
- o_2 is the outcome where you get a free trip to Disneyland (which would normally cost $500) and a C in the class and
- o_3 is the outcome where you get a $150 gift certificate at Amazon.com and a B in the class.

If you are risk neutral, what sum of money would you consider to be just as good as the lottery?

Exercise 2.3 Given the choice between getting $18 for sure or playing the lottery

$$\begin{pmatrix} \$10 & \$20 & \$30 \\ \frac{3}{10} & \frac{5}{10} & \frac{2}{10} \end{pmatrix}$$

James – who likes money (that is, prefers more money to less) – chooses to get $18 for sure. Is he risk neutral?

Exercise 2.4 Find the expected value of the following lottery

$$\begin{pmatrix} 24 & 12 & 48 & 6 \\ \frac{1}{6} & \frac{2}{6} & \frac{1}{6} & \frac{2}{6} \end{pmatrix}.$$

2.7 Exercises

Exercise 2.5 Consider the lottery $\begin{pmatrix} o_1 & o_2 & o_3 \\ \frac{1}{4} & \frac{1}{2} & \frac{1}{4} \end{pmatrix}$ where

- o_1 = you get an invitation to have dinner at the White House,
- o_2 = you get (for free) a puppy of your choice,
- o_3 = you get $600.

What is the expected value of this lottery?

Exercise 2.6 Consider the following money lottery

$$L = \begin{pmatrix} \$10 & \$15 & \$18 & \$20 & \$25 & \$30 & \$36 \\ \frac{3}{12} & \frac{1}{12} & 0 & \frac{3}{12} & \frac{2}{12} & 0 & \frac{3}{12} \end{pmatrix}$$

(a) What is the expected value of the lottery?

(b) Ann prefers more money to less and has transitive preferences. She says that, between getting $20 for certain and playing the above lottery, she would prefer $20 for certain. What is her attitude to risk?

(c) Bob prefers more money to less and has transitive preferences. He says that, given the same choice as Ann, he would prefer playing the lottery. What is his attitude to risk?

Exercise 2.7 Sam has a debilitating illness and has been offered two mutually exclusive courses of action:

(1) take some well-known drugs which have been tested for a long time, or

(2) take a new experimental drug.

If he chooses (1) then for certain his pain will be reduced to a bearable level. If he chooses (2) then he has a 50% chance of being completely cured and a 50% chance of no benefits from the drug and possibly some harmful side effects. He chose (1). What is his attitude to risk?

Exercise 2.8 Shirley owns a house worth $200,000. The value of the building is $75,000 and the value of the land is $125,000. In the area where she lives there is a 10% probability that a fire will completely destroy the building (on the other hand, the land would not be affected by a fire). An insurance company offers a policy that covers the full replacement cost of the building in the event of fire (that is, there is no deductible). The premium for this policy is $7,500 per year. What attitude to risk must Shirley have in order to purchase the insurance policy? [Hint: think in terms of wealth levels.]

Exercise 2.9 Bill's entire wealth consists of the money in his bank account: $12,000. Bill's friend Bob claims to have discovered a great investment opportunity, which would require an investment of $10,000. Bob does not have any money and asks Bill to provide the $10,000. According to Bob, the investment could yield a return of $150,000, in which case Bob will return the initial $10,000 to Bill and then give him 50% of the remaining $140,000. According to Bob the probability that the investment will be successful is 12% and the probability that the initial investment of $10,000 will be completely lost is 88%. Bill decides to go ahead with the investment and gives $10,000 to Bob. What is Bill's attitude to risk?

2.7.2 Exercises for Section 2.3: Certainty equivalent and risk premium

Exercise 2.10 In Section 2.3 we defined three relations over money lotteries: the strict preference relation (denoted by $\succ$), the indifference relation (denoted by $\sim$) and the 'at least as good' relation (denoted by $\succsim$). As a matter of fact, one can simply postulate just one relation, the 'at least as good' relation $\succsim$, and derive the other two from it as follows:

- $L_1 \succ L_2$ if and only if $L_1 \succsim L_2$ and it is **not** the case that $L_2 \succsim L_1$,
- $L_1 \sim L_2$ if and only if $L_1 \succsim L_2$ and also $L_2 \succsim L_1$.

Recall that a relation $\succsim$ over a set $\mathscr{L}$ of money lotteries is *complete* if, for every two lotteries $L_1, L_2 \in \mathscr{L}$, either $L_1 \succsim L_2$ or $L_2 \succsim L_1$ (or both) and is *transitive* if, for every three lotteries $L_1, L_2, L_3 \in \mathscr{L}$, if $L_1 \succsim L_2$ and $L_2 \succsim L_3$ then $L_1 \succsim L_3$.

Prove that if the 'at least as good' relation $\succsim$ is complete and transitive then the derived 'strict preference' relation $\succ$ is also transitive, that is, if $L_1 \succ L_2$ and $L_2 \succ L_3$ then $L_1 \succ L_3$.

Exercise 2.11 As in Exercise 2.10 take the 'at least as good' relation $\succsim$ as primitive and derive from it the indifference relation $\sim$. Prove that if the 'at least as good' relation $\succsim$ is transitive then the derived indifference relation $\sim$ is also transitive, that is, if $L_1 \sim L_2$ and $L_2 \sim L_3$ then $L_1 \sim L_3$.

Exercise 2.12 As in Exercise 2.10 take the 'at least as good' relation $\succsim$ as primitive and derive from it the 'strict preference' relation $\succ$ and the indifference relation $\sim$. Prove that if the 'at least as good' relation $\succsim$ is transitive then if $L_1 \succ L_2$ and $L_2 \sim L_3$ then $L_1 \succ L_3$.

Exercise 2.13 As in Exercise 2.10 take the 'at least as good' relation $\succsim$ as primitive and derive from it the 'strict preference' relation $\succ$ and the indifference relation $\sim$. Prove that if the 'at least as good' relation $\succsim$ is transitive then if $L_1 \sim L_2$ and $L_2 \succ L_3$ then $L_1 \succ L_3$.

2.7.3 Exercises for Section 2.4: Insurance: basic concepts

Exercise 2.14 Tom's entire wealth consists of a boat which is worth $38,000. He is worried about the possibility of a hurricane damaging the boat. Typically, restoring a damaged boat costs $25,000. Unfortunately, because of global warming, the probability of a hurricane hitting his area is not negligible: it is 12%. The diagrams requested below should all be drawn, as usual, in the cartesian plane where on the horizontal axis you measure wealth in the bad state (W_1) and on the vertical axis wealth in the good state (W_2). Call such a diagram a "wealth diagram".

(a) Represent the no-insurance option (NI) as a point in a wealth diagram.

(b) Suppose that an insurance company offers the following insurance contract, call it B: the premium is $2,000 and the deductible is $9,000. Represent contract B in the wealth diagram of Part (a).

(c) Suppose that another insurance company offers the following full-insurance contract, call it C: the premium is $3,000. Represent contract C in the wealth diagram of Part (a).

(d) If Tom is risk neutral, how will he rank the three options: NI, B and C?

(e) If Tom is risk averse, has transitive preferences and prefers more money to less, how will he rank the three options: NI, B and C?

Exercise 2.15 Refer to the diagram shown in Figure 2.12.

(a) Calculate the potential loss ℓ.

(b) Calculate the premium h_A and the deductible d_A of contract A.

(c) Calculate the premium h_B and the deductible d_B of contract B.

(d) For each of the two contracts state whether it is a partial-insurance contract or a full-insurance contract.

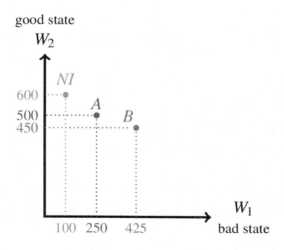

Figure 2.12: The diagram for Exercise 2.15

2.7.4 Exercises for Section 2.5: Isoprofit lines

Exercise 2.16 Consider again the information given in Exercise 2.14: Tom's entire wealth consists of a boat which is worth $38,000; he is worried about the possibility of a hurricane damaging the boat, in which case it would cost him $25,000 to repair the boat; the probability of a hurricane hitting his area is 12%. He is considering two insurance contracts: contract B, with premium $2,000 and deductible $9,000, and contract C, with premium $3,000 and zero deductible.

(a) If Tom were to purchase contract B, what would the expected profit be for the insurance company?

(b) If Tom were to purchase contract C, what would the expected profit be for the insurance company?

(c) What is the slope of an isoprofit line?

(d) Find the equation of the isoprofit line that goes through contract B and draw it in a wealth diagram.

(e) Find the equation of the isoprofit line that goes through contract C and draw it in a wealth diagram.

Exercise 2.17 Consider again the information given in Exercise 2.15 (shown in Figure 2.12). Assume that the probability of loss is 20%.

(a) Calculate the expected profit from contract A.

(b) Calculate the expected profit from contract B.

(c) Draw the zero-profit line.

(d) Draw the isoprofit line that goes through contract A.

(e) Draw the isoprofit line that goes through contract B.

Exercise 2.18 The equation of the zero-profit line is $W_2 = 8,100 - \frac{1}{9}W_1$. The individual's initial wealth is $7,600.

(a) What is the probability of loss?

(b) Calculate the potential loss ℓ.

(c) Find a full-insurance contract, call it A, that yields a profit of $40.

(d) Find a contract, call it B, that lies on the isoprofit line through A and has a deductible of $1,500.

(e) Find a contract, call it C, with deductible $d = 2,000$ that yields a profit of $25.

(f) Write the equation of the isoprofit line that goes through contract A (in the wealth diagram).

(g) Write the equation of the isoprofit line that goes through contract C (in the wealth diagram).

2.7 Exercises

Exercise 2.19 Consider the wealth diagram shown in Figure 2.13. Let $p = 0.2$.

(a) Interpret each point (including *NI*) as an insurance contract and express it in terms of premium and deductible.

(b) Calculate the expected profit from each contract.

(c) Find the equation of the isoprofit line that goes through each contract (including the one that goes through point *NI*).

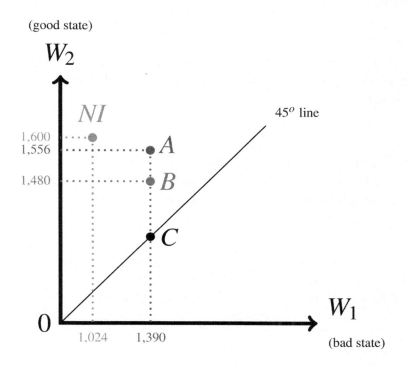

Figure 2.13: The wealth diagram for Exercise 2.19

Exercise 2.20 In a wealth diagram

(a) show the subset of the set of insurance contracts that contains the contracts that yield non-negative profits to the insurer (recall that the set of insurance contracts is the shaded triangle shown in Figure 2.1 on page 22),

(b) of all the contracts that yield non-negative profits to the insurer, find the one that is most preferred by a risk-averse individual and explain why there is only one such contract,

(c) of all the contracts that yield non-negative profits to the insurer, find the ones that are most preferred by a risk-neural individual.

Exercise 2.21 In a wealth diagram draw an isoprofit line and pick a partial-insurance contract $A = \left(W_1^A, W_2^A\right)$ on this line. Next, pick an insurance contract $B = \left(W_1^B, W_2^B\right)$ which is *vertically below A*, so that $W_1^B = W_1^A$ and $W_2^B < W_2^A$. Prove that $\pi(B) > \pi(A)$.

2.7.5 Exercises for Section 2.6: Profitable insurance requires risk aversion

Exercise 2.22 Prove that a risk-neutral individual is indifferent between no insurance and a full-insurance contract that yields zero profits to the insurance company.

Exercise 2.23 Prove that a risk-loving individual strictly prefers no insurance to a "fair" full-insurance contract (that is, a full-insurance contract that yields zero profits to the insurance company).

Exercise 2.24 Ann has an initial wealth of $24,000 and faces a potential loss of $15,000 with probability 20%. The risk premium of the no-insurance lottery for Ann is $2,000. If Ann is offered full insurance for a premium of $4,920 will she take it?

Exercise 2.25 Bob has an initial wealth of $18,000 and faces a potential loss of $10,000. The risk premium of the no-insurance lottery for Bob is $900. The maximum premium that he is willing to pay for full insurance is $4,000. What is the probability of loss?

2.8 Solutions to Exercises

Solution to Exercise 2.1.
(a) The expected value is

$$\frac{3}{12}10 + \frac{1}{12}15 + 0\,(18) + \frac{3}{12}20 + \frac{2}{12}25 + 0\,(30) + \frac{3}{12}36 = \frac{263}{12} = \$21.92.$$

(b) A risk-neutral person is indifferent between the lottery and $21.92 for sure. Assuming that she prefers more money to less, she will prefer $23 to $21.92. Thus, if her preferences are transitive, she will prefer $23 to the lottery. □

Solution to Exercise 2.2. One might be tempted to compute the "expected value" $\frac{3}{10}100 + \frac{5}{10}500 + \frac{2}{10}150 = 310$ and answer: $310. However, this answer would be wrong, because the given lottery is not a money lottery: the outcomes are not just sums of money (they do involve sums of money but also what grade you get in the class). The definition of risk neutrality can only be applied to money lotteries. □

2.8 Solutions to Exercises

Solution to Exercise 2.3. The expected value of the lottery is $\frac{3}{10}10 + \frac{5}{10}20 + \frac{2}{10}30 = 19$. If James were risk-neutral he would consider the lottery to be just as good as getting $19 for sure and would therefore choose the lottery (since getting $19 is better than getting $18). Hence, he is *not* risk neutral. □

Solution to Exercise 2.4 The expected value of the lottery $\begin{pmatrix} 24 & 12 & 48 & 6 \\ \frac{1}{6} & \frac{2}{6} & \frac{1}{6} & \frac{2}{6} \end{pmatrix}$ is $\frac{1}{6}24 + \frac{2}{6}12 + \frac{1}{6}48 + \frac{2}{6}6 = 18$. □

Solution to Exercise 2.5 This was a trick question! There is no expected value because the outcomes are not numbers. □

Solution to Exercise 2.6

(a) As already computed in Exercise 2.1, the expected value of the lottery

$$L = \begin{pmatrix} \$10 & \$15 & \$18 & \$20 & \$25 & \$30 & \$36 \\ \frac{3}{12} & \frac{1}{12} & 0 & \frac{3}{12} & \frac{2}{12} & 0 & \frac{3}{12} \end{pmatrix}$$

is $\mathbb{E}[L] = \frac{3}{12}10 + \frac{1}{12}15 + 0\,(18) + \frac{3}{12}20 + \frac{2}{12}25 + 0\,(30) + \frac{3}{12}36 = \frac{263}{12} = \$21.92$.

(b) Since Ann prefers more money to less, she prefers $21.92 to $20 ($21.92 ≻ $20). She said that she prefers $20 to lottery L ($20 ≻ L$). Thus, since her preferences are transitive, she prefers $21.92 to lottery L ($21.92 ≻ L$). Hence, she is risk averse.

(c) The answer is: we cannot tell. First of all, since Bob prefers more money to less, he prefers $21.92 to $20 ($21.92 ≻ $20). Bob could be risk neutral, because a risk neutral person would be indifferent between L and $21.92 ($L \sim \$21.92$); since Bob prefers $21.92 to $20 and has transitive preferences, if risk neutral he would prefer L to $20. However, Bob could also be risk loving: a risk-loving person prefers L to $21.92 ($L \succ \$21.92$) and we know that he prefers $21.92 to $20; thus, by transitivity, he would prefer L to $20. But Bob could also be risk averse: he could consistently prefer $21.92 to L and L to $20 (for example, he could consider L to be just as good as $20.50). □

Solution to Exercise 2.7 Just like Exercise 2.5, this was a trick question! Here the basic outcomes are not sums of money but states of health. Since the described choice is not one between money lotteries, the definitions of risk aversion/neutrality/love are not applicable. □

Solution to Exercise 2.8 The decision not to buy insurance is the decision to face the following lottery: with probability 0.9 Shirley's wealth will be $200,000, with probability 0.1 it will be $125,000. The expected value of this lottery is: $0.9(200,000) + 0.1(125,000) = \$192,500$. The insurance policy guarantees a wealth of $200,000 - 7,500 = 192,500$. Hence Shirley will buy the insurance policy if she is risk-averse, will be indifferent between buying and not buying if she is risk-neutral and will prefer not to buy if she is risk-loving. □

Solution to Exercise 2.9 If Bill refuses to invest, his wealth is $12,000$ for sure. If Bill gives $10,000$ to Bob to invest then he faces the following lottery: $L = \begin{pmatrix} \$2,000 & \$82,000 \\ 0.88 & 0.12 \end{pmatrix}$. The expected value of L is $\mathbb{E}[L] = \frac{88}{100}2,000 + \frac{12}{100}82,000 = \$11,600$. If Bill were risk averse he would prefer $\$11,600$ for sure to the investment (lottery L) and obviously he will prefer $\$12,000$ to $\$11,600$; thus he would prefer $\$12,000$ for sure to the investment; since he decides to go ahead with the investment he is not risk averse. If Bill were risk neutral he would be indifferent between $\$11,600$ for sure and the investment (lottery L) and obviously he will prefer $\$12,000$ to $\$11,600$; thus he would prefer $\$12,000$ for sure to the investment; since he decides to go ahead with the investment he is not risk neutral either. Hence Bill is risk-loving. □

Solution to Exercise 2.10 Let $L_1, L_2, L_3 \in \mathscr{L}$ be such that $L_1 \succ L_2$ and $L_2 \succ L_3$. We need to show that $L_1 \succ L_3$. Since $L_1 \succ L_2$, $L_1 \succsim L_2$ and since $L_2 \succ L_3$, $L_2 \succsim L_3$. Thus, by transitivity of $\succsim$, $L_1 \succsim L_3$. It remains to prove that it is not the case that $L_3 \succsim L_1$. Suppose that $L_3 \succsim L_1$; then, since $L_1 \succsim L_2$ it would follow from transitivity of $\succsim$ that $L_3 \succsim L_2$, contradicting the hypothesis that $L_2 \succ L_3$. □

Solution to Exercise 2.11 Let $L_1, L_2, L_3 \in \mathscr{L}$ be such that $L_1 \sim L_2$ and $L_2 \sim L_3$. We need to show that $L_1 \sim L_3$. Since $L_1 \sim L_2$, $L_1 \succsim L_2$ and since $L_2 \sim L_3$, $L_2 \succsim L_3$; thus, by transitivity of $\succsim$, $L_1 \succsim L_3$. Similarly, since $L_1 \sim L_2$, $L_2 \succsim L_1$ and since $L_2 \sim L_3$, $L_3 \succsim L_2$; thus, by transitivity of $\succsim$, $L_3 \succsim L_1$. It follows from $L_1 \succsim L_3$ and $L_3 \succsim L_1$ that $L_1 \sim L_3$. □

Solution to Exercise 2.12 Let $L_1, L_2, L_3 \in \mathscr{L}$ be such that $L_1 \succ L_2$ and $L_2 \sim L_3$. We need to show that $L_1 \succ L_3$. Since $L_1 \succ L_2$, $L_1 \succsim L_2$ and since $L_2 \sim L_3$, $L_2 \succsim L_3$; thus, by transitivity of $\succsim$, $L_1 \succsim L_3$. It remains to show that it is not the case that $L_3 \succsim L_1$. Suppose that $L_3 \succsim L_1$; then, in conjunction with $L_1 \succsim L_3$, we get that $L_3 \sim L_1$; since, by hypothesis, $L_2 \sim L_3$, it would follow from transitivity of $\sim$ (proved in Exercise 2.11) that $L_1 \sim L_2$ contradicting the hypothesis that $L_1 \succ L_2$. □

Solution to Exercise 2.13 Let $L_1, L_2, L_3 \in \mathscr{L}$ be such that $L_1 \sim L_2$ and $L_2 \succ L_3$. We need to show that $L_1 \succ L_3$. Since $L_1 \sim L_2$, $L_1 \succsim L_2$ and since $L_2 \succ L_3$, $L_2 \succsim L_3$; thus, by transitivity of $\succsim$, $L_1 \succsim L_3$. It remains to show that it is not the case that $L_3 \succsim L_1$. Suppose that $L_3 \succsim L_1$; then, in conjunction with $L_1 \succsim L_3$, we get that $L_3 \sim L_1$; since, by hypothesis, $L_2 \sim L_1$, it would follow from transitivity of $\sim$ (proved in Exercise 2.11) that $L_2 \sim L_3$ contradicting the hypothesis that $L_2 \succ L_3$. □

2.8 Solutions to Exercises

Solution to Exercise 2.14

(a) See Figure 2.14.

(b) $W_1^B = 38,000 - 2,000 - 9,000 = 27,000$ and $W_2^B = 38,000 - 2,000 = 36,000$. Contract B is shown in Figure 2.14.

(c) $W_1^C = 38,000 - 3,000 = 35,000 = W_2^C$. Contract C is shown in Figure 2.12.

(d) NI represents the lottery $\begin{pmatrix} 13,000 & 38,000 \\ \frac{12}{100} & \frac{88}{100} \end{pmatrix}$ whose expected value is $\frac{12}{100} 13,000 + \frac{88}{100} 38,000 = 35,000$. Contract B represents the lottery $\begin{pmatrix} 27,000 & 36,000 \\ \frac{12}{100} & \frac{88}{100} \end{pmatrix}$ whose expected value is $\frac{12}{100} 27,000 + \frac{88}{100} 36,000 = 34,920$. Contract C represents the lottery $\begin{pmatrix} 35,000 \\ 1 \end{pmatrix}$ whose expected value is $35,000$. Thus if Tom is risk neutral then he is indifferent between NI and C and prefers either of them to B.

(e) By risk aversion, Tom strictly prefers C to NI. He also strictly prefers C to B: since he prefers more money to less, he prefers \$35,000 to \$34,920 and, by risk aversion, he prefers \$34,920 for sure to B; hence, by transitivity, he prefers C to B. On the other hand, we cannot tell how he ranks NI relative to B. □

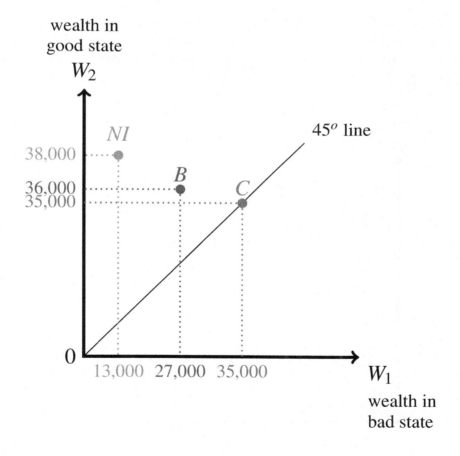

Figure 2.14: The diagram for Exercise 2.14

Solution to Exercise 2.15

(a) $\ell = 600 - 100 = 500$.

(b) $h_A = 600 - 500 = 100$, $d_A = 500 - 250 = 250$.

(c) $h_B = 600 - 450 = 150$, $d_B = 450 - 425 = 25$.

(d) Both contracts are partial-insurance contracts (neither of them lies on the 45° line). □

Solution to Exercise 2.16

(a) $\pi(B) = h_B - p\ell + p\, d_B = 2,000 - \frac{12}{100} 25,000 + \frac{12}{100} 9,000 = 80$.

(b) $\pi(C) = h_C - p\ell = 3,000 - \frac{12}{100} 25,000 = 0$.

(c) The slope of each isoprofit line is $-\frac{p}{1-p} = -\frac{\frac{12}{100}}{\frac{88}{100}} = -\frac{3}{22} = -0.136$.

(d) Since isoprofit lines are straight lines with slope $-\frac{3}{22}$, they are of the form $W_2 = a - \frac{3}{22} W_1$. To find the value of a replace W_2 with $36,000$ and W_1 with $27,000$ and solve for a to get $a = \frac{436,500}{11} = 39,681.82$. The isoprofit line is shown in Figure 2.15.

(e) This is the zero-profit line and thus it goes through the no-insurance point NI. Again, it is of the form $W_2 = a - \frac{3}{22} W_1$. To find the value of a replace both W_1 and W_2 with $35,000$ and solve for a to get $a = \frac{437,500}{11} = 39,772.73$. The isoprofit line is shown in Figure 2.15. □

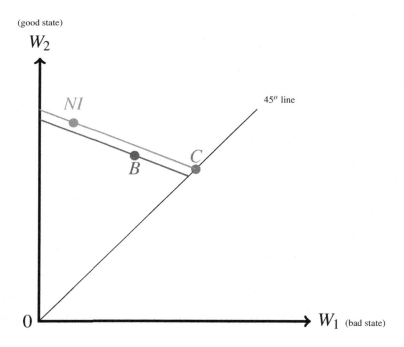

Figure 2.15: The diagram for Exercise 2.16

Solution to Exercise 2.17

(a) $\pi(A) = h_A - p(\ell - d_A) = 100 - \frac{1}{5}(500 - 250) = 50$.

(b) $\pi(B) = h_B - p(\ell - d_B) = 150 - \frac{1}{5}(500 - 25) = 55$.

(c) See Figure 2.16. All three profit lines have a slope of $-\frac{0.2}{0.8} = -\frac{1}{4}$. The equation of the zero-profit line is $W_2 = 625 - \frac{1}{4}W_1$.

(d) See Figure 2.16. The equation of the line is $W_2 = 562.5 - \frac{1}{4}W_1$.

(e) See Figure 2.16. The equation of the line is $W_2 = 556.25 - \frac{1}{4}W_1$. □

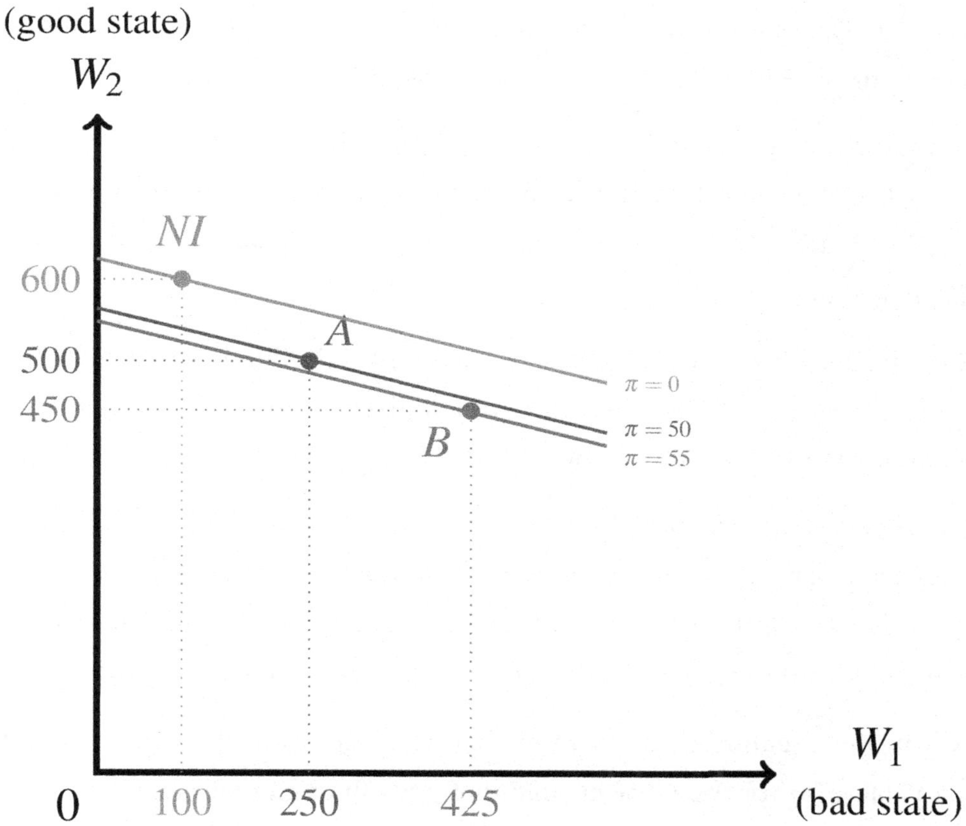

Figure 2.16: The diagram for Exercise 2.17

Solution to Exercise 2.18

(a) Let p be the probability of loss. We know that the slope of any isoprofit line is $-\frac{p}{1-p}$. Thus, since the slope of the zero-profit line is $-\frac{1}{9}$, it must be that $\frac{p}{1-p} = \frac{1}{9}$. Solving for p we get that $p = \frac{1}{10}$.

(b) The no-insurance point is on the zero-profit line. We know that the vertical coordinate of the no-insurance point is $W_0 = 7,600$. Thus, to find the horizontal coordinate, which is equal to $W_0 - \ell$, we must solve the equation $7,600 = 8,100 - \frac{1}{9}W_1$ which gives $W_1 = 4,500$. Thus $\ell = 7,600 - 4,500 = 3,100$.

(c) A full-insurance contract with premium h yields a profit of $h - p\ell = h - \frac{1}{10}3,100 = h - 310$. Thus we want h to solve the equation $h - 310 = 40$. Hence contract A has a premium of 350 (and, of course, zero deductible).

(d) A contract with premium h and deductible $1,500$ yields a profit of $h - p\ell + 1,500p = h - 310 + 150 = h - 160$. Hence, since B is on the same isoprofit line as A, it must be that $h - 160 = 40$, that is, $h = 200$. Thus contract B has a premium of 200 and a deductible of 1,500.

(e) Similar reasoning as in Part (d): we need $h - p\ell + 2,000p$ to be equal to 25. Hence we must solve $h - 310 + 200 = 25$, which gives $h = 135$. Thus contract C has a premium of 135 and a deductible of 2,000.

(f) The equation of an isoprofit line is of the form $W_2 = a - \frac{1}{9}W_1$. To find the value of a for the isoprofit line that goes through contract A we must solve $7,600 - 350 = a - \frac{1}{9}(7,600 - 350)$ to get $a = \frac{72,500}{9} = 8,055.56$. Thus the equation of the isoprofit line that goes through contract A is $W_2 = 8,055.56 - \frac{1}{9}W_1$.

(g) Again, the equation of an isoprofit line is of the form $W_2 = a - \frac{1}{9}W_1$. To find the value of a for the isoprofit line that goes through contract C we must solve $7,600 - 135 = a - \frac{1}{9}(7,600 - 135 - 2,000)$ to get $a = \frac{72,650}{9} = 8,072.22$. Thus the equation the isoprofit line that goes through contract C is $W_2 = 8,072.22 - \frac{1}{9}W_1$.

2.8 Solutions to Exercises

Solution to Exercise 2.19

(a) First of all, note that the initial wealth is $W_0 = 1,600$ and the potential loss is $\ell = 1,600 - 1,024 = 576$. Let us write each point as a pair (h,d) where $h = W_0 - W_2$ is the premium and $d = W_2 - W_1$ is the deductible. Thus

$NI = (0, 576)$,

$A = (1600 - 1556, \ 1556 - 1390) = (44, 166)$,

$B = (1600 - 1480, \ 1480 - 1390) = (120, 90)$,

$C = (1600 - 1390, \ 0) = (210, 0)$.

(b) The expected profit from contract (h,d) is $\pi = h - p(\ell - d)$. Thus $\pi(NI) = 0$, $\pi(A) = -38$, $\pi(B) = 22.8$ and $\pi(C) = 94.8$.

(c) All the isoprofit lines are straight lines and all have the same slope given by $-\frac{p}{1-p} = -\frac{\frac{1}{5}}{\frac{4}{5}} = -\frac{1}{4}$. Thus starting at a point (W_1, W_2), if you reduce W_1 to 0 then the vertical coordinate changes to $W_2 + \frac{1}{4}W_1$, yielding the vertical intercept. Applying this to point NI we get that by reducing the horizontal coordinate by 1,024, the vertical coordinate increases by $\frac{1,024}{4} = 256$ to $1,600 + 256 = 1,856$. Hence the equation of the isoprofit line that goes through point NI (which is the zero-profit line) is $W_2 = 1,856 - \frac{1}{4}W_1$. Applying the same procedure we get that

Equation of isoprofit line through A: $W_2 = 1,903.5 - \frac{1}{4}W_1$

Equation of isoprofit line through B: $W_2 = 1,827.5 - \frac{1}{4}W_1$

Equation of isoprofit line through C: $W_2 = 1,737.5 - \frac{1}{4}W_1$

Solution to Exercise 2.20

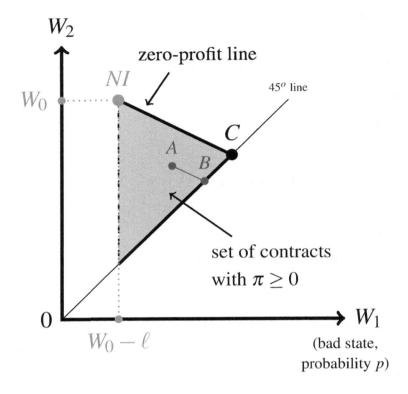

Figure 2.17: The diagram for Exercise 2.20

(a) The set of contracts that yield non-negative profits is shown as a shaded triangle in Figure 2.17.

(b) Contract C shown in Figure 2.17 is the contract that is most preferred by a risk-averse individual among the contracts in the shaded triangle. C is a full-insurance contract with premium $h = p\ell$ guaranteeing a wealth of $W_0 - p\ell$. Any other contract on the zero-profit line is worse than contract C because it gives rise to a non-degenerate lottery with expected value $W_0 - p\ell$. Any other contract on the thick part of the 45° line is worse than contract C because it has a higher premium (while still being a full-insurance contract). Finally, any contract, say A, inside the shaded area lies on an isoprofit line that goes through a contract which is on the thick part of the 45° line below point C, call this point B (see Figure 2.17); then B is better than A (since it guarantees the expected value of A) but is worse than C, so that C is better than A.

(c) The contracts on the thick line from NI to C: the individual is indifferent among all these contracts, because they correspond to lotteries that have the same expected value as the NI lottery. On the other hand, contracts below this line have an expected value which is less than the expected value of the NI lottery and thus are worse than NI.

2.8 Solutions to Exercises

Solution to Exercise 2.21 Let contract B be vertically below contract A as shown in Figure 2.18

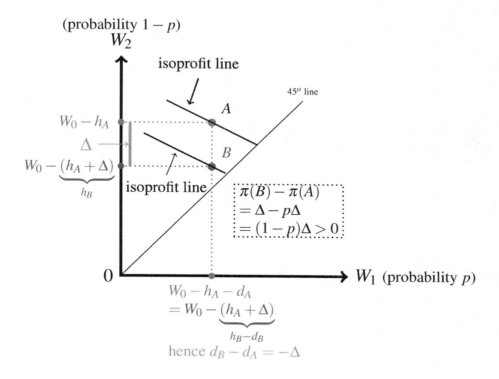

Figure 2.18: The diagram for Exercise 2.21

Then $W_1^B = W_1^A$ and $W_2^B < W_2^A$. From the latter we deduce that the premium of contract B is higher than the premium of contract A. Let $\Delta = W_2^A - W_2^B > 0$ be the amount by which B's premium exceeds A's premium. From the fact that $W_1^B = W_1^A$ we calculate the difference between the deductible of contract B and the deductible of contract A as follows:

$$\underbrace{\overbrace{W_2^B}^{=W_2^A-\Delta} - \overbrace{W_1^B}^{=W_1^A}}_{d_B} = \underbrace{W_2^A - W_1^A}_{d_A} - \Delta,$$

so that

$$d_B - d_A = -\Delta.$$

Thus, when contract B is vertically below contract A, then h_B is greater than h_A and, letting Δ be the amount by which h_B exceeds h_A ($\Delta = h_B - h_A$), $d_B - d_A = -\Delta$, that is, the deductible of contract B is *less than* the deductible of contract A by an amount equal to Δ. From this we deduce that contract B yields higher profits that contract A, because it yields an extra \$$\Delta$ for sure (the premium is received with probability 1) and involves an extra payment of \$$\Delta$ to the insured only with probability p (the payment is made with probability $p < 1$), that is,[13]

$$\pi(B) - \pi(A) = \Delta - p\Delta = (1-p)\Delta > 0.$$

---

[13]This conclusion can be verified directly, as follows: $\pi(B) = W_0 - W_2^B - p\ell + p(W_2^B - W_1^B)$ and

Solution to Exercise 2.22 The no-insurance option corresponds to the wealth lottery $NI = \begin{pmatrix} W_0 & W_0 - \ell \\ 1-p & p \end{pmatrix}$ whose expected value is

$$\mathbb{E}[NI] = W_0 - p\ell. \tag{2.10}$$

Suppose that the individual is **risk neutral** and is offered a full-insurance contract $(h, 0)$ which yields zero profits, that is,

$$h - p\ell = 0 \quad \text{or, equivalently,} \quad h = p\ell. \tag{2.11}$$

For the potential customer, such a contract corresponds to the wealth lottery $C = \begin{pmatrix} W_0 - h \\ 1 \end{pmatrix}$ whose expected value is

$$\mathbb{E}[C] = W_0 - h \underbrace{=}_{\text{using (2.10) and (2.11)}} \mathbb{E}[NI]. \tag{2.12}$$

By risk neutrality, the individual is indifferent between NI and $\mathbb{E}[NI]$ for sure ($NI \sim \mathbb{E}[NI]$) and is also indifferent between C and $\mathbb{E}[NI]$ for sure (since – by (2.12) – C and $\mathbb{E}[NI]$ for sure are the same contract):

$$NI \sim \mathbb{E}[NI] \sim C.$$

Assuming that the individual's preferences are transitive, it follows that

$$NI \sim C.$$

$\pi(A) = W_0 - W_2^A - p\ell + p(W_2^A - W_1^A)$ so that (recall that $W_1^B = W_1^A$ and thus $pW_1^B = pW_1^A$)

$$\pi(B) - \pi(A) = (W_2^A - W_2^B) - p(W_2^A - W_2^B) = (1-p)\underbrace{(W_2^A - W_2^B)}_{\Delta}.$$

2.8 Solutions to Exercises

Solution to Exercise 2.23 The proof is a simple modification of the proof for Exercise 2.22: the no-insurance option corresponds to the wealth lottery $NI = \begin{pmatrix} W_0 & W_0 - \ell \\ 1-p & p \end{pmatrix}$ whose expected value is

$$\mathbb{E}[NI] = W_0 - p\ell. \tag{2.13}$$

Suppose that the individual is **risk loving** and is offered a full-insurance contract $(h, 0)$ that yields zero profits, that is,

$$h = p\ell. \tag{2.14}$$

For the potential customer, such a contract corresponds to the wealth lottery $C = \begin{pmatrix} W_0 - h \\ 1 \end{pmatrix}$ which is the same as $\begin{pmatrix} \mathbb{E}[C] \\ 1 \end{pmatrix} = \mathbb{E}[C] = W_0 - h \underset{\text{by (2.14)}}{=} \mathbb{E}[NI]$. Since the individual is risk loving, he prefers NI to $\mathbb{E}[NI]$ for sure ($NI \succ \mathbb{E}[NI]$) and is indifferent between C and $\mathbb{E}[NI]$ for sure, since it is the same lottery ($C \sim \mathbb{E}[NI]$); thus $NI \succ \mathbb{E}[NI] \sim C$. Assuming that the individual's preferences are transitive, it follows that $NI \succ C$.

Solution to Exercise 2.24 The maximum premium that Ann is willing to pay for full insurance is $h_{max} = p\ell + R_{NI} = \frac{1}{5}15,000 + 2,000 = 5,000$. Since she is offered full insurance at a lower premium, namely 4,920, she will take it (she is better off with full insurance at this premium than with no insurance).

Solution to Exercise 2.25 The maximum premium that Bob is willing to pay for full insurance is $h_{max} = p\ell + R_{NI} = p10,000 + 900$. We are told that this is equal to 4,000. Thus, to find p we solve the equation $p10,000 + 900 = 4,000$ whose solution is $p = \frac{3,100}{10,000} = 0.31$.

3. Expected Utility Theory

3.1 Expected utility: theorems

As noted in the previous chapter, with the exception of risk-neutral individuals, even if we restrict attention to money lotteries we are not able to say much – in general – about how an individual would choose among lotteries. What we need is a theory of "rational" preferences over lotteries that

(1) is general enough to cover lotteries whose outcomes are not necessarily sums of money and

(2) is capable of accounting for different attitudes to risk in the case of money lotteries.

One such theory is the theory of expected utility, to which we now turn.

The theory of expected utility was developed by the founders of Game Theory, namely John von Neumann and Oskar Morgenstern, in their 1944 book *Theory of Games and Economic Behavior*. In a rather unconventional way, we shall first (in this section) state the main result of the theory (which we split into two theorems) and then (in the following section) explain the assumptions (or axioms) behind that result. The reader who is not interested in understanding the conceptual foundations of expected utility theory, but wants to understand what the theory says and how it can be used, can study this section and skip the next.

Let O be a set of *basic outcomes*. Note that a basic outcome need not be a sum of money: it could be the state of an individual's health, or whether the individual under consideration receives an award, or whether it will rain on the day of a planned outdoor party, etc. Let $\mathscr{L}(O)$ be the set of *simple lotteries* (or probability distributions) over O.

We will assume throughout this chapter that O is a finite set: $O = \{o_1, o_2, ..., o_m\}$ ($m \geq 1$). Thus, an element of $\mathscr{L}(O)$ is of the form $\begin{pmatrix} o_1 & o_2 & ... & o_m \\ p_1 & p_2 & ... & p_m \end{pmatrix}$ with $0 \leq p_i \leq 1$, for all $i = 1, 2, ..., m$, and $p_1 + p_2 + ... + p_m = 1$. We will use the symbol L (with or without subscript) to denote an element of $\mathscr{L}(O)$, that is, a simple lottery. Lotteries are used to represent situations of uncertainty. For example, if $m = 4$ and the individual faces the lottery $L = \begin{pmatrix} o_1 & o_2 & o_3 & o_4 \\ \frac{2}{5} & 0 & \frac{1}{5} & \frac{2}{5} \end{pmatrix}$ then she knows that, eventually, the outcome will be one and only one of o_1, o_2, o_3, o_4, but does not know which one; furthermore, she is able to quantify her uncertainty by assigning probabilities to these outcomes. We interpret these probabilities either as objectively obtained from relevant (past) data or as subjective estimates by the individual, as explained in Chapter 2 (Section 2.1).

The assignment of *zero probability* to a particular basic outcome is taken to be an expression of *belief, not impossibility*: the individual is confident that the outcome will not arise, but she cannot rule out that outcome on logical grounds or by appealing to the laws of nature.

Among the elements of $\mathscr{L}(O)$ there are the degenerate lotteries that assign probability 1 to one basic outcome: for example, if $m = 4$ one degenerate lottery is $\begin{pmatrix} o_1 & o_2 & o_3 & o_4 \\ 0 & 0 & 1 & 0 \end{pmatrix}$. To simplify the notation we will often denote degenerate lotteries as basic outcomes, that is, instead of writing $\begin{pmatrix} o_1 & o_2 & o_3 & o_4 \\ 0 & 0 & 1 & 0 \end{pmatrix}$ we will simply write o_3. Thus, in general, the degenerate lottery $\begin{pmatrix} o_1 & ... & o_{i-1} & o_i & o_{i+1} & ... & o_m \\ 0 & 0 & 0 & 1 & 0 & 0 & 0 \end{pmatrix}$ will be denoted by o_i. As another simplification, we will often omit those outcomes that are assigned zero probability. For example, if $m = 4$, the lottery $\begin{pmatrix} o_1 & o_2 & o_3 & o_4 \\ \frac{1}{3} & 0 & \frac{2}{3} & 0 \end{pmatrix}$ will be written more simply as $\begin{pmatrix} o_1 & o_3 \\ \frac{1}{3} & \frac{2}{3} \end{pmatrix}$.

Throughout this chapter we shall call the individual under consideration the Decision-Maker, or *DM* for short. The theory of expected utility assumes that the *DM* has a complete and transitive ranking $\succsim$ of the elements of $\mathscr{L}(O)$ (indeed, this is one of the axioms listed in the next section). As in Chapter 2, the interpretation of $L \succsim L'$ is that the *DM* considers L to be at least as good as L'. By completeness, given any two lotteries L and L', either $L \succ L'$ (the *DM* prefers L to L') or $L' \succ L$ (the *DM* prefers L' to L) or $L \sim L'$ (the *DM* is indifferent between L and L'). Furthermore, by transitivity, for any three lotteries L_1, L_2 and L_3, if $L_1 \succsim L_2$ and $L_2 \succsim L_3$, then $L_1 \succsim L_3$. Besides completeness and transitivity, a number of other "rationality" constraints are postulated on the ranking $\succsim$ of the elements of $\mathscr{L}(O)$; these constraints are the so-called Expected Utility Axioms and are discussed in

3.1 Expected utility: theorems

the next section.

> **Definition 3.1.1** A ranking $\succsim$ of the elements of $\mathscr{L}(O)$ that satisfies the Expected Utility Axioms (listed in the next section) is called a *von Neumann-Morgenstern ranking*.

The two theorems in this section are the key results in the theory of expected utility.

> **Theorem 3.1.1** [von Neumann-Morgenstern, 1944].
> Let $O = \{o_1, o_2, ..., o_m\}$ be a set of basic outcomes and $\mathscr{L}(O)$ the set of simple lotteries over O. If $\succsim$ is a von Neumann-Morgenstern ranking of the elements of $\mathscr{L}(O)$ then there exists a function $U : O \to \mathbb{R}$, called a *von Neumann-Morgenstern utility function*, that assigns a number (called *utility*) to every basic outcome and is such that, for any two lotteries $L = \begin{pmatrix} o_1 & o_2 & ... & o_m \\ p_1 & p_2 & ... & p_m \end{pmatrix}$ and $L' = \begin{pmatrix} o_1 & o_2 & ... & o_m \\ q_1 & q_2 & ... & q_m \end{pmatrix}$,
>
> $$L \succ L' \text{ if and only if } \mathbb{E}[U(L)] > \mathbb{E}[U(L')], \quad \text{and}$$
>
> $$L \sim L' \text{ if and only if } \mathbb{E}[U(L)] = \mathbb{E}[U(L')]$$
>
> where
>
> $$U(L) = \begin{pmatrix} U(o_1) & U(o_2) & ... & U(o_m) \\ p_1 & p_2 & ... & p_m \end{pmatrix}, U(L') = \begin{pmatrix} U(o_1) & U(o_2) & ... & U(o_m) \\ q_1 & q_2 & ... & q_m \end{pmatrix},$$
>
> $\mathbb{E}[U(L)]$ is the expected value of the lottery $U(L)$ and $\mathbb{E}[U(L')]$ is the expected value of the lottery $U(L')$, that is,
>
> $$\mathbb{E}[U(L)] = p_1 U(o_1) + p_2 U(o_2) + ... + p_m U(o_m), \text{ and}$$
>
> $$\mathbb{E}[U(L')] = q_1 U(o_1) + q_2 U(o_2) + ... + q_m U(o_m).$$
>
> $\mathbb{E}[U(L)]$ is called the *expected utility* of lottery L (and $\mathbb{E}[U(L')]$ the expected utility of lottery L').
>
> We say that any function $U : O \to \mathbb{R}$ that satisfies the property that, for any two lotteries L and L', $L \succsim L'$ if and only if $\mathbb{E}[U(L)] \geq \mathbb{E}[U(L')]$ *represents the preferences* (or ranking) $\succsim$.

Before we comment on Theorem 3.1.1 we give an example of how one can use it. Theorem 3.1.1 sometimes allows us to predict an individual's choice between two lotteries C and D if we know how that individual ranks two different lotteries A and B.

For example, suppose we observe that Susan is faced with the choice between lotteries A and B below and she says that she prefers A to B:

$$A = \begin{pmatrix} o_1 & o_2 & o_3 \\ 0 & 0.25 & 0.75 \end{pmatrix} \qquad B = \begin{pmatrix} o_1 & o_2 & o_3 \\ 0.2 & 0 & 0.8 \end{pmatrix}$$

With this information we can predict which of the following two lotteries C and D she will choose, if she has von Neumann-Morgenstern preferences:

$$C = \begin{pmatrix} o_1 & o_2 & o_3 \\ 0.8 & 0 & 0.2 \end{pmatrix} \qquad D = \begin{pmatrix} o_1 & o_2 & o_3 \\ 0 & 1 & 0 \end{pmatrix} = o_2.$$

Let U be a von Neumann-Morgenstern utility function whose existence is guaranteed by Theorem 3.1.1. Let $U(o_1) = a$, $U(o_2) = b$ and $U(o_3) = c$ (where a, b and c are numbers). Then, since Susan prefers A to B, the expected utility of A must be greater than the expected utility of B: $0.25b + 0.75c > 0.2a + 0.8c$. This inequality is equivalent to $0.25b > 0.2a + 0.05c$ or, dividing both sides by 0.25, $b > 0.8a + 0.2c$. It follows from this and Theorem 3.1.1 that Susan prefers D to C, because the expected utility of D is b and the expected utility of C is $0.8a + 0.2c$. Note that, in this example, we merely used the fact that a von Neumann-Morgenstern utility function *exists*, even though we do not know what the values of this function are.

Theorem 3.1.1 is an example of a "representation theorem" and is a generalization of a similar result for the case of the ranking of a finite set of basic outcomes O. It is not difficult to prove that if $\succsim$ is a complete and transitive ranking of O then there exists a function $U : O \to \mathbb{R}$, called a utility function, such that, for any two basic outcomes $o, o' \in O$, $U(o) \geq U(o')$ if and only if $o \succsim o'$. Now, it is quite possible that an individual has a complete and transitive ranking of O, is fully aware of her ranking and yet she is not able to answer the question "what is your utility function?", perhaps because she has never heard about utility functions. A utility function is a *tool* that we can use to represent her ranking, nothing more than that. The same applies to von Neumann-Morgenstern rankings: Theorem 3.1.1 tells us that if an individual has a von Neumann-Morgenstern ranking of the set of lotteries $\mathscr{L}(O)$ then there exists a von Neumann-Morgenstern utility function that we can use to represent her preferences, but it would not make sense for us to ask the individual "what is your von Neumann-Morgenstern utility function?" (indeed this was a question that could not even be conceived before von Neumann and Morgenstern stated and proved Theorem 3.1.1 in 1944!).

Theorem 3.1.1 tells us that a von Neumann-Morgenstern utility function exists; the next theorem can be used to actually construct such a function, by asking the individual to answer a few questions, formulated in a way that is fully comprehensible to her (that is, without using the word 'utility'). The theorem says that, although there are many utility functions that represent a given von Neumann-Morgenstern ranking, once you know one

3.1 Expected utility: theorems

function you "know them all", in the sense that there is a simple operation that transforms one function into the other.

> **Theorem 3.1.2** [von Neumann-Morgenstern, 1944].
> Let $\succsim$ be a von Neumann-Morgenstern ranking of the set of basic lotteries $\mathscr{L}(O)$, where $O = \{o_1, o_2, ..., o_m\}$. Then the following are true.
>
> **(A)** If $U : O \to \mathbb{R}$ is a von Neumann-Morgenstern utility function that represents $\succsim$, then, for any two real numbers a and b, with $a > 0$, the function $V : O \to \mathbb{R}$ defined by $V(o_i) = aU(o_i) + b$ (for every $i = 1, \ldots, m$) is also a von Neumann-Morgenstern utility function that represents $\succsim$.
>
> **(B)** If $U : O \to \mathbb{R}$ and $V : O \to \mathbb{R}$ are two von Neumann-Morgenstern utility functions that represent $\succsim$, then there exist two real numbers a and b, with $a > 0$, such that $V(o_i) = aU(o_i) + b$ (for every $i = 1, \ldots, m$).

Proof. The proof of Part A of Theorem 3.1.2 is very simple. Let a and b be two numbers, with $a > 0$. The hypothesis is that $U : O \to \mathbb{R}$ is a von Neumann-Morgenstern utility function that represents $\succsim$, that is, that, for any two lotteries $L = \begin{pmatrix} o_1 & \cdots & o_m \\ p_1 & \cdots & p_m \end{pmatrix}$ and $L' = \begin{pmatrix} o_1 & \cdots & o_m \\ q_1 & \cdots & q_m \end{pmatrix}$,

$$L \succsim L' \text{ if and only if } p_1 U(o_1) + \ldots + p_m U(o_m) \geq q_1 U(o_1) + \ldots + q_m U(o_m) \quad (3.1)$$

Multiplying both sides of inequality (3.1) by $a > 0$ and adding $(p_1 + \cdots + p_m)b$ to the left-hand side and $(q_1 + \cdots + q_m)b$ to the right-hand side[1] we obtain

$$p_1 [aU(o_1) + b] + \ldots + p_m [aU(o_m) + b] \geq q_1 [aU(o_1) + b] + \ldots + q_m [aU(o_m) + b] \quad (3.2)$$

Defining $V(o_i) = aU(o_i) + b$, it follows from (3.1) and (3.2) that

$$L \succsim L' \text{ if and only if } p_1 V(o_1) + \ldots + p_m V(o_m) \geq q_1 V(o_1) + \ldots + q_m V(o_m),$$

that is, the function V is a von Neumann-Morgenstern utility function that represents the ranking $\succsim$. The proof of Part B will be given later, after introducing more notation and some observations. ∎

---

[1] Note that $(p_1 + \cdots + p_m) = (q_1 + \cdots + q_m) = 1$.

Suppose that the *DM* has a von Neumann-Morgenstern ranking of the set of lotteries $\mathscr{L}(O)$. Since among the lotteries there are the degenerate ones that assign probability 1 to a single basic outcome, it follows that the *DM* has a complete and transitive ranking of the basic outcomes. We shall write o_{best} for a best basic outcome, that is, a basic outcome which is at least as good as any other basic outcome ($o_{best} \succsim o$, for every $o \in O$) and o_{worst} for a worst basic outcome, that is, a basic outcome such that every other outcome is at least as good as it ($o \succsim o_{worst}$, for every $o \in O$). Note that there may be several best outcomes (then the *DM* would be indifferent among them) and several worst outcomes; then o_{best} will denote an arbitrary best outcome and o_{worst} an arbitrary worst outcome. We shall assume throughout that the *DM* is not indifferent among all the outcomes, that is, we shall assume that $o_{best} \succ o_{worst}$.

We now show that, in virtue of Theorem 3.1.2, among the von Neumann-Morgenstern utility functions that represent a given von Neumann-Morgenstern ranking $\succsim$ of $\mathscr{L}(O)$, there is one that assigns the value 1 to the best basic outcome(s) and the value 0 to the worst basic outcome(s). To see this, consider an arbitrary von Neumann-Morgenstern utility function $F: O \to \mathbb{R}$ that represents $\succsim$ and define $G: O \to \mathbb{R}$ as follows: for every $o \in O$, $G(o) = F(o) - F(o_{worst})$. Then, by Theorem 3.1.2 (with $a = 1$ and $b = -F(o_{worst})$), G is also a utility function that represents $\succsim$ and, by construction, $G(o_{worst}) = F(o_{worst}) - F(o_{worst}) = 0$; note also that, since $o_{best} \succ o_{worst}$, it follows that $G(o_{best}) > 0$. Finally, define $U: O \to \mathbb{R}$ as follows: for every $o \in O$, $U(o) = \frac{G(o)}{G(o_{best})}$. Then, by Theorem 3.1.2 (with $a = \frac{1}{G(o_{best})}$ and $b = 0$), U is a utility function that represents $\succsim$ and, by construction, $U(o_{worst}) = 0$ and $U(o_{best}) = 1$. For example, if there are six basic outcomes and the ranking of the basic outcomes is $o_3 \sim o_6 \succ o_1 \succ o_4 \succ o_2 \sim o_5$, then one can take as o_{best} either o_3 or o_6 and as o_{worst} either o_2 or o_5; furthermore, if F is given by

$$\begin{pmatrix} o_1 & o_2 & o_3 & o_4 & o_5 & o_6 \\ 2 & -2 & 8 & 0 & -2 & 8 \end{pmatrix}$$ then G is the function $$\begin{pmatrix} o_1 & o_2 & o_3 & o_4 & o_5 & o_6 \\ 4 & 0 & 10 & 2 & 0 & 10 \end{pmatrix}$$ and U is the function $$\begin{pmatrix} o_1 & o_2 & o_3 & o_4 & o_5 & o_6 \\ 0.4 & 0 & 1 & 0.2 & 0 & 1 \end{pmatrix}.$$

Definition 3.1.2 Let $U: O \to \mathbb{R}$ be a utility function that represents a given von Neumann-Morgenstern ranking $\succsim$ of the set of lotteries $\mathscr{L}(O)$. We say that U is *normalized* if $U(o_{worst}) = 0$ and $U(o_{best}) = 1$.

The transformations described above show how to normalize any given utility function. Armed with the notion of a normalized utility function we can now complete the proof of Theorem 3.1.2.

3.1 Expected utility: theorems

Proof of Part B of Theorem 3.1.2. Let $F: O \to \mathbb{R}$ and $G: O \to \mathbb{R}$ be two von Neumann-Morgenstern utility functions that represent a given von Neumann-Morgenstern ranking of $\mathscr{L}(O)$. Let $U: O \to \mathbb{R}$ be the normalization of F and $V: O \to \mathbb{R}$ be the normalization of G. First we show that it must be that $U = V$, that is, $U(o) = V(o)$ for every $o \in O$. Suppose, by contradiction, that there is an $\hat{o} \in O$ such that $U(\hat{o}) \neq V(\hat{o})$. Without loss of generality we can assume that $U(\hat{o}) > V(\hat{o})$. Construct the following lottery: $L = \begin{pmatrix} o_{best} & o_{worst} \\ \hat{p} & 1-\hat{p} \end{pmatrix}$ with $\hat{p} = U(\hat{o})$ (recall that U is normalized and thus takes on values in the interval from 0 to 1). Then $\mathbb{E}[U(L)] = \mathbb{E}[V(L)] = U(\hat{o})$. Hence, according to U it must be that $\hat{o} \sim L$ (this follows from Theorem 3.1.1), while according to V it must be (again, by Theorem 3.1.1) that $L \succ \hat{o}$ (since $\mathbb{E}[V(L)] = U(\hat{o}) > V(\hat{o})$). Then U and V cannot be two representations of the same ranking. Now let $a_1 = \frac{1}{F(o_{best})-F(o_{worst})}$ and $b_1 = -\frac{F(o_{worst})}{F(o_{best})-F(o_{worst})}$. Note that $a_1 > 0$. Then it is easy to verify that, for every $o \in O$, $U(o) = a_1 F(o) + b_1$. Similarly let $a_2 = \frac{1}{G(o_{best})-G(o_{worst})}$ and $b_2 = -\frac{G(o_{worst})}{G(o_{best})-G(o_{worst})}$; again, $a_2 > 0$ and, for every $o \in O$, $V(o) = a_2 G(o) + b_2$. We can invert the latter transformation and obtain that, for every $o \in O$, $G(o) = \frac{V(o)}{a_2} - \frac{b_2}{a_2}$. Thus, we can transform F into U, which – as proved above – is the same as V, and then transform V into G thus obtaining the following transformation of F into G:

$$G(o) = aF(o) + b \text{ where } a = \frac{a_1}{a_2} > 0 \text{ and } b = \frac{b_1 - b_2}{a_2}.$$

∎

Ⓡ Theorem 3.1.2 is often stated as follows: a utility function that represents a von Neumann-Morgenstern ranking $\succsim$ of $\mathscr{L}(O)$ is *unique up to a positive affine transformation*. An affine transformation is a function $f: \mathbb{R} \to \mathbb{R}$ of the form $f(x) = ax + b$ with $a, b \in \mathbb{R}$. The affine transformation is positive if $a > 0$.
Because of Theorem 3.1.2, a von Neumann-Morgenstern utility function is usually referred to as a *cardinal* utility function.

Theorem 3.1.1 guarantees the existence of a utility function that represents a given von Neumann-Morgenstern ranking $\succsim$ of $\mathscr{L}(O)$ and Theorem 3.1.2 characterizes the set of such functions. Can one actually construct a utility function that represents a given ranking? The answer is affirmative: if there are m basic outcomes one can construct an individual's von Neumann-Morgenstern utility function by asking her at most $(m-1)$ questions. The first question is "what is your ranking of the basic outcomes?". Then we can construct the normalized utility function by first assigning the value 1 to the best outcome(s) and the value 0 to the worst outcome(s). This leaves us with at most

$(m-2)$ values to determine. For this we appeal to one of the axioms discussed in the next section, namely the Continuity Axiom, which says that, for every basic outcome o_i there is a probability $p_i \in [0,1]$ such that the *DM* is indifferent between o_i for certain and the lottery that gives a best outcome with probability p_i and a worst outcome with probability $(1-p_i)$: $o_i \sim \begin{pmatrix} o_{best} & o_{worst} \\ p_i & 1-p_i \end{pmatrix}$. Thus, for each basic outcome o_i for which a utility has not been determined yet, we should ask the individual to tell us the value of p_i such that $o_i \sim \begin{pmatrix} o_{best} & o_{worst} \\ p_i & 1-p_i \end{pmatrix}$; then we can set $U_i(o_i) = p_i$, because the expected utility of the lottery $\begin{pmatrix} o_{best} & o_{worst} \\ p_i & 1-p_i \end{pmatrix}$ is $p_i U_i(o_{best}) + (1-p_i) U_i(o_{worst}) = p_i(1) + (1-p_i)0 = p_i$.

■ **Example 3.1** Suppose that there are five basic outcomes, that is, $O = \{o_1, o_2, o_3, o_4, o_5\}$ and the *DM*, who has von Neumann-Morgenstern preferences, tells us that her ranking of the basic outcomes is as follows: $o_2 \succ o_1 \sim o_5 \succ o_3 \sim o_4$. Then we can begin by assigning utility 1 to the best outcome o_2 and utility 0 to the worst outcomes o_3 and o_4: $\begin{pmatrix} \text{outcome:} & o_1 & o_2 & o_3 & o_4 & o_5 \\ \text{utility:} & ? & 1 & 0 & 0 & ? \end{pmatrix}$. There is only one value left to be determined, namely the utility of o_1 (which is also the utility of o_5, since $o_1 \sim o_5$). To find this value, we ask the *DM* to tell us what value of p makes her indifferent between the lottery $L = \begin{pmatrix} o_2 & o_3 \\ p & 1-p \end{pmatrix}$ and outcome o_1 with certainty. Suppose that her answer is: 0.4. Then her normalized von Neumann-Morgenstern utility function is

$$\begin{pmatrix} \text{outcome:} & o_1 & o_2 & o_3 & o_4 & o_5 \\ \text{utility:} & 0.4 & 1 & 0 & 0 & 0.4 \end{pmatrix}.$$

Knowing this, we can predict her choice among any set of lotteries over these five basic outcomes. ■

Test your understanding of the concepts introduced in this section, by going through the exercises in Section 3.3.2 at the end of this chapter.

3.2 Expected utility: the axioms

We can now turn to the list of rationality axioms proposed by von Neumann and Morgenstern. This section makes heavy use of mathematical notation and, as mentioned in the previous section, if the reader is not interested in understanding in what sense the theory of expected utility captures the notion of rationality, he/she can skip it without affecting his/her ability to understand the rest of this book.

Let $O = \{o_1, o_2, \ldots, o_m\}$ be the set of basic outcomes and $\mathscr{L}(O)$ the set of simple lotteries, that is, the set of probability distributions over O. Let $\succsim$ be a binary relation on $\mathscr{L}(O)$. We say that $\succsim$ is a *von Neumann-Morgenstern ranking* of $\mathscr{L}(O)$ if it satisfies the following four axioms or properties.

Axiom 1 [Completeness and transitivity]. $\succsim$ is complete (for every two lotteries L and L' either $L \succsim L'$ or $L' \succsim L$ or both) and transitive (for any three lotteries L_1, L_2 and L_3, if $L_1 \succsim L_2$ and $L_2 \succsim L_3$ then $L_1 \succsim L_3$).

As noted in the previous section, Axiom 1 implies that there is a complete and transitive ranking of the basic outcomes. Recall that o_{best} denotes a best basic outcome and o_{worst} denotes a worst basic outcome and that we are assuming that $o_{best} \succ o_{worst}$, that is, that the DM is not indifferent among all the basic outcomes.

Axiom 2 [Monotonicity]. $\begin{pmatrix} o_{best} & o_{worst} \\ p & 1-p \end{pmatrix} \succsim \begin{pmatrix} o_{best} & o_{worst} \\ q & 1-q \end{pmatrix}$ if and only if $p \geq q$.

Axiom 3 [Continuity]. For every basic outcome o_i there is a $p_i \in [0,1]$ such that $o_i \sim \begin{pmatrix} o_{best} & o_{worst} \\ p_i & 1-p_i \end{pmatrix}$.

Before we introduce the last axiom we need to define a compound lottery.

Definition 3.2.1 A *compound lottery* is a lottery of the form $\begin{pmatrix} x_1 & x_2 & \ldots & x_r \\ p_1 & p_2 & \ldots & p_r \end{pmatrix}$ where each x_i is either an element of O or an element of $\mathscr{L}(O)$.

For example, let $m = 4$. Then $L = \begin{pmatrix} o_1 & o_2 & o_3 & o_4 \\ \frac{2}{5} & 0 & \frac{1}{5} & \frac{2}{5} \end{pmatrix}$ is a simple lottery (an element of

$\mathscr{L}(O))$, while

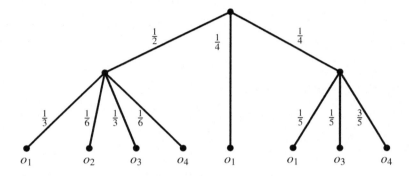

is a compound lottery.[2] The compound lottery C can be viewed graphically as a tree, as shown in Figure 3.1.

[Figure: tree diagram for compound lottery C]

Figure 3.1: A compound lottery

Next we define the simple lottery $L(C)$ corresponding to a compound lottery C. Before introducing the formal definition, we shall explain in an example how to construct such a simple lottery. Continuing with the example of the compound lottery C given above and illustrated in Figure 3.1, first we replace a sequence of edges with a single edge and associate with it the product of the probabilities along the sequence of edges, as shown in Figure 3.2.

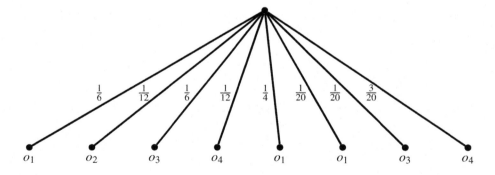

Figure 3.2: Simplification of Figure 3.1 obtained by merging paths into simple edges and associating with the simple edges the products of the probabilities along the path.

---

[2]With $r = 3$, $x_1 = \begin{pmatrix} o_1 & o_2 & o_3 & o_4 \\ \frac{1}{3} & \frac{1}{6} & \frac{1}{3} & \frac{1}{6} \end{pmatrix}$, $x_2 = o_1$, $x_3 = \begin{pmatrix} o_1 & o_2 & o_3 & o_4 \\ \frac{1}{5} & 0 & \frac{1}{5} & \frac{3}{5} \end{pmatrix}$, $p_1 = \frac{1}{2}, p_2 = \frac{1}{4}$ and $p_3 = \frac{1}{4}$.

3.2 Expected utility: the axioms

Then we add up the probabilities of each outcome, as shown in Figure 3.3. Thus, the simple lottery $L(C)$ that corresponds to C is $L(C) = \begin{pmatrix} o_1 & o_2 & o_3 & o_4 \\ \frac{28}{60} & \frac{5}{60} & \frac{13}{60} & \frac{14}{60} \end{pmatrix}$, namely the lottery shown in Figure 3.3.

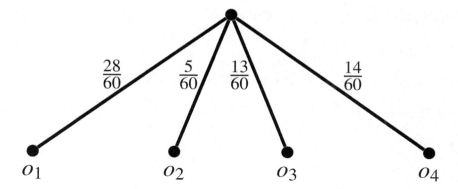

Figure 3.3: Simplification of Figure 3.2 obtained by adding, for each outcome, the probabilities of that outcome.

Definition 3.2.2 Given a compound lottery $C = \begin{pmatrix} x_1 & x_2 & \dots & x_r \\ p_1 & p_2 & \dots & p_r \end{pmatrix}$ the *corresponding simple lottery* $L(C) = \begin{pmatrix} o_1 & o_2 & \dots & o_m \\ q_1 & q_2 & \dots & q_m \end{pmatrix}$ is defined as follows. First of all, for $i = 1, \dots, m$ and $j = 1, \dots, r$, define

$$o_i(x_j) = \begin{cases} 1 & \text{if } x_j = o_i \\ 0 & \text{if } x_j = o_k \text{ with } k \neq i \\ s_i & \text{if } x_j = \begin{pmatrix} o_1 & \dots & o_{i-1} & o_i & o_{i+1} & \dots & o_m \\ s_1 & \dots & s_{i-1} & s_i & s_{i+1} & \dots & s_m \end{pmatrix} \end{cases}$$

Then $q_i = \sum_{j=1}^{r} p_j o_i(x_j)$.

Continuing the above example where

$$C = \begin{pmatrix} \begin{pmatrix} o_1 & o_2 & o_3 & o_4 \\ \frac{1}{3} & \frac{1}{6} & \frac{1}{3} & \frac{1}{6} \end{pmatrix} & o_1 & \begin{pmatrix} o_1 & o_2 & o_3 & o_4 \\ \frac{1}{5} & 0 & \frac{1}{5} & \frac{3}{5} \end{pmatrix} \\ \frac{1}{2} & \frac{1}{4} & \frac{1}{4} \end{pmatrix}$$

we have that

$$r = 3, \quad x_1 = \begin{pmatrix} o_1 & o_2 & o_3 & o_4 \\ \frac{1}{3} & \frac{1}{6} & \frac{1}{3} & \frac{1}{6} \end{pmatrix}, \quad x_2 = o_1 \text{ and } x_3 = \begin{pmatrix} o_1 & o_2 & o_3 & o_4 \\ \frac{1}{5} & 0 & \frac{1}{5} & \frac{3}{5} \end{pmatrix},$$

so that

$$o_1(x_1) = \tfrac{1}{3}, \quad o_1(x_2) = 1, \quad \text{and} \quad o_1(x_3) = \tfrac{1}{5}$$

and thus $q_1 = \frac{1}{2}\left(\frac{1}{3}\right) + \frac{1}{4}(1) + \frac{1}{4}\left(\frac{1}{5}\right) = \frac{28}{60}$. Similarly, $q_2 = \frac{1}{2}\left(\frac{1}{6}\right) + \frac{1}{4}(0) + \frac{1}{4}(0) = \frac{1}{12} = \frac{5}{60}$, $q_3 = \frac{1}{2}\left(\frac{1}{3}\right) + \frac{1}{4}(0) + \frac{1}{4}\left(\frac{1}{5}\right) = \frac{13}{60}$ and $q_4 = \frac{1}{2}\left(\frac{1}{6}\right) + \frac{1}{4}(0) + \frac{1}{4}\left(\frac{3}{5}\right) = \frac{14}{60}$.

Axiom 4 [Independence or substitutability]. Consider an arbitrary basic outcome o_i and an arbitrary simple lottery $L = \begin{pmatrix} o_1 & \cdots & o_{i-1} & o_i & o_{i+1} & \cdots & o_m \\ p_1 & \cdots & p_{i-1} & p_i & p_{i+1} & \cdots & p_m \end{pmatrix}$. If $\hat{L}$ is a simple lottery such that $o_i \sim \hat{L}$, then $L \sim M$ where M is the simple lottery corresponding to the compound lottery $C = \begin{pmatrix} o_1 & \cdots & o_{i-1} & \hat{L} & o_{i+1} & \cdots & o_m \\ p_1 & \cdots & p_{i-1} & p_i & p_{i+1} & \cdots & p_m \end{pmatrix}$ obtained by replacing o_i with $\hat{L}$ in L.

We can now prove the first theorem of the previous section.

Proof of Theorem 3.1.1. To simplify the notation, throughout this proof we will assume that we have renumbered the basic outcomes in such a way that $o_{best} = o_1$ and $o_{worst} = o_m$. First of all, for every basic outcome o_i, let $u_i \in [0,1]$ be such that $o_i \sim \begin{pmatrix} o_1 & o_m \\ u_i & 1-u_i \end{pmatrix}$. The existence of such a value u_i is guaranteed by the Continuity Axiom (Axiom 3); clearly $u_1 = 1$ and $u_m = 0$. Now consider an arbitrary lottery

$$L_1 = \begin{pmatrix} o_1 & \cdots & o_m \\ p_1 & \cdots & p_m \end{pmatrix}.$$

First we show that

$$L_1 \sim \begin{pmatrix} o_1 & o_m \\ \sum_{i=1}^{m} p_i u_i & 1 - \sum_{i=1}^{m} p_i u_i \end{pmatrix} \tag{3.3}$$

This is done through a repeated application of the Independence Axiom (Axiom 4), as follows. Consider the compound lottery

$$\mathscr{C}_2 = \begin{pmatrix} o_1 & \begin{pmatrix} o_1 & o_m \\ u_2 & 1-u_2 \end{pmatrix} & o_3 & \cdots & o_m \\ p_1 & p_2 & p_3 & \cdots & p_m \end{pmatrix}$$

obtained by replacing o_2 in lottery L_1 with the lottery $\begin{pmatrix} o_1 & o_m \\ u_2 & 1-u_2 \end{pmatrix}$ that the DM

3.2 Expected utility: the axioms

considers to be just as good as o_2. The simple lottery corresponding to $\mathscr{C}_2$ is

$$L_2 = \begin{pmatrix} o_1 & o_3 & \ldots & o_{m-1} & o_m \\ p_1 + p_2 u_2 & p_3 & \ldots & p_{m-1} & p_m + p_2(1-u_2) \end{pmatrix}.$$

Note that o_2 is assigned probability 0 in L_2 and thus we have omitted it. By Axiom 4, $L_1 \sim L_2$. Now apply the same argument to L_2: let

$$\mathscr{C}_3 = \begin{pmatrix} o_1 & \begin{pmatrix} o_1 & o_m \\ u_3 & 1-u_3 \end{pmatrix} & \ldots & o_{m-1} & o_m \\ p_1 + p_2 u_2 & p_3 & \ldots & p_{m-1} & p_m + p_2(1-u_2) \end{pmatrix}$$

whose corresponding simple lottery is

$$L_3 = \begin{pmatrix} o_1 & \ldots & o_m \\ p_1 + p_2 u_2 + p_3 u_3 & \ldots & p_m + p_2(1-u_2) + p_3(1-u_3) \end{pmatrix}.$$

Note, again, that o_3 is assigned probability zero in L_3. By Axiom 4, $L_2 \sim L_3$; thus, by transitivity (since $L_1 \sim L_2$ and $L_2 \sim L_3$) we have that $L_1 \sim L_3$. Repeating this argument we get that $L_1 \sim L_{m-1}$, where

$$L_{m-1} = \begin{pmatrix} o_1 & o_m \\ p_1 + p_2 u_2 + \ldots + p_{m-1} u_{m-1} & p_m + p_2(1-u_2) + \ldots + p_{m-1}(1-u_{m-1}) \end{pmatrix}.$$

Since $u_1 = 1$ (so that $p_1 u_1 = p_1$) and $u_m = 0$ (so that $p_m u_m = 0$),

$$p_1 + p_2 u_2 + \ldots + p_{m-1} u_{m-1} = \sum_{i=1}^{m} p_i u_i$$

and

$$p_2(1-u_2) + \ldots + p_{m-1}(1-u_{m-1}) + p_m = \sum_{i=2}^{m} p_i - \sum_{i=2}^{m-1} p_i u_i = p_1 + \sum_{i=2}^{m} p_i - \sum_{i=2}^{m-1} p_i u_i - p_1$$

$$= \underset{\text{(since } u_1=1 \text{ and } u_m=0)}{} \sum_{i=1}^{m} p_i - \sum_{i=2}^{m-1} p_i u_i - p_1 u_1 - p_m u_m = \underset{\left(\text{since } \sum\limits_{i=1}^{m} p_i = 1\right)}{} 1 - \sum_{i=1}^{m} p_i u_i.$$

Thus, $L_{m-1} = \begin{pmatrix} o_1 & o_m \\ \sum_{i=1}^{m} p_i u_i & 1 - \sum_{i=1}^{m} p_i u_i \end{pmatrix}$, which proves (3.3). Now define the following utility function $U : \{o_1, ..., o_m\} \to [0, 1]$: $U(o_i) = u_i$, where, as before, for every basic outcome o_i, $u_i \in [0, 1]$ is such that $o_i \sim \begin{pmatrix} o_1 & o_m \\ u_i & 1 - u_i \end{pmatrix}$. Consider two arbitrary lotteries $L = \begin{pmatrix} o_1 & ... & o_m \\ p_1 & ... & p_m \end{pmatrix}$ and $L' = \begin{pmatrix} o_1 & ... & o_m \\ q_1 & ... & q_m \end{pmatrix}$. We want to show that $L \succsim L'$ if and only if $\mathbb{E}[U(L)] \geq \mathbb{E}[U(L')]$, that is, if and only if $\sum_{i=1}^{m} p_i u_i \geq \sum_{i=1}^{m} q_i u_i$. By (3.3), $L \sim M$, where

$M = \begin{pmatrix} o_1 & o_m \\ \sum_{i=1}^{m} p_i u_i & 1 - \sum_{i=1}^{m} p_i u_i \end{pmatrix}$ and also $L' \sim M'$, where $M' = \begin{pmatrix} o_1 & o_m \\ \sum_{i=1}^{m} q_i u_i & 1 - \sum_{i=1}^{m} q_i u_i \end{pmatrix}$.

Thus, by transitivity of $\succsim$, $L \succsim L'$ if and only if $M \succsim M'$; by the Monotonicity Axiom (Axiom 2), $M \succsim M'$ if and only if $\sum_{i=1}^{m} p_i u_i \geq \sum_{i=1}^{m} q_i u_i$. ∎

The following example, known as the *Allais paradox*, suggests that one should view expected utility theory as a "prescriptive" or "normative" theory (that is, as a theory about how rational people *should* choose) rather than as a descriptive theory (that is, as a theory about the *actual* behavior of individuals). In 1953 the French economist Maurice Allais published a paper regarding a survey he had conducted in 1952 concerning a hypothetical decision problem. Subjects "with good training in and knowledge of the theory of probability, so that they could be considered to behave rationally" were asked to rank the following pairs of lotteries:

$$A = \begin{pmatrix} \$5 \text{ Million} & \$0 \\ \frac{89}{100} & \frac{11}{100} \end{pmatrix} \text{ versus } B = \begin{pmatrix} \$1 \text{ Million} & \$0 \\ \frac{90}{100} & \frac{10}{100} \end{pmatrix}$$

and

$$C = \begin{pmatrix} \$5 \text{ Million} & \$1 \text{ Million} & \$0 \\ \frac{89}{100} & \frac{10}{100} & \frac{1}{100} \end{pmatrix} \text{ versus } D = \begin{pmatrix} \$1 \text{ Million} \\ 1 \end{pmatrix}.$$

3.2 Expected utility: the axioms

Most subjects reported the following ranking: $A \succ B$ and $D \succ C$. Such ranking violates the axioms of expected utility. To see this, let $O = \{o_1, o_2, o_3\}$ with $o_1 = \$5$ Million, $o_2 = \$1$ Million and $o_3 = \$0$. Let us assume that the individual in question prefers more money to less, so that $o_1 \succ o_2 \succ o_3$ and has a von Neumann-Morgenstern ranking of the lotteries over $\mathscr{L}(O)$. Let $u_2 \in (0, 1)$ be such that $D \sim \begin{pmatrix} \$5 \text{ Million} & \$0 \\ u_2 & 1 - u_2 \end{pmatrix}$ (the existence of such u_2 is guaranteed by the Continuity Axiom). Then, since $D \succ C$, by transitivity

$$\begin{pmatrix} \$5 \text{ Million} & \$0 \\ u_2 & 1 - u_2 \end{pmatrix} \succ C. \tag{3.4}$$

Let C' be the simple lottery corresponding to the compound lottery

$$\begin{pmatrix} \$5 \text{ Million} & \begin{pmatrix} \$5 \text{ Million} & \$0 \\ u_2 & 1 - u_2 \end{pmatrix} & \$0 \\ \frac{89}{100} & \frac{10}{100} & \frac{1}{100} \end{pmatrix}.$$

Then $C' = \begin{pmatrix} \$5 \text{ Million} & \$0 \\ \frac{89}{100} + \frac{10}{100} u_2 & 1 - \left(\frac{89}{100} + \frac{10}{100} u_2\right) \end{pmatrix}.$

By the Independence Axiom, $C \sim C'$ and thus, by (3.4) and transitivity,

$$\begin{pmatrix} \$5 \text{ Million} & \$0 \\ u_2 & 1 - u_2 \end{pmatrix} \succ \begin{pmatrix} \$5 \text{ Million} & \$0 \\ \frac{89}{100} + \frac{10}{100} u_2 & 1 - \left(\frac{89}{100} + \frac{10}{100} u_2\right) \end{pmatrix}.$$

Hence, by the Monotonicity Axiom, $u_2 > \frac{89}{100} + \frac{10}{100} u_2$, that is,

$$u_2 > \frac{89}{90}. \tag{3.5}$$

Let B' be the simple lottery corresponding to the following compound lottery, constructed from B by replacing the basic outcome '$1 Million' with $\begin{pmatrix} \$5 \text{ Million} & \$0 \\ u_2 & 1 - u_2 \end{pmatrix}$:

$$\begin{pmatrix} \begin{pmatrix} \$5 \text{ Million} & \$0 \\ u_2 & 1 - u_2 \end{pmatrix} & \$0 \\ \frac{90}{100} & \frac{10}{100} \end{pmatrix}.$$

Then

$$B' = \begin{pmatrix} \$5 \text{ Million} & \$0 \\ \frac{90}{100} u_2 & 1 - \frac{90}{100} u_2 \end{pmatrix}.$$

By the Independence Axiom, $B \sim B'$; thus, since $A \succ B$, by transitivity, $A \succ B'$ and therefore, by the Monotonicity Axiom, $\frac{89}{100} > \frac{90}{100}u_2$, that is, $u_2 < \frac{89}{90}$, contradicting (3.5).

Thus, if one finds the expected utility axioms compelling as axioms of rationality, then one cannot consistently express a preference for A over B and also a preference for D over C.

Another well-known paradox is the *Ellsberg paradox*. Suppose that you are told that an urn contains 30 red balls and 60 more balls that are either blue or yellow. You don't know how many blue or how many yellow balls there are, but the number of blue balls plus the number of yellow ball equals 60 (they could be all blue or all yellow or any combination of the two). The balls are well mixed so that each individual ball is as likely to be drawn as any other. You are given a choice between bets A and B, where

A = you get \$100 if you pick a red ball and nothing otherwise,

B = you get \$100 if you pick a blue ball and nothing otherwise.

Many subjects in experiments state a strict preference for A over B: $A \succ B$. Consider now the following bets:

C = you get \$100 if you pick a red or yellow ball and nothing otherwise,

D = you get \$100 if you pick a blue or yellow ball and nothing otherwise.

Do the axioms of expected utility constrain your ranking of C and D? Many subjects in experiments state the following ranking: $A \succ B$ and $D \succsim C$. All such people violate the axioms of expected utility. The fraction of red balls in the urn is $\frac{30}{90} = \frac{1}{3}$. Let p_2 be the fraction of blue balls and p_3 the fraction of yellow balls (either of these can be zero: all we know is that $p_2 + p_3 = \frac{60}{90} = \frac{2}{3}$). Then A, B, C and D can be viewed as the following lotteries:

$$A = \begin{pmatrix} \$100 & \$0 \\ \frac{1}{3} & p_2 + p_3 \end{pmatrix}, \quad B = \begin{pmatrix} \$100 & \$0 \\ p_2 & \frac{1}{3} + p_3 \end{pmatrix}$$

$$C = \begin{pmatrix} \$100 & \$0 \\ \frac{1}{3} + p_3 & p_2 \end{pmatrix}, \quad D = \begin{pmatrix} \$100 & \$0 \\ p_2 + p_3 = \frac{2}{3} & \frac{1}{3} \end{pmatrix}$$

Let U be the normalized von Neumann-Morgenstern utility function that represents the individual's ranking; then $U(\$100) = 1$ and $U(0) = 0$. Thus,

$$\mathbb{E}[U(A)] = \tfrac{1}{3}, \quad \mathbb{E}[U(B)] = p_2, \quad \mathbb{E}[U(C)] = \tfrac{1}{3} + p_3, \quad \text{and} \quad \mathbb{E}[U(D)] = p_2 + p_3 = \tfrac{2}{3}.$$

Hence, $A \succ B$ if and only if $\frac{1}{3} > p_2$, which implies that $p_3 > \frac{1}{3}$, so that $\mathbb{E}[U(C)] = \frac{1}{3} + p_3 > \mathbb{E}[U(D)] = \frac{2}{3}$ and thus $C \succ D$ (similarly, $B \succ A$ if and only if $\frac{1}{3} < p_2$, which implies that $\mathbb{E}[U(C)] < \mathbb{E}[U(D)]$ and thus $D \succ C$).

Test your understanding of the concepts introduced in this section, by going through the exercises in Section 3.3.2 at the end of this chapter.

3.3 Exercises

The solutions to the following exercises are given in Section 3.4 at the end of this chapter.

3.3.1 Exercises for Section 3.1: Expected utility: theorems

Exercise 3.1 Ben is offered a choice between the following two money lotteries:

$$A = \begin{pmatrix} \$4,000 & \$0 \\ 0.8 & 0.2 \end{pmatrix} \quad \text{and} \quad B = \begin{pmatrix} \$3,000 \\ 1 \end{pmatrix}.$$

He says he strictly prefers B to A. Which of the following two lotteries, C and D, will Ben choose if he satisfies the axioms of expected utility and prefers more money to less?

$$C = \begin{pmatrix} \$4,000 & \$0 \\ 0.2 & 0.8 \end{pmatrix}, \quad D = \begin{pmatrix} \$3,000 & \$0 \\ 0.25 & 0.75 \end{pmatrix}.$$

■

Exercise 3.2 There are three basic outcomes, o_1, o_2 and o_3. Ann satisfies the axioms of expected utility theory and her preferences over lotteries involving these three outcomes can be represented by the following von Neumann-Morgenstern utility function:

$$V(o_2) = a > V(o_1) = b > V(o_3) = c.$$

Normalize the utility function.

■

Exercise 3.3 Consider the following lotteries:

$$L_1 = \begin{pmatrix} \$3000 & \$500 \\ \frac{5}{6} & \frac{1}{6} \end{pmatrix}, \quad L_2 = \begin{pmatrix} \$3000 & \$500 \\ \frac{2}{3} & \frac{1}{3} \end{pmatrix},$$

$$L_3 = \begin{pmatrix} \$3000 & \$2000 & \$1000 & \$500 \\ \frac{1}{4} & \frac{1}{4} & \frac{1}{4} & \frac{1}{4} \end{pmatrix}, \quad L_4 = \begin{pmatrix} \$2000 & \$1000 \\ \frac{1}{2} & \frac{1}{2} \end{pmatrix}.$$

Jennifer says that she is indifferent between lottery L_1 and getting $\$2,000$ for certain. She is also indifferent between lottery L_2 and getting $\$1,000$ for certain. Finally, she says that between L_3 and L_4 she would chose L_3. Is she rational according to the theory of expected utility? [Assume that she prefers more money to less.]

■

Exercise 3.4 Consider the following basic outcomes:

- o_1 = a Summer internship at the White House,
- o_2 = a free one-week vacation in Europe,
- o_3 = \$800,
- o_4 = a free ticket to a concert.

Rachel says that her ranking of these outcomes is $o_1 \succ o_2 \succ o_3 \succ o_4$. She also says that (1) she is indifferent between $\begin{pmatrix} o_2 \\ 1 \end{pmatrix}$ and $\begin{pmatrix} o_1 & o_4 \\ \frac{4}{5} & \frac{1}{5} \end{pmatrix}$ and (2) she is indifferent between $\begin{pmatrix} o_3 \\ 1 \end{pmatrix}$ and $\begin{pmatrix} o_1 & o_4 \\ \frac{1}{2} & \frac{1}{2} \end{pmatrix}$. If she satisfies the axioms of expected utility theory, which of the two lotteries $L_1 = \begin{pmatrix} o_1 & o_2 & o_3 & o_4 \\ \frac{1}{8} & \frac{2}{8} & \frac{3}{8} & \frac{2}{8} \end{pmatrix}$ and $L_2 = \begin{pmatrix} o_1 & o_2 & o_3 \\ \frac{1}{5} & \frac{3}{5} & \frac{1}{5} \end{pmatrix}$ will she choose?

Exercise 3.5 Consider the following lotteries:

$$L_1 = \begin{pmatrix} \$30 & \$28 & \$24 & \$18 & \$8 \\ \frac{2}{10} & \frac{1}{10} & \frac{1}{10} & \frac{2}{10} & \frac{4}{10} \end{pmatrix} \quad \text{and} \quad L_2 = \begin{pmatrix} \$30 & \$28 & \$8 \\ \frac{1}{10} & \frac{4}{10} & \frac{5}{10} \end{pmatrix}.$$

(a) Which lottery would a risk neutral person choose?

(b) Paul's von Neumann-Morgenstern utility-of-money function is $U(\$m) = ln(m)$, where ln denotes the natural logarithm. Which lottery would Paul choose?

Exercise 3.6 There are five basic outcomes. Jane has a von Neumann-Morgenstern ranking of the set of lotteries over basic outcomes that can be represented by either of the following utility functions U and V:
$$\begin{pmatrix} o_1 & o_2 & o_3 & o_4 & o_5 \\ U: & 44 & 170 & -10 & 26 & 98 \\ V: & 32 & 95 & 5 & 23 & 59 \end{pmatrix}.$$

(a) Show how to normalize each of U and V and verify that you get the same normalized utility function.

(b) Show how to transform U into V with a positive affine transformation of the form $x \mapsto ax + b$ with $a, b \in \mathbb{R}$ and $a > 0$.

3.3 Exercises

Exercise 3.7 Consider the following lotteries: $L_3 = \begin{pmatrix} \$28 \\ 1 \end{pmatrix}, L_4 = \begin{pmatrix} \$10 & \$50 \\ \frac{1}{2} & \frac{1}{2} \end{pmatrix}$.

(a) Ann has the following von Neumann-Morgenstern utility function: $U_{Ann}(\$m) = \sqrt{m}$. How does she rank the two lotteries?

(b) Bob has the following von Neumann-Morgenstern utility function: $U_{Bob}(\$m) = 2m - \frac{m^4}{100^3}$. How does he rank the two lotteries?

(c) Verify that both Ann and Bob are risk averse, by determining what they would choose between lottery L_4 and its expected value for certain.

3.3.2 Exercises for Section 3.2: Expected utility: the axioms

Exercise 3.8 Let $O = \{o_1, o_2, o_3, o_4\}$. Find the simple lottery corresponding to the following compound lottery

$$\left(\begin{pmatrix} o_1 & o_2 & o_3 & o_4 \\ \frac{2}{5} & \frac{1}{10} & \frac{3}{10} & \frac{1}{5} \end{pmatrix} \quad o_2 \quad \begin{pmatrix} o_1 & o_3 & o_4 \\ \frac{1}{5} & \frac{1}{5} & \frac{3}{5} \end{pmatrix} \quad \begin{pmatrix} o_2 & o_3 \\ \frac{1}{3} & \frac{2}{3} \end{pmatrix} \right)$$
$$\frac{1}{8} \frac{1}{4} \frac{1}{8} \frac{1}{2}$$

Exercise 3.9 Let $O = \{o_1, o_2, o_3, o_4\}$. Suppose that the *DM* has a von Neumann-Morgenstern ranking of $\mathscr{L}(O)$ and states the following indifference:

$$o_1 \sim \begin{pmatrix} o_2 & o_4 \\ \frac{1}{4} & \frac{3}{4} \end{pmatrix} \quad \text{and} \quad o_2 \sim \begin{pmatrix} o_3 & o_4 \\ \frac{3}{5} & \frac{2}{5} \end{pmatrix}.$$

Find a lottery that the *DM* considers just as good as

$$L = \begin{pmatrix} o_1 & o_2 & o_3 & o_4 \\ \frac{1}{3} & \frac{2}{9} & \frac{1}{9} & \frac{1}{3} \end{pmatrix}.$$

Do not add any information to what is given above (in particular, do not make any assumptions about which outcome is best and which is worst).

Exercise 3.10 — More difficult. Would you be willing to pay more in order to reduce the probability of dying within the next hour from one sixth to zero or from four sixths to three sixths? Unfortunately, this is not a hypothetical question: you accidentally entered the office of a mad scientist and have been overpowered and tied to a chair. The mad scientist has put six glasses in front of you, numbered 1 to 6, and tells you that one of them contains a deadly poison and the other five contain a harmless liquid. He says that he is going to roll a die and make you drink from the glass whose number matches the number that shows up from the rolling of the die. You beg to be exempted and he asks you "what is the largest amount of money that you would be willing to pay to replace the glass containing the poison with one containing a harmless liquid?". Interpret this question as "what sum of money x makes you indifferent between

(1) leaving the poison in whichever glass contains it and rolling the die, and

(2) reducing your wealth by $\$x$ and rolling the die after the poison has been replaced by a harmless liquid". Your answer is: $\$X$.

Then he asks you "suppose that instead of one glass with poison there had been four glasses with poison (and two with a harmless liquid); what is the largest amount of money that you would be willing to pay to replace one glass with poison with a glass containing a harmless liquid (and thus roll the die with 3 glasses with poison and 3 with a harmless liquid)?". Your answer is: $\$Y$.

Show that if $X > Y$ then you do not satisfy the axioms of Expected Utility Theory.

[Hint: think about what the basic outcomes are; assume that you do not care about how much money is left in your estate if you die and that, when alive, you prefer more money to less.]

3.4 Solutions to Exercises

Solution to Exercise 3.1 Since Ben prefers B to A, he must prefer D to C.
Proof. Let U be a von Neumann-Morgenstern utility function that represents Ben's preferences. Let $U(\$4,000) = a, U(\$3,000) = b$ and $U(\$0) = c$. Since Ben prefers more money to less, $a > b > c$. Then $\mathbb{E}[U(A)] = 0.8U(\$4,000) + 0.2U(\$0) = 0.8a + 0.2c$ and $\mathbb{E}[U(B)] = U(\$3,000) = b$. Since Ben prefers B to A, it must be that $b > 0.8a + 0.2c$. Let us now compare C and D: $\mathbb{E}[U(C)] = 0.2a + 0.8c$ and $\mathbb{E}[U(D)] = 0.25b + 0.75c$. Since $b > 0.8a + 0.2c$, $0.25b > 0.25(0.8a + 0.2c) = 0.2a + 0.05c$ and thus, adding $0.75c$ to both sides, we get that $0.25b + 0.75c > 0.2a + 0.8c$, that is, $\mathbb{E}[U(D)] > \mathbb{E}[U(C)]$, so that $D \succ C$. Note that the proof would have been somewhat easier if we had taken the normalized utility function, so that $a = 1$ and $c = 0$. □

3.4 Solutions to Exercises

Solution to Exercise 3.2 Define the function U as follows: $U(x) = \frac{1}{a-c}V(x) - \frac{c}{a-c} = \frac{V(x)-c}{a-c}$ (note that, by hypothesis, $a > c$ and thus $\frac{1}{a-c} > 0$). Then U represents the same preferences as V. Then $U(o_2) = \frac{V(o_2)-c}{a-c} = \frac{a-c}{a-c} = 1$, $U(o_1) = \frac{V(o_1)-c}{a-c} = \frac{b-c}{a-c}$, and $U(o_3) = \frac{V(o_3)-c}{a-c} = \frac{c-c}{a-c} = 0$. Note that, since $a > b > c$, $0 < \frac{b-c}{a-c} < 1$. □

Solution to Exercise 3.3 We can take the set of basic outcomes to be $\{\$3000, \$2000, \$1000, \$500\}$. Suppose that there is a von Neumann-Morgenstern utility function U that represents Jennifer's preferences. We can normalize it so that $U(\$3000) = 1$ and $U(\$500) = 0$. Since Jennifer is indifferent between L_1 and $\$2000$, $U(\$2000) = \frac{5}{6}$ (since the expected utility of L_1 is $\frac{5}{6}(1) + \frac{1}{6}(0) = \frac{5}{6}$). Since she is indifferent between L_2 and $\$1000$, $U(\$1000) = \frac{2}{3}$ (since the expected utility of L_2 is $\frac{2}{3}(1) + \frac{1}{3}(0) = \frac{2}{3}$). Thus, $\mathbb{E}[U(L_3)] = \frac{1}{4}(1) + \frac{1}{4}\left(\frac{5}{6}\right) + \frac{1}{4}\left(\frac{2}{3}\right) + \frac{1}{4}(0) = \frac{5}{8}$ and $\mathbb{E}[U(L_4)] = \frac{1}{2}\left(\frac{5}{6}\right) + \frac{1}{2}\left(\frac{2}{3}\right) = \frac{3}{4}$. Since $\frac{3}{4} > \frac{5}{8}$, Jennifer should prefer L_4 to L_3. Hence, she is not rational according to the theory of expected utility. □

Solution to Exercise 3.4 Normalize her utility function so that $U(o_1) = 1$ and $U(o_4) = 0$. Then, since Rachel is indifferent between $\begin{pmatrix} o_2 \\ 1 \end{pmatrix}$ and $\begin{pmatrix} o_1 & o_4 \\ \frac{4}{5} & \frac{1}{5} \end{pmatrix}$, we have that $U(o_2) = \frac{4}{5}$. Similarly, since she is indifferent between $\begin{pmatrix} o_3 \\ 1 \end{pmatrix}$ and $\begin{pmatrix} o_1 & o_4 \\ \frac{1}{2} & \frac{1}{2} \end{pmatrix}$, $U(o_3) = \frac{1}{2}$. Then the expected utility of $L_1 = \begin{pmatrix} o_1 & o_2 & o_3 & o_4 \\ \frac{1}{8} & \frac{2}{8} & \frac{3}{8} & \frac{2}{8} \end{pmatrix}$ is $\frac{1}{8}(1) + \frac{2}{8}\left(\frac{4}{5}\right) + \frac{3}{8}\left(\frac{1}{2}\right) + \frac{2}{8}(0) = \frac{41}{80} = 0.5125$, while the expected utility of $L_2 = \begin{pmatrix} o_1 & o_2 & o_3 \\ \frac{1}{5} & \frac{3}{5} & \frac{1}{5} \end{pmatrix}$ is $\frac{1}{5}(1) + \frac{3}{5}\left(\frac{4}{5}\right) + \frac{1}{5}\left(\frac{1}{2}\right) = \frac{39}{50} = 0.78$. Hence, she prefers L_2 to L_1. □

Solution to Exercise 3.5

(a) The expected value of L_1 is $\frac{2}{10}(30) + \frac{1}{10}(28) + \frac{1}{10}(24) + \frac{2}{10}(18) + \frac{4}{10}(8) = 18$ and the expected value of L_2 is $\frac{1}{10}(30) + \frac{4}{10}(28) + \frac{5}{10}8 = 18.2$. Hence, a risk-neutral person would prefer L_2 to L_1.

(b) The expected utility of L_1 is $\frac{1}{5}\ln(30) + \frac{1}{10}\ln(28) + \frac{1}{10}\ln(24) + \frac{1}{5}\ln(18) + \frac{2}{5}\ln(8) = 2.741$ while the expected utility of L_2 is $\frac{1}{10}\ln(30) + \frac{2}{5}\ln(28) + \frac{1}{2}\ln(8) = 2.713$. Thus, Paul would choose L_1 (since he prefers L_1 to L_2). □

Solution to Exercise 3.6

(a) To normalize U first add 10 to each value and then divide by 180. Denote the normalization of U by $\bar{U}$. Then

$$\bar{U}: \begin{array}{ccccc} o_1 & o_2 & o_3 & o_4 & o_5 \\ \frac{54}{180}=0.3 & \frac{180}{180}=1 & \frac{0}{180}=0 & \frac{36}{180}=0.2 & \frac{108}{180}=0.6 \end{array}$$

To normalize V first subtract 5 from each value and then divide by 90. Denote the normalization of V by $\bar{V}$. Then

$$\bar{V}: \begin{array}{ccccc} o_1 & o_2 & o_3 & o_4 & o_5 \\ \frac{27}{90}=0.3 & \frac{90}{90}=1 & \frac{0}{90}=0 & \frac{18}{90}=0.2 & \frac{54}{90}=0.6 \end{array}$$

(b) The transformation is of the form $V(o) = aU(o) + b$. To find the values of a and b plug in two sets of values and solve the system of equations $\begin{cases} 44a+b=32 \\ 170a+b=95 \end{cases}$. The solution is $a = \frac{1}{2}$, $b = 10$. Thus, $V(o) = \frac{1}{2}U(o) + 10$. □

Solution to Exercise 3.7

(a) Ann prefers L_3 to L_4 ($L_3 \succ_{Ann} L_4$). In fact, $\mathbb{E}[U_{Ann}(L_3)] = \sqrt{28} = 5.2915$ while $\mathbb{E}[U_{Ann}(L_4)] = \frac{1}{2}\sqrt{10} + \frac{1}{2}\sqrt{50} = 5.1167$.

(b) Bob prefers L_4 to L_3 ($L_4 \succ_{Bob} L_3$). In fact, $\mathbb{E}[U_{Bob}(L_3)] = 2(28) - \frac{28^4}{100^3} = 55.3853$ while $\mathbb{E}[U_{Bob}(L_4)] = \frac{1}{2}\left[2(10) - \frac{10^4}{100^3}\right] + \frac{1}{2}\left[2(50) - \frac{50^4}{100^3}\right] = 56.87$.

(c) The expected value of lottery L_4 is $\frac{1}{2}10 + \frac{1}{2}50 = 30$; thus, a risk-averse person would strictly prefer $30 with certainty to lottery L_4. We saw in Part (a) that for Ann the expected utility of lottery L_4 is 5.1167; the utility of $30 is $\sqrt{30} = 5.4772$. Thus, Ann would indeed choose $30 for certain over the lottery L_4. We saw in Part (b) that for Bob the expected utility of lottery L_4 is 56.87; the utility of $30 is $2(30) - \frac{30^4}{100^3} = 59.19$. Thus, Bob would indeed choose $30 for certain over the lottery L_4. □

Solution to Exercise 3.8 The simple lottery is $\begin{pmatrix} o_1 & o_2 & o_3 & o_4 \\ \frac{18}{240} & \frac{103}{240} & \frac{95}{240} & \frac{24}{240} \end{pmatrix}$. For example, the probability of o_2 is computed as follows: $\frac{1}{8}\left(\frac{1}{10}\right) + \frac{1}{4}(1) + \frac{1}{8}(0) + \frac{1}{2}\left(\frac{1}{3}\right) = \frac{103}{240}$. □

3.4 Solutions to Exercises

Solution to Exercise 3.9 Using the stated indifference, use lottery L to construct the compound lottery

$$\left(\begin{array}{cccc} \begin{pmatrix} o_2 & o_4 \\ \frac{1}{4} & \frac{3}{4} \end{pmatrix} & \begin{pmatrix} o_3 & o_4 \\ \frac{3}{5} & \frac{2}{5} \end{pmatrix} & o_3 & o_4 \\ \frac{1}{3} & \frac{2}{9} & \frac{1}{9} & \frac{1}{3} \end{array} \right),$$

whose corresponding simple lottery is $L' = \begin{pmatrix} o_1 & o_2 & o_3 & o_4 \\ 0 & \frac{1}{12} & \frac{11}{45} & \frac{121}{180} \end{pmatrix}$. Then, by the Independence Axiom, $L \sim L'$. □

Solution to Exercise 3.10 Let W be your initial wealth. The basic outcomes are:

1. you do not pay any money, do not die and live to enjoy your wealth W (denote this outcome by A_0),

2. you pay $\$Y$, do not die and live to enjoy your remaining wealth $W - Y$ (call this outcome A_Y),

3. you pay $\$X$, do not die and live to enjoy your remaining wealth $W - X$ (call this outcome A_X),

4. you die (call this outcome D); this could happen because (a) you do not pay any money, roll the die and drink the poison or (b) you pay $\$Y$, roll the die and drink the poison; we assume that you are indifferent between these two outcomes.

Since, by hypothesis, $X > Y$, your ranking of these outcomes must be $A_0 \succ A_Y \succ A_X \succ D$. If you satisfy the von Neumann-Morgenstern axioms, then your preferences can be represented by a von Neumann-Morgenstern utility function U defined on the set of basic outcomes. We can normalize your utility function by setting $U(A_0) = 1$ and $U(D) = 0$. Furthermore, it must be that

$$U(A_Y) > U(A_X). \tag{3.6}$$

The maximum amount $\$P$ that you are willing to pay is that amount that makes you indifferent between (1) rolling the die with the initial number of poisoned glasses and (2) giving up $\$P$ and rolling the die with one less poisoned glass.

Thus – based on your answers – you are indifferent between the two lotteries

$$\begin{pmatrix} D & A_0 \\ \frac{1}{6} & \frac{5}{6} \end{pmatrix} \text{ and } \begin{pmatrix} A_X \\ 1 \end{pmatrix}$$

and you are indifferent between the two lotteries:

$$\begin{pmatrix} D & A_0 \\ \frac{4}{6} & \frac{2}{6} \end{pmatrix} \quad \text{and} \quad \begin{pmatrix} D & A_Y \\ \frac{3}{6} & \frac{3}{6} \end{pmatrix}.$$

Thus,

$$\underbrace{\tfrac{1}{6}U(D) + \tfrac{5}{6}U(A_0)}_{=\tfrac{1}{6}0 + \tfrac{5}{6}1 = \tfrac{5}{6}} = U(A_X) \quad \text{and} \quad \underbrace{\tfrac{4}{6}U(D) + \tfrac{2}{6}U(A_0)}_{=\tfrac{4}{6}0 + \tfrac{2}{6}1 = \tfrac{2}{6}} = \underbrace{\tfrac{3}{6}U(D) + \tfrac{3}{6}U(A_Y)}_{=\tfrac{3}{6}0 + \tfrac{3}{6}U(A_Y)}.$$

Hence, $U(A_X) = \tfrac{5}{6}$ and $U(A_Y) = \tfrac{2}{3} = \tfrac{4}{6}$, so that $U(A_X) > U(A_Y)$, contradicting (3.6). □

4. Money lotteries revisited

4.1 von Neumann Morgenstern preferences over money lotteries

In this section we revisit the notions of risk aversion/neutrality/love in the context of von Neumann-Morgenstern preferences. From now on we will use the abbreviation "vNM" for "von Neumann Morgenstern" and, unless explicitly stated otherwise, we will assume that the individual in question has vNM preferences.

4.1.1 The vNM utility-of-money function of a risk-neutral agent

Recall from Chapter 2 (Section 2.2) that, given a money lottery $L = \begin{pmatrix} \$m_1 & \$m_2 & \dots & \$m_n \\ p_1 & p_2 & \dots & p_n \end{pmatrix}$, an individual is said to be risk neutral relative to L if she is indifferent between L and the expected value of L for sure: $L \sim \begin{pmatrix} \$\mathbb{E}[L] \\ 1 \end{pmatrix}$. If the individual has vNM preferences over money lotteries then, by Theorem 3.1.1 (Chapter 3), there exists a utility function U (that assigns a real number to each sums of money) such that

$$\underbrace{L \sim \begin{pmatrix} \$\mathbb{E}[L] \\ 1 \end{pmatrix}}_{L \text{ is as good as } \mathbb{E}[L]} \quad \text{if and only if} \quad \mathbb{E}[U(L)] = U(\mathbb{E}[L]), \text{ that is, if and only if,}$$

$$\underbrace{p_1 U(m_1) + \dots + p_n U(m_n)}_{\mathbb{E}[U(L)]} = U\left(\underbrace{p_1 m_1 + \dots + p_n m_n}_{\mathbb{E}[L]} \right). \tag{4.1}$$

It is clear that one utility function that satisfies (4.1) is the identity function $U(m) = m$. In fact, when U is the identity function

$$p_1 U(m_1) + \dots + p_n U(m_n) = p_1 m_1 + \dots + p_n m_n = U(p_1 m_1 + \dots + p_n m_n). \tag{4.2}$$

The utility-of-money function $U(m) = m$ represents the vNM preferences of an individual who is risk neutral relative to all money lotteries, or risk neutral for short. Hence, by Theorem 3.1.1 (Chapter 3), any function of the form $U(m) = am + b$ with $a > 0$ is an alternative vNM utility function representing the preferences of a risk-neutral person.

In Chapter 3 we assumed that the set of possible monetary outcomes (over which lotteries were defined) was finite. If we allow for any non-negative amount of money then the vNM utility-of-money function of a risk-neutral individual is represented by the 45° line, as shown in Figure 4.1.

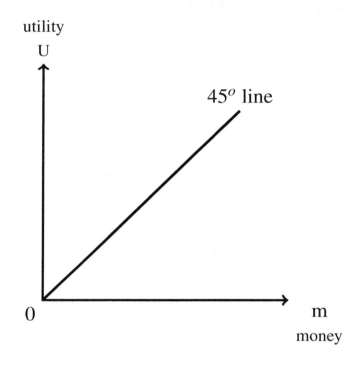

Figure 4.1: The identity function $U(m) = m$ represents the vNM preferences of a risk-neutral individual.

4.1.2 Concavity and risk aversion

In Chapter 2 we said that, given a non-degenerate money lottery $L = \begin{pmatrix} \$m_1 & \$m_2 & \ldots & \$m_n \\ p_1 & p_2 & \ldots & p_n \end{pmatrix}$, an individual is defined to be risk averse relative to L if she prefers the expected value of L for sure to the lottery: $\mathbb{E}[L] \succ L$.[1] If the individual has vNM preferences over money lotteries then, by Theorem 3.1.1 (Chapter 3), there exists a utility-of-money function U

---

[1] It would be more precise to write $\begin{pmatrix} \$\mathbb{E}[L] \\ 1 \end{pmatrix} \succ L$ instead of $\mathbb{E}[L] \succ L$, but from now on we shall use the latter, simpler, notation.

4.1 von Neumann Morgenstern preferences over money lotteries

such that

$$\mathbb{E}[L] \succ L \quad \text{if and only if} \quad U(\mathbb{E}[L]) > \mathbb{E}[U(L)], \text{that is, if and only if,}$$

$$U\Big(\underbrace{p_1 m_1 + \ldots + p_n m_n}_{\mathbb{E}[L]}\Big) > \underbrace{p_1 U(m_1) + \ldots + p_n U(m_n)}_{\mathbb{E}[U(L)]}. \tag{4.3}$$

The inequality in (4.3) is shown graphically in Figure 4.2 when $n = 2$, that is, with reference to the lottery $L = \begin{pmatrix} \$m_1 & \$m_2 \\ p & 1-p \end{pmatrix}$ with $m_1 < m_2$ and $0 < p < 1$.

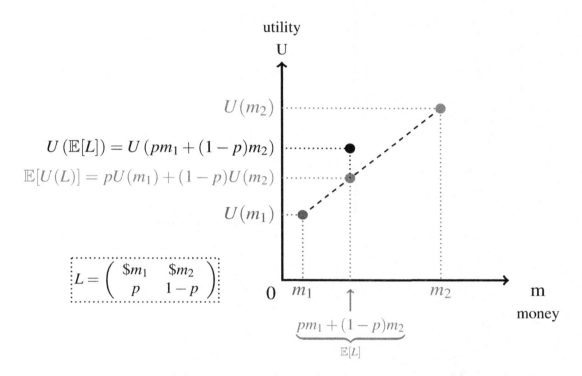

Figure 4.2: A graphical representation of the inequality $U(\mathbb{E}[L]) > \mathbb{E}[U(L)]$, that is $U(pm_1 + (1-p)m_2) > pU(m_1) + (1-p)U(m_2)$.

In Figure 4.2, the point $pm_1 + (1-p)m_2$ is a point on the horizontal axis between m_1 and m_2 (the closer to m_1, the closer p is to 1). Since the individual is assumed to prefer more money to less, $U(m_1) < U(m_2)$. The point $pU(m_1) + (1-p)U(m_2)$ is a point on the vertical axis between $U(m_1)$ and $U(m_2)$. To find that point, draw a straight-line segment from the point $(m_1, U(m_1))$ to the point $(m_2, U(m_2))$ (the dashed line in Figure 4.2) and go vertically up from the point $pm_1 + (1-p)m_2$ on the horizontal axis to the dashed line and from there horizontally to the vertical axis. By (4.3) this point must be below the point $U(pm_1 + (1-p)m_2)$.

It follows from the above discussion that, if we draw a continuous vNM utility-of-money function for a risk-averse individual, the corresponding curve must lie *above* the straight-line segment joining any two points on the graph, as shown in Figure 4.3. This property is know as *strict concavity*.

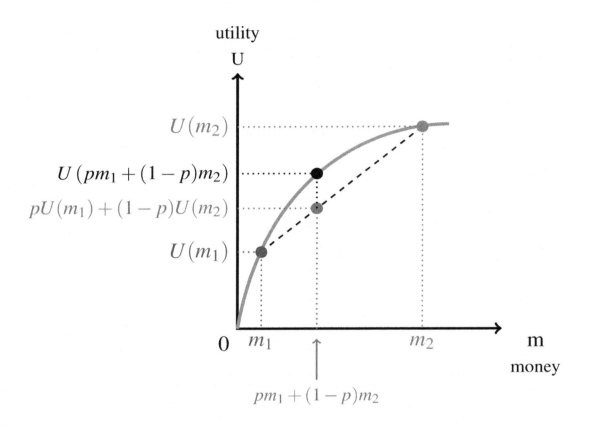

Figure 4.3: The utility function of a risk-averse individual is strictly concave.

Definition 4.1.1 A function $f : \mathbb{R}^+ \to \mathbb{R}$ (where $\mathbb{R}^+$ denotes the set of non-negative real numbers) is *stricly concave* if, for every $x, y \in \mathbb{R}$ and for every $p \in (0, 1)$,

$$f(px + (1-p)y) > pf(x) + (1-p)f(y).$$

(R) The vNM utility-of-money function of a risk-averse individual (that is, of an individual who is risk averse relative to every non-degenerate money lottery) is strictly concave.

4.1.3 Convexity and risk loving

Given a non-degenerate money lottery $L = \begin{pmatrix} \$m_1 & \$m_2 & \ldots & \$m_n \\ p_1 & p_2 & \ldots & p_n \end{pmatrix}$, a risk-loving individual prefers the lottery L to its expected value for sure: $L \succ \mathbb{E}[L]$. If the individual has vNM preferences over money lotteries then, by Theorem 3.1.1 (Chapter 3), there exists a utility-of-money function U such that

$$L \succ \mathbb{E}[L] \quad \text{if and only if} \quad \mathbb{E}[U(L)] > U(\mathbb{E}[L]), \quad \text{that is, if and only if,}$$

$$\underbrace{p_1 U(m_1) + \ldots + p_n U(m_n)}_{\mathbb{E}[U(L)]} > U\left(\underbrace{p_1 m_1 + \ldots + p_n m_n}_{\mathbb{E}[L]}\right). \tag{4.4}$$

An argument similar to the one used in the previous section leads to the conclusion that, if we draw a continuous vNM utility-of-money function for a risk-loving individual, the graph must lie *below* the straight-line segment joining any two points on the graph, as shown in Figure 4.4. This property is know as *strict convexity*.

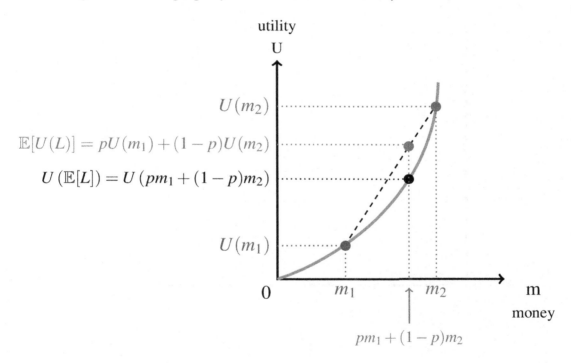

Figure 4.4: The utility function of a risk-averse individual is strictly concave.

Definition 4.1.2 A function $f : \mathbb{R}^+ \to \mathbb{R}$ is *strictly convex* if, for every $x, y \in \mathbb{R}$ and for every $p \in (0, 1)$,
$$f(px + (1-p)y) < pf(x) + (1-p)f(y).$$

ⓇThe vNM utility-of-money function of a risk-loving individual (that is, of an individual who is risk loving relative to every non-degenerate money lottery) is strictly convex.

4.1.4 Mixtures of risk attitudes

While we will tend to concentrate on risk neutrality and risk aversion – and we will typically assume that an individual is risk-neutral or risk-averse relative to *every* non-degenerate money lottery – it is possible for people to display different attitudes to risk for different money lotteries. Consider, for example, an individual whose vNM utility-of-money function is as shown in Figure 4.5. This individual displays risk love for money lotteries that involve small sums of money, risk neutrality for lotteries involving intermediate sums of money and risk aversion for lotteries involving "big stakes": the function is strictly convex for values of m between 0 and m_1, a straight line for values of m between m_1 and m_2 and strictly concave for values of m larger than m_2. Such an individual might be willing to buy a Powerball lottery ticket for \$1 (thus displaying risk love) while at the same time purchasing fire insurance for her house worth \$400,000 (thus displaying risk aversion).

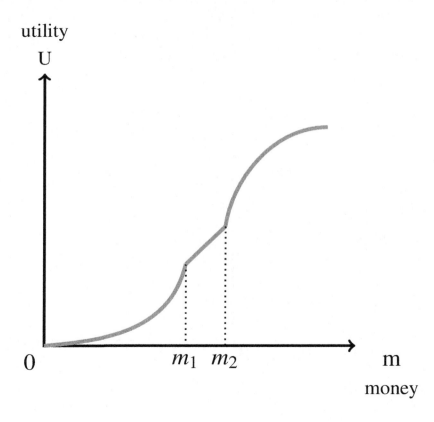

Figure 4.5: The utility function of an individual with different attitudes to risk for different lotteries.

4.1.5 Attitude to risk and the second derivative of the utility function

If the vNM utility-of-money function of an individual is a smooth function (or, at least, twice differentiable) then we can relate the attitude to risk (that is, the shape of the graph of the function) to the second-derivative of the utility function, using the following result from calculus.

Let $f : \mathbb{R}^+ \to \mathbb{R}$ be a twice differentiable function, then

- f is strictly concave if and only if $\frac{d^2 f}{dx^2}(x) < 0$, for every $x \in \mathbb{R}^+$,

- f is strictly convex if and only if $\frac{d^2 f}{dx^2}(x) > 0$, for every $x \in \mathbb{R}^+$,

- the graph of f is a straight line if and only if $\frac{d^2 f}{dx^2}(x) = 0$, for every $x \in \mathbb{R}^+$.

For example, an individual whose vNM utility-of-money function is $U(m) = \sqrt{m}$ is risk averse, since $\frac{dU}{dm} = \frac{1}{2\sqrt{m}}$ and thus $\frac{d^2 U}{dm^2} = -\frac{1}{4\sqrt{m^3}}$ which is negative for every $m > 0$. Figure 4.6 shows the graph of this function.

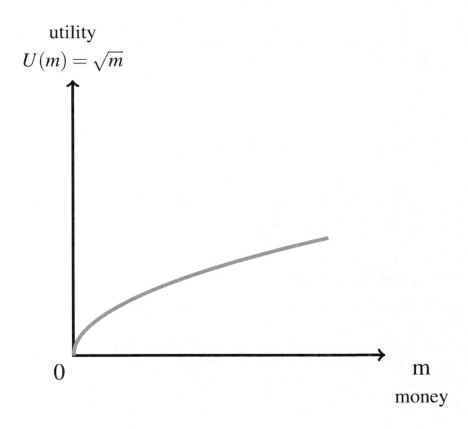

Figure 4.6: The graph of the utility function $U(m) = \sqrt{m}$.

On the other hand, an individual whose vNM utility-of-money function is $U(m) = \frac{m^2}{8}$ is risk averse, since $\frac{dU}{dm} = \frac{m}{4}$ and thus $\frac{d^2U}{dm^2} = \frac{1}{4} > 0$. Figure 4.7 shows the graph of this function.

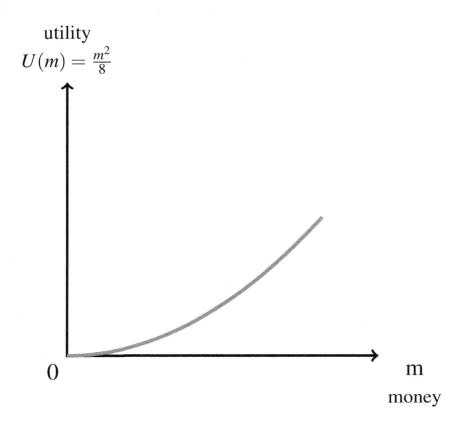

Figure 4.7: The graph of the utility function $U(m) = \frac{m^2}{8}$.

Test your understanding of the concepts introduced in this section, by going through the exercises in Section 4.5.1 at the end of this chapter.

4.2 Measures of risk aversion

Let us now focus on the case of risk aversion. Is it possible to measure the degree of risk aversion of an individual?

One possible measure of risk aversion is provided by the notion of *risk premium* defined in Chapter 2 (Section 2.3), which we can now re-write using the notion of expected utility.

Consider an individual, whose initial wealth is $\$W \geq 0$, and a non-degenerate money lottery $M = \begin{pmatrix} \$x_1 & \$x_2 & \ldots & \$x_n \\ p_1 & p_2 & \ldots & p_n \end{pmatrix}$ (if $x_i < 0$ then we assume that $|x_i| \leq W$, that is, if x_i represents a loss then we assume that the loss is not larger than the initial wealth). As usual, let $\mathbb{E}[M] = p_1 x_1 + \cdots + p_n x_n$ be the expected value of M. In terms of wealth levels, lottery M corresponds to the non-degenerate lottery $L = \begin{pmatrix} \$(W+x_1) & \$(W+x_2) & \ldots & \$(W+x_n) \\ p_1 & p_2 & \ldots & p_n \end{pmatrix}$

4.2 Measures of risk aversion

(given our assumption about the size of potential losses, $W + x_i \geq 0$, for every $i = 1, \ldots, n$), whose expected value is

$$\mathbb{E}[L] = W + \mathbb{E}[M].$$

If the individual has vNM preferences represented by the utility-of-money function $U(m)$, the expected utility of L is

$$\mathbb{E}[U(L)] = p_1 U(W + x_1) + \cdots + p_n U(W + x_n).$$

The risk premium associated with lottery L and utility function U is that amount of money R_{LU} such that the agent is indifferent between lottery L and the sum of money $\$(\mathbb{E}[L] - R_{LU})$ for sure:

$$U(\mathbb{E}[L] - R_{LU}) = \mathbb{E}[U(L)].$$

Thus R_{LU} is the maximum amount that an individual with vNM utility function U is willing to forego to exchange the risky prospect L for a non-risky (i.e. certain) one with the same expected value.

For example, consider the money lottery

$$M = \begin{pmatrix} \$11 & \$20 \\ \frac{3}{5} & \frac{2}{5} \end{pmatrix}$$

whose expected value is $\mathbb{E}[M] = \frac{3}{5} 11 + \frac{2}{5} 20 = \$14.6$, and an individual whose initial wealth is $W = \$5$ and whose vNM preferences can be represented by the utility-of-money function $U(m) = \sqrt{m}$. Then, in terms of wealth levels, the individual is facing the lottery

$$L = \begin{pmatrix} \$16 & \$25 \\ \frac{3}{5} & \frac{2}{5} \end{pmatrix}$$

whose expected value is $\mathbb{E}[L] = \$(14.6 + 5) = \$19.6$; the expected utility of lottery L is $\mathbb{E}[U(L)] = \frac{3}{5}\sqrt{16} + \frac{2}{5}\sqrt{25} = 4.4$. Thus, for this lottery and this individual, the risk premium is the solution to the equation $\sqrt{19.6 - R_{LU}} = 4.4$, which is $R_{LU} = \$0.24$.

On the other hand, if the individual's initial wealth is $\$110$ then lottery M corresponds to the wealth lottery

$$L' = \begin{pmatrix} \$121 & \$130 \\ \frac{3}{5} & \frac{2}{5} \end{pmatrix}$$

whose expected value is $\mathbb{E}[L'] = \$(14.6 + 110) = \$124.6$; the expected utility of lottery L' is $\mathbb{E}[U(L')] = \frac{3}{5}\sqrt{121} + \frac{2}{5}\sqrt{130} = 11.1607$. Hence, for this lottery and this individual, the risk premium is the solution to the equation $\sqrt{124.6 - R_{L'U}} = 11.1607$, which is $R_{L'U} = \$0.0388$.

Thus – as measured by the risk premium– the degree of risk aversion (incorporated in a given vNM utility function U) towards a given money lottery M, varies with the individual's initial wealth. In the above example, when the individual's initial wealth is only $\$5$, she is prepared to avoid the risky prospect M by reducing the expected value of the corresponding wealth lottery by an amount of up to 24 cents, but if her initial wealth is $\$110$ then she is only prepared to reduce the expected value of the corresponding wealth lottery by up to 4 cents.

From now on we will use the expression *wealth lottery* to refer to a lottery whose outcomes are levels of wealth for the individual (such as lotteries L and L' above, constructed from the money lottery M by adding the individual's initial wealth to every outcome in M).

The reader should try to prove the following: suppose that, given a wealth lottery L and a vNM utility function U, the risk premium is \$$r$; then the risk premium remains \$$r$ if the utility-of-money function U is replaced by a positive affine transformation V of U, that is, for every m, $V(m) = aU(m) + b$, with $a > 0$. In other words, if, for every m, $V(m) = aU(m) + b$, with $a > 0$, then $R_{LV} = R_{LU}$.

Instead of comparing, *for a fixed utility function*, the risk premium of a given money lottery across different levels of initial wealth, we can also compare the risk premium, *for a fixed wealth lottery*, for different utility functions (representing different preferences, hence different individuals). Figure 4.8 shows the risk premium for the wealth lottery $L = \begin{pmatrix} \$m_1 & \$m_2 \\ p & 1-p \end{pmatrix}$ and two different utility functions, U and V. Let R_{LU} be the risk premium associated with U and R_{LV} be the risk premium associated with V; then $R_{LV} = [pm_1 + (1-p)m_2] - \hat{m}_V > R_{LU} = [pm_1 + (1-p)m_2] - \hat{m}_U$, where $\hat{m}_V$ is the certainty equivalent of lottery L for V and $\hat{m}_U$ is the certainty equivalent of lottery L for U (see Chapter 2, Section 2.3 for the notion of certainty equivalent).

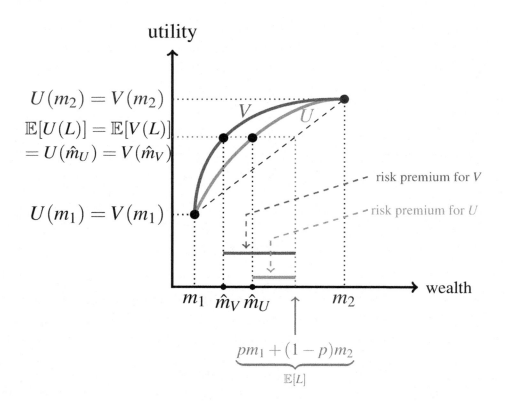

Figure 4.8: The graphs of two utility functions U and V and the risk premia corresponding to the wealth lottery that gives \$$m_1$ with probability p and \$$m_2$ with probability $(1-p)$.

4.2 Measures of risk aversion

Let us now focus on the issue of comparing different utility functions in terms of the the extent to which they express risk aversion. Using the notion of risk premium, one possibility is given in the following definition.

Definition 4.2.1 Let U and V be two concave vNM utility-of-money functions. We say that V incorporates *more* risk aversion than U if, for every non-degenerate wealth lottery L, $R_{LV} \geq R_{LU}$ (with strict inequality for at least one lottery).

Since we identified risk aversion with concavity of the vNM utility function, it seems that the more concave the utility function, the more risk averse the individual is. This intuition is confirmed in Figure 4.8 (on page 88): V is more concave than U and indeed it incorporates more risk aversion, as measured by the size of the risk premium.

Since we identified concavity with negativity of the second derivative of the utility function, one might be tempted to conclude that an individual with vNM utility-of-money function V is more risk-averse than an individual with vNM utility-of-money function U if, in absolute value, the second derivative of V is larger than the second derivative of U: $\left|\frac{d^2V}{dm^2}\right| > \left|\frac{d^2U}{dm^2}\right|$.

Unfortunately, this is not correct, because it violates the requirement that, if V is a positive affine transformation of U, then V and U represent the same preferences and thus the same degree of risk aversion (as was pointed out in the remark on page 88). For example, let $V(m) = 2U(m)$, for every $m \geq 0$. Then, for every m, $\left|\frac{d^2V}{dm^2}(m)\right| = \left|2\frac{d^2U}{dm^2}(m)\right| > \left|\frac{d^2U}{dm^2}(m)\right|$ and yet V and U represent the same preferences.

An expression involving the second derivative of the utility function is the following, which is known as the *Arrow-Pratt measure of absolute risk aversion*, denoted by $A_U(m)$:[2]

$$A_U(m) = -\frac{U''(m)}{U'(m)}.$$

The minus sign makes this expression positive (since $U'(m) > 0$, because the individual is assumed to prefer more money to less, and $U''(m) < 0$, since the individual is assumed to be risk averse).

Note that the Arrow-Pratt measure of absolute risk aversion is a *local* measure, since it varies with the amount of money considered; that is, typically, if $m_1 \neq m_2$ then $A_U(m_1) \neq A_U(m_2)$.

Let us verify that the Arrow-Pratt measure of risk aversion *is* invariant to affine transformations. Let a and b be real numbers, with $a > 0$, and let $V(m) = aU(m) + b$, for every $m \geq 0$. Then $V'(m) = aU'(m)$ and $V''(m) = aU''(m)$, so that $\frac{V''(m)}{V'(m)} = \frac{aU''(m)}{aU'(m)} = \frac{U''(m)}{U'(m)}$ and thus $A_V(m) = A_U(m)$.

Using the Arrow-Pratt measure of risk aversion we can introduce a second definition of "more risk averse".

---

[2] We denote the first derivative of U interchangeably by either $U'(m)$ or $\frac{dU}{dm}(m)$ and the second derivative interchangeably by either $U''(m)$ or $\frac{d^2U}{dm^2}(m)$

Definition 4.2.2 Let U and V be two concave vNM utility-of-money functions. We say that V incorporates *more* risk aversion than U if, for every level of wealth $m > 0$, $A_V(m) \geq A_U(m)$ (with strict inequality for at least one m).

For example, according to Definition 4.2.2, which of $\sqrt{m}$ and $\ln(m)$ incorporates greater risk aversion? Let us compute the Arrow-Pratt measure of risk aversion for these two functions.

Since $\frac{d}{dm}\sqrt{m} = -\frac{1}{2\sqrt{m}}$ and $\frac{d^2}{dm^2}\sqrt{m} = -\frac{1}{4\sqrt{m^3}}$, $A_{\sqrt{}}(m) = \frac{1}{2m}$.

On the other hand, since $\frac{d}{dm}\ln(m) = \frac{1}{m}$ and $\frac{d^2}{dm^2}\ln(m) = -\frac{1}{m^2}$, $A_{\ln}(m) = \frac{1}{m}$.

Thus, since, for every $m > 0$, $\frac{1}{m} > \frac{1}{2m}$ we have that, for every $m > 0$, $A_{\ln}(m) > A_{\sqrt{}}(m)$ and thus, according to Definition 4.2.2, the utility function $\ln(m)$ incorporates more risk aversion than the utility function $\sqrt{m}$.

Note that, in general, there may be utility functions U and V that cannot be ranked according to Definition 4.2.2. For example, it may be that case $A_U(m) > A_V(m)$ for values of m in some interval and $A_U(m) < A_V(m)$ for values of m in some other interval: see Exercise 4.11.

Yet a third definition of "more risk averse" relies on the intuition that "more concave" means "more risk averse":

Definition 4.2.3 Let U and V be two concave vNM utility-of-money functions. We say that V incorporates *more* risk aversion than U if there exists a strictly increasing and concave function $f : \mathbb{R} \to \mathbb{R}$ such that, for every $m \geq 0$, $V(m) = f(U(m))$. In this case we say that V is a *concave transformation* of U.

For example, since $\ln(x)$ is a strictly increasing, concave function, $V(m) = \ln(\sqrt{m})$ is a concave transformation of $U(m) = \sqrt{m}$ and thus, according to Definition 4.2.3, V incorporates more risk aversion than U.

Of course, having three different definitions of greater risk aversion is rather confusing: which of the three is the "correct" definition? Furthermore, while the condition in Definition 4.2.2 is somewhat easier to verify, the condition in Definition 4.2.1 is not very practical, since it would require considering all possible wealth lotteries, and the condition in Definition 4.2.3 is also hard to verify: how can one tell if one function is a concave transformation of another? Luckily, it turns out that the three definitions are in fact equivalent. The following theorem was proved by John Pratt in 1964.[3]

---

[3] John W. Pratt, Risk aversion in the small and in the large, *Econometrica*, Vol. 32, No. 1/2, 1964, pp. 122-136.

4.2 Measures of risk aversion

> **Theorem 4.2.1** Let $U(m)$ and $V(m)$ be two functions. Then the following conditions are equivalent:
>
> 1. $R_{LV} \geq R_{LU}$, for every non-degenerate wealth lottery L.
> 2. $A_V(m) \geq A_U(m)$, for every m.
> 3. There exists a strictly increasing and concave function $f : \mathbb{R} \to \mathbb{R}$ such that $V(m) = f(U(m))$, for every $m \geq 0$.

The Arrow-Pratt measure of absolute risk aversion is not invariant to a change in the units of measurement. For example, if the agent's vNM utility-of-money function is $U(m) = \sqrt{m}$, where m is wealth measured in dollars, then her Arrow-Pratt measure of absolute risk aversion is, as we saw above, $A_{\sqrt{}}(m) = \frac{1}{2m}$; for example, when the agent's wealth is $10, her Arrow-Pratt measure of absolute risk aversion is $A_{\sqrt{}}(10) = \frac{1}{2(10)} = \frac{1}{20} = 0.05$. Suppose now that we want to change our units of measurement from dollars to cents. The utility function then would be written as $V(y) = \sqrt{y}$ where y is wealth measured in cents (thus $y = 100m$) and her Arrow-Pratt measure of absolute risk aversion is $A_{\sqrt{}}(y) = \frac{1}{2y}$; so that when $y = 1,000\,cents$, that is, $10, her Arrow-Pratt measure of absolute risk aversion is $A_{\sqrt{}}(1,000) = \frac{1}{2(1,000)} = \frac{1}{2,000} = 0.0005$: a different number, despite the fact that we are looking at the same preferences and the same wealth.

A related measure of risk aversion, which is immune from this problem (that is, is invariant to changes in units of measurement) is the *Arrow-Pratt measure of relative risk aversion*, denoted by $r_U(m)$:

$$r_U(m) = -m \frac{U''(m)}{U'(m)}.$$

Thus $r_U(m) = m A_U(m)$.

While the Arrow-Pratt measure of *absolute* risk aversion measures the rate at which marginal utility (that is, the first derivative of the utility function) decreases when wealth is increased by one monetary unit (e.g. $1), the Arrow-Pratt measure of *relative* risk aversion measures the rate at which marginal utility decreases when wealth is increased by 1%.[4]

> Test your understanding of the concepts introduced in this section, by going through the exercises in Section 4.5.2 at the end of this chapter.

---

[4] In other words, $r_U(m)$ is the absolute value of the elasticity of marginal utility, $U'(m)$, with respect to m.

4.3 Some noteworthy utility functions

In the previous section we considered some specific utility-of-money functions.

For the square root function $\sqrt{m}$ we found that the Arrow-Pratt measure of absolute risk aversion is $A_{\sqrt{}}(m) = \frac{1}{2m}$, which is decreasing in m. Thus an individual with this vNM utility function displays less and less risk aversion as her wealth increases.[5]

The natural logarithm function $\ln(m)$ is similar: the Arrow-Pratt measure of absolute risk aversion is also decreasing in m: $A_{\ln}(m) = \frac{1}{m}$.[6]

Consider now the following utility-of-money function, whose graph is shown in Figure 4.9:

$$U(m) = 1 - e^{-m} = 1 - \frac{1}{e^m}.$$

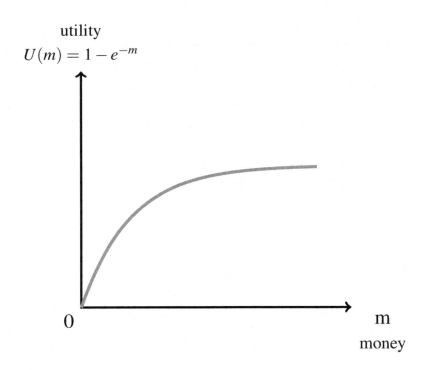

Figure 4.9: The graphs of the utility function $U(m) = 1 - e^{-m}$.

Since $\frac{d}{dm}(1 - e^{-m}) = e^{-m}$ and $\frac{d^2}{dm^2}(1 - e^{-m}) = -e^{-m}$ it follows that the Arrow-Pratt measure of absolute risk aversion for this function is a constant:

$$A(m) = -\frac{-e^{-m}}{e^{-m}} = 1.$$

---

[5] On the other hand, the Arrow-Pratt measure of *relative* risk aversion is constant: $r_{\sqrt{}}(m) = mA_{\sqrt{}}(m) = m\frac{1}{2m} = \frac{1}{2}$.

[6] And the Arrow-Pratt measure of *relative* risk aversion is constant: $r_{\ln}(m) = mA_{\ln}(m) = m\frac{1}{m} = 1$.

Indeed, this is a special case of the class of CARA (Constant Absolute Risk Aversion) utility functions, which is the class of functions of the form

$$U(m) = 1 - e^{-\lambda m} = 1 - \frac{1}{e^{\lambda m}}$$

where λ is a positive constant. In fact, $\frac{d}{dm}\left(1 - e^{-\lambda m}\right) = \lambda e^{-\lambda m}$ and $\frac{d^2}{dm^2}\left(1 - e^{-\lambda m}\right) = -\lambda^2 e^{-\lambda m}$ so that the Arrow-Pratt measure of absolute risk aversion is equal to λ.

We saw above that the utility function $\ln(m)$ is characterized by constant relative risk aversion. That is not the only function with this property. The class of CRRA (Constant Relative Risk Aversion) utility functions contains, besides the natural logarithm function,[7] the functions of the form

$$U(m) = \frac{m^{(1-\lambda)}}{1-\lambda} \quad \text{with } \lambda > 0, \lambda \neq 1.$$

For these functions the Arrow-Pratt measure of absolute risk aversion is $A_U(m) = \frac{\lambda}{m}$ so that the Arrow-Pratt measure of relative risk aversion is $r_U(m) = mA_U(m) = \lambda$.

> Test your understanding of the concepts introduced in this section, by going through the exercises in Section 4.5.3 at the end of this chapter.

4.4 Higher risk

In the previous section we answered the following questions:

- For a given money lottery M involving changes in wealth, how does a risk-averse individual view the corresponding wealth lottery at different levels of initial wealth? Typically (but not necessarily), individuals display less risk aversion as their initial wealth increases.
- How can we determine if one individual, whose utility-of-money function is $U(m)$, is more or less risk averse than another individual, whose utility-of-money function is $V(m)$? We considered three alternative definitions of "more risk averse" and saw that they are equivalent.

In this section we ask a different question, namely: when can we say that a money lottery, L, is "more risky" than another money lottery, M?

In order to address this issue we fix a set of non-negative monetary prizes, $\$m_1, \ldots, \$m_n$ with the convention that they are ordered from smallest to largest, that is,

$$0 \leq m_1 < m_2 < \cdots < m_n.$$

A lottery over $\{m_1, m_2, \ldots, m_n\}$ coincides with a probability distribution over this set.

---

[7] And, more generally, the logarithmic functions $\log_a(m)$ with $a > 1$.

Let L be one such lottery, whose probabilities are $\{p_1, p_2, \ldots, p_n\}$ (p_i is the probability of prize \$$m_i$, for every $i = 1, 2, \ldots, n$)[8] and let M be another lottery, whose probabilities are $\{q_1, q_2, \ldots, q_n\}$:

$$L = \begin{pmatrix} \$m_1 & \$m_2 & \ldots & \$m_n \\ p_1 & p_2 & \ldots & p_n \end{pmatrix} \quad \text{and} \quad M = \begin{pmatrix} \$m_1 & \$m_2 & \ldots & \$m_n \\ q_1 & q_2 & \ldots & q_n \end{pmatrix}.$$

⊛ Note that we allow for the possibility that some of the p_i's and q_i's are zero.

We shall denote by $P : \{m_1, m_2, \ldots, m_n\} \to [0,1]$ the *cumulative* distribution corresponding to the distribution $\{p_1, p_2, \ldots, p_n\}$ and by $Q : \{m_1, m_2, \ldots, m_n\} \to [0,1]$ the *cumulative* distribution corresponding to the distribution $\{q_1, q_2, \ldots, q_n\}$, that is, for every $i = 1, 2, \ldots, n$ (denoting $P(m_i)$ by P_i and $Q(m_i)$ by Q_i)

$$P_i = p_1 + \cdots + p_i \quad \text{and} \quad Q_i = q_1 + \cdots + q_i$$

(clearly, $P_1 = p_1$, $Q_1 = q_1$ and $P_n = Q_n = 1$). For example, if

$$L = \begin{pmatrix} \$12 & \$26 & \$40 & \$58 & \$80 & \$96 \\ \frac{1}{20} & \frac{7}{20} & 0 & \frac{4}{20} & 0 & \frac{8}{20} \end{pmatrix}$$

then the corresponding cumulative distribution is as follows:

	\$12	\$26	\$40	\$58	\$80	\$96
cumulative P:	$\frac{1}{20}$	$\frac{8}{20}$	$\frac{8}{20}$	$\frac{12}{20}$	$\frac{12}{20}$	$\frac{20}{20}$

4.4.1 First-order stochastic dominance

The following definition captures one (rather obvious) way in which a lottery M can be viewed as unambiguously better than another lottery L.

Definition 4.4.1 Given two lotteries

$$L = \begin{pmatrix} \$m_1 & \$m_2 & \ldots & \$m_n \\ p_1 & p_2 & \ldots & p_n \end{pmatrix} \quad \text{and} \quad M = \begin{pmatrix} \$m_1 & \$m_2 & \ldots & \$m_n \\ q_1 & q_2 & \ldots & q_n \end{pmatrix}$$

we say that *L first-order stochastically dominates M* (and write $L >_{FSD} M$) if

$$P_i \leq Q_i \quad \text{for ever } i = 1, 2, \ldots, n, \text{ with at least one strict inequality.}$$

---

[8]Thus p is a function $p : \{m_1, \ldots, m_n\} \to [0,1]$ and, for every $i = 1, \ldots, m$, we denote $p(m_i)$ by p_i.

4.4 Higher risk

For example,

$$L = \begin{pmatrix} \$26 & \$40 & \$58 & \$80 & \$96 \\ \frac{7}{20} & 0 & \frac{3}{20} & \frac{1}{20} & \frac{9}{20} \end{pmatrix} >_{FSD} M = \begin{pmatrix} \$26 & \$40 & \$58 & \$80 & \$96 \\ \frac{7}{20} & 0 & \frac{4}{20} & 0 & \frac{9}{20} \end{pmatrix}$$

as can be seen from the cumulative distributions:

		$26	$40	$58	$80	$96
cumulative for L,	P:	$\frac{7}{20}$	$\frac{7}{20}$	$\frac{10}{20}$	$\frac{11}{20}$	1
cumulative for M,	Q:	$\frac{7}{20}$	$\frac{7}{20}$	$\frac{11}{20}$	$\frac{11}{20}$	1

It should be clear that if lottery L first-order stochastically dominates lottery M, then L assigns higher probabilities to higher prizes relative to M. It follows that the expected value of L is greater than the expected value of M: $\mathbb{E}[L] > \mathbb{E}[M]$; thus a risk-neutral person prefers L to M. However, the same is true for any attitude to risk.[9]

Theorem 4.4.1 Let L and M be two money lotteries (over the same set of prizes). Then

$$L >_{FSD} M$$

if and only if

$$\mathbb{E}[U(L)] > \mathbb{E}[U(M)], \text{ for every strictly increasing utility function } U.$$

4.4.2 Mean preserving spread and second-order stochastic dominance

The notion of first-order stochastic dominance does not really capture the fact that a money lottery is less risky than another one; it captures a different notion, namely that of a money lottery being unambiguously better than another one. On the other hand, the notion of *second-order* stochastic dominance does capture the property of being unambiguously less risky. Second-order stochastic dominance is based on the notion of a "mean preserving spread".

Intuitively, a mean preserving spread of a probability distribution is an operation that takes probability from a point and moves it to each side of that point in such a way that the expected value remains the same.

---

[9]The theorem can be proved using Abel's Lemma, which says that if $a_1, \ldots, a_n$ and $b_1, \ldots, b_n$ are real numbers, then, letting $A_i = a_1 + \cdots + a_i$ and $B_i = b_1 + \cdots + b_i$, $\sum_{i=1}^{n} a_i b_i = \sum_{i=1}^{n-1} A_i(b_i - b_{i+1}) + A_n b_n$ (see https://planetmath.org/abelslemma). To prove Theorem 4.4.1 using Abel's Lemma, let $a_i = q_i - p_i$ and $b_i = U(m_i)$.

Chapter 4. Money lotteries revisited

Let L be the following money lottery, whose expected value is $\mathbb{E}[L] = 5$:

$$L = \begin{pmatrix} \$2 & \$3 & \$4 & \$5 & \$9 \\ \frac{1}{3} & 0 & \frac{1}{3} & 0 & \frac{1}{3} \end{pmatrix}.$$

Now let us construct a new lottery M by taking the probability assigned to the prize \$4, namely $\frac{1}{3}$, and spreading it equally between the prizes \$3 and \$5, as shown inn Figure 4.10. It is easy to check that the expected value of M is the same as the expected value of L, namely 5.

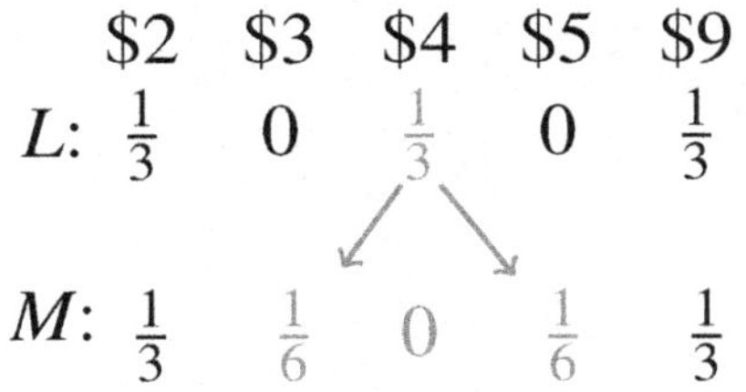

$$\begin{array}{cccccc} & \$2 & \$3 & \$4 & \$5 & \$9 \\ L: & \frac{1}{3} & 0 & \frac{1}{3} & 0 & \frac{1}{3} \\ & & \swarrow & & \searrow & \\ M: & \frac{1}{3} & \frac{1}{6} & 0 & \frac{1}{6} & \frac{1}{3} \end{array}$$

Figure 4.10: A mean-preserving spread.

Intuitively, a risk-averse person should dislike the change from L to M because it involves more risk: the prize of \$4 has been replaced with a non-degenerate "sub-lottery" with expected value of \$4. By definition of risk aversion, the sub-lottery is worse than its expected value.

To perform a 'worsening" of lottery L it is not even necessary to spread out the entire probability of prize \$4; for example, we could merely take away half that probability, namely $\frac{1}{6}$, and spread it equally between the prizes \$3 and \$5 thus obtaining the alternative lottery

$$M' = \begin{pmatrix} \$2 & \$3 & \$4 & \$5 & \$9 \\ \frac{1}{3} & \frac{1}{12} & \frac{1}{6} & \frac{1}{12} & \frac{1}{3} \end{pmatrix}.$$

It is easy to check that also the expected value of M' is 5. In Exercise 4.18 the reader is asked to verify that an individual with utility-of-money function $U(m) = \sqrt{m}$ strictly prefers L to M' and M' to M.

In fact, according to the next definition, M is a mean-preserving spread of M', which, in turn, is a mean-preserving spread of L.

Before giving the formal definition of a mean-preserving spread, let us gain some intuition, as follows. Start with a lottery

$$L = \begin{pmatrix} \$m_1 & \$m_2 & \dots & \$m_n \\ p_1 & p_2 & \dots & p_n \end{pmatrix}$$

and fix three monetary prizes m_i, m_j and m_k with $m_i < m_j < m_k$ and assume that m_j has positive probability in L, that is, $p_j > 0$. Since m_j is strictly between m_i and m_k, there is a $\delta \in (0,1)$ such that $m_j = (1-\delta)m_i + \delta m_k$, in fact

$$\delta = \frac{m_j - m_i}{m_k - m_i}. \qquad (\blacklozenge)$$

4.4 Higher risk

Now focus on the part of lottery L that involves the three prizes m_i, m_j and m_k:

$$\begin{pmatrix} \ldots & \$m_i & \ldots & \$m_j & \ldots & \$m_k & \ldots \\ \ldots & \$p_i & \ldots & \$p_j & \ldots & \$p_k & \ldots \end{pmatrix}$$

Let $\alpha \in (0,1)$ and let us reduce the probability of m_j from p_j to $p_j - \alpha p_j$ and spread the probability αp_j between m_i and m_k in the proportions $(1-\delta)$ and δ, respectively, where δ is given by ($\blacklozenge$). This is shown in Figure 4.11.

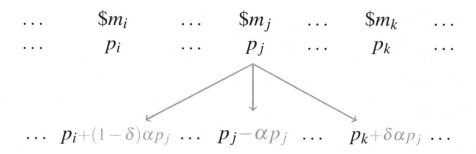

Figure 4.11: A mean-preserving spread.

Let M be the new lottery so constructed. Thus L and M differ **only** in the probabilities assigned to prizes m_i, m_j and m_k. The contribution of these prizes to the calculation of the expected value of the initial lottery L is

$$p_i m_i + p_j m_j + p_k m_k$$

while the contribution of these prizes to the calculation of the expected value of the new lottery M is

$$\left[p_i + (1-\delta)\alpha p_j\right] m_i + \left[p_j - \alpha p_j\right] m_j + \left[p_k + \delta \alpha p_j\right] m_k$$

$$= p_i m_i + p_j m_j + p_k m_k + \alpha p_j \underbrace{\left[(1-\delta)m_i + \delta m_k - m_j\right]}_{=0 \text{ because } (1-\delta)m_i + \delta m_k = m_j}$$

$$= p_i m_i + p_j m_j + p_k m_k.$$

Hence $\mathbb{E}[L] = \mathbb{E}[M]$.

We are now ready to give the definition of a mean-preserving spread.[10]

---

[10] The notion of a mean preserving spread of a probability distribution was introduced by Michael Rothschild and Joseph Stiglitz in "Increasing risk I: A definition", *Journal of Economic Theory*, 1970, Vol. 2, pp. 225-243. Their definition involved re-assigning probabilities across *four* different points, but that definition is equivalent to one that is based on reassigning probabilities across *three* different points, as shown by Eric Rasmusen and Emmanuel Petrakis, "Defining the mean-preserving spread: 3-pt versus 4-pt", in: *Decision making under risk and uncertainty: new models and empirical findings*, edited by John Geweke, Amsterdam: Kluwer, 1992. Rasmusen and Petrakis' definition is different from ours, but equivalent to it. Their definition is as follows. Take three points a_1, a_2, a_3 with $a_1 < a_2 < a_3$; a mean-preserving spread is a triple of probabilities $\gamma_1, \gamma_2, \gamma_3$ such that (1) $\gamma_1 + \gamma_3 = \gamma_2 \leq p_2$ (where p_2 is the initial probability of a_2) and (2) $\gamma_1 a_1 - \gamma_2 a_2 + \gamma_3 a_3 = 0$. The initial probability of a_i is p_i and the modified probabilities are $p_1 + \gamma_1, p_2 - \gamma_2, p_3 + \gamma_3$. To convert it into our definition let $\alpha = \frac{\gamma_1 + \gamma_3}{p_2}$ and $\delta = \frac{a_2 - a_1}{a_3 - a_1}$. Invert the operations to go from our definition to theirs.

Definition 4.4.2 Let

$$L = \begin{pmatrix} \$m_1 & \$m_2 & \ldots & \$m_n \\ p_1 & p_2 & \ldots & p_n \end{pmatrix} \quad \text{and} \quad M = \begin{pmatrix} \$m_1 & \$m_2 & \ldots & \$m_n \\ q_1 & q_2 & \ldots & q_n \end{pmatrix}.$$

be two money lotteries. We say that *M is obtained from L by a mean-preserving spread*, and write

$$L \to_{MPS} M$$

if there are three prizes m_i, m_j, m_k with $m_i < m_j < m_k$ such that:

(1) for very $t \in \{1, \ldots, n\} \setminus \{i, j, k\}$, $q_t = p_t$ and

(2) for some $\alpha \in (0, 1]$

$$q_i = p_i + (1-\delta)\alpha p_j, \quad q_j = p_j - \alpha p_j, \quad q_k = p_k + \delta \alpha p_j \quad \text{with } \delta = \frac{m_j - m_i}{m_k - m_i}.$$

Definition 4.4.3 Let

$$L = \begin{pmatrix} \$m_1 & \$m_2 & \ldots & \$m_n \\ p_1 & p_2 & \ldots & p_n \end{pmatrix} \quad \text{and} \quad M = \begin{pmatrix} \$m_1 & \$m_2 & \ldots & \$m_n \\ q_1 & q_2 & \ldots & q_n \end{pmatrix}.$$

be two money lotteries. We say that *L second-order stochastically dominates M* and write

$$L >_{SSD} M$$

if M can be obtained from L by a finite sequence of mean-preserving spreads, that is, if there is a sequence of money lotteries $\langle L_1, L_2, \ldots, L_m \rangle$ (with $m \geq 2$) such that:

(1) $L_1 = L$,

(2) $L_m = M$ and

(3) for every $i = 1, \ldots, m-1$, $L_i \to_{MPS} L_{i+1}$.

As remarked above, a risk-averse person ought to be made worse off by a mean preserving spread. This intuition is confirmed by the following theorem.[11]

> **Theorem 4.4.2** Let L and M be two money lotteries (over the same set of prizes). Then
>
> $$L >_{SSD} M$$
>
> if and only if
>
> $\mathbb{E}[U(L)] > \mathbb{E}[U(M)]$, for every strictly increasing and concave utility function U.

> Test your understanding of the concepts introduced in this section, by going through the exercises in Section 4.5.4 at the end of this chapter.

4.5 Exercises

The solutions to the following exercises are given in Section 4.6 at the end of this chapter.

4.5.1 Exercises for Section 4.1: vNM preferences over money lotteries

> **Exercise 4.1** Jennifer's von Neumann-Morgenstern utility-of-money function is $U(m) = 20\sqrt{m} - 4$. Consider the following lottery, where the outcomes are possible levels of wealth for Jennifer:
>
> $$L = \begin{pmatrix} \$8 & \$18 & \$24 & \$28 & \$30 \\ \frac{2}{5} & \frac{1}{5} & \frac{1}{10} & \frac{1}{10} & \frac{1}{5} \end{pmatrix}$$
>
> (a) What is the expected value of L?
> (b) What is the expected utility of L?
> (c) Calculate $\frac{d}{dm}U(m)$.
> (d) Calculate $\frac{d^2}{dm^2}U(m)$.
> (e) Is Jennifer risk-averse, risk-neutral or risk-loving?

---

[11]This result is best known to economists from the 1970 paper by Rothschild and Stiglitz mentioned in Footnote 10. However, in a later article (Michael Rothschild and Joseph Stiglitz, Addendum to 'Increasing risk I: A definition', *Journal of Economic Theory*, 1972, Vol. 5, p. 306) the authors themselves acknowledged that their main result could have been derived from earlier contributions by mathematicians.

Exercise 4.2 Consider again the wealth lottery of Exercise 4.1, but a different agent: Jim, whose vNM utility-of-money function is $U(m) = \sqrt{m}$. Answer the same questions as in Exercise 4.1 but referring to Jim. ■

Exercise 4.3 What attitude to risk is incorporated in the following vNM utility-of-money functions? Base your answer on the sign of the second derivative of the utility function.
  (a) $\ln(m+1)$
  (b) $8 + m^{1.65}$
  (c) $2 + 7m$. ■

Exercise 4.4 Let m denote the amount of money (measured in millions of dollars) and suppose that it varies in the interval $[0,1]$. John's utility-of-money function is given by:
$$U(m) = -m^2 + 2m - 4.$$
  (a) What is John's attitude to risk?

Jenny, on the other hand, has the following utility function:
$$V(m) = -3\left(m^2 - 2m\right).$$
  (b) What is Jenny's attitude to risk?
  (c) Do John and Jenny have the same preferences?
  (d) Give an example of two utility functions that incorporate the same attitude to risk but do not represent the same preferences for lotteries. ■

4.5.2 Exercises for Section 4.2: Measures of risk aversion

Exercise 4.5 As in Exercise 4.1, consider Jennifer, whose vNM utility-of-money function is $U(m) = 20\sqrt{m} - 4$, and the lottery
$$L = \begin{pmatrix} \$8 & \$18 & \$24 & \$28 & \$30 \\ \frac{2}{5} & \frac{1}{5} & \frac{1}{10} & \frac{1}{10} & \frac{1}{5} \end{pmatrix}$$

  (a) Calculate the risk premium for lottery L for Jennifer.
  (b) Calculate Jennifer's Arrow-Pratt measure of absolute risk aversion for $m = 900$ and for $m = 1{,}600$. ■

4.5 Exercises

Exercise 4.6 As in Exercise 4.2, consider Jim, whose vNM utility-of-money function is $V(m) = \sqrt{m}$, and the lottery

$$L = \begin{pmatrix} \$8 & \$18 & \$24 & \$28 & \$30 \\ \frac{2}{5} & \frac{1}{5} & \frac{1}{10} & \frac{1}{10} & \frac{1}{5} \end{pmatrix}$$

(a) Calculate the risk premium for lottery L for Jim.

(b) Calculate Jim's Arrow-Pratt measure of absolute risk aversion for $m = 900$ and for $m = 1,600$.

Exercise 4.7 As in Exercise 4.4, let m denote the amount of money, measured in millions of dollars, and suppose that it varies in the interval $[0,1]$. John's utility-of-money function is given by: $U(m) = -m^2 + 2m - 4$ while Jenny's utility function is: $V(m) = -3\left(m^2 - 2m\right)$. Calculate the Arrow-Pratt measures of absolute and relative risk aversion for John and Jenny and compare them.

Exercise 4.8 Amy faces the wealth lottery $\begin{pmatrix} \$24 & \$12 & \$48 \\ \frac{2}{6} & \frac{3}{6} & \frac{1}{6} \end{pmatrix}$ and tells you that she considers it equivalent to getting $18 for sure.

(a) Calculate the risk premium for lottery L for Amy.

(b) What is Amy's attitude to risk?

(c) Could Amy's vNM utility-of-money function be $U(m) = \sqrt{m}$?

Exercise 4.9 Bill is risk neutral.

(a) How does he rank the following lotteries?

$$L_1 = \begin{pmatrix} \$24 & \$12 & \$48 & \$6 \\ \frac{1}{6} & \frac{2}{6} & \frac{1}{6} & \frac{2}{6} \end{pmatrix} \quad L_2 = \begin{pmatrix} \$180 & \$0 & \$90 \\ \frac{1}{20} & \frac{17}{20} & \frac{2}{20} \end{pmatrix}$$

(b) What is the risk premium associated with lottery L_1 for Bill?

(c) What is the risk premium associated with lottery L_2 for Bill?

Exercise 4.10 Consider the following money lottery, where the outcomes are *changes* in wealth:

$$M = \begin{pmatrix} -\$50 & \$120 \\ \frac{1}{4} & \frac{3}{4} \end{pmatrix}.$$

Berta's vNM utility-of-money function is $U(m) = \ln(m)$.

(a) Suppose that Berta's inital wealth is \$80. Write the wealth lottery corresponding to lottery M above and calculate the risk premium for this lottery for Berta.

(b) Suppose that Berta's inital wealth is \$200. Write the wealth lottery corresponding to lottery M above and calculate the risk premium for this lottery for Berta.

Exercise 4.11 Consider the wealth lottery $L = \begin{pmatrix} \$120 & \$180 & \$260 \\ \frac{2}{5} & \frac{2}{5} & \frac{1}{5} \end{pmatrix}$ and the following vNM utility-of-money functions defined for $m \in [0, 300]$:

$$U(m) = \sqrt{m} \quad \text{and} \quad V(m) = -\left(\frac{m}{10} - 36\right)^2 + \frac{m}{20} + 1,400.$$

(a) Write an equation whose solution gives R_{LU} (the risk premium for lottery L and utility function U) and verify that the solution is $R_{LU} = 3.6949$.

(b) Write an equation whose solution gives R_{LV} (the risk premium for lottery L and utility function V) and verify that the solution is $R_{LV} = 6.848$.

(c) Using the Arrow-Pratt measure of absolute risk aversion, which of U and V incorporates greater risk aversion?

4.5.3 Exercises for Section 4.3: Some noteworthy utility functions

Exercise 4.12 Plot the following utility functions in the same diagram:

$$U(m) = 1 - e^{-m} \quad \text{and} \quad V(m) = 1 - e^{-3m}.$$

Exercise 4.13 Consider the utility-of-money function $U(m) = m^a$, where a is a constant such that $0 < a < 1$. For this function is the Arrow-Pratt measure of absolute risk aversion decreasing, constant or increasing?

Exercise 4.14 Consider the quadratic utility-of-money function $U(m) = cm - \frac{m^2}{2}$, where c is a positive constant and $m \in [0, c)$. For this function is the Arrow-Pratt measure of absolute risk aversion decreasing, constant or increasing?

4.5.4 Exercises for Section 4.4: Higher risk

Exercise 4.15 Consider the following lotteries:

$$L = \begin{pmatrix} \$26 & \$40 & \$58 & \$80 & \$96 \\ \frac{6}{20} & \frac{4}{20} & \frac{2}{20} & \frac{1}{20} & \frac{7}{20} \end{pmatrix} \quad \text{and} \quad M = \begin{pmatrix} \$26 & \$40 & \$58 & \$80 & \$96 \\ \frac{5}{20} & \frac{4}{20} & \frac{2}{20} & \frac{2}{20} & \frac{7}{20} \end{pmatrix}$$

Does one dominate the other in terms of first-order stochastic dominance?

Exercise 4.16 Consider the following lotteries:

$$L = \begin{pmatrix} \$26 & \$40 & \$58 & \$80 & \$96 \\ \frac{6}{20} & \frac{4}{20} & \frac{2}{20} & 0 & \frac{8}{20} \end{pmatrix} \quad \text{and} \quad M = \begin{pmatrix} \$26 & \$40 & \$58 & \$80 & \$96 \\ \frac{5}{20} & \frac{4}{20} & \frac{2}{20} & \frac{2}{20} & \frac{7}{20} \end{pmatrix}$$

Does one dominate the other in terms of first-order stochastic dominance?

Exercise 4.17 Consider the lotteries of Exercise 4.16. Since it is not the case that M dominates L in terms of first-order stochastic dominance, by Theorem 4.4.1 there must be an increasing utility-of-money function U such that $\mathbb{E}[U(L)] > \mathbb{E}[U(M)]$. Construct such a function. Note that you don't need to define a function over the entire set of non-negative real numbers: it is enough to define a function over the set $\{26, 40, 58, 80, 96\}$.

Exercise 4.18 Consider the following lotteries, which were discussed at the beginning of Section 4.4.2:

$$L = \begin{pmatrix} \$2 & \$3 & \$4 & \$5 & \$9 \\ \frac{1}{3} & 0 & \frac{1}{3} & 0 & \frac{1}{3} \end{pmatrix}$$

$$M' = \begin{pmatrix} \$2 & \$3 & \$4 & \$5 & \$9 \\ \frac{1}{3} & \frac{1}{12} & \frac{1}{6} & \frac{1}{12} & \frac{1}{3} \end{pmatrix} \quad \text{and} \quad M = \begin{pmatrix} \$2 & \$3 & \$4 & \$5 & \$9 \\ \frac{1}{3} & \frac{1}{6} & 0 & \frac{1}{6} & \frac{1}{3} \end{pmatrix}.$$

Show that an individual with utility-of-money function $U(m) = \sqrt{m}$ strictly prefers L to M' and M' to M.

Exercise 4.19 Consider the following lotteries:

$$L = \begin{pmatrix} \$4 & \$16 & \$25 & \$36 & \$49 \\ \frac{3}{40} & \frac{9}{40} & \frac{18}{40} & \frac{8}{40} & \frac{2}{40} \end{pmatrix} \quad \text{and} \quad M = \begin{pmatrix} \$4 & \$16 & \$25 & \$36 & \$49 \\ \frac{23}{200} & \frac{9}{40} & \frac{3}{8} & \frac{8}{40} & \frac{17}{200} \end{pmatrix}.$$

(a) Calculate $\mathbb{E}[L]$.

(b) Calculate $\mathbb{E}[M]$.

(c) Calculate the expected utility of L for an individual whose utility-of-money function is $U(m) = \sqrt{m}$.

(d) Calculate the expected utility of M for an individual whose utility-of-money function is $U(m) = \sqrt{m}$.

(e) Show that M is a mean-preserving spread of L according to Definition 4.4.2.

■

Exercise 4.20 Show that $L >_{SSD} M$, where

$$L = \begin{pmatrix} \$6 & \$23 & \$44 & \$51 & \$70 \\ \frac{1}{3} & \frac{1}{12} & \frac{1}{6} & \frac{1}{12} & \frac{1}{3} \end{pmatrix} \quad \text{and} \quad M = \begin{pmatrix} \$6 & \$23 & \$44 & \$51 & \$70 \\ \frac{77}{192} & \frac{11}{94} & 0 & 0 & \frac{4349}{9024} \end{pmatrix}$$

by constructing a two-step mean-preserving spread from L to M.
[Hint: in the first step take the probability assigned to $44 and re-allocate it to $6 and $70.]

■

4.6 Solutions to Exercises

Solution to Exercise 4.1

(a) The expected value of L is $\frac{2}{10} \times 30 + \frac{1}{10} \times 28 + \frac{1}{10} \times 24 + \frac{2}{10} \times 18 + \frac{4}{10} \times 8 = 18$.

(b) The expected utility of L is

$$\tfrac{2}{10}(20\sqrt{30}-4) + \tfrac{1}{10}(20\sqrt{28}-4) + \tfrac{1}{10}(20\sqrt{24}-4) + \tfrac{2}{10}(20\sqrt{18}-4) + \tfrac{4}{10}(20\sqrt{8}-4)$$

$$= 77.88.$$

(c) $\frac{d}{dm}(20\sqrt{m}-4) = 20\frac{1}{2\sqrt{m}} = \frac{10}{\sqrt{m}}$.

(d) $\frac{d^2}{dm^2}(20\sqrt{m}-4) = 10\left(-\frac{1}{2}\right)m^{-\frac{3}{2}} = -\frac{5}{\sqrt{m^3}} < 0$, for every $m > 0$.

(e) Jennifer is risk-averse since the second derivative of her utility function is negative for every $m > 0$. □

4.6 Solutions to Exercises

Solution to Exercise 4.2

(a) The expected value is, of course, the same, namely 18.

(b) The expected utility of L is

$$\tfrac{2}{10}\sqrt{30}+\tfrac{1}{10}\sqrt{28}+\tfrac{1}{10}\sqrt{24}+\tfrac{2}{10}\sqrt{18}+\tfrac{4}{10}\sqrt{8}=4.094.$$

Note that this is equal to $\frac{77.88}{20}+\frac{1}{5}$ (recall that 77.88 was the expected utility for Jennifer). Indeed, Jim's utility function, call it V, can be obtained from Jennifer's utility function, call it $U(m)$, **by applying the following affine transformation** $V(m)=\frac{1}{20}U(m)+\frac{1}{5}$; hence Jennifer and Jim have the same preferences.

(c) $\frac{d\sqrt{m}}{dm}=\frac{1}{2\sqrt{m}}$.

(d) $\frac{d^2\sqrt{m}}{dm^2}=-\frac{1}{4\sqrt{m^3}}$.

(e) Jim is risk-averse (he has the same preferences as Jennifer). □

Solution to Exercise 4.3

(a) $\frac{d^2}{dm^2}\ln(m+1)=-\frac{1}{(m+1)^2}<0$, for every $m\geq 0$. Thus risk aversion.

(b) $\frac{d^2}{dm^2}(8+m^{1.65})=\frac{1.0725}{m^{0.35}}>0$, for every $m>0$. Thus risk love.

(c) $\frac{d^2}{dm^2}(2+7m)=0$. Thus risk neutrality. □

Solution to Exercise 4.4

(a) $U''(m)=-2<0$. Thus John is risk averse.

(b) $V''(m)=-6<0$. Thus Jenny is risk averse.

(c) Since $V(m)=3U(m)+12$, that is, V is an affine transformation of U, John and Jenny have the same preferences.

(d) There are, of course, many examples. One example is $U(m)=\sqrt{m}$ and $V(m)=\ln(m+1)$. □

Solution to Exercise 4.5

(a) Recall from Exercise 4.1 that the expected value of L is 18. The risk premium is the value of R that solves the equation $20\sqrt{18-R}-4=77.88$. The solution is $R=\$1.24$.

(b) The Arrow-Pratt measure of absolute risk aversion is

$$A(m)=-\frac{U''(m)}{U'(m)}=-\frac{-\frac{5}{\sqrt{m^3}}}{\frac{10}{\sqrt{m}}}=\frac{1}{2m}$$

Thus $A(900)=\frac{1}{1,800}$ and $A(1,600)=\frac{1}{3,200}$. □

Solution to Exercise 4.6

(a) Again, the expected value of L is 18. The risk premium is the value of R that solves the equation $\sqrt{18-R} = 4.094$. The solution is $R = \$1.24$: the same as for Jennifer (as it should be, since they have the same preferences).

(b) The Arrow-Pratt measure of absolute risk aversion is

$$A(m) = -\frac{V''(m)}{V'(m)} = -\frac{-\frac{1}{4\sqrt{m^3}}}{\frac{1}{2\sqrt{m}}} = \frac{1}{2m}$$

the same as for Jennifer (as it should be, since they have the same preferences). Thus $A(900) = \frac{1}{1,800}$ and $A(1,600) = \frac{1}{3,200}$. □

Solution to Exercise 4.7

We already know from Exercise 4.4 that John and Jennifer have the same preferences. This is confirmed by the fact that the Arrow-Pratt measures are the same for both individuals:

$$A_U(m) = A_V(m) = \frac{1}{1-m} \quad \text{and} \quad r_U(m) = r_V(m) = \frac{m}{1-m}.$$

□

Solution to Exercise 4.8

(a) The expected value of lottery $\begin{pmatrix} \$24 & \$12 & \$48 \\ \frac{2}{6} & \frac{3}{6} & \frac{1}{6} \end{pmatrix}$ is $\frac{2}{6}24 + \frac{3}{6}12 + \frac{1}{6}48 = 22$. Thus the risk premium is $\$(22-18) = \$4$.

(b) Amy is risk-averse since she considers the lottery to be equivalent to a sum of money which is *less* than the expected value of the lottery (hence she prefers the expected value of the lottery for sure to the lottery).

(c) If $U(m)$ is Amy's vNM utility-of-money function, then it must be that $U(18) = \mathbb{E}[U(L)]$, where $\mathbb{E}[U(L)] = \frac{2}{6}U(24) + \frac{3}{6}U(12) + \frac{1}{6}U(48)$. Since $\sqrt{18} = 4.2426$, while $\frac{2}{6}\sqrt{24} + \frac{3}{6}\sqrt{12} + \frac{1}{6}\sqrt{48} = 4.5197$, it cannot be that $U(m) = \sqrt{m}$. □

Solution to Exercise 4.9

(a) The expected value of both lotteries is 18, hence Bill is indifferent between the two.

(b) Zero.

(c) Zero. □

4.6 Solutions to Exercises

Solution to Exercise 4.10

(a) When Berta's initial wealth is $80, the corresponding wealth lottery is $L = \begin{pmatrix} \$30 & \$200 \\ \frac{1}{4} & \frac{3}{4} \end{pmatrix}$, whose expected value is $157.5. The risk premium is given by the solution to

$$\ln(157.5 - R) = \tfrac{1}{4}\ln(30) + \tfrac{3}{4}\ln(200)$$

which is $33.0304.

(b) When Berta's initial wealth is $200, the corresponding wealth lottery is $L = \begin{pmatrix} \$150 & \$320 \\ \frac{1}{4} & \frac{3}{4} \end{pmatrix}$, whose expected value is $277.5. The risk premium is given by the solution to

$$\ln(277.5 - R) = \tfrac{1}{4}\ln(150) + \tfrac{3}{4}\ln(320)$$

which is $12.7199. □

Solution to Exercise 4.11 We are considering the wealth lottery $L = \begin{pmatrix} \$120 & \$180 & \$260 \\ \frac{2}{5} & \frac{2}{5} & \frac{1}{5} \end{pmatrix}$. The expected value of L is 172.

(a) R_{LU} is the solution to $\sqrt{172-R} = \tfrac{2}{5}\sqrt{120} + \tfrac{2}{5}\sqrt{180} + \tfrac{1}{5}\sqrt{260}$. The solution is $R_{LU} = 3.6949$.

(b) R_{LV} is the solution to

$$-\left(\tfrac{172-R}{10} - 36\right)^2 + \tfrac{172-R}{20} + 1{,}400 =$$
$$\tfrac{2}{5}\left[-\left(\tfrac{120}{10} - 36\right)^2 + \tfrac{120}{20} + 1{,}400\right]$$
$$+ \tfrac{2}{5}\left[-\left(\tfrac{180}{10} - 36\right)^2 + \tfrac{180}{20} + 1{,}400\right]$$
$$+ \tfrac{1}{5}\left[-\left(\tfrac{260}{10} - 36\right)^2 + \tfrac{260}{20} + 1{,}400\right].$$

The solution is $R_{LV} = 6.848$.

(c) $A_U(m) = \tfrac{1}{2m}$ and $A_V(m) = \tfrac{1}{362.5-m}$. The two are equal when $m = 120.833$, $A_U(m) > A_V(m)$ for $m \in (0, 120.833)$ and $A_U(m) < A_V(m)$ for $m \in (120.833, 300]$. Thus U incorporates greater risk aversion than V for values of m in the interval $(0, 120.833)$ and less risk aversion than V in the interval $(120.833, 300]$. □

Solution to Exercise 4.12 See Figure 4.12.

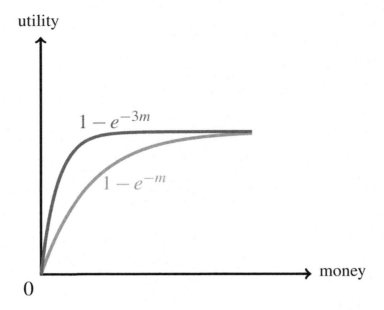

Figure 4.12: The graphs of $1 - e^{-m}$ and $1 - e^{-3m}$.

Solution to Exercise 4.13

$\frac{d}{dm} m^a = \frac{a}{m^{1-a}}$ and $\frac{d^2}{dm^2} m^a = \frac{-a(1-a)}{m^{2-a}}$. Thus $A(m) = \frac{1-a}{m}$ which is decreasing in m.

Solution to Exercise 4.14

$\frac{d}{dm}\left(cm - \frac{m^2}{2}\right) = c - m$ and $\frac{d^2}{dm^2}\left(cm - \frac{m^2}{2}\right) = -1$. Thus $A(m) = \frac{1}{c-m}$ which is *increasing* in m. In fact, $\frac{d}{dm}\left(\frac{1}{c-m}\right) = \frac{1}{(c-m)^2} > 0$.

Solution to Exercise 4.15

The lotteries are:

$$M = \begin{pmatrix} \$26 & \$40 & \$58 & \$80 & \$96 \\ \frac{5}{20} & \frac{4}{20} & \frac{2}{20} & \frac{2}{20} & \frac{7}{20} \end{pmatrix} \text{ and } L = \begin{pmatrix} \$26 & \$40 & \$58 & \$80 & \$96 \\ \frac{6}{20} & \frac{4}{20} & \frac{2}{20} & \frac{1}{20} & \frac{7}{20} \end{pmatrix}$$

By constructing the corresponding cumulative distribution functions one can see that $M >_{FSD} L$ ($Q_i \leq P_i$ for every $i = 1, \ldots, 5$ and $Q_3 < P_3$):

		$m_1 = \$26$	$m_2 = \$40$	$m_3 = \$58$	$m_4 = \$80$	$m_5 = \$96$
cumulative for L,	P :	$\frac{6}{20}$	$\frac{10}{20}$	$\frac{12}{20}$	$\frac{13}{20}$	1
cumulative for M,	Q :	$\frac{5}{20}$	$\frac{9}{20}$	$\frac{11}{20}$	$\frac{13}{20}$	1

4.6 Solutions to Exercises

Solution to Exercise 4.16

The lotteries are:

$$L = \begin{pmatrix} \$26 & \$40 & \$58 & \$80 & \$96 \\ \frac{6}{20} & \frac{4}{20} & \frac{2}{20} & 0 & \frac{8}{20} \end{pmatrix} \quad \text{and} \quad M = \begin{pmatrix} \$26 & \$40 & \$58 & \$80 & \$96 \\ \frac{5}{20} & \frac{4}{20} & \frac{2}{20} & \frac{2}{20} & \frac{7}{20} \end{pmatrix}$$

By constructing the corresponding cumulative distribution functions one can see that, according to the criterion of first-order dominance, it is neither the case that L dominates M (since, for example, $P_1 = \frac{6}{20} > Q_1 = \frac{5}{20}$) nor the case that M dominates L (since $Q_4 = \frac{13}{20} > P_4 = \frac{12}{20}$):

	$26	$40	$58	$80	$96
cumulative for L, P:	$\frac{6}{20}$	$\frac{10}{20}$	$\frac{12}{20}$	$\frac{12}{20}$	1
cumulative for M, Q:	$\frac{5}{20}$	$\frac{9}{20}$	$\frac{11}{20}$	$\frac{13}{20}$	1

□

Solution to Exercise 4.17

The lotteries are:

$$L = \begin{pmatrix} \$26 & \$40 & \$58 & \$80 & \$96 \\ \frac{6}{20} & \frac{4}{20} & \frac{2}{20} & 0 & \frac{8}{20} \end{pmatrix} \quad \text{and} \quad M = \begin{pmatrix} \$26 & \$40 & \$58 & \$80 & \$96 \\ \frac{5}{20} & \frac{4}{20} & \frac{2}{20} & \frac{2}{20} & \frac{7}{20} \end{pmatrix}$$

Since L assigns an additional probability of $\frac{1}{20}$ to $96 (relative to M), it is sufficient to have a "big jump" in utility going from $80 to $96. For example, consider the following utility function:

	$26	$40	$58	$80	$96
Utility U:	1	2	3	4	10

Then $\mathbb{E}[U(L)] = \frac{6}{20}1 + \frac{4}{20}2 + \frac{2}{20}3 + \frac{8}{20}10 = 5$ and $\mathbb{E}[U(M)] = \frac{5}{20}1 + \frac{4}{20}2 + \frac{2}{20}3 + +\frac{2}{20}4 + \frac{7}{20}10 = 4.85$. Thus an individual with this (strictly increasing) utility function prefers lottery L to lottery M. One can also easily construct a strictly increasing utility function according to which lottery M is preferred to lottery L (big jump at $80, small jump at $96). □

Solution to Exercise 4.18

The lotteries are:

$$L = \begin{pmatrix} \$2 & \$3 & \$4 & \$5 & \$9 \\ \frac{1}{3} & 0 & \frac{1}{3} & 0 & \frac{1}{3} \end{pmatrix}$$

$$M' = \begin{pmatrix} \$2 & \$3 & \$4 & \$5 & \$9 \\ \frac{1}{3} & \frac{1}{12} & \frac{1}{6} & \frac{1}{12} & \frac{1}{3} \end{pmatrix} \quad \text{and} \quad M = \begin{pmatrix} \$2 & \$3 & \$4 & \$5 & \$9 \\ \frac{1}{3} & \frac{1}{6} & 0 & \frac{1}{6} & \frac{1}{3} \end{pmatrix}.$$

$$\mathbb{E}[U(L)] = \tfrac{1}{3}\sqrt{2} + \tfrac{1}{3}\sqrt{4} + \tfrac{1}{3}\sqrt{9} = 2.1381$$
$$> E[U(M')] = \tfrac{1}{3}\sqrt{2} + \tfrac{1}{12}\sqrt{3} + \tfrac{1}{6}\sqrt{4} + \tfrac{1}{12}\sqrt{5} + \tfrac{1}{3}\sqrt{9} = 2.1354$$
$$> E[U(M)] = \tfrac{1}{3}\sqrt{2} + \tfrac{1}{6}\sqrt{3} + \tfrac{1}{16}\sqrt{5} + \tfrac{1}{3}\sqrt{9} = 2.1328.$$

□

Solution to Exercise 4.19

The lotteries are:

$$L = \begin{pmatrix} \$4 & \$16 & \$25 & \$36 & \$49 \\ \frac{3}{40} & \frac{9}{40} & \frac{18}{40} & \frac{8}{40} & \frac{2}{40} \end{pmatrix} \quad \text{and} \quad M = \begin{pmatrix} \$4 & \$16 & \$25 & \$36 & \$49 \\ \frac{23}{200} & \frac{9}{40} & \frac{3}{8} & \frac{8}{40} & \frac{17}{200} \end{pmatrix}.$$

(a) $\mathbb{E}[L] = \frac{3}{40}4 + \frac{9}{40}16 + \frac{18}{40}25 + \frac{8}{40}36 + \frac{2}{40}49 = 24.8$.

(b) $\mathbb{E}[M] = \frac{23}{200}4 + \frac{9}{40}16 + \frac{3}{8}25 + \frac{8}{40}36 + \frac{17}{200}49 = 24.8$.

(c) $\mathbb{E}[U(L)] = \frac{3}{40}\sqrt{4} + \frac{9}{40}\sqrt{16} + \frac{18}{40}\sqrt{25} + \frac{8}{40}\sqrt{36} + \frac{2}{40}\sqrt{49} = 4.85$

(d) $\mathbb{E}[U(M)] = \frac{23}{200}\sqrt{4} + \frac{9}{40}\sqrt{16} + \frac{3}{8}\sqrt{25} + \frac{8}{40}\sqrt{36} + \frac{17}{200}\sqrt{49} = 4.8$.

(e) We have that $m_1 = 4, m_2 = 16, m_3 = 25, m_4 = 36, m_5 = 49$, $p_2 = q_2$ and $p_4 = q_4$. Thus the change involves prizes m_1, m_3 and m_5, that is, $i = 1, j = 3, k = 5$. To find α solve $\frac{18}{40} - \alpha\frac{18}{40} = \frac{3}{8}$ which gives $\alpha = \frac{1}{6}$. Then verify that $p_1 + \left(1 - \frac{m_3 - m_1}{m_5 - m_1}\right)\alpha p_3 = q_1$ and $p_5 + \left(\frac{m_3 - m_1}{m_5 - m_1}\right)\alpha p_3 = q_5$; indeed $\frac{3}{40} + \left(1 - \frac{25-4}{49-4}\right)\frac{1}{6}\left(\frac{18}{40}\right) = \frac{23}{200}$ and $\frac{2}{40} + \left(\frac{25-4}{49-4}\right)\frac{1}{6}\left(\frac{18}{40}\right) = \frac{17}{200}$ □

Solution to Exercise 4.20

The lotteries are:

$$L = \begin{pmatrix} \$6 & \$23 & \$44 & \$51 & \$70 \\ \frac{1}{3} & \frac{1}{12} & \frac{1}{6} & \frac{1}{12} & \frac{1}{3} \end{pmatrix} \quad \text{and} \quad M = \begin{pmatrix} \$6 & \$23 & \$44 & \$51 & \$70 \\ \frac{77}{192} & \frac{11}{94} & 0 & 0 & \frac{4349}{9024} \end{pmatrix}.$$

Let us perform a first mean-preserving spread (MPS) on L by reducing the probability of $m_3 = 44$ to 0 (hence $\alpha = 1$) and spreading it out to $m_1 = 6$ and $m_5 = 70$ (thus $\delta = \frac{44-6}{70-6} = \frac{38}{64}$); then the probability of m_1 becomes $\frac{1}{3} + \left(1 - \frac{38}{64}\right)\frac{1}{6} = \frac{77}{192}$ and the probability of m_5 becomes $\frac{1}{3} + \left(\frac{38}{64}\right)\frac{1}{6} = \frac{83}{192}$. Call the resulting lottery M'. Then

$$M' = \begin{pmatrix} \$6 & \$23 & \$44 & \$51 & \$70 \\ \frac{77}{192} & \frac{1}{12} & 0 & \frac{1}{12} & \frac{83}{192} \end{pmatrix}.$$

Now perform a second MPS on M' by reducing the probability of $m_4 = 51$ to 0 (hence $\alpha = 1$) and spreading it out to $m_2 = 23$ and $m_5 = 70$ (thus $\delta = \frac{51-23}{70-23} = \frac{28}{47}$); then the probability of m_2 becomes $\frac{1}{12} + \left(1 - \frac{28}{47}\right)\frac{1}{12} = \frac{11}{94}$ and the probability of m_5 becomes

4.6 Solutions to Exercises

$\frac{83}{192} + \left(\frac{28}{47}\right)\frac{1}{12} = \frac{4349}{9024}$ thus yielding

$$M = \begin{pmatrix} \$6 & \$23 & \$44 & \$51 & \$70 \\ \frac{77}{192} & \frac{11}{94} & 0 & 0 & \frac{4349}{9024} \end{pmatrix}.$$

It can be verified that $\mathbb{E}[L] = \mathbb{E}[M'] = \mathbb{E}[M] = 38.8333$. □

5. Insurance: Part 2

5.1 Binary lotteries and indifference curves

In this chapter we complete the analysis of insurance that we started in Chapter 2 by considering the point view of the potential customer. Before we do so, we need to develop the analysis of binary money lotteries, which are lotteries that involve only two prizes.

Fix a value of p (with $0 < p < 1$) and consider all the lotteries of the form

$$\begin{pmatrix} \$x & \$y \\ p & 1-p \end{pmatrix} \quad \text{with } x \geq 0 \text{ and } y \geq 0.$$

Thus we think of x and y as variables, while **p is a constant**.

We can identify a binary lottery with a point (x,y) in the positive quadrant of the cartesian plane. If $x = y$ then the lottery (x,x) lies on the 45°-line out of the origin and represents the situation where the individual gets x with probability p and x with probability $(1-p)$, that is, she gets x for sure; if $x > y$ the point lies below the 45°-line and if $x < y$ the point lies above the 45°-line.

Consider an individual whose utility-of-money function is $U(m)$. We assume that $U'(m) > 0$ (for every $m \geq 0$), that is, that the individual prefers more money to less. Given a lottery (x,y), the individual's expected utility is given by: $pU(x) + (1-p)U(y)$. Given two lotteries $A = (x_1, y_1)$ and $B = (x_2, y_2)$, the individual will prefer A to B if and only if

$$\mathbb{E}[U(A)] = pU(x_1) + (1-p)U(y_1) > \mathbb{E}[U(B)] = pU(x_2) + (1-p)U(y_2),$$

she will prefer B to A if the above inequality is reversed and will be indifferent between A and B if $\mathbb{E}[U(A)] = \mathbb{E}[U(B)]$. For example, if $p = \frac{1}{4}$ and the individual is risk neutral (so that we can take the identity function $U(m) = m$ as her vNM utility function) then the individual will be indifferent among the following lotteries, since their expected value is the same (namely 85): (130, 70), (100, 80), (85, 85) and (16, 108).

Definition 5.1.1 An *indifference curve* is a set of points (lotteries) in the (x,y) plane among which the individual is indifferent. For every point (x,y) there is an indifference curve that goes through that point. Since $U'(m) > 0$, for every m, each indifference curve will be downward-sloping.[a]

---

[a]In order for expected utility to remain constant, if one coordinate is increased then the other coordinate must be decreased.

We want to relate the shape of the indifference curves of an individual to her attitude towards risk.

5.1.1 Case 1: risk neutrality

As remarked above, for a risk-neutral person we can take the identity function $U(m) = m$ as her vNM utility-of-money function, so that expected utility and expected value coincide. Fix an arbitrary lottery $A = (x_A, y_A)$ and let us try to find another lottery $B = (x_B, y_B)$ that lies on the same indifference curve. Then it must be that $px_A + (1-p)y_A = px_B + (1-p)y_B$ which can be written as

$$\underbrace{\frac{\overbrace{y_A - y_B}^{rise}}{\underbrace{x_A - x_B}_{run}}} = -\frac{p}{1-p}.$$

Thus indifference curves are straight lines with slope $-\frac{p}{1-p}$, as shown in Figure 5.1.

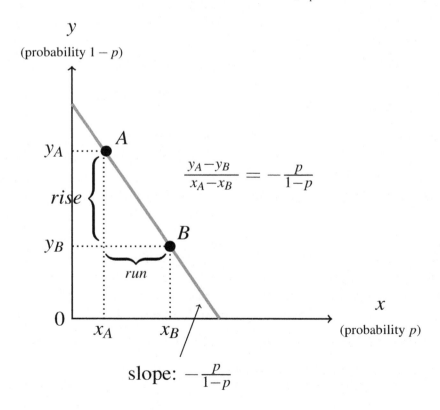

Figure 5.1: An indifference curve for a risk-neutral individual.

5.1 Binary lotteries and indifference curves

5.1.2 Case 2: risk aversion

Now consider the case of a risk-averse individual. Recall from Chapter 4 that the utility-of-money function $U(m)$ of a risk-averse individual is strictly concave, that is, for every $x > 0$ and $y > 0$ and for every $t \in (0,1)$,

$$U(tx + (1-t)y) > tU(x) + (1-t)U(y). \tag{5.1}$$

We now show that, if we take two lotteries A and B that yield the same expected utility (so that they lie on the same indifference curve), then all the lotteries on the line segment joining A and B (apart from A and B themselves) correspond to higher levels of expected utility than A and B. Hence, since the utility function is assumed to be strictly increasing, it follows that the indifference curve to which A and B belong, must lie *below* the line segment that joins A and B, that is, the indifference curve must be convex towards the origin.

As before, fix an arbitrary $p \in (0,1)$ and consider all the lotteries of the form

$$\begin{pmatrix} \$x & \$y \\ p & 1-p \end{pmatrix}$$

which can be identified with points in the positive quadrant of the cartesian plane (x, y).

Let $A = (x_A, y_A)$ and $B = (x_B, y_B)$ lie on the same indifference curve, that is,

$$\underbrace{pU(x_A) + (1-p)U(y_A)}_{=\mathbb{E}[U(A)]} = \underbrace{pU(x_B) + (1-p)U(y_B)}_{=\mathbb{E}[U(B)]} = \hat{u}.$$

Fix an arbitrary $t \in (0,1)$ and consider the point $C = tA + (1-t)B$ on the line segment joining A and B, which represents the lottery

$$C = \begin{pmatrix} tx_A + (1-t)x_B & ty_A + (1-t)y_B \\ p & 1-p \end{pmatrix}.$$

Then

$$\mathbb{E}[U(C)] = p\,U(tx_A + (1-t)x_B) + (1-p)\,U(ty_A + (1-t)y_B). \tag{5.2}$$

By (5.1),

$$U(tx_A + (1-t)x_B) > tU(x_A) + (1-t)U(x_B) \tag{5.3}$$
$$U(ty_A + (1-t)y_B) > tU(y_A) + (1-t)U(y_B). \tag{5.4}$$

Thus, from (5.2)-(5.4) we get that

$$\mathbb{E}[U(C)] > p\left[tU(x_A) + (1-t)U(x_B)\right] + (1-p)\left[tU(y_A) + (1-t)U(y_B)\right]$$

$$= t\left[pU(x_A) + (1-p)U(y_A)\right] + (1-t)\left[pU(x_B) + (1-p)U(y_B)\right]$$

$$= t\mathbb{E}[U(A)] + (1-t)\mathbb{E}[U(B)]$$

$$= t\hat{u} + (1-t)\hat{u} = \hat{u}.$$

All of this is illustrated in Figure 5.2.

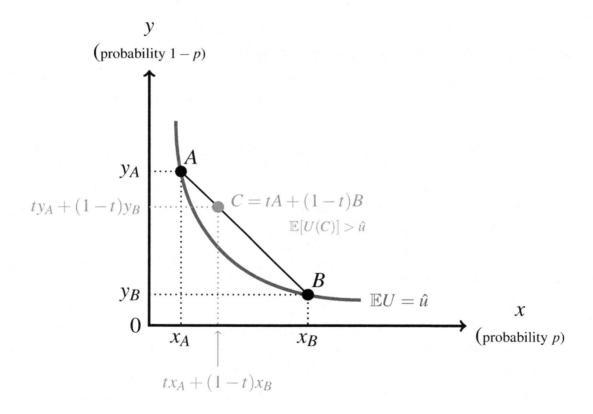

Figure 5.2: Indifference curves for a risk-averse individual are convex.

5.1 Binary lotteries and indifference curves

5.1.3 Case 3: risk love

Now consider the case of a risk-loving individual. Recall from Chapter 4 that the utility-of-money function $U(m)$ of a risk-loving individual is strictly convex, that is, for every $x > 0$ and $y > 0$ and for every $t \in (0,1)$,

$$U(tx + (1-t)y) < tU(x) + (1-t)U(y). \tag{5.5}$$

With an argument similar to the one used in the previous section, one can show that, if we take two lotteries A and B that yield the same expected utility – so that they lie on the same indifference curve – all the lotteries on the line segment joining A and B (apart from A and B themselves) correspond to *lower* levels of expected utility than A and B. Hence, since the utility function is assumed to be strictly increasing, it follows that the indifference curve to which A and B belong, must lie *above* the line segment that joins A and B, that is, the indifference curve must be concave towards the origin, as shown in Figure 5.3.

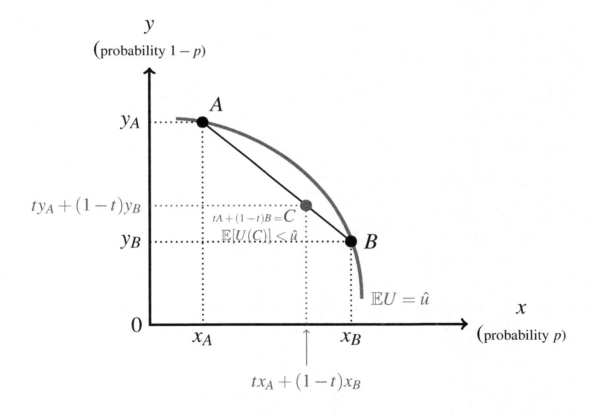

Figure 5.3: Indifference curves for a risk-loving individual are concave.

5.1.4 The slope of an indifference curve

We saw above that the indifference curves of a risk-neutral individual are straight lines and thus have a constant slope, which is equal to $-\frac{p}{1-p}$. On the other hand, the indifference curves of a risk-averse individual are convex towards the origin and thus do *not* have a constant slope: indeed the slope decreases as we move along the curve in the direction of an increase in the horizontal coordinate (and a decrease in the vertical coordinate). For a risk-loving individual the opposite is true: the slope of an indifference curve increases as we move along the curve in the direction of an increase in the horizontal coordinate.

How can we compute the slope of an indifference curve at a point? Let $A = (x_A, y_A)$ and consider a point B on the same indifference curve as A, so that $\mathbb{E}[U(A)] = \mathbb{E}[U(B)]$. Let us choose this point B to be "very close" to A, so that $B = (x_A + \delta, y_A + \varepsilon)$ with δ and ε close to 0 (one must be positive and the other negative). By hypothesis,

$$\underbrace{pU(x_A) + (1-p)U(y_A)}_{\mathbb{E}[U(A)]} = \underbrace{pU(x_A + \delta) + (1-p)U(y_A + \varepsilon)}_{\mathbb{E}[U(B)]} \tag{5.6}$$

Since B is close to A (that is, δ and ε are small), we can approximate the values of $U(x_A + \delta)$ and $U(y_A + \varepsilon)$ using the derivative of U (that is, using a first-order Taylor expansion):

$$\begin{aligned} U(x_A + \delta) &= U(x_A) + U'(x_A)\,\delta \\ U(y_A + \varepsilon) &= U(y_A) + U'(y_A)\,\varepsilon. \end{aligned} \tag{5.7}$$

Replacing (5.7) into (5.6) we get

$$\begin{aligned} pU(x_A) + (1-p)U(y_A) &= p\left[U(x_A) + U'(x_A)\delta\right] + (1-p)\left[U(y_A) + U'(y_A)\varepsilon\right] \\ &= pU(x_A) + (1-p)U(y_A) + pU'(x_A)\delta + (1-p)U'(y_A)\varepsilon \end{aligned} \tag{5.8}$$

from which we get that

$$pU'(x_A)\delta + (1-p)U'(y_A)\varepsilon = 0,$$

that is,

$$\underbrace{\frac{\overbrace{\varepsilon}^{\text{rise}}}{\underbrace{\delta}_{\text{run}}}} = -\frac{p}{1-p}\frac{U'(x_A)}{U'(y_A)}.$$

Thus the slope of an indifference curve at a point $A = (x_A, y_A)$ is given by[1]

$$\boxed{-\frac{p}{1-p}\frac{U'(x_A)}{U'(y_A)}} \tag{5.9}$$

---

[1] Alternatively, one can derive the slope of an indifference curve at a point by using the implicit function theorem, which says the following. Let $F : \mathbb{R}^2 \to \mathbb{R}$ be a continuously differentiable function and $(x_0, y_0) \in \mathbb{R}^2$ a point such that $F(x_0, y_0) = c$; if $\frac{\partial F}{\partial y}(x_0, y_0) \neq 0$ then there is an interval $(x_0 - \varepsilon, x_0 + \varepsilon)$ and a differentiable function $f : (x_0 - \varepsilon, x_0 + \varepsilon) \to \mathbb{R}$ such that (1) $F(x_0, f(x_0)) = y_0$, (2) $F(x, f(x)) = c$ for every $x \in (x_0 - \varepsilon, x_0 + \varepsilon)$ and (3) $f'(x_0) = -\frac{\frac{\partial F}{\partial x}(x_0, y_0)}{\frac{\partial F}{\partial y}(x_0, y_0)}$. To apply the implicit function theorem in this context, let $F(x, y) = pU(x) + (1-p)U(y)$ and let $A = (x_A, y_A)$ be a point where $pU(x_A) + (1-p)U(y_A) = \hat{u}$.

5.1 Binary lotteries and indifference curves

In the case of risk neutrality U' is constant and thus $U'(x_A) = U'(y_A)$ so that $\frac{U'(x_A)}{U'(y_A)} = 1$; hence the slope becomes $-\frac{p}{1-p}$ at every point, consistently with what we saw above.

Now let us see what (5.9) implies for a concave utility-of-money function, that is, for the case of **risk aversion**. When the utility function is *concave*, the second derivative is negative ($U''(m) < 0$), which means that *the first derivative is decreasing*, that is,

$$\text{if} \quad m_1 < m_2 \quad \text{then} \quad U'(m_1) > U'(m_2) \quad \left(\text{or} \quad \frac{U'(m_1)}{U'(m_2)} > 1\right),$$

as shown in Figure 5.4.

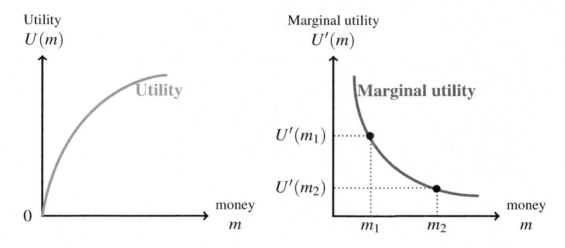

Figure 5.4: When the utility function is concave, marginal utility is decreasing.

At a point $A = (x, y)$ **above** the $45°$ line (where $x < y$) we have that $\frac{U'(x)}{U'(y)} > 1$ so that

$$-\frac{p}{1-p}\frac{U'(x)}{U'(y)} < -\frac{p}{1-p} \quad \text{or} \quad \frac{p}{1-p}\frac{U'(x)}{U'(y)} > \frac{p}{1-p}.$$

Hence the indifference curve is **steeper** than the straight line with slope $-\frac{p}{1-p}$.

Conversely, at a point $A = (x, y)$ **below** the $45°$ line (where $x > y$) we have that $\frac{U'(x)}{U'(y)} < 1$ so that

$$-\frac{p}{1-p}\frac{U'(x)}{U'(y)} > -\frac{p}{1-p} \quad \text{or} \quad \frac{p}{1-p}\frac{U'(x)}{U'(y)} < \frac{p}{1-p}.$$

Hence the indifference curve is **less steep** than the straight line with slope $-\frac{p}{1-p}$.

Finally at a point **on** the $45°$ line (where $x = y$) we have that $\frac{U'(x)}{U'(y)} = 1$ so that

$$-\frac{p}{1-p}\frac{U'(x)}{U'(y)} = -\frac{p}{1-p};$$

hence the straight line with slope $-\frac{p}{1-p}$ is **tangent to** the indifference curve.

■ **Example 5.1** This example is illustrated in Figure 5.5. Let $p = \frac{2}{5}$ and $U(m) = \sqrt{m}$ and consider all the lotteries of the form $\begin{pmatrix} \$x & \$y \\ \frac{2}{5} & \frac{3}{5} \end{pmatrix}$. Since, $U'(m) = \frac{1}{2\sqrt{m}}$, $\frac{U'(x)}{U'(y)} = \frac{\sqrt{y}}{\sqrt{x}}$ (for $x > 0$ and $y > 0$).

Consider three points: (25,100), (64,64) and (121,36). The expected utility of these three lotteries is the same, namely 8; hence these three points belong to the same indifference curve.[2]

- Point (64,64) is on the 45° line and the slope of the indifference curve at that point is

$$-\frac{p}{1-p}\left(\frac{\sqrt{64}}{\sqrt{64}}\right) = -\frac{p}{1-p} = -\frac{2}{3}.$$

- Point (25,100) is above the 45° line and the slope of the indifference curve at that point is

$$-\frac{p}{1-p}\left(\frac{\sqrt{100}}{\sqrt{25}}\right) = -\frac{2}{3}\left(\frac{10}{5}\right) = -\frac{4}{3}.$$

- Point (121,36) is below the 45° line and the slope of the indifference curve at that point is

$$-\frac{p}{1-p}\left(\frac{\sqrt{36}}{\sqrt{121}}\right) = -\frac{2}{3}\left(\frac{6}{11}\right) = -\frac{4}{11}.$$

■

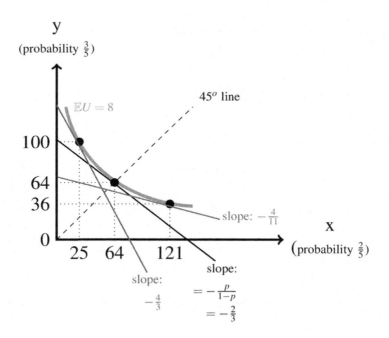

Figure 5.5: The graph for Example 5.1.

---

[2]The equation of the indifference curve is obtained by solving for y the equation $\frac{2}{5}\sqrt{x} + \frac{3}{5}\sqrt{y} = 8$. The solution is $y = \frac{4}{9}(20 - \sqrt{x})^2$.

We will omit the case of risk love (convex utility function, concave indifference curves). The reader should convince himself/herself that in this case an indifference curve is less steep than the line of slope $-\frac{p}{1-p}$ at a point above the 45° line and steeper at a point below the 45° line.

> Test your understanding of the concepts introduced in this section, by going through the exercises in Section 5.5.1 at the end of this chapter.

5.2 Back to insurance

We can now return to the topic of insurance, which we partially analyzed in Chapter 2. We begin by recalling the general set-up.

Consider an individual whose current wealth is $\$W_0$. She faces the possibility of a loss in the amount of $\$\ell$ ($0 < \ell \leq W_0$) with probability p ($0 < p < 1$). An insurance contract can be expressed as a pair of wealth levels (W_1, W_2), where W_1 is wealth in the bad state (if the loss occurs) and W_2 is wealth in the good state (if the loss does not occur); the amount $(W_0 - W_2)$ is the contract's premium and the amount $W_2 - W_1$ is the deductible. If $W_1 = W_2$ the contract offers full insurance, while if $W_1 < W_2$ the contract offers partial insurance.

We saw in Chapter 2 that, through any point in the (W_1, W_2) plane, we can draw an isoprofit line which contains all the contracts that yield the same profit to the insurer. Recall that

$$\text{isoprofit lines are straight lines with slope } -\frac{p}{1-p}.$$

The isoprofit line that goes through the no-insurance point $NI = (W_0 - \ell, W_0)$ is the zero-profit line. Points below the zero-profit line represent profitable contracts, while points above the zero-profit line correspond to contracts that would involve a loss for the insurer. Thus no insurer would be willing to offer a contract that lies above the zero-profit line.

We can now ask the question: what contracts would be acceptable to the individual under consideration?

If the individual purchases insurance contract (W_1, W_2) then she faces the following money lottery:

$$\begin{pmatrix} \$W_1 & \$W_2 \\ p & 1-p \end{pmatrix}.$$

We focus on a risk-averse individual who has von Neumann-Morgenstern preferences, so that her preferences over possible insurance contracts can be represented by means of a vNM utility-of-money function $U(m)$ (which is increasing and strictly concave). A contract (W_1, W_2) will be acceptable to the individual if it yields at least as high an expected utility as the no-insurance option, that is, if

$$pU(W_1) + (1-p)U(W_2) \geq pU(W_0 - \ell) + (1-p)U(W_0).$$

Using the tools developed in this chapter, we can draw the individual's indifference curve that goes through the no-insurance point *NI*: it will be a decreasing and convex curve; we shall call it the *reservation indifference curve*. Points below the reservation indifference curve represent contracts that would yield lower expected utility than the no-insurance option; thus the individual would reject any such contracts, if offered to her. Only contracts represented by points on or above the reservation indifference curve will be acceptable to the individual.

Thus the set of *mutually beneficial insurance contracts* is given by the area bounded below by the reservation indifference curve, bounded above by the zero-profit line and bounded on the right by the 45^0 line; it is shown as a shaded area in Figure 5.6.

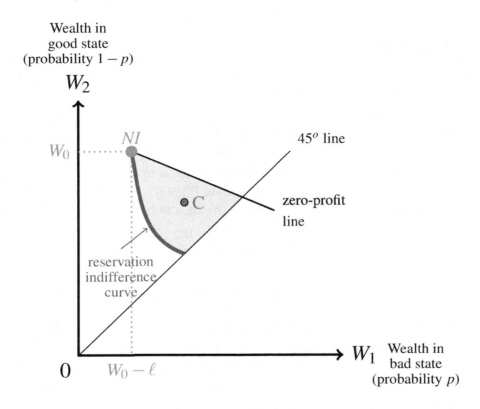

Figure 5.6: The shaded area is the set of mutually beneficial insurance contracts.

Contract *C* in Figure 5.6 is above the reservation indifference curve and thus yields higher expected utility than the no-insurance option (that is, *C* is strictly preferred to *NI* by the potential customer) and is below the zero-profit line and thus yields positive profit to the insurer.

In Figure 5.6 the reservation indifference curve that goes through the no-insurance (*NI*) point is steeper at that point than the zero-profit line. This follows from the analysis in Section 5.1.4. Indeed this is true of any point that lies above the 45° line. Let $A = (W_1^A, W_2^A)$ be a contract that lies above the 45° line. Then, by (5.9) the slope, at point *A*, of the indifference curve that goes through *A* is equal to

$$\boxed{-\frac{p}{1-p}\left(\frac{U'(W_1^A)}{U'(W_2^A)}\right)} \qquad (5.10)$$

5.2 Back to insurance

Recall that the slope of the isoprofit line that goes through any point in the wealth diagram is $-\frac{p}{1-p}$. By the remark on page 119,

- At any point **above** the 45° line the indifference curve is steeper than the isoprofit line that goes through that point.

- At any point **on** the 45° line the indifference curve is tangent to (has the same slope as) the isoprofit line that goes through that point.

This is shown in Figure 5.7. Any contract that lies in the area above the indifference curve that goes through contract A and below the isoprofit line through A, such as point B in Figure 5.7, represents a contract that is better than A for the potential customer (B yields higher expected utility than A) and is better than A for the insurance company (B yields higher profits than A).

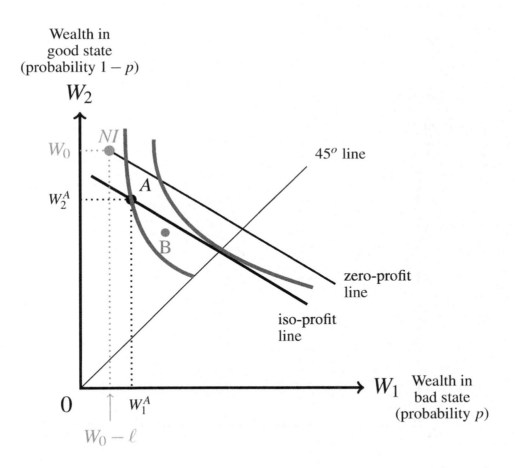

Figure 5.7: The relative slope of an indifference curve and an isoprofit line.

5.2.1 The profit-maximizing contract for a monopolist

Without making use of expected utility theory, we showed in Chapter 2 (Section 2.6.3) that a profit-maximizing monopolist would offer a full-insurance contract to a potential customer, at a premium that makes her indifferent between insuring and not insuring. We can now confirm this result with the tools developed in this chapter. Consider an arbitrary partial-insurance contract that is acceptable to the potential customer (that is, that lies on or above the reservation indifference curve), such as point A in Figure 5.7. Such a contract is not profit maximizing, because the monopolist could replace it with a contract above the indifference curve through A and below the iso-profit line through A (such as contract B in Figure 5.7) and (1) the potential customer would be even happier with the new contract and (2) the monopolist would increase its profits. Since this argument applies to *any* partial-insurance contract (that is, to any point above the 45° line), we deduce that a profit-maximizing monopolist would offer a full-insurance contract.[3] Of all the full-insurance contracts that are acceptable to the potential customer (that is, that are not below the reservation indifference curve) the one that yields the highest profit to the insurer is at the intersection of the reservation indifference curve and the 45° line: contract C in Figure 5.8. The corresponding premium, denoted by h^{max}, is such that:

$$U(W_0 - h_{max}) = pU(W_0 - \ell) + (1-p)U(W_0). \tag{5.11}$$

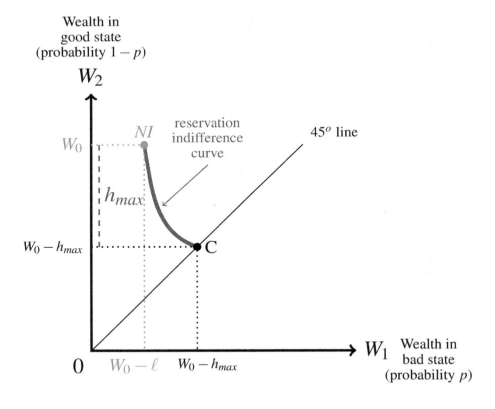

Figure 5.8: Contract C is the full-insurance contract that would be offered by a monopolist.

---

[3]Recall that, at any point on the 45° line, the indifference curve is tangent to the isoprofit line.

5.2 Back to insurance

Recall the definition of risk premium, R_L, of a money lottery L: it is the amount by which the expected value of lottery L can be reduced to leave the individual indifferent between the amount $\$(\mathbb{E}[L] - R_L)$ for sure and the lottery itself. Using this definition and (5.11) it is clear that, since $\mathbb{E}[NI] = W_0 - p\ell$,

$$h_{max} = p\ell + R_{NI}$$

where $NI = \begin{pmatrix} W_0 - \ell & W_0 \\ p & 1-p \end{pmatrix}$ is the no-insurance lottery. That is, h_{max} is equal to the *expected loss plus the risk premium of the no-insurance lottery.*

For example, if $W_0 = 1,600$, $\ell = 700$, $p = \frac{1}{10}$ and $U(m) = \sqrt{m}$ then h_{max} is given by the solution to the equation

$$\sqrt{1,600 - h} = \frac{1}{10}\sqrt{1,600 - 700} + \frac{9}{10}\sqrt{1,600}$$

which is $h^{max} = 79$. Hence the risk premium of the *NI* lottery is

$$R_{NI} = h_{max} - p\ell = 79 - \frac{1}{10}700 = \$9.$$

5.2.2 Perfectly competitive industry with free entry

Without making use of expected utility theory, we showed in Chapter 2 (Section 2.6.4) that, at an equilibrium in a perfectly competitive industry with free entry, all the insurance firms offer the same contract, namely the full insurance contract with "fair" premium equal to the expected loss $p\ell$. We can now confirm this result with the tools developed in this chapter.

Recall that a free-entry competitive equilibrium is a situation where

1. each firm in the industry makes zero profits, and

2. there is no unexploited profit opportunity in the industry, that is, there is no currently-not-offered contract that would attract some custmers and yield positive profit to a firm that offered that contract.

By the zero-profit condition (Point 1), any equilibrium contract must be on the zero-profit line. By the no-profitable-opportunity condition (Point 2), it cannot be a partial-insurance contract, such as contract A in Figure 5.9, because a new entrant (or an existing firm) could offer a contract in the region above the indifference curve through point A and below the iso-profit line through point A, such as contract B in Figure 5.9; such a contract would induce all those customers who were purchasing contract A to switch to B and would yield positive profits to the insurance firm offering it. The only contract that is immune to this is the contract at the intersection of the zero-profit line and the 45° line (contract D in Figure 5.9).

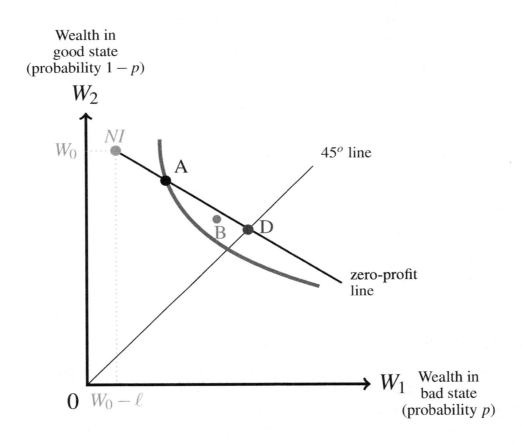

Figure 5.9: Contract D is the full-insurance contract that would be offered at a free-entry competitive equilibrium.

Test your understanding of the concepts introduced in this section, by going through the exercises in Section 5.5.2 at the end of this chapter.

5.3 Choosing from a menu of contracts

It is often the case that insurance companies offer, not just a single contract, but a menu of contracts and potential customers are allowed to choose which contract to purchase from this menu. Typically, customers are given a choice between a higher premium with higher coverage (= lower deductible) or a lower premium with lower coverage (= higher deductible). The offered menu consists of either a list of contracts or a formula that relates premium to deductible. In this section we discuss how the potential customer chooses a contract from a given menu.

5.3.1 Choosing from a finite menu

In the case where the menu consists of a finite list of contracts, the potential customer will first determine which of the offered contracts is best for her (that is, yields the highest expected utility) then choose the best contract, provided that it is better than the no-insurance alternative.

For example, consider an individual whose initial wealth is $1,000. He faces a potential loss of $400, with probability 20% and has the following vNM utility-of-money function $U(m) = \sqrt{m}$. Suppose that the insurance company offers the following options:

	premium	deductible
Contract 1:	$82	0
Contract 2:	$62	$100
Contract 3:	$40	$200

The expected utility of each contract is as follows:

Contract 1: $\sqrt{1,000 - 82} = 30.2985$

Contract 2: $0.2\sqrt{1,000 - 162} + 0.8\sqrt{1,000 - 62} = 30.2911$

Contract 3: $0.2\sqrt{1,000 - 240} + 0.8\sqrt{1,000 - 40} = 30.3007$

This *if* he decides to insure, he will choose Contract 3. To see if he does decide to insure we need to compare the expected utility of the best contract, namely Contract 3, with the expected utility of no insurance, which is $0.2\sqrt{1,000 - 400} + 0.8\sqrt{1,000} = 30.1972$. Since Contract 3 (the best of the three offered contracts) is better than no insurance, he will purchase Contract 3.

5.3.2 Choosing from a continuum of options

Suppose now that the insurance company offers a continuum of options in the form of a formula relating premium and deductible. For example, consider an individual who is facing a potential loss of $4,100 and is told by the insurance company that she can choose any deductible $d \in [0, 4100]$; the corresponding premium h is then calculated according to the following formula:

$$h = 820 - \frac{1}{5}d. \tag{5.12}$$

Thus the following are some of the many possible contracts that the individual can choose from:

deductible	premium
0	$820
$100	$800
$140	$792
$260	$768
...	...

The set of possible choices is infinite, since any $d \in [0, 4100]$ can be chosen by the individual. Thus we can think of (5.12) as a line, similar to the budget line faced by a consumer. We shall call it the *insurance budget line*.

It is useful to translate the line of equation (5.12) – which is expressed in terms of premium and deductible – into a line in the wealth diagram (W_1, W_2). This is easily done by recalling that $h = W_0 - W_2$ and $d = W_2 - W_1$:

$$W_0 - W_2 = 820 - \frac{1}{5}(W_2 - W_1), \quad \text{that is,} \quad W_2 = \left(\frac{5W_0}{4} - 1025\right) - \frac{W_1}{4}. \tag{5.13}$$

For example, if $W_0 = 6,000$ then (5.13) becomes $W_0 - W_2 = 820 - \frac{1}{5}(W_2 - W_1)$, that is,

$$W_2 = 6,475 - \frac{W_1}{4}. \tag{5.14}$$

Note that the line (in the wealth space) corresponding to equation (5.14) goes through the no-insurance point $NI = (1900, 6000)$; in fact, replacing W_1 with the value 1900 in (5.14) we get $W_2 = 6000$.

5.3 Choosing from a menu of contracts

The insurance budget line of equation (5.14) is shown in Figure 5.10.

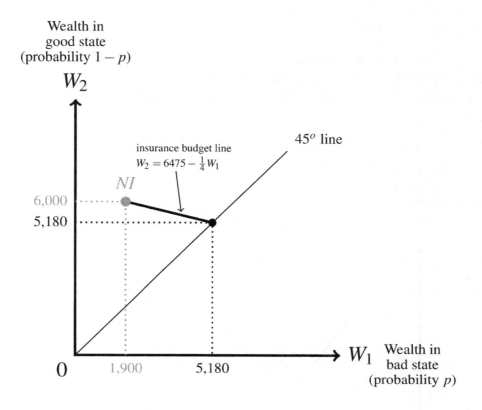

Figure 5.10: The insurance budget line $W_2 = 6,475 - \frac{W_1}{4}$.

We will consider insurance budget lines defined by equations of the form

$$h = a - bd \qquad \text{with } a > 0,\ b > 0,\ d \in [0, \ell] \text{ and } a - b\ell \geq 0, \tag{5.15}$$

which – translated into the wealth space (by replacing h with $(W_0 - W_2)$ and d with $(W_2 - W_1)$) – becomes

$$W_2 = \frac{W_0 - a}{1 - b} - \frac{b}{1 - b} W_1. \tag{5.16}$$

If (5.15) is such that $a - b\ell = 0$ then the insurance budget line in the wealth space (defined by (5.16)) goes through the no-insurance point $NI = (W_0 - \ell, W_0)$,[4] while if $a - b\ell > 0$ then the insurance budget line in the wealth space (defined by (5.16)) goes through a point vertically below NI.[5]

---

[4] For example, the zero-profit line falls into this category.
[5] For example, an isoprofit line corresponding to a positive level of profit will fall into this category.

What contract, if any, would the individual choose from the insurance budget line?

We start with the case where the insurance budget line goes through the *NI* point. There are three cases to consider.

Case 1: the reservation indifference curve is, at *NI*, as steep as, or less steep than, the insurance budget line, as shown in Figure 5.11. It follows that the entire insurance budget line lies below the reservation indifference curve and thus **the individual will choose not to insure**.

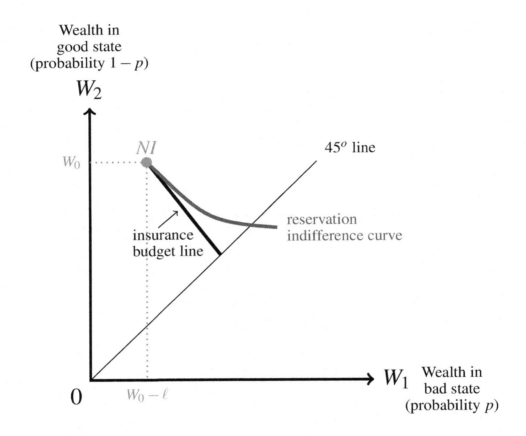

Figure 5.11: Case 1: the insurance budget line lies below the reservation indifference curve.

In the example above, where $W_0 = 6,000$, $\ell = 4,100$ and the insurance budget line is given by the equation $W_2 = 6,475 - \frac{W_1}{4}$, we will be in Case 1 if and only if

$$\frac{p}{1-p}\left(\frac{U'(1,900)}{U'(6,000)}\right) \leq \frac{1}{4}.$$

For instance, if $U(m) = \ln(m)$, then Case 1 occurs if and only if $p \leq \frac{19}{259} = 0.0734$.

5.3 Choosing from a menu of contracts

> For Cases 2 and 3 below we assume that the reservation indifference curve is steeper at *NI* than the insurance budget line.

Case 2: the indifference curve that goes through the point at the intersection of the 45° line and the insurance budget line is steeper than, or as steep as, the insurance budget line at that point, as shown in Figure 5.12.[6]

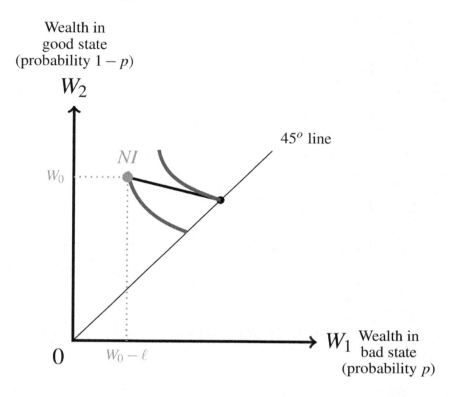

Figure 5.12: Case 2: the individual chooses full insurance.

In this case, insurance is better than no insurance and the best contract (that is, the contract that yields the highest expected utility) is the **full insurance** contract (the point at the intersection of the 45° line and the insurance budget).

In the example above, where the insurance budget line is given by the equation $W_2 = 6,475 - \frac{W_1}{4}$, we will be in Case 2 if and only if (recall that the slope of any indifference curve at any point on the 45° line is $-\frac{p}{1-p}$)

$$\frac{p}{1-p} \geq \frac{1}{4} \quad \text{i.e.} \quad p \geq \frac{1}{5}.$$

---

[6] The indifference curve will be, at that point, as steep as the insurance budget line if and only if the insurance budget line is the zero-profit line, since that slope will be $-\frac{p}{1-p}$. It is steeper if and only if the insurance budget line is less steep than the zero-profit line, which implies that all the contracts on the insurance budget line – with the exception of the *NI* point – yield negative profits; thus it is unlikely that an insurance company would offer such menu (unless it is subsidized by the government).

Case 3: the indifference curve that goes through the point at the intersection of the 45° line and the insurance budget line is less steep than the insurance budget line at that point, as shown in Figure 5.13.

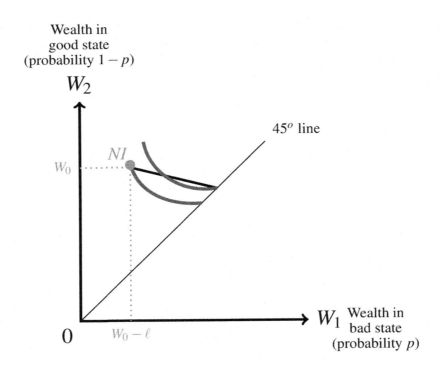

Figure 5.13: Case 3: the individual chooses partial insurance.

In this case, there are partial-insurance contracts on the insurance budget line that are better than full insurance (and than no insurance). Thus the individual will choose a partial insurance contract.

Which of the many partial-insurance contracts will she choose? It cannot be a contract where the indifference curve through it is either steeper, or less steep, than the insurance budget line: in the former case there would be contracts on the budget line to the right of that contract that would be better and in the latter case there would be contracts on the budget line to the left of that contract that would be better. Hence the best contract is the one at which the slope of the indifference curve at that point is equal to the slope of the insurance budget line, that is, it is a contract at which the indifference curve through it is *tangent to* the insurance budget line: it is that contract $C = (W_1^C, W_2^C)$ such that, letting $W_2 = \alpha - \beta W_1$ be the equation of the budget line (with $\alpha > 0$ and $\beta > 0$),

$$W_2^C = \alpha - \beta W_1^C \quad \text{and} \quad \frac{p}{1-p}\left(\frac{U'(W_1^C)}{U'(W_2^C)}\right) = \beta. \tag{5.17}$$

5.3 Choosing from a menu of contracts

The optimal contract (which satisfies (5.17)) is shown in Figure 5.14.

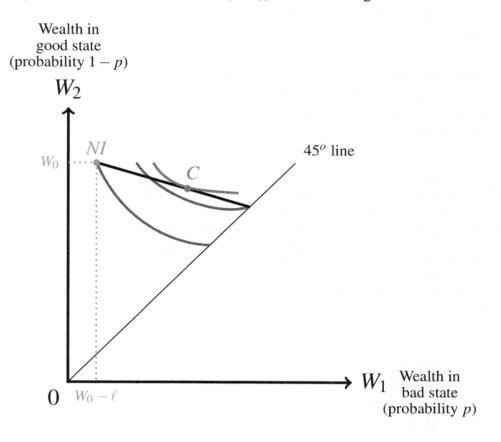

Figure 5.14: The best contract in Case 3.

In the example above, where $W_0 = 6,000$, $\ell = 4,100$ and the insurance budget line is given by the equation $W_2 = 6,475 - \frac{W_1}{4}$, we will be in Case 3 if and only if[7]

$$\frac{p}{1-p}\left(\frac{U'(1,900)}{U'(6,000)}\right) > \frac{1}{4} \quad \text{and} \quad \frac{p}{1-p} < \frac{1}{4}.$$

For instance, if $U(m) = \ln(m)$, then Case 3 occurs if and only if $p > \frac{19}{259}$ and $p < \frac{1}{5}$, that is, if and only if $p \in \left[\frac{19}{259}, \frac{1}{5}\right]$. Fix a value of p in this range and continue to assume that $U(m) = \ln(m)$. Then the optimal contract $C = (W_1^C, W_2^C)$ is given by the solution to

$$W_2 = 6,475 - \frac{W_1}{4} \quad \text{and} \quad \frac{p}{1-p}\left(\frac{W_2}{W_1}\right) = \frac{1}{4}.$$

For example, if $p = \frac{1}{7}$ then the optimal contract is $C = (3700, 5550)$, that is, the individual will choose a deductible of $5,550 - 3,700 = \$1,850$ with a corresponding premium of $6,000 - 5,550 = \$450$.

---

[7] The first inequality says that the reservation indifference curve is steeper at NI than the insurance budget line. The second inequality says that the indifference curve that goes through the point on the 45° line that lies on the insurance budget line is less steep at that point than the budget line.

So far we have assumed that the insurance budget line goes through the no-insurance point *NI*. If it does not then, given the assumptions stated in (5.15) on page 129, it will go through a point vertically below the no-insurance point. There are several possibilities.

A **first possibility** is that the insurance budget line lies entirely below the reservation indifference curve (this situation is similar to Case 1 considered above). In such a case the individual will choose not to insure, since any of the offered contracts yields a lower expected utility than no insurance.

A **second possibility** is that there are points on the insurance budget line that are above the reservation indifference curve, as well as points that are below the reservation indifference curve. This case can be further subdivided into two sub-cases.

The **first sub-case** is that there is only one point of intersection between the insurance budget line and the reservation indifference curve, as shown in Figure 5.15. In this case the entire segment of the budget line to the right of the intersection point lies above the reservation indifference curve.

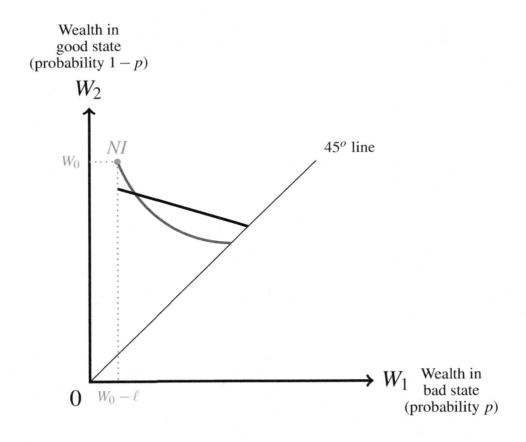

Figure 5.15: The case where the insurance budget line does not go through *NI*.

5.3 Choosing from a menu of contracts

In this case,

- if the indifference curve that goes through the point at the intersection of the 45° line and the insurance budget line is - at that point - *steeper than, or as steep as,* the insurance budget line (as shown in the left panel of Figure 5.16), then the best contract for the individual is the full-insurance contract;

- if the indifference curve that goes through the point at the intersection of the 45° line and the insurance budget line is - at that point - *less steep than* the insurance budget line (as shown in the right panel of Figure 5.16), then the best contract for the individual is a partial-insurance contract, namely a point at which there is a tangency between the budget line and the indifference curve that goes through that point (point C in the right panel of Figure 5.16).

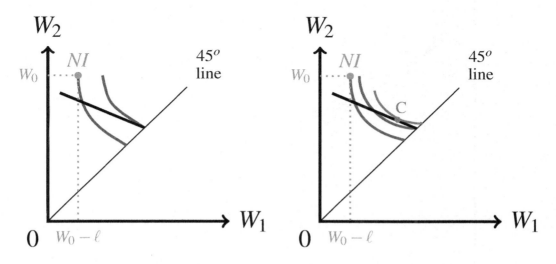

Figure 5.16: In the case on the left the individual chooses full insurance, in the case on the right partial insurance.

For example, let $W_0 = 3,600$, $\ell = 1,100$ and $p = \frac{1}{5}$. Suppose that the insurance company is willing to offer any contact that yields a profit of \$10. Then premium and deductible are related by the equation $h - p(\ell - d) = 10$, that is, $h = 230 - \frac{d}{5}$. Let us translate it into a line in the wealth space: $3,600 - W_2 = 230 - \frac{1}{5}(W_2 - W_1)$, that is,

$$W_2 = 4,212.5 - \frac{W_1}{4}.$$

This is the equation of the isoprofit line corresponding to a profit-level of 10. Call B the point of intersection of the budget line and the 45° line. Then the slope of the isoprofit line is equal to the slope, at point B, of the indifference curve that goes through point B. Hence we are in the subcase shown in the left panel of Figure 5.16 and the individual will choose the full-insurance contract, with a premium of \$230 (assuming, of course, that the utility-of-money function is such that the reservation indifference curve crosses the insurance budget line).

On the other hand, if the insurance budget line is steeper than an isoprofit line, then we are in the case shown in the right panel of Figure 5.16 and the individual will choose a partial-insurance contract.

The **second sub-case** is that there are two points of intersection between the insurance budget line and the reservation indifference curve, as shown in Figure 5.17.

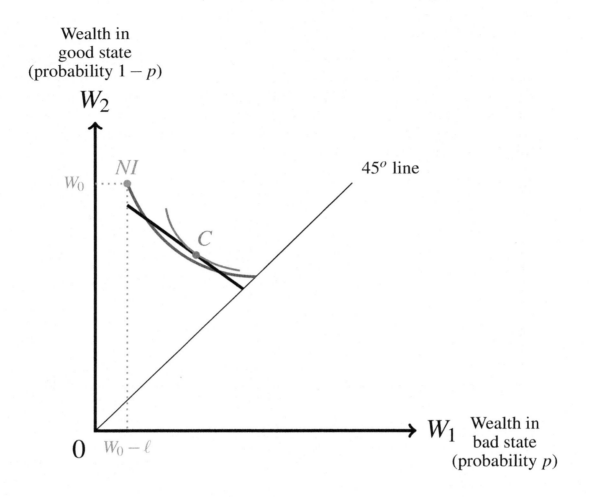

Figure 5.17: In this case the individual chooses partial insurance.

In this case the individual will choose a partial-insurance contract, namely the contract on the insurance budget line at which there is a tangency between the budget line and the indifference curve that goes through that point (shown as point C in Figure 5.17).

We will not consider cases where the insurance budget line does not cover the entire range $[0, \ell]$ of possible deductibles and is thus a smaller segment than considered so far; it should be clear, however, that the method would be the same, namely based on comparing the relative slopes of indifference curves and the budget line. An example of this is given in Exercise 5.16.

5.3 Choosing from a menu of contracts

We can summarize the discussion of this section as follows. Let

$$W_2 = \alpha - \beta W_1$$

be the equation of the insurance budget line (with $\alpha > 0$ and $\beta > 0$). To determine whether the individual will buy insurance and, if so, what contract she will choose, we can proceed as follows.[8]

Let B be the full-insurance contract on the insurance budget line (thus $W_1^B = W_2^B = \frac{\alpha}{1+\beta}$) and recall that the slope, at point B, of the indifference curve that goes through B is $\frac{p}{1-p}$ (where, as usual, p denotes the probability of loss).

1. If $\mathbb{E}[U(B)] \geq \mathbb{E}[U(NI)]$, then the individual will buy insurance[9] and

    (a) if $\frac{p}{1-p} \geq \beta$ she will choose the full-insurance contract B;

    (b) if $\frac{p}{1-p} < \beta$ she will choose partial insurance, namely that contract $C = (W_1^C, W_2^C)$ such that

    $$W_2^C = \alpha - \beta W_1^C \quad \text{and} \quad \frac{p}{1-p}\left(\frac{U'(W_1^C)}{U'(W_2^C)}\right) = \beta.$$

2. If $\mathbb{E}[U(B)] < \mathbb{E}[U(NI)]$ then

    (a) if the insurance budget line does not intersect the reservation indifference curve, that is, if the there is no solution to the equation

    $$pU(W_0 - \ell) + (1-p)U(W_0) = pU(W_1) + (1-p)U(\alpha - \beta W_1)$$

    in the range $(W_0 - \ell, W_0)$, then the individual will not buy insurance;

    (b) if the insurance budget line intersects the reservation indifference curve at two points, that is, if the there are two solutions to the equation

    $$pU(W_0 - \ell) + (1-p)U(W_0) = pU(W_1) + (1-p)U(\alpha - \beta W_1)$$

    in the range $(W_0 - \ell, W_0)$, then the individual will choose partial insurance, namely the contract $C = (W_1^C, W_2^C)$ such that

    $$W_2^C = \alpha - \beta W_1^C \quad \text{and} \quad \frac{p}{1-p}\left(\frac{U'(W_1^C)}{U'(W_2^C)}\right) = \beta.$$

Test your understanding of the concepts introduced in this section, by going through the exercises in Section 5.5.3 at the end of this chapter.

---

[8] The reader should convince herself/himself that, indeed, the following steps cover all the cases considered in this section.

[9] Here and elsewhere we are implicitly assuming that if the individual is indifferent between insuring and not insuring then she will choose to insure.

5.4 Mutual insurance

After an exceptional spate of wildfires in the western United States in 2017 and 2018, several insurance companies notified residents in brush-heavy areas that their homeowner-insurance policies would not be renewed because the location of their homes posed an unacceptable fire risk. For example, on August 6, 2018, CBS News reported that[10]

> facing mounting losses, some property insurers are pulling back from selling policies in California and other western states where wildfire risk is elevated. In California alone, damages had mounted to at least $12 billion by early 2018.

Clearly, the unavailability of insurance makes a risk-averse individual worse off. Is there anything that he/she can do mitigate the welfare loss due to the inability to but insurance?

Imagine that Ann and Bob are friends who live in high-risk areas that insurers have decided to no longer cover. To make things simple, imagine that Ann and Bob have the same initial wealth $\$W_0$ and their homes are of equal value, so that they both face the same potential loss of $\$\ell$ if a fire occurs; furthermore, assume that they face the same probability p of a fire occurring. Without insurance they both face the same money lottery, namely

$$NI = \begin{pmatrix} W_0 & W_0 - \ell \\ 1-p & p \end{pmatrix}$$

One possible course of action for Ann and Bob is to resort to *mutual-insurance*, that is, to insure each other by signing the following contract:

> I agree to the following:
> 1. in the event that we both suffer a loss (due to a fire) or in the event that none of us suffers a loss, then no transfer of money will take place between us,
> 2. in the event that only one of us suffers a loss of $\$\ell$ (due to a fire), the other one (who did not suffer a loss) will give $\$\frac{\ell}{2}$ to the person who suffered the loss, that is, will cover 50% of his/her loss.

Would such a contract make them better off relative to no insurance? Let us assume they leave in locations that are far apart, so that the event of a fire in Ann's area can plausibly be treated as independent of the event of a fire in Bob's area. When two events are independent, the probability of them jointly occurring is equal to the product of the individual probabilities. Thus the probabilities can be computed as follows:

event:	no fire	fire only at Ann's	fire only at Bob's	fire at both locations
probability:	$(1-p)^2$	$p(1-p)$	$p(1-p)$	p^2

Thus, each individual will suffers a loss of $\$\frac{\ell}{2}$ (either in the form of a payment to a less lucky friend or in the form of a loss of ℓ followed by a reimbursement, in the amount of $\frac{\ell}{2}$,

---
[10] https://www.cbsnews.com/news/california-wildfires-property-insurers-cancel-policies-because-of-risk/

5.4 Mutual insurance

from the luckier friend) with probability $2p(1-p)$, so that the contract will give rise to the following money lottery for each of them ('MI' stands for 'Mutual Insurance'):

$$MI = \begin{pmatrix} W_0 & W_0 - \frac{\ell}{2} & W_0 - \ell \\ (1-p)^2 & 2p(1-p) & p^2 \end{pmatrix}$$

Assuming that Ann has vNM preferences over money lotteries and prefers more money to less (a similar argument applies to Bob), we can represent her preferences by means of a normalized vNM utility function as follows, with $0 < a < 1$:

$$\begin{array}{cccc} \text{money:} & W_0 & W_0 - \frac{\ell}{2} & W_0 - \ell \\ \text{utility:} & 1 & a & 0 \end{array}$$

Then the expected utilities of the two lotteries are:

$$\mathbb{E}[U(NI)] = 1 - p, \quad \text{and}$$

$$\mathbb{E}[U(MI)] = (1-p)^2 + 2p(1-p)a = (1-p)[1 + p(2a-1)].$$

Consider first the case where Ann is risk neutral. Then it must be that $a = \frac{1}{2}$. In fact, the lottery $\begin{pmatrix} W_0 - \frac{\ell}{2} \\ 1 \end{pmatrix}$ and the lottery $\begin{pmatrix} W_0 & W_0 - \ell \\ \frac{1}{2} & \frac{1}{2} \end{pmatrix}$ have the same expected value, namely $W_0 - \frac{\ell}{2}$ and thus Ann must be indifferent between them. The expected utility of the former is a and the expected utility of the latter is $\frac{1}{2}$; thus $a = \frac{1}{2}$. When $a = \frac{1}{2}$, $(2a-1) = 0$ and thus $\mathbb{E}[U(NI)] = \mathbb{E}[U(MI)]$ so that Ann does not gain from signing the contract: with the contract she is as well off as without the contract.

Next consider first the case where Ann is risk averse. Then it must be that $a > \frac{1}{2}$. In fact, the lottery $\begin{pmatrix} W_0 - \frac{\ell}{2} \\ 1 \end{pmatrix}$, whose expected utility is a, gives for sure the expected value of the lottery $\begin{pmatrix} W_0 & W_0 - \ell \\ \frac{1}{2} & \frac{1}{2} \end{pmatrix}$, whose expected utility is $\frac{1}{2}$. By definition of risk aversion, Ann prefers the former lottery to the latter. Hence $a > \frac{1}{2}$. When $a > \frac{1}{2}$, $(2a-1) > 0$ and thus $(1-p)[1 + p(2a-1)] > 1 - p$ so that $\mathbb{E}[U(MI)] > E[U(NI)]$, that is, Ann is better off with the contract than without the contract.

Thus we have shown that two *risk-averse individuals can make themselves better off by signing a mutual-insurance agreement*, according to which they share the losses equally.

The astute reader will have realized that there was no need for a detailed proof of the fact that a risk-averse individual will prefer lottery *MI* to lottery *NI*, since it follows from the analysis of Chapter 4 (Section 4.4.2): lottery *NI* can be obtained from lottery *MI* by means of a mean-preserving spread. First of all, the reader should verify that $\mathbb{E}[NI] = \mathbb{E}[MI] = W_0 - p\ell$. Secondly, by taking the probability of outcome $(W_0 - \frac{\ell}{2})$, namely $2p(1-p)$, and spreading it equally to each of the other outcomes we obtain lottery *NI*; in fact, $(1-p)^2 + \frac{1}{2}2p(1-p) = 1 - p$ and $p^2 + \frac{1}{2}2p(1-p) = p$.

> Test your understanding of the concepts introduced in this section, by going through the exercises in Section 5.5.4 at the end of this chapter.

5.5 Exercises

The solutions to the following exercises are given in Section 5.6 at the end of this chapter.

5.5.1 Exercises for Section 5.1: Binary lotteries and indifference curves

Exercise 5.1 Consider all the lotteries of the form $\begin{pmatrix} \$x & \$y \\ \frac{1}{3} & \frac{2}{3} \end{pmatrix}$ with $x \geq 0$ and $y \geq 0$.
Assume that the individual in question is risk neutral.

(a) Write the equation of the indifference curve that goes through point $(x=6, y=10)$.

(b) Write the equation of the indifference curve that goes through point $(10,8)$.

(c) Write the equation of the indifference curve that goes through point $(4,9)$.

Exercise 5.2 Consider all the lotteries of the form $\begin{pmatrix} \$x & \$y \\ \frac{1}{3} & \frac{2}{3} \end{pmatrix}$ with $x \geq 0$ and $y \geq 0$.
Consider an individual with von Neumann-Morgenstern utility-of-money function $U(m) = \ln(m)$.

(a) Calculate the expected utility of lottery $A = \begin{pmatrix} \$10 & \$40 \\ \frac{1}{3} & \frac{2}{3} \end{pmatrix}$.

(b) Calculate the expected utility of lottery $B = \begin{pmatrix} \$10 & \$10 \\ \frac{1}{3} & \frac{2}{3} \end{pmatrix}$.

(c) Calculate the slope of the indifference curve at point $A = (10, 40)$.

(d) Calculate the slope of the indifference curve at point $B = (10, 10)$.

(e) In the (x,y)-plane draw the indifference curve that goes to point $A = (10,40)$ and the indifference curve that goes to point $B = (10, 10)$.

Exercise 5.3 Repeat Parts (a)-(e) of the previous question for the case of an individual who is risk neutral.

5.5 Exercises

Exercise 5.4 Consider all the lotteries of the form $\begin{pmatrix} \$x & \$y \\ \frac{2}{3} & \frac{1}{3} \end{pmatrix}$ with $x \geq 0$ and $y \geq 0$. Consider an individual with von Neumann-Morgenstern utility-of-money function $U(m) = \ln(m)$.

(a) Write an equation whose solutions give the set of lotteries that the individual considers just as good as lottery $A = \begin{pmatrix} \$4 & \$4 \\ \frac{2}{3} & \frac{1}{3} \end{pmatrix}$.

(b) Solve the equation of Part (a) and obtain a function $y = f(x)$ whose graph is the indifference curve that goes through point $(4,4)$.

(c) Write an equation whose solutions give the set of lotteries that the individual considers just as good as lottery $B = \begin{pmatrix} \$9 & \$4 \\ \frac{2}{3} & \frac{1}{3} \end{pmatrix}$.

(d) Solve the equation of Part (c) and obtain a function $y = g(x)$ whose graph is the indifference curve that goes through point $(9,4)$.

(e) Calculate the slope of the indifference curve at point $A = (4,4)$.

(f) Calculate the slope of the indifference curve at point $B = (9,4)$.

■

Exercise 5.5 Consider all the lotteries of the form $\begin{pmatrix} \$x & \$y \\ \frac{1}{5} & \frac{4}{5} \end{pmatrix}$ with $x \geq 0$ and $y \geq 0$. Let $A = (100, 25)$, $B = (4, 49)$ and $C = (40, 40)$.

(a) Draw the indifference curves that go through points A, B and C for an individual with von Neumann-Morgenstern utility-of-money function $U(m) = \sqrt{m}$.

(b) Draw the indifference curves that go through points A, B and C for a risk-neutral individual.

■

5.5.2 Exercises for Section 5.2: Back to insurance

Exercise 5.6 Adam's current wealth is $80,000. With probability $\frac{1}{20}$ he faces a loss of $30,000. His vNM utility-of-money function is $U(m) = \ln(m)$.

(a) Calculate the slope of Adam's reservation indifference curve at the no-insurance point NI.

(b) Calculate the slope of the iso-profit curve that goes through point NI.

(c) Calculate the maximum premium that Adam is willing to pay for full insurance.

(d) Calculate the increase in Adam's utility relative to no insurance if he obtains full insurance at the "fair" premium (that is, at a premium that yields zero profits to the insurer).

(e) Consider contract $A = (80,000 - h,\ 80,000 - h)$. Calculate the slope at point A of Adam's indifference curve that goes through point A.

■

Exercise 5.7 Frank has a wealth of W_0. With probability $p = \frac{1}{10}$ he faces a loss of $\$\ell$. The maximum he is willing to pay for full insurance is $800. The risk premium associated with the lottery corresponding to no insurance is $500.

(a) What is the value of ℓ?

(b) What is the maximum profit that a monopolist can make by selling insurance to Frank?

Exercise 5.8 Bob owns a house. The value of the land is $75,000 while the value of the building is $110,000. The rest of his wealth consists of the balance of his bank account, which is $10,000. Thus his current wealth is $195,000. Bob lives in an area where there is a 5% probability that a fire will completely destroy his house during any year (while the land will not be affected by a fire). Bob's utility function is given by:

$$U(m) = 800 - (20 - m)^2$$

where $m \in [0, 20]$ denotes money measured in $10,000 (thus, for example, $m = 11$ means $110,000).

(a) What is Bob's expected loss if he does not insure?

(b) What is Bob's expected *wealth* if he does not insure?

(c) What is Bob's expected *utility* if he does not insure?

(d) What is Bob's expected utility if he purchases an insurance contract with premium $1,200 and deductible $20,000?

(e) What is the slope of Bob's reservation indifference curve at the no-insurance point?

(f) Let A be the point in the wealth diagram that corresponds to the insurance contract with premium $1,200 and deductible $20,000. What is the slope, at point A, of Bob's indifference curve that goes through point A?

(g) Does the indifference curve that goes through point A of Part (f) lie above or below the reservation indifference curve?

(h) What is the maximum premium that Bob would be willing to pay for full insurance?

Exercise 5.9 Beth's vNM utility-of-money function is $U(m) = \alpha - \beta e^{-m}$, where α and β are positive constants. [Recall that $e \approx 2.71828$ and $\frac{d}{dx}e^x = e^x$.]

(a) What is Beth's attitude to risk?

(b) What is Beth's Arrow-Pratt measure of absolute risk aversion?

(c) Show that if Beth's initial wealth is W_0 and she is faced with a potential loss ℓ with probability p, the maximum premium that she is willing to pay for full insurance is the same whatever her initial wealth, that is, it is independent of W_0.

5.5.3 Exercises for Section 5.3: Choosing from a menu of contracts

Exercise 5.10 Barbara has a wealth of $80,000 and faces a potential loss of $20,000 with probability 10%. Her utility-of-money function is $U(m) = \sqrt{m}$. An insurance company offers her the following menu of contracts:

	premium	deductible
Contract 1:	$2,340	$500
Contract 2:	$2,280	$1,000
Contract 3:	$2,220	$1,500
Contract 4:	$2,160	$2,000

(a) What is Barbara's expected utility if she does not insure?

(b) For each contract calculate the corresponding expected utility and determine which contract, if any, Barbara will choose.

Exercise 5.11 You have the following vNM utility-of-money function: $U(m) = \ln(m)$. Your initial wealth is $10,000 and you face a potential loss of $4,000 with probability $\frac{1}{6}$. An insurance company offers you the following menu of choices: if you choose deductible d (with $0 \le d \le 4,000$) then your premium is $h = 800 - 0.2d$.

(a) Translate the equation $h = 800 - 0.2d$ into an equation in terms of wealth levels.

(b) Compare the slope of the reservation indifference curve at the no-insurance point NI to the slope of the insurance budget line. Are there contracts that are better for you than no insurance?

(c) Which contract will you choose from the menu?

(d) Compare expected utility if you do not insure with expected utility if you purchase the best contract from the menu.

(e) What is the insurance company's expected profit from the contract of Part (c)?

(f) Prove the result of Part (c) directly by expressing expected utility as a function of the deductible d and by maximizing that expression.

Exercise 5.12 You have the following vNM utility-of-money function: $U(m) = \sqrt{m}$. Your initial wealth is $576 and you face a potential loss of $176 with probability $\frac{1}{16}$. An insurance company offers you the following menu of choices: if you choose deductible d (with $0 \le d \le 176$) then your premium is $h = \frac{1}{9}(176 - d)$.

(a) Translate the equation $h = \frac{1}{9}(176 - d)$ into an equation in terms of wealth levels.

(b) Compare the slope of the reservation indifference curve at the no-insurance point NI to the slope of the insurance budget line. Are there contracts that are better for you than no insurance?

Exercise 5.13 [Note: in this exercise the data is the same as in Exercise 5.12, but we have changed the probability of loss from $\frac{1}{16}$ to $\frac{1}{7}$.]

Your vNM utility-of-money function is $U(m) = \sqrt{m}$; your initial wealth is \$576 and you face a potential loss of \$176 with probability $\frac{1}{7}$. An insurance company offers you the following menu of choices: if you choose deductible d (with $0 \le d \le 176$) then your premium is $h = \frac{1}{9}(176 - d)$.

(a) Translate the equation $h = \frac{1}{9}(176 - d)$ into an equation in terms of wealth levels.

(b) Compare the slope of the reservation indifference curve at the no-insurance point *NI* to the slope of the insurance budget line. Are there contracts that are better for you than no insurance?

(c) Which contract will you choose from the menu?

(d) Compare expected utility if you do not insure with expected utility if you purchase the best contract from the menu.

(e) What is the insurance company's expected profit from the contract of Part (c)?

(f) Confirm the result of Part (c) by expressing expected utility as a function of the deductible d and by finding the maximum of that function in the interval $[0, 400]$.

Exercise 5.14 David's vNM utility-of-money function is $U(m) = 1 - (m+1)^{-1}$, where m is money measured in thousands of dollars (thus, for example, $m = 6$ means \$6,000).

(a) What is David's attitude to risk?

(b) Calculate the Arrow-Pratt measure of absolute risk aversion for David.

David's initial wealth is \$8,000 and he faces a potential loss of \$3,000 with probability $\frac{1}{10}$. An insurance company offers him insurance at the following terms:

choose the amount (of your potential loss) that you would like to be covered (thus a number in the range from 0 to 3,000); for every dollar of **coverage** you will pay \$$\gamma$ as premium (with $0 < \gamma < 1$).

(c) Write an equation that expresses the premium in terms of the deductible. [Recall that the deductible is that part of the loss that is **not** covered.].

(d) Translate the equation of Part (c) into an equation in terms od David's wealth levels.

(e) Does the insurance budget line of Part (d) go through the no-insurance point *NI*?

(f) For what values of γ will David choose not to insure?

(g) For what values of γ will Davis purchase full insurance?

(h) Assuming that the value of γ is in the range where David chooses partial insurance, write a system of two equations whose solution gives the contract that David will choose.

5.5 Exercises

Exercise 5.15 Anna's vNM utility-of-money function is $U(m) = \ln(m)$. Her initial wealth is \$3,600 and she faces a potential loss of \$2,700 with 25% probability. An insurance company is offering Anna any contract such that premium h and deductible d satisfy the following equation: $h = 810 - \frac{3}{10}d$.

(a) Translate the equation $h = 810 - \frac{3}{10}d$ into an equation in terms of wealth levels.

(b) Does the equation found in Part (a) correspond to an isoprofit line?

(c) Does the insurance budget line of Part (a) go through the no-insurance point?

(d) Are there any contracts on the insurance budget line that Anna prefers to no insurance?

(e) What is the best contract on the insurance budget line for Anna?

(f) Calculate Anna's expected utility at the following points:
   (1) NI (no insurance),
   (2) the full-insurance contracts that belongs to the budget line, and
   (3) the contract found in Part (e).

(g) Prove the result of Part (e) directly by expressing expected utility as a function of the deductible d and by maximizing that expression.

Exercise 5.16 Kate has an initial wealth of $W_0 = \$1,600$ and faces a potential loss of $\ell = \$576$ with probability 20%. Her von Neumann-Morgenstern utility-of-money function is $U(m) = \sqrt{m}$. An insurance company is offering the following menu of contracts:

$$h = 152 - \frac{3}{10}d.$$

However, the deductible is restricted to the interval $[0, 360]$ (hence the largest deductible is 360 rather than 576).

Let $A = (W_1^A, W_2^A)$ be the point in wealth space corresponding to the contract $(h = 44, d = 360)$.

(a) Translate the insurance budget line $h = 152 - \frac{3}{10}d$ ($d \in [0, 360]$) into a budget line in wealth space (give the range of values).

(b) Does contract A lie on, below or above the reservation indifference curve?

(c) Calculate the slope, at point A, of the indifference curve that goes through A, compare it to the slope of the insurance budget line and deduce which contract from the offered menu will be chosen by Kate.

5.5.4 Exercises for Section 5.4: Mutual insurance

Exercise 5.17 Carla and Don have the same initial wealth, namely $32,400, and face the same potential loss, namely $18,000, with the same probability, namely $\frac{1}{5}$.

Carla's vNM utility-of-money function is

$$U_C(m) = \sqrt{m}$$

while Don's is

$$U_D(m) = 1 - \frac{1}{\frac{m}{10,000} + 1}.$$

They are unable to obtain insurance on the market, so they have decided to write a mutual insurance contract, according to which any losses are shared equally between them.

Assuming that the event that Carla suffers a loss is independent of the event that Don suffers a loss, show that signing the mutual insurance contract has made each of them better off relative to no insurance. ■

Exercise 5.18 Ann, Carla and Dana have the same initial wealth, namely $40,000, and face the same potential loss, namely $30,000, with the same probability, namely $\frac{1}{5}$. They have the same vNM preferences, represented by the vNM utility-of-money function $U(m) = \sqrt{m}$. They are unable to obtain insurance on the market and have decided to sign a mutual insurance contract, according to which any losses suffered by any of them will be shared equally by all three of them. Assume that the event that any of them suffers a loss is independent of the event(s) that the other(s) also suffer a loss.

(a) Calculate the probabilities of the following events:
  1. All three of them suffer a loss.
  2. Exactly two of them suffer a loss.
  3. Exactly one of them suffers a loss.
  4. None of them suffers a loss.

(b) Show that each of them is better off with the mutual insurance contract relative to no insurance. ■

Exercise 5.19 In this exercise we consider the benefit of mutual insurance when independence fails to hold: one person suffering a loss makes it more likely that the other person would also suffer a loss.

We consider two individuals, Albert an Ben, who have the same initial wealth, namely $40,000, and face the same potential loss of $30,000 due to wildfire, with the same probability, namely $\frac{1}{5}$. They have the same vNM preferences, represented by the vNM utility-of-money function $U(m) = \sqrt{m}$.

Since they live not far apart from each other if a fire occurs at one of the two properties then the probability that there will be a fire at the other property is greater than $\frac{1}{5}$. If the events were independent then the probabilities would be as follows:

fire at both	fire at one only	no fires
$\frac{1}{25}$	$\frac{8}{25}$	$\frac{16}{25}$

However, due to correlation, the probabilities are as follows:

fire at both	fire at one only	no fires
$\frac{3}{30}$	$\frac{7}{30}$	$\frac{20}{30}$

Suppose that Albert and Ben are unable to obtain insurance on the market. Are they better off with no insurance or with a mutual insurance agreement (according to which any losses suffered by either of them will be shared equally by both)? ■

5.6 Solutions to Exercises

Solution to Exercise 5.1

The slope of every indifference curve is $-\frac{\frac{1}{3}}{\frac{2}{3}} = -\frac{1}{2}$. Thus the equation of any indifference curve is of the form $y = a - \frac{1}{2}x$.

(a) To find the value of a for the indifference curve that goes through point (6,10) solve the equation $10 = a - \frac{1}{2}6$ to get $a = 13$. Thus the equation of the indifference curve that goes through point (6,10) is $y = 13 - \frac{1}{2}x$.

(b) To find the value of a for the indifference curve that goes through point (10,8) solve the equation $8 = a - \frac{1}{2}10$ to get $a = 13$. Thus the equation of the indifference curve that goes through point (10,8) is $y = 13 - \frac{1}{2}x$. Hence the two lotteries (6,10) and (10,8) lie on the same indifference curve; indeed, they have the same expected value, namely $\frac{26}{3}$.

(c) To find the value of a for the indifference curve that goes through point (4,9) solve the equation $9 = a - \frac{1}{2}4$ to get $a = 11$. Thus the equation of the indifference curve that goes through point (4,9) is $y = 11 - \frac{1}{2}x$. □

Solution to Exercise 5.2

(a) The expected utility of lottery $A = \begin{pmatrix} \$10 & \$40 \\ \frac{1}{3} & \frac{2}{3} \end{pmatrix}$ is $\frac{1}{3}\ln(10) + \frac{2}{3}\ln(40) = 3.227$.

(b) The expected utility of lottery $B = \begin{pmatrix} \$10 & \$10 \\ \frac{1}{3} & \frac{2}{3} \end{pmatrix}$ is $\frac{1}{3}\ln(10) + \frac{2}{3}\ln(10) = 3.303$.

(c) The indifference curve that goes through $A = (10, 40)$ is the set of lotteries that yield an expected utility of 3.227. It is a convex curve since the utility function U incorporates risk aversion. The slope of the indifference curve at point A is equal to

$$-\frac{p}{1-p}\left(\frac{U'(10)}{U'(40)}\right) = -\frac{\frac{1}{3}}{\frac{2}{3}}\left(\frac{\frac{1}{10}}{\frac{1}{40}}\right) = -2.$$

(d) Similarly, the indifference curve that goes through $B = (10, 10)$ is the set of lotteries that yield an expected utility of 2.303. It is a convex curve. The slope of the indifference curve at point B is equal to

$$-\frac{p}{1-p}\frac{U'(10)}{U'(10)} = -\frac{\frac{1}{3}}{\frac{2}{3}}\frac{\frac{1}{10}}{\frac{1}{10}} = -\frac{1}{2}.$$

(e) The two indifference curves are shown in Figure 5.18. □

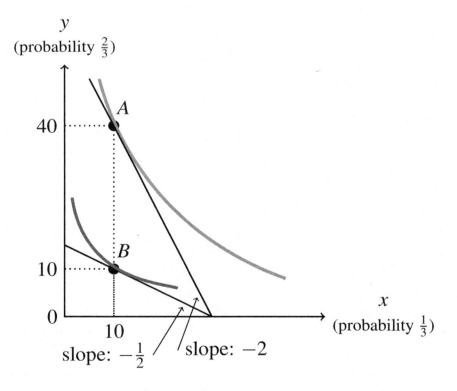

Figure 5.18: The graph for Part (e) of Exercise 5.2.

Solution to Exercise 5.3

Since the individual is risk neutral, we can take his/her utility-of-money function to be the identity function $U(m) = m$. Thus the expected utility of a lottery coincides with the expected value.

(a) The expected utility (= value) of lottery $A = \begin{pmatrix} \$10 & \$40 \\ \frac{1}{3} & \frac{2}{3} \end{pmatrix}$ is $\frac{1}{3}10 + \frac{2}{3}40 = 30$.

(b) The expected utility of lottery $B = \begin{pmatrix} \$10 & \$10 \\ \frac{1}{3} & \frac{2}{3} \end{pmatrix}$ is $\frac{1}{3}10 + \frac{2}{3}10 = 10$.

(c) The indifference curve that goes through $A = (10, 40)$ is the set of lotteries that yield an expected utility (= value) of 30. It is a straight line because of risk neutrality. The slope of the indifference curve at point A is equal to

$$-\frac{p}{1-p}\left(\frac{U'(10)}{U'(40)}\right) = -\frac{\frac{1}{3}}{\frac{2}{3}}\left(\frac{1}{1}\right) = -\frac{1}{2}.$$

(d) Similarly, the indifference curve that goes through $B = (10, 10)$ is the set of lotteries that yield an expected utility (= value) of 10. It is a straight line because of risk neutrality. The slope of the indifference curve at point B is equal to

$$-\frac{p}{1-p}\left(\frac{U'(10)}{U'(10)}\right) = -\frac{\frac{1}{3}}{\frac{2}{3}}1 = -\frac{1}{2}.$$

(e) The two indifference curves are shown in Figure 5.19. □

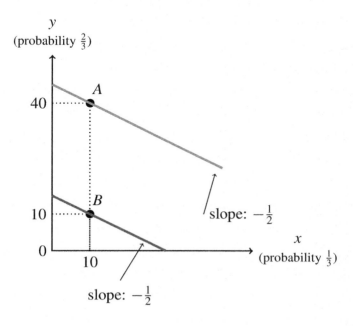

Figure 5.19: The graph for Part (e) of Exercise 5.3.

Solution to Exercise 5.4

(a) $\frac{2}{3}\ln(x) + \frac{1}{3}\ln(y) = \ln(4)$.

(b) First of all, rewrite the above equation as $2\ln(x) + \ln(y) = 3\ln(4)$, from which we get that $e^{(2\ln(x)+\ln(y))} = e^{3\ln(4)}$. Now, $e^{(2\ln(x)+\ln(y))} = e^{2\ln(x)} e^{\ln(y)} = \left(e^{\ln(x)}\right)^2 y = x^2 y$. Similarly, $e^{3\ln(4)} = 4^3 = 64$. Thus the equation becomes $x^2 y = 64$ from which we get $\boxed{y = \dfrac{64}{x^2}}$.

(c) $\frac{2}{3}\ln(x) + \frac{1}{3}\ln(y) = \frac{2}{3}\ln(9) + \frac{1}{3}\ln(4)$.

(d) Repeating the steps of Part (b): from $2\ln(x) + \ln(y) = 2\ln(9) + \ln(4)$ we get $e^{(2\ln(x)+\ln(y))} = e^{(2\ln(9)+\ln(4))}$, which becomes $x^2 y = 9^2 \cdot 4$ which yields $\boxed{y = \dfrac{324}{x^2}}$.

(e) The slope of the indifference curve at point $A = (4,4)$ is equal to[11]

$$-\frac{p}{1-p}\left(\frac{U'(4)}{U'(4)}\right) = -\frac{\frac{2}{3}}{\frac{1}{3}} \cdot 1 = -2.$$

(f) The slope of the indifference curve at point $B = (9,4)$ is equal to[12]

$$-\frac{p}{1-p}\left(\frac{U'(9)}{U'(4)}\right) = -\frac{\frac{2}{3}}{\frac{1}{3}}\left(\frac{\frac{1}{9}}{\frac{1}{4}}\right) = -\frac{8}{9}.$$

□

---

[11] Alternatively, using the function $f(x) = \frac{64}{x^2}$ of Part (b), $f'(x) = -\frac{128}{x^3}$ so that $f'(4) = -\frac{128}{4^3} = -2$.

[12] Alternatively, using the function $g(x) = \frac{324}{x^2}$ of Part (d), $g'(x) = -\frac{648}{x^3}$ so that $g'(9) = -\frac{648}{9^3} = -\frac{8}{9}$.

5.6 Solutions to Exercises

Solution to Exercise 5.5

(a) $\mathbb{E}[U(A)] = \frac{1}{5}\sqrt{100} + \frac{4}{5}\sqrt{25} = 2 + 4 = 6$ and $\mathbb{E}[U(B)] = \frac{1}{5}\sqrt{4} + \frac{4}{5}\sqrt{49} = 6$. Thus A and B lie on the same indifference curve. On the other hand, $\mathbb{E}[U(C)] = \sqrt{40} = 6.3246$. Thus C lies on a higher indifference curve. See Figure 5.20.[13]

(b) The expected value of A, B and C is the same, namely 40. Thus the three points lie on the same indifference curve, which is a straight line with slope $-\frac{1}{4}$. □

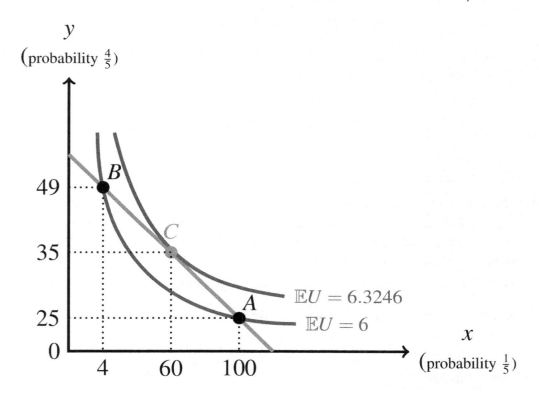

Figure 5.20: The graph for Exercise 5.5.

---

[13] Note that the scale of the axes has been distorted to make the qualitative properties of the graph easier to see.

Solution to Exercise 5.6

(a) $NI = (50000, 80000)$ and $\frac{d}{dm}\ln(m) = \frac{1}{m}$. Thus the slope of the reservation indifference curve at NI is

$$-\frac{\frac{1}{20}}{\frac{19}{20}}\left(\frac{\frac{1}{50,000}}{\frac{1}{80,000}}\right) = -\frac{8}{95} = -0.0842.$$

(b) The slope of *every* isoprofit line is $-\frac{\frac{1}{20}}{\frac{19}{20}} = -\frac{1}{19} = 0.0526$.

(c) The maximum premium that Adam is willing to pay for full insurance is given by the solution to the equation

$$\ln(80,000-h) = \frac{1}{20}\ln(50,000) + \frac{19}{20}\ln(80,000)$$

which is $h_{max} = \$1,858.10$

(d) The fair premium is equal to $\frac{1}{20}(30,000) = 1,500$. If Adam does not insure, his expected utility is $\frac{1}{20}\ln(50,000) + \frac{19}{20}\ln(80,000) = 11.2663$. If Adam obtains full insurance at premium $\$1,500$, his utility is $\ln(80,000-1,500) = 11.2709$. Thus the increase in utility is $11.2709 - 11.2663 = 0.0046$.

(e) The slope of *any* indifference curve at *any* point on the 45° line is equal to the slope of any isoprofit line, namely $-\frac{\frac{1}{20}}{\frac{19}{20}} = -\frac{1}{19} = 0.0526$. □

Solution to Exercise 5.7

(a) If Frank does not buy insurance he faces the lottery $\begin{pmatrix} W_0 & W_0-\ell \\ \frac{9}{10} & \frac{1}{10} \end{pmatrix}$ whose expected value is $W_0 - \frac{1}{10}\ell$. If h_{max} is the maximum premium that he is willing to pay for full insurance [that is, h_{max} is the solution to the equation $U(W_0-h) = \frac{9}{10}U(W_0) + \frac{1}{10}U(W_0-\ell)$] and R_{NI} is the risk premium associated with the no-insurance lottery [that is, R_{NI} is the solution to the equation $U(W_0 - \frac{1}{10}\ell - R) = \frac{9}{10}U(W_0) + \frac{1}{10}U(W_0-\ell)$], then $h_{max} = \frac{1}{10}\ell + R_{NI}$. Thus we have the following equation

$$800 = \frac{1}{10}\ell + 500,$$

whose solution is $\ell = 3,000$.

(b) The monopolist would sell Frank the full-insurance contract with premium $\$800$ and thus make an expected profit equal to $800 - \frac{1}{10}3,000 = \$500$. □

5.6 Solutions to Exercises

Solution to Exercise 5.8

(a) Bob's expected loss is $\frac{5}{100} 110,000 = \$5,500$.

(b) Bob's expected wealth if he does not insure is $195,000 - 5,500 = \$189,500$.

(c) Bob's expected utility if he does not insure is

$$\frac{5}{100}\left[800 - (20 - 8.5)^2\right] + \frac{95}{100}\left[800 - (20 - 19.5)^2\right] = 793.15.$$

(d) The insurance contract with premium $\$1,200$ and deductible $\$20,000$ corresponds to the following point in the wealth diagram: $(173{,}800,\ 193{,}800)$. The corresponding expected utility is

$$\frac{5}{100}\left[800 - (20 - 17.38)^2\right] + \frac{95}{100}\left[800 - (20 - 19.38)^2\right] = 799.29.$$

(e) $U'(m) = 40 - 2m$. Thus the slope of Bob's reservation indifference curve at the no-insurance point is

$$-\frac{\frac{5}{100}}{\frac{95}{100}}\left(\frac{40 - 2(8.5)}{40 - 2(19.5)}\right) = -1.2105.$$

(f) From Part (d) we have that $A = (173{,}800,\ 193{,}800)$. The slope, at point A, of Bob's indifference curve that goes through point A is

$$-\frac{5}{95}\left(\frac{40 - 2(17.38)}{40 - 2(19.38)}\right) = -0.2224.$$

(g) Since $\mathbb{E}[U(A)] = 799.29 > 793.15 = \mathbb{E}[U(NI)]$, the indifference curve that goes through point A lies above reservation indifference curve.

(h) The maximum premium that Bob would be willing to pay for full insurance is given by the solution to the equation $U(W_0 - h) = \mathbb{E}[U(NI)]$, that is, $800 - [20 - (19.5 - h)]^2 = 793.15$, which is 2.1173, that is, $\$21,173$ (slightly less than four times the expected loss). □

Solution to Exercise 5.9

(a) $U'(m) = \beta e^{-m} > 0$ and $U''(m) = -\beta e^{-m} < 0$, thus Beth is risk averse.

(b) $A(m) = -\frac{U''(m)}{U'(m)} = 1$, a constant.

(c) The maximum premium h_{max} is determined by the solution to

$$U(W_0 - h) = pU(W_0 - \ell) + (1-p)U(W_0), \quad \text{that is,}$$

$$\begin{aligned}
\alpha - \beta e^{(-W_0 + h)} &= p\left(\alpha - \beta e^{(-W_0 + \ell)}\right) + (1-p)\left(\alpha - \beta e^{-W_0}\right) \\
&= p\alpha + (1-p)\alpha - \beta\left[pe^{(-W_0+\ell)} + (1-p)e^{-W_0}\right] \\
&= \alpha - \beta\left[pe^{-W_0}e^{\ell} + (1-p)e^{-W_0}\right] \\
&= \alpha - \beta e^{-W_0}\left[pe^{\ell} + 1 - p\right].
\end{aligned}$$

Subtracting α from both sides and multiplying by $-\frac{1}{\beta}$ we get

$$e^{-W_0}e^h = e^{-W_0}\left[pe^{\ell} + 1 - p\right],$$

and multiplying both sides by e^{W_0}, we are left with

$$e^h = pe^{\ell} + 1 - p.$$

Thus $h_{max} = \ln(pe^{\ell} + 1 - p)$, independent of W_0. □

Solution to Exercise 5.10

(a) Barbara's expected utility if she does not insure is: $0.9\sqrt{80,000} + 0.1\sqrt{60,000} = 279.053$.

(b) Barbara's expected utility from a contract with premium h and deductible d is $0.1\sqrt{80,000 - h - d} + 0.9\sqrt{80,000 - h}$. Thus,

	premium	deductible	expected utility
Contract 1:	2,340	500	$0.1\sqrt{77,160} + 0.9\sqrt{77,660} = 278.5856$
Contract 2:	2,280	1,000	$0.1\sqrt{76,720} + 0.9\sqrt{77,720} = 278.6031$
Contract 3:	2,220	1,500	$0.1\sqrt{76,280} + 0.9\sqrt{77,780} = 278.6204$
Contract 4:	2,160	2,000	$0.1\sqrt{75,840} + 0.9\sqrt{77,840} = 278.6375$

None of the contracts gives her higher expected utility than no insurance. Hence she will not buy insurance. □

5.6 Solutions to Exercises

Solution to Exercise 5.11

(a) Letting $h = 10,000 - W_2$ and $d = W_2 - W_1$ we get $10,000 - W_2 = 800 - 0.2(W_2 - W_1)$, that is

$$W_2 = 11,500 - \frac{1}{4}W_1.$$

(b) From Part (a) we have that the slope of the insurance budget line is $-\frac{1}{4}$. The slope of the reservation indifference curve at $NI = (6000, 10000)$ is

$$-\frac{\frac{1}{6}}{\frac{5}{6}}\left(\frac{\frac{1}{6,000}}{\frac{1}{10,000}}\right) = -\frac{1}{3}.$$

Thus the reservation indifference curve is steeper, at NI, than the insurance budget line and, therefore, there are contracts that are better than no insurance.

(c) Since the slope of any indifference curve at any point on the 45° line is equal to $-\frac{\frac{1}{6}}{\frac{5}{6}} = -\frac{1}{5}$, the indifference curve that goes through the point at the intersection of the insurance budget line and the 45° line is less steep than the insurance budget line and thus we are in Case 3 of Section 5.3.2 and the optimal contract is given by the solution to the following two equations:

$$W_2 = 11,500 - \frac{1}{4}W_1 \quad \text{and} \quad -\frac{\frac{1}{6}}{\frac{5}{6}}\left(\frac{\frac{1}{W_1}}{\frac{1}{W_2}}\right) = -\frac{1}{4}$$

which is $W_1 = 7,666.67$ and $W_2 = 9,583.33$. Thus the chosen deductible is

$$d = 9,583.33 - 7,666.67 = \$1,916.66$$

and the corresponding premium is

$$h = 10,000 - 9,583.33 = \$416.67.$$

(d) Expected utility from no insurance is $\frac{1}{6}\ln(6,000) + \frac{5}{6}\ln(10,000) = 9.1252$, while expected utility from the contract of Part (c) is $\frac{1}{6}\ln(7,666.67) + \frac{5}{6}\ln(9,583.33) = 9.1306$.

(e) Expected profits from the contract of Part (c) is $416.67 - \frac{1}{6}(4,000 - 1,916.66) = \$69.45$.

(f) Expected utility from contract (h,d) is: $\frac{1}{6}\ln(10,000 - h - d) + \frac{5}{6}\ln(10,000 - h)$. Replacing h with $800 - 0.2d$ we get the following function:

$$f(d) = \frac{1}{6}\ln(10,000 - 800 + 0.2d - d) + \frac{5}{6}\ln(10,000 - 800 + 0.2d)$$
$$= \frac{1}{6}\ln(9,200 - 0.8d) + \frac{5}{6}\ln(9,200 + 0.2d).$$

To maximize this function we must solve the equation $f'(d) = 0$, that is

$$\frac{1}{6}\left(\frac{1}{9,200 - 0.8d}\right)(-0.8) + \frac{5}{6}\left(\frac{1}{9,200 + 0.2d}\right)0.2 = 0$$

The solution is $d = \frac{5,750}{3} = 1,916.66$ with corresponding premium $h = 800 - 0.2(1,916.67) = 416.67$, confirming the conclusion of Part (c). □

Chapter 5. Insurance: Part 2

Solution to Exercise 5.12

(a) Letting $h = 576 - W_2$ and $d = W_2 - W_1$ we get $576 - W_2 = \frac{1}{9}(176 - W_2 + W_1)$, that is
$$W_2 = 626 - \frac{1}{8}W_1.$$

(b) From Part (a) we have that the slope of the insurance budget line is $-\frac{1}{8}$. The slope of the reservation indifference curve at $NI = (400, 576)$ is
$$-\frac{\frac{1}{16}}{\frac{15}{16}}\left(\frac{\frac{1}{2\sqrt{400}}}{\frac{1}{2\sqrt{576}}}\right) = -\frac{2}{25}.$$

Thus the reservation indifference curve is less steep, at NI, than the insurance budget line and, therefore, the insurance budget line lies below the reservation indifference curve, that is, there are no contracts that are better than no insurance. Thus we are in Case 1 of Section 5.3.2 and your best decision is not to insure. □

Solution to Exercise 5.13

(a) The answer is, of course, the same as in Exercise 5.12: $W_2 = 626 - \frac{1}{8}W_1$.

(b) The slope of the insurance budget line is $-\frac{1}{8}$. The slope of the reservation indifference curve at $NI = (400, 576)$ is
$$-\frac{\frac{1}{7}}{\frac{6}{7}}\left(\frac{\frac{1}{2\sqrt{400}}}{\frac{1}{2\sqrt{576}}}\right) = -\frac{1}{5}.$$

Thus the reservation indifference curve is steeper, at NI, than the insurance budget line and, therefore, there are contracts that are better than no insurance.

(c) Since the slope of any indifference curve at any point on the 45° line is equal to $-\frac{\frac{1}{7}}{\frac{6}{7}} = -\frac{1}{6}$, the indifference curve that goes through the point at the intersection of the insurance budget line and the 45° line is steeper than the insurance budget line and thus we are in Case 2 of Section 5.3.2 and the optimal contract is given by the full-insurance contract (the point of intersection between the insurance budget line and the 45° line), that is, by the solution to the following two equations:
$$W_2 = 626 - \frac{1}{8}W_1 \quad \text{and} \quad W_2 = W_1$$
which is $W_1 = W_2 = \frac{5,008}{9} = 556.44$. Thus the chosen deductible is zero and the premium is $h = 576 - 556.44 = \$19.56$.

(d) Expected utility from no insurance is $\frac{1}{7}\sqrt{400} + \frac{6}{7}\sqrt{576} = 23.4286$, while expected utility from the contract of Part (c) is $\sqrt{556.44} = 23.589$.

(e) Expected profits from the contract of Part (c) is $19.56 - \frac{1}{7}400 = -\$37.58$, thus a loss.

(f) Expected utility from contract (h,d) is: $\frac{1}{7}\sqrt{576-h-d}+\frac{6}{7}\sqrt{576-h}$. Replacing h with $\frac{1}{9}(176-d)$ we get the following function:

$$f(d) = \frac{1}{7}\sqrt{576-\frac{176}{9}+\frac{1}{9}d-d}+\frac{6}{7}\sqrt{576-\frac{176}{9}+\frac{1}{9}d}$$
$$= \frac{1}{7}\sqrt{556.44-\frac{8}{9}d}+\frac{6}{7}\sqrt{556.44+\frac{1}{9}d}.$$

We know from Part (c) that the maximum of the function $f(d)$ is achieved at a corner (that is, not in the interior of the interval $[0,400]$) and thus it cannot be found by solving the equation $f'(d)=0$ (indeed, the solution to this equation is -398.36 which is outside the interval $[0,400]$). Another way to see that the solution is at a corner, is to calculate the value $f'(d)$ at $d=0$: $f'(0)=-0.0007<0$, indicating that increasing the deductible from 0 reduces expected utility. □

Solution to Exercise 5.14

(a) The utility function is $U(m)=1-\frac{1}{m+1}$. Thus $U'(m)=\frac{1}{(m+1)^2}$ and $U''(m)=-\frac{2}{(m+1)^3}$. Since $U''(m)<0$ (given that $m \geq 0$), David is risk averse.

(b) The Arrow-Pratt measure of risk aversion is $A_U(m) = -\frac{U''(m)}{U'(m)} = \frac{2}{m+1}$.

(c) Since coverage = loss − deductible, the equation is $h=\gamma(\ell-d)=\gamma(3000-d)$.

(d) Replacing h with $W_0 - W_2 = 8,000 - W_2$ and $d = (W_2 - W_1)$ in the equation of Part (c) we get
$$W_2 = \frac{8,000-3,000\gamma}{1-\gamma} - \frac{\gamma}{1-\gamma}W_1.$$

(e) Yes: replacing W_1 with $5,000$ ($=W_0 - \ell = 8,000 - 3,000$, the horizontal coordinate of NI) in the above equation we get $W_2 = 8,000$ (the vertical coordinate of NI).

(f) David will choose not to insure when the insurance budget line is steeper than the reservation indifference curve at the NI point, that is, when (recall that money is measure in thousands of dollars)
$$\frac{\gamma}{1-\gamma} > \frac{p}{1-p}\left(\frac{U'(5)}{U'(8)}\right) = \frac{1}{9}\left(\frac{(8+1)^2}{(5+1)^2}\right) = \frac{9}{36} = \frac{1}{4}.$$
Solving $\frac{\gamma}{1-\gamma} > \frac{1}{4}$ we get $\gamma > \frac{1}{5}$.

(g) David will choose full insurance when the slope of the indifference curve at the offered full-insurance contract (which is $-\frac{p}{1-p} = -\frac{1}{9}$) is, in absolute value, greater than or equal to the slope of the budget line (which is $-\frac{\gamma}{1-\gamma}$). Solving $\frac{1}{9} \geq \frac{\gamma}{1-\gamma}$ we get $\gamma \leq \frac{1}{10}$.

(h) David will choose partial insurance when
   1. he prefers insurance to no insurance (that is, as seen in Part (f), when $\gamma < \frac{1}{5}$) and
   2. the slope of the indifference curve at the offered full-insurance contract is, in absolute value, less than the slope of the budget line (that is, as seen in Part (g), when $\gamma > \frac{1}{10}$).

Thus David will choose partial insurance when

$$\frac{1}{10} < \gamma < \frac{1}{5}.$$

Assume that $\frac{1}{10} < \gamma < \frac{1}{5}$. Then David will choose that contract $C = \left(W_1^C, W_2^C\right)$ at which there is a tangency between the budget line and the indifference curve through C, that is, C must satisfy the following equations (recall that wealth levels are expressed in dollars while the argument of the utility function is expressed in thousands of dollars):

$$W_2 = \frac{8,000 - 3,000\gamma}{1-\gamma} - \frac{\gamma}{1-\gamma}W_1 \quad \text{and} \quad \frac{1}{9}\left[\frac{\left(\frac{W_2^C}{1,000}+1\right)^2}{\left(\frac{W_1^C}{1,000}+1\right)^2}\right] = \frac{\gamma}{1-\gamma}.$$

□

Solution to Exercise 5.15

(a) Replacing h with $W_0 - W_2 = 3,600 - W_2$ and d with $(W_2 - W_1)$ in the equation $h = 810 - \frac{3}{10}d$ we get

$$W_2 = \frac{27,900}{7} - \frac{3}{7}W_1.$$

(b) No, because the slope of an isoprofit line is $-\frac{p}{1-p} = -\frac{\frac{1}{4}}{\frac{3}{4}} = -\frac{1}{3} \neq -\frac{3}{7}$.

(c) Yes: replacing W_1 in the equation of Part (a) with 900 ($= W_0 - \ell = 3,600 - 2,700$, the horizontal coordinate of NI) we get $W_2 = 3,600$ ($= W_0$, the vertical coordinate of NI).

(d) Yes, because the absolute value of the slope of the reservation indifference curve at NI, namely $\frac{1}{3}\frac{3,600}{900} = \frac{4}{3}$ (recall that $U(m) = \ln(m)$ and $U'(m) = \frac{1}{m}$) is greater than the absolute value of the slope of the insurance budget line, namely $\frac{3}{7}$.

(e) Since the slope of the indifference curve at the full-insurance contract is $-\frac{1}{3}$, which is less – in absolute value – than the slope of the budget line (in absolute value), the best contract is a partial-insurance contract. It is found by solving the following equations:

$$W_2 = \frac{27,900}{7} - \frac{3}{7}W_1 \quad \text{and} \quad \frac{1}{3}\left(\frac{W_2}{W_1}\right) = \frac{3}{7}.$$

The solution is: $W_1 = 2,325$ and $W_2 = \frac{20,925}{7} = 2,989.29$. Thus the premium is $h = 3,600 - 2,989.29 = 610.71$ and the deductible is $d = 2,989.29 - 2,325 = 664.29$.

5.6 Solutions to Exercises

(f) Let F be the full-insurance contract (obtained by solving the equation $W_1 = \frac{27,900}{7} - \frac{3}{7}W_1$) and B the contract of Part (e). Then

$$NI = (900, 3600), \quad F = (2790, 2790) \quad \text{and} \quad B = (2325, 2989.29)$$

Thus

- $\mathbb{E}[U(NI)] = \frac{1}{4}\ln(900) + \frac{3}{4}\ln(3,600) = 7.8421.$
- $\mathbb{E}[U(F)] = \ln(2,790) = 7.9338.$
- $\mathbb{E}[U(B)] = \frac{1}{4}\ln(2,325) + \frac{3}{4}\ln(2989.29) = 7.94.$

(g) Expected utility from contract (h,d) is: $\frac{1}{4}\ln(3,600 - h - d) + \frac{3}{4}\ln(3,600 - h)$. Replacing h with $810 - \frac{3}{10}d$ we get the following function:

$$f(d) = \tfrac{1}{4}\ln(3,600 - 810 + 0.3d - d) + \tfrac{3}{4}\ln(3,600 - 810 + 0.3d)$$
$$= \tfrac{1}{4}\ln(2,790 - 0.7d) + \tfrac{3}{4}\ln(2,790 + 0.3d).$$

To maximize this function we must solve the equation $f'(d) = 0$, that is

$$\frac{0.225}{2,790 + 0.3d} - \frac{0.175}{2,790 - 0.7d} = 0$$

The solution is $d = 664.29$ with corresponding premium $h = 610.71$, confirming the conclusion of Part (e). □

Solution to Exercise 5.16

Contract A is the following point in the (W_1, W_2) space: $W_2^A = 1,600 - 44 = 1,556$, $W_1^A = 1,556 - 360 = 1,196$, that is, $A = (1196, 1556)$.

(a) Replacing h with $(1,600 - W_2)$ and d with $(W_2 - W_1)$ in the equation $h = 152 - \frac{3}{10}d$ we get

$$W_2 = \frac{14,480}{7} - \frac{3}{7}W_1.$$

(b) $\mathbb{E}[U(NI)] = \frac{1}{5}\sqrt{1,024} + \frac{4}{5}\sqrt{1600} = 38.4$ and $\mathbb{E}[U(A)] = \frac{1}{5}\sqrt{1,196} + \frac{4}{5}\sqrt{1,556} = 38.4736$. Thus point A lies above the reservation indifference curve.

(c) The slope of the indifference curve that goes through point A is, at point A, equal to

$$-\frac{p}{1-p}\left(\frac{U'(1,196)}{U'(1,556)}\right) = \frac{1}{4}\left(\frac{\sqrt{1,556}}{\sqrt{1,196}}\right) = -0.2852.$$

Since $0.2852 < \frac{3}{7} = 0.4286$, the indifference curve is less steep, at point A, than the insurance budget line; thus the insurance budget line lies below the indifference curve that goes through point A and, therefore, the best contract on the budget line is contract A. □

Solution to Exercise 5.17

For both Carla and Don, no insurance corresponds to the lottery

$$NI = \begin{pmatrix} \$14,400 & \$32,400 \\ \frac{1}{5} & \frac{4}{5} \end{pmatrix}$$

whose expected utility is:

for Carla: $\frac{1}{5}\sqrt{14,400} + \frac{4}{5}\sqrt{32,400} = 168$

for Don: $\frac{1}{5}\left(1 - \frac{1}{1.44+1}\right) + \frac{4}{5}\left(1 - \frac{1}{3.24+1}\right) = 0.7294$.

Mutual insurance corresponds to the lottery

$$MI = \begin{pmatrix} \$14,400 & \$23,400 & \$32,400 \\ \frac{1}{25} & \frac{8}{25} & \frac{16}{25} \end{pmatrix}$$

whose expected utility is:

for Carla: $\frac{1}{25}\sqrt{14,400} + \frac{8}{25}\sqrt{23,400} + \frac{16}{25}\sqrt{32,400} = 168.9506$

for Don: $\frac{1}{25}\left(1 - \frac{1}{1.44+1}\right) + \frac{8}{25}\left(1 - \frac{1}{2.34+1}\right) + \frac{16}{25}\left(1 - \frac{1}{3.24+1}\right) = 0.7369$.

Thus they are both better off with mutual insurance than with no insurance. □

Solution to Exercise 5.18

(a) The probabilities are as follows:

3 losses	2 losses	1 loss	no losses
$\left(\frac{1}{5}\right)^3 = \frac{1}{125}$	$3\left(\frac{1}{5}\right)^2 \frac{4}{5} = \frac{12}{125}$	$3\frac{1}{25}\left(\frac{4}{5}\right)^2 = \frac{48}{125}$	$\left(\frac{4}{5}\right)^3 = \frac{64}{125}$

(b) Expected utility from no insurance is

$$\mathbb{E}[U(NI)] = \frac{1}{5}\sqrt{10,000} + \frac{4}{5}\sqrt{40,000} = 180$$

while expected utility from mutual insurance is

$$\mathbb{E}[U(MI)] = \frac{1}{125}\sqrt{10,000} + \frac{12}{125}\sqrt{40,000 - \frac{1}{3}60,000}$$

$$+ \frac{48}{125}\sqrt{40,000 - \frac{1}{3}30,000} + \frac{64}{125}\sqrt{40,000}$$

$$= 183.29.$$

Thus mutual insurance is better than no insurance for each of them. □

5.6 Solutions to Exercises

Solution to Exercise 5.19

Expected utility from no insurance is

$$\mathbb{E}[U(NI)] = \frac{1}{5}\sqrt{10,000} + \frac{4}{5}\sqrt{40,000} = 180.$$

Expected utility form a mutual insurance (*MI*) agreement is

$$\mathbb{E}[U(MI)] = \frac{3}{30}\sqrt{10,000} + \frac{7}{30}\sqrt{40,000 - \tfrac{1}{2}30,000} + \frac{20}{30}\sqrt{40,000} = 180.23.$$

Thus mutual insurance would still be preferred by both to no insurance. □

II Risk Sharing

6 Risk Sharing and Efficiency 165
- 6.1 Sharing an uncertain surplus
- 6.2 The Edgeworth box
- 6.3 Points of tangency
- 6.4 Pareto efficient contracts on the sides of the Edgeworth box
- 6.5 The Edgeworth box when the parties have positive initial wealth
- 6.6 More than two outcomes
- 6.7 Exercises
- 6.8 Solutions to Exercises

6. Risk Sharing and Efficiency

6.1 Sharing an uncertain surplus

In this chapter we will consider contractual relationships between two parties, one called the *Principal* and the other the *Agent*. The Principal hires the Agent to perform a task, whose outcome is a surplus (a sum of money) that is to be divided between the two parties, according to the terms of the contract. If there were no uncertainty concerning the surplus, then the terms of the contract would merely reflect the relative bargaining power of the two parties. Instead, we are interested in the case where the size of the surplus is partly affected by random factors and thus is *ex ante* uncertain. In such a case there are two issues that arise in determining the type of contract that will be agreed upon: the relative bargaining power of the parties and the *allocation of risk between the two parties*. This chapter will focus on the latter issue.

The following are examples of the contractual relationships considered in this chapter.

- A client (the Principal) hires a lawyer (the Agent) to sue a third party for damages. The surplus is the amount that will be awarded by the jury or the judge. Typically, this amount cannot be determined in advance with certainty: it may depend on the type of evidence that the defendant will produce during the trial, on the composition and leaning of the jury, etc. There are several types of contracts that the client and the lawyer could sign: they could agree on a fixed payment to the lawyer (that is, independent of the awarded damages), or they could agree that the lawyer will retain a specified percentage of the awarded damages, or they could agree that the client will be guaranteed a certain amount and the lawyer will keep the residual amount.

- The owner of a store (the Principal) hires a sales assistant (the Agent) to run the store. The surplus is the profit generated during a specified period of time. The size of the profit is typically affected by random factors which are not under the control of either party, such as the number of customers that will show up during that period of time. Again, many contractual possibilities arise: the employee (the Agent) could be hired at a fixed salary, or could be offered a percentage of the profits generated by the store, or could be guaranteed a base salary as well as a percentage of the profits, etc.

- A landowner (the Principal) gives his land to a farmer (the Agent) to cultivate. The surplus is the sale value of the crop. The size and the value of the crop depend on random factors, such as the weather and the market price. A possible contractual arrangement is to have the Agent give a part of the crop to the Principal as rent (this is called sharecropping). Another possible contractual arrangement is for the Principal to pay a fixed salary to the Agent and keep the crop for himself. There are, of course, several alternative contracts that could be agreed upon.

- The shareholders of a firm (the Principal) hire a manager (the Agent) to run the firm. The surplus is the profit generated by the firm, which can vary depending on such factors as the cost of inputs, the intensity of competition, the state of the economy, etc. Possible compensation schemes are: a fixed salary to the manager, stock options, bonuses, etc.

We assume that the Principal and the Agent are able to agree on the possible levels of surplus, denoted by $X_1, X_2, \ldots, X_n$ ($n \geq 2$) and are able to assign probabilities to them, denoted by $p_1, p_2, \ldots, p_n$. Thus if they enter into a contractual relationship they will, together, generate the money lottery

$$\begin{pmatrix} \$X_1 & \$X_2 & \ldots & \$X_n \\ p_1 & p_2 & \ldots & p_n \end{pmatrix}$$

with $X_i > 0$ and $0 < p_i < 1$, for all $i = 1, 2, \ldots, n$, and $p_1 + p_2 + \cdots + p_n = 1$.

We will describe a possible contract between the two parties as a list of n sums of money $w_1, w_2, \ldots, w_n$ with the interpretation of w_i ($i = 1, \ldots, n$) as the amount of money that will be paid *to the Agent* if the surplus turns out to be X_i. Unless we explicitly state otherwise, we shall assume that, for all $i = 1, \ldots, n$,

$$0 \leq w_i \leq X_i.$$

A contract $C = (w_1, w_2, \ldots, w_n)$ is viewed differently by the two parties:

- for the Agent the contract corresponds to the money lottery

$$\begin{pmatrix} \$w_1 & \ldots & \$w_n \\ p_1 & \ldots & p_n \end{pmatrix}$$

- while for the Principal the contract corresponds to the money lottery

$$\begin{pmatrix} \$(X_1 - w_1) & \ldots & \$(X_n - w_n) \\ p_1 & \ldots & p_n \end{pmatrix}.$$

6.2 The Edgeworth box

As in previous chapters, we use the following notation: if C and D are two contracts and j is one of the parties to the contract (thus $j \in \{P, A\}$, where P denotes the Principal and A the Agent),

$C \succ_j D$ means that party j strictly prefers C to D.

$C \sim_j D$ means that party j is indifferent between C and D.

$C \succsim_j D$ means that party j considers C to be at least as good as D (that is, either $C \succ_j D$ or $C \sim_j D$).

> **Definition 6.1.1** Let C and D be two possible contracts. We say that C *Pareto dominates* D (or that D is *Pareto dominated* by C) if one party prefers C to D and the other considers C to be at least as good as D, that is, if
> - either $C \succ_P D$ and $C \succsim_A D$,
> - or $C \succsim_P D$ and $C \succ_A D$.
>
> We say that a contract is *Pareto efficient* if there is no other contract that Pareto dominates it.[a]
>
> ---
> [a]The notions of Pareto dominance and Pareto efficiency are named after the Italian economist Vilfredo Pareto (1848-1923) who introduced them.

Thus a contract C is Pareto efficient if and only if, for every other contract D, if one of party prefers D to C then the other Party prefers C to D. Clearly, it would be irrational for the parties to sign a Pareto dominated contract, since there is another contract that one of the parties prefers and the other also prefers or considers to be just as good. Our objective is to characterize the set of Pareto efficient contracts.

> Test your understanding of the concepts introduced in this section, by going through the exercises in Section 6.7.1 at the end of this chapter.

6.2 The Edgeworth box

In order to be able to illustrate with figures, we shall - until Section 6.6 - focus on the case where $n = 2$, that is where there are only two possible levels of surplus. Thus we can think in terms of two possible states: the "good" state where the surplus is $\$X^g$ and the "bad" state where the surplus is $\$X^b$, with

$$X^g > X^b > 0.$$

A contract is specified as a pair (w^g, w^b) where w^g is what the agent gets in the good state (so that the Principal gets the residual amount $X^g - w^g$) and w^b is what the Agent gets in the bad state (so that the Principal gets the difference: $X^b - w^b$). The set of possible contracts can be represented graphically by means of an Edgeworth box, which is a rectangle whose long side is equal to X^g and whose short side is equal to X^b, as shown in Figure 6.1.[1]

---
[1]The Edgeworth box is named after the English economist Francis Ysidro Edgeworth (1845-1926) who introduced it as a way of representing possible distributions of resources between two individuals.

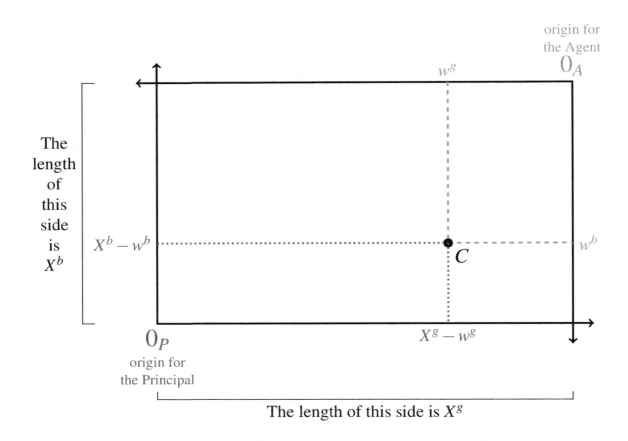

Figure 6.1: The Edgeworth box representing the set of possible divisions of the uncertain surplus between the Principal and the Agent.

The lower left-hand corner of the box is taken to be the origin for the Principal and the upper right-hand corner to be the origin for the Agent. Any point in the box represents a possible contract. Consider, for example, point C in Figure 6.1. Going vertically up from C to the top horizontal side of the box one obtains the amount w^g (measured from the origin 0_A for the Agent) that the Agent receives if the surplus turns out to be X^g, while going vertically down from point C to the bottom horizontal side of the box one obtains the amount $(X^g - w^g)$ (measured from the origin 0_P for the Principal) that goes to the Principal if the surplus turns out to be X^g. Similarly, going horizontally from point C to the right vertical side of the box one can read the amount w^b that goes to the Agent if the surplus turns out to be X^b, while going horizontally to the left vertical side one can read the amount $(X^b - w^b)$ that goes to the Principal when the surplus is X^b.

6.2 The Edgeworth box

What about points *outside* the Edgeworth box? Do they represent feasible contracts? For example, suppose that $X^g = 1,000$ and $X^b = 600$ and consider the contract $(w^g = 300, w^b = -200)$ which is shown as point D in Figure 6.2.

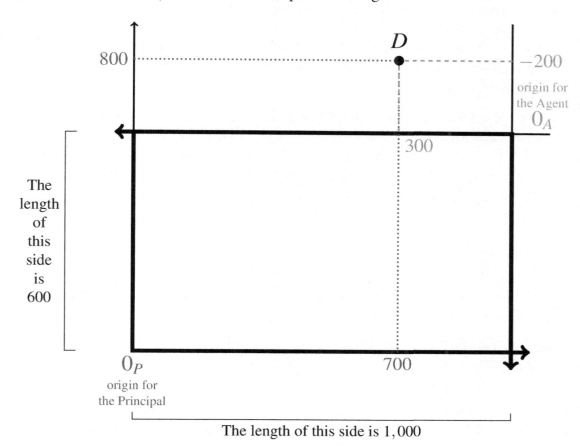

Figure 6.2: A contract outside the Edgeworth box.

How is such a contract to be interpreted? If the outcome is $1,000 then the Agent will get $300 and the rest, namely $700, will go to the Principal; on the other hand, if the outcome is $600 then the Agent will give $200 to the Principal so that the Principal will get the entire surplus of $600 plus the additional sum of $200 contributed by the Agent, for a total of $800. Is such a contractual arrangement feasible? Only if the Agent has an initial wealth which is greater than or equal to $200 so that she can draw from that wealth to make a payment to the Principal in case the outcome turns out to be $600.

For the time being we shall assume that neither the Principal nor the Agent have independent funds from which they can draw to make payments to the other party:

> until Section 6.5 we will assume that both the Principal and the Agent have zero initial wealth so that contracts outside the Edgeworth box are not feasible.

Two possible types of contracts in the Edgeworth box are worth highlighting.

- The first type are contracts that guarantee the Agent a fixed income, no matter what the surplus turns out to be: these are contracts of the form (w^g, w^b) with $w^g = w^b$. The set of such contracts is represented by the 45° line out of the origin for the Agent. Contract D in Figure 6.3 is an example of a fixed-income, or income-certainty, contract for the Agent.

- The second type are contracts that guarantee the Principal a fixed income, no matter what the surplus turns out to be: these are contracts of the form (w^g, w^b) with $X^g - w^g = X^b - w^b$. The set of such contracts is represented by the 45° line out of the origin for the Principal. Contract E in Figure 6.3 is an example of a fixed-income, or income-certainty, contract for the Principal.

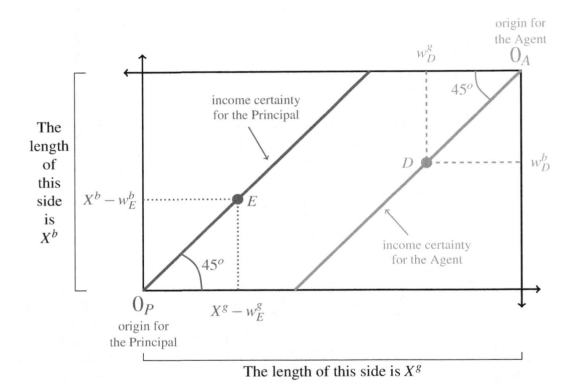

Figure 6.3: Contract $D = (w_D^g, w_D^b)$ is such that $w_D^g = w_D^b$ and thus guarantees income certainty to the Agent. Contract $E = (w_E^g, w_E^b)$ is such that $X^g - w_E^g = X^b - w_E^b$ and thus guarantees income certainty to the Principal.

We shall assume that both the Principal and the Agent have preferences over money lotteries that satisfy the axioms of Expected Utility Theory (see Chapter 5) and can thus be represented by von Neumann-Morgenstern utility-of-money functions: $U_P(m)$ for the Principal and $U_A(m)$ for the Agent.

For example, suppose that the Principal is risk averse with utility function $U_P(m) = \sqrt{m}$, while the Agent is risk neutral, so that we can take her utility function to be the identity function: $U_A(m) = m$. Suppose that in the good state the surplus is $X^g = \$1,000$ and in the bad state the surplus is $X^b = \$600$; furthermore the probability of the good state is $p^g = \frac{1}{3}$ (so that probability of the bad state is $p^b = \frac{2}{3}$). Would it be rational for the these two individuals to sign the contract $C = (w^g = 400, w^b = 400)$ that guarantees income certainty to the Agent? If they did sign such a contract, the Principal's expected utility would be $\mathbb{E}[U_P(C)] = \frac{1}{3}\sqrt{1,000-400} + \frac{2}{3}\sqrt{600-400} = 17.5931$ and the Agent's utility would be $U_A(400) = 400$. Consider the alternative contract $D = (w^g = 676, w^b = 276)$. With this contract, the Principal gets the same amount of money no matter what the state (namely, $1,000 - 676 = 324$ in the good state and $600 - 276 = 324$ in the bad state) and thus his utility is $\sqrt{324} = 18$, while the Agent has an expected utility of $\frac{1}{3}676 + \frac{2}{3}276 = 409.33$. Hence both parties strictly prefer contract D to contract C and thus it would be irrational for them to agree on contract C. In other words, contract C is not a rational choice because there is another contract, namely D, that Pareto dominates it.

In order to identify the set of Pareto efficient contracts, we need to add indifference curves to the Edgeworth box.

Recall from Chapter 5 that the indifference curves of a risk-averse individual are convex towards the origin. Figure 6.4 illustrates the case of a risk-averse Principal.

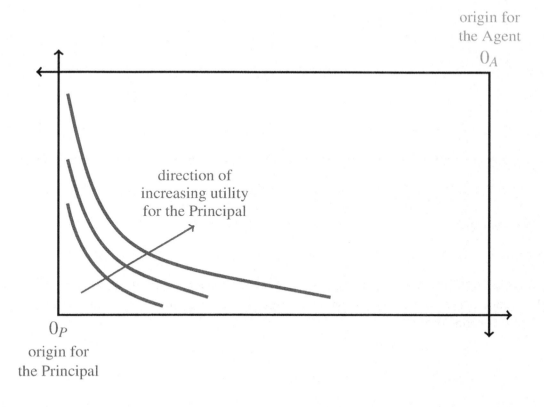

Figure 6.4: Indifference curves of a risk-averse Principal. Higher indifference curves (that is, indifference curves farther away from the origin for the Principal) correspond to higher levels of utility for the Principal.

In Chapter 5 we also saw that the indifference curves of a risk-neutral individual are straight lines. Figure 6.5 illustrates the case of a risk-neutral Agent.

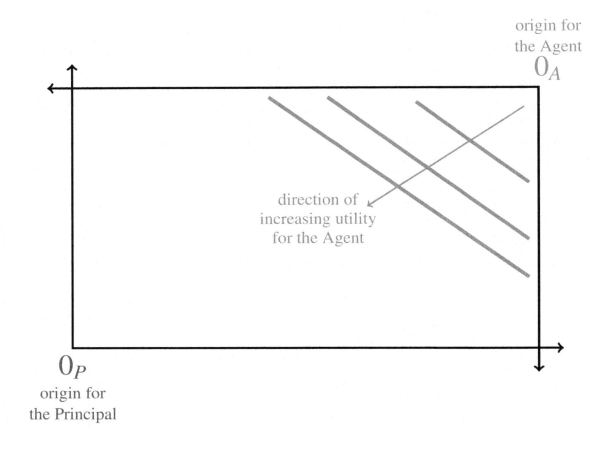

Figure 6.5: Indifference curves of a risk-neutral Agent. Lower indifference curves (that is, indifference curves farther away from the origin for the Agent) correspond to higher levels of utility for the Agent.

6.2 The Edgeworth box

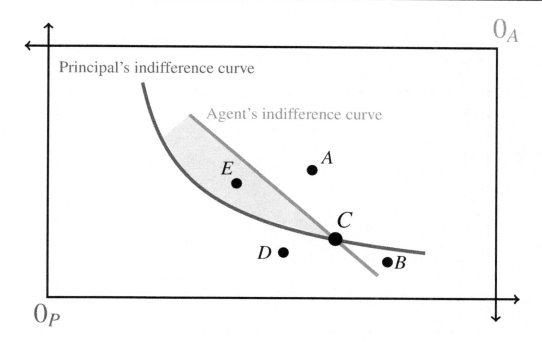

Figure 6.6: Contract C is not Pareto efficient.

We now show that *any contract at which the indifference curve of the Principal and the indifference curve of the Agent cross cannot be Pareto efficient.* Consider again the case where the Principal is risk averse and the Agent is risk neutral. Contract C in Figure 6.6 is a contract at which the indifference curves of the two parties cross.

Let us compare alternative contracts to contract C. The terms "above" and "below" are to be understood as taking the point of view of the origin for the Principal (the bottom, left-hand side of the box).

- Any contract, such as contract A, that lies above the Principal's indifference curve through C and above the Agent's indifference curve through C, is preferred to C by the Principal, but considered to be worse than C by the Agent: $A \succ_P C$ and $C \succ_A A$.

- Any contract, such as contract B, that lies below the Principal's indifference curve through C and above the Agent's indifference curve through C, is considered to be worse than C by both Principal and Agent: $C \succ_P B$ and $C \succ_A B$.

- Any contract, such as contract D, that lies below both indifference curves, is considered to be worse than C by the Principal but better than C by the Agent: $C \succ_P D$ and $D \succ_A C$.

- Finally, any contract, such as contract E, that lies between the two indifference curves, is *preferred to contract C by both parties*: $E \succ_P C$ and $E \succ_A C$.

Thus, whenever the indifference curves of the two parties that go through a contract C cross at point C, the area between the two curves (the shaded area in Figure 6.6) represents contracts that are preferred by both the Principal and the Agent to contract C. Hence C is Pareto dominated by any of those contracts, implying that C is not Pareto efficient.

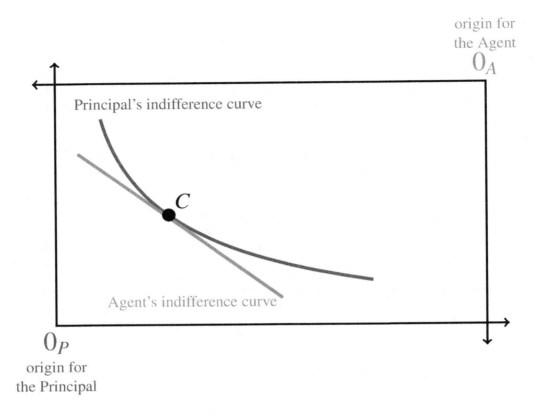

Figure 6.7: Contract C is **Pareto efficient**.

On the other hand, a contract at which the two indifference curves are tangent must be Pareto efficient. Contract C in Figure 6.7 is an example of such a contract: any other contract must be either above the Principal's indifference curve, in which case it is worse than C for the Agent, or below the Agent's indifference curve, in which case it is worse than C for the Principal, or between the two indifference curves, in which case it is worse than C for both parties.

Thus we conclude that

> any contract at which the indifference curves are tangent is **Pareto efficient**.

In the next section we identify the set of points where the indifference curves of Principal and Agent are tangent.

> Test your understanding of the concepts introduced in this section, by going through the exercises in Section 6.7.2 at the end of this chapter.

6.3 Points of tangency

We will consider four separate cases.

6.3.1 Risk averse Principal and risk neutral Agent

Let us begin with the case where the Principal is risk averse, so that his indifference curves are convex towards the origin for the Principal, and the Agent's indifference curves are straight lines.

Recall from Chapter 5 that the indifference curves of a risk-neutral individual are straight lines with slope (since we are measuring the outcome of the good state on the horizontal axis):

$$-\frac{p^g}{1-p^g} \qquad (6.1)$$

where p^g is the probability of the good state. On the other hand, the slope of the Principal's indifference curve at a contract where the Agent gets w^g in the good state (so that the Principal gets $X^g - w^g$) and w^b in the bad state (so that the Principal gets $X^b - w^b$) is (recall that $U_P(\cdot)$ is the utility-of-money function of the Principal and $U'_P(\cdot)$ is its first derivative):

$$-\frac{p^g}{1-p^g}\frac{U'_P(X^g - w^g)}{U'_P(X^b - w^b)}. \qquad (6.2)$$

If the two indifference curves are tangent at point $C = (w^g, w^b)$ then they have the same slope there, that is, it must be that

$$-\frac{p^g}{1-p^g} = -\frac{p^g}{1-p^g}\frac{U'_P(X^g - w^g)}{U'_P(X^b - w^b)} \qquad (6.3)$$

which requires that

$$\frac{U'_P(X^g - w^g)}{U'_P(X^b - w^b)} = 1, \text{ that is, that } U'_P(X^g - w^g) = U'_P(X^b - w^b).$$

Since the Principal is risk averse, the second derivative of his utility function is negative, which means that the first derivative is strictly decreasing; hence

$$U'_P(X^g - w^g) = U'_P(X^b - w^b) \text{ if and only if } X^g - w^g = X^b - w^b,$$

that is, *if and only if point $C = (w^g, w^b)$ lies on the 45° line out of the origin for the Principal*, as shown in Figure 6.8.

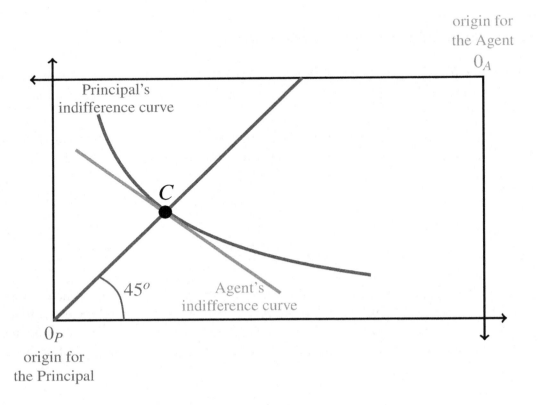

Figure 6.8: When the Principal is risk averse and the Agent is risk neutral, the 45° line out of the origin for the Principal is the set of points where there is a tangency between the Principal's indifference curve and the Agent's indifference curve.

6.3.2 Risk neutral Principal and risk averse Agent

Now consider the symmetric case where the Principal is risk neutral and the Agent is risk averse. In this case the Principal's indifference curves are straight lines with slope $-\frac{p^g}{1-p^g}$, while the Agent's indifference curves are convex towards the origin for the Agent. The slope of the Agent's indifference curve at contract $C = (w^g, w^b)$ is

$$-\frac{p^g}{1-p^g} \frac{U'_A(w^g)}{U'_A(w^b)}$$

where $U_A(\cdot)$ is the utility-of-money function of the Agent and $U'_A(\cdot)$ is its first derivative. As before, if the two indifference curves are tangent at point $C = (w^g, w^b)$ then they have the same slope there, that is, it must be that

$$-\frac{p^g}{1-p^g} = -\frac{p^g}{1-p^g} \frac{U'_A(w^g)}{U'_A(w^b)} \tag{6.4}$$

6.3 Points of tangency

which requires that

$$\frac{U'_A(w^g)}{U'_A(w^b)} = 1, \text{ that is, that } U'_A(w^g) = U'_A(w^b).$$

Since the Agent is risk averse, the second derivative of her utility function is negative, which means that the first derivative is strictly decreasing; hence

$$U'_A(w^g) = U'_A(w^b) \text{ if and only if } w^g = w^b,$$

that is, *if and only if point $C = (w^g, w^b)$ lies on the 45° line out of the origin for the Agent*, as shown in Figure 6.9.

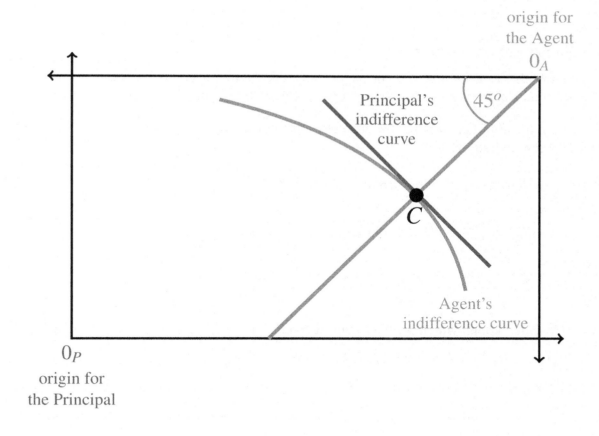

Figure 6.9: When the Agent is risk averse and the Principal is risk neutral, the 45° line out of the origin for the Agent is the set of points where there is a tangency between the Principal's indifference curve and the Agent's indifference curve.

6.3.3 A general principle

From the analysis of Sections 6.3.1 and 6.3.2 we can draw a general principle concerning the optimal (i.e. Pareto efficient) allocation of risk between two individuals, one of whom is risk averse and the other is risk neutral:

> When one party is risk neutral and the other is risk averse,
> a contract $C = (w^g, w^b)$ such that $0 < w^g < X^g$ and $0 < w^b < X^b$
> is Pareto efficient if and only if *all the risk is borne by the risk-neutral party*,
> so that the risk-averse party is guaranteed a fixed income.

The reason why the above principle requires the restriction that $0 < w^g < X^g$ and $0 < w^b < X^b$ will be explained in Section 6.4.

6.3.4 Both parties risk averse

When both the Principal and the Agent are risk averse, a tangency between the two indifference curves can only occur at a point strictly between the two 45° lines.

Recall from Chapter 5 that the absolute value of the slope of the indifference curve of a risk-averse individual is

$$\begin{aligned} &\text{grater than } \tfrac{p^g}{1-p^g} &&\text{at a point } above \text{ the } 45^o \text{ line} \\ &\text{equal to } \tfrac{p^g}{1-p^g} &&\text{at a point } on \text{ the } 45^o \text{ line} \\ &\text{less than } \tfrac{p^g}{1-p^g} &&\text{at a point } below \text{ the } 45^o \text{ line.} \end{aligned} \tag{6.5}$$

Consider a point which is *above* (such as point A in Figure 6.10) or *on* (such as point B in Figure 6.10) the 45° line out of the origin for the Principal. Then, by (6.5), the slope of the Principal's indifference curve at that point is greater than (point A), or equal to (point B), $\frac{p^g}{1-p^g}$; on the other hand, from the point of view of the Agent, that point is below her 45° line and thus the slope of her indifference curve at that point is, in absolute value, less than $\frac{p^g}{1-p^g}$. Hence the Principal's indifference curve is steeper at that point than the Agent's indifference curve, so that the two curves are not tangent and thus the contract is not Pareto efficient (any contract between the two indifference curves Pareto dominates it).

6.3 Points of tangency

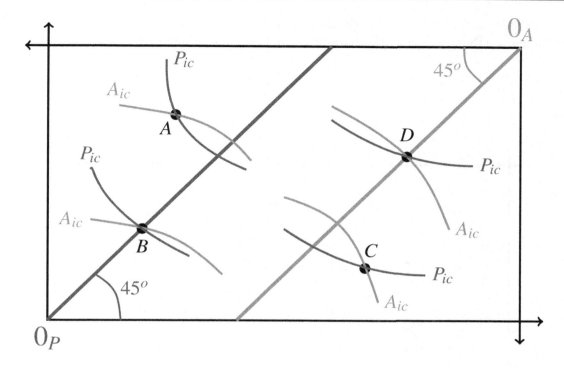

Figure 6.10: When both the Principal and the Agent are risk averse a tangency between the Principal's indifference curve and the Agent's indifference curve cannot occur at points that are not between the two 45° lines. A_{ic} stands for "indifference curve of the Agent" and P_{ic} stands for "indifference curve of the Principal".

Similarly, consider a point which is *below* (such as point C in Figure 6.10) or *on* (such as point D in Figure 6.10) the 45° line out of the origin for the Agent. Then, by (6.5), the slope of the Agent's indifference curve at that point is greater than (point C), or equal to (point D), $\frac{p^g}{1-p^g}$; on the other hand, from the point of view of the Principal, that point is below his 45° line and thus the slope of his indifference curve at that point is, in absolute value, less than $\frac{p^g}{1-p^g}$. Hence the Principal's indifference curve is less steep at that point than the Agent's indifference curve, so that the two curves are not tangent and thus the contract is not Pareto efficient (any contract between the two indifference curves Pareto dominates it).

A Pareto efficient contract is shown as point E in Figure 6.11. It lies between the two 45° lines and thus involves risk-sharing: neither party is guaranteed a fixed income.

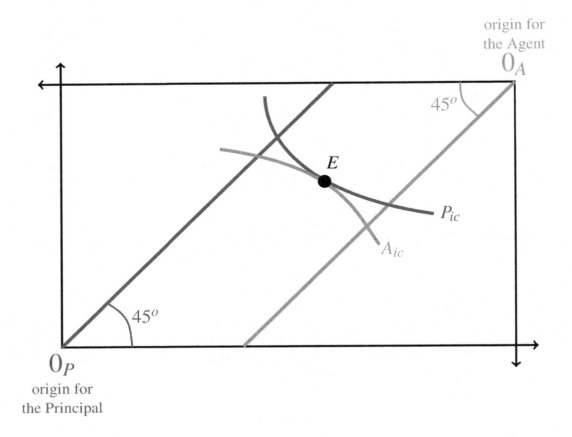

Figure 6.11: Contract E is Pareto efficient and involves risk-sharing. A_{ic} stands for "indifference curve of the Agent" and P_{ic} stands for "indifference curve of the Principal".

If $E = (w^g, w^b)$ is a contract at which there is a tangency between the indifference curve of the Principal and the indifference curve of the Agent, then it must be that

$$-\frac{p^g}{1-p^g}\frac{U'_P(X^g - w^g)}{U'_P(X^b - w^b)} = -\frac{p^g}{1-p^g}\frac{U'_A(w^g)}{U'_P(w^b)}$$

that is,

$$\frac{U'_P(X^g - w^g)}{U'_P(X^b - w^b)} = \frac{U'_A(w^g)}{U'_A(w^b)}. \tag{6.6}$$

Equation (6.6) is necessary and sufficient for a contract $E = (w^g, w^b)$ with $0 < w^g < X^g$ and $0 < w^b < X^b$ to be Pareto efficient and provides us with a quick test for Pareto efficiency.

6.3 Points of tangency

For example, suppose that

- the surplus in the good state is $X^g = \$1,000$ and the surplus in the bad state be $X^b = \$321$,
- the Principal's von Neumann-Morgenstern utility-of-money function is $U_P(m) = \sqrt{m}$ and
- the Agent's von Neumann-Morgenstern utility-of-money function is $U_A(m) = \ln(m)$.

Is Contract $C = (600, 200)$ Pareto efficient? We need to check if (6.6) is satisfied at point C. Since

$$\frac{U'_P(X^g - w^g))}{U'_P(X^b - w^b)} = \frac{\frac{1}{2\sqrt{400}}}{\frac{1}{2\sqrt{121}}} = \frac{11}{20}$$

and

$$\frac{U'_A(w^g)}{U'_A(w^b)} = \frac{\frac{1}{600}}{\frac{1}{200}} = \frac{1}{3}$$

and $\frac{11}{20} \neq \frac{1}{3}$, contract C is *not* Pareto efficient.

6.3.5 Both parties risk neutral

The only case that remains to be considered is the case where both Principal and Agent are risk neutral. We want to show that in this case *every contract is Pareto efficient*.

There are several ways to prove this. First of all, when an individual is risk neutral he/she prefers one money lottery to another if and only if the expected value of the first is greater than the expected value of the second. Pick an arbitrary contract $C = (w_C^g, w_C^b)$. To show that it is Pareto efficient it is sufficient to show that, for every other contract $D = (w_D^g, w_D^b)$, if the Principal prefers D to C then the Agent prefers C to D. Being risk neutral, the Principal prefers D to C if and only if

$$p^g(X^g - w_D^g) + (1 - p^g)(X^b - w_D^b) > p^g(X^g - w_C^g) + (1 - p^g)(X^b - w_C^b)$$

that is, if and only if

$$\begin{aligned} & p^g X^g - p^g w_D^g + (1 - p^g) X^b - (1 - p^g) w_D^b \\ & > p^g X^g - p^g w_C^g + (1 - p^g) X^b - (1 - p^g) w_C^b. \end{aligned} \quad (6.7)$$

Subtracting $p^g X^g + (1 - p^g) X^b$ from both sides of (6.7) we get

$$-p^g w_D^g - (1 - p^g) w_D^b > -p^g w_C^g - (1 - p^g) w_C^b$$

that is,

$$p^g w_C^g + (1 - p^g) w_C^b > p^g w_D^g + (1 - p^g) w_D^b. \quad (6.8)$$

The left-hand side of (6.8) is the expected value of the money lottery for the Agent corresponding to contract C and the right-hand side of (6.8) is the expected value of the money lottery for the Agent corresponding to contract D. Thus we conclude that contract D is preferred to contract C by the Principal if and only if the Agent has the opposite ranking, that is, she prefers C to D.

An alternative proof that any contract is Pareto efficient makes use of the tangency argument: when both parties are risk neutral, their indifference curves are straight line with slope $-\frac{p^g}{1-p^g}$ and thus the indifference curve of the Principal that goes through a point C coincides with the indifference curve of the Agent that goes to point C and thus the two are tangent.

6.3.6 Pareto efficiency for contracts in the interior of the Edgeworth box

A contract $C = (w^g, w^b)$ is in the interior of the Edgeworth box if and only if

$$0 < w^g < X^g \quad \text{and} \quad 0 < w^b < X^b.$$

Let us focus on contracts that are in the interior of the Edgeworth box. We showed in Section 6.3.4 that, for such contracts, equality (6.6) (page 180) is necessary and sufficient for Pareto efficiency when both parties are risk averse. We now show that, for contracts in the interior of the Edgeworth box, equality (6.6) is necessary and sufficient for Pareto efficiency no matter what the risk attitude of the parties, that is, in *all* cases.

First of all, note that when an individual is risk neutral, we can take the identity function as his von Neumann-Morgenstern utility-of-money function, that is, we can take $U(m) = m$. Hence $U'(m) = 1$ and, for any two sums of money m_1 and m_2, $\frac{U'(m_1)}{U'(m_2)} = 1$. Thus

- If the Principal is risk averse and the Agent is risk neutral (Section 6.3.1), equation (6.6) reduces to

$$\frac{U'_P(X^g - w^g)}{U'_P(X^b - w^b)} = 1$$

which requires (as shown in Section 6.3.1) that $X^g - w^g = X^b - w^b$, that is, the Principal (the risk-averse party) must be guaranteed a fixed income.

- If the Principal is risk neutral and the Agent is risk averse (Section 6.3.2), (6.6) reduces to

$$1 = \frac{U'_A(w^g)}{U'_A(w^b)}$$

which requires (as shown in Section 6.3.2) that $w^g = w^b$, that is, the Agent (the risk-averse party) must be guaranteed a fixed income.

- If both Principal and Agent are risk neutral, then equation (6.6) reduces to $1 = 1$, which is true at every point.

Hence we conclude this section with a general principle:

> A contract $C = (w^g, w^b)$ such that $0 < w^g < X^g$ and $0 < w^b < X^b$
> is Pareto efficient if and only if $\frac{U'_P(X^g - w^g)}{U'_P(X^b - w^b)} = \frac{U'_A(w^g)}{U'_A(w^b)}$.

> Test your understanding of the concepts introduced in this section, by going through the exercises in Section 6.7.3 at the end of this chapter.

6.4 Pareto efficient contracts on the sides of the Edgeworth box

In the previous section we focused on Pareto efficient contracts in the interior of the Edgeworth box: these are the contracts where there is a tangency between the indifference curve of the Principal and the indifference curve of the Agent. In this section we show that there are also contracts on the sides of the Edgeworth box that are Pareto efficient, even though the indifference curves of the two parties are not tangent there.

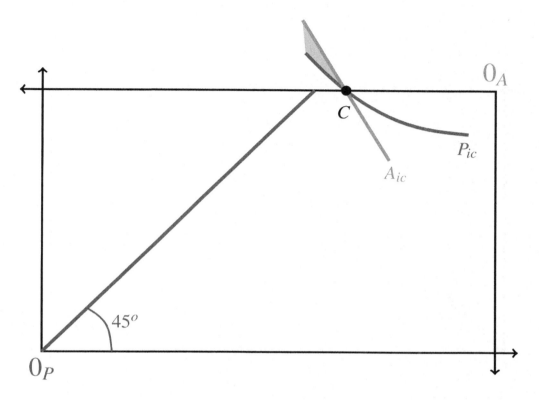

Figure 6.12: Contract C satisfies Pareto efficiency subject to the constraint that only contracts in the Edgeworth box are feasible. A_{ic} stands for "indifference curve of the Agent" and P_{ic} stands for "indifference curve of the Principal".

6.4.1 Risk averse Principal and risk neutral Agent

Let us revisit the case of Section 6.3.1, where the Principal is risk averse (so that his indifference curves are convex towards the origin for the Principal) and the Agent is risk neutral (so that her indifference curves are straight lines). Consider a point, such as point C in Figure 6.12, on the upper side of the Edgeworth box to the right of the point at which the 45° line out of the origin for the Principal intersects that side. From (6.5) (page 178) we know that at such a point the indifference curve of the Agent is steeper than the indifference curve of the Principal, as shown in Figure 6.12. Thus there would potentially be contracts that are Pareto superior to contract C (all those in the shaded area in Figure 6.12, that is, all those that lie between the two indifference curves). However, such contracts are not feasible, because they lie outside the Edgeworth box. Thus there are no contracts *in the Edgeworth box* that are Pareto superior to C; in other words, contract C satisfies Pareto efficiency subject to the constraint that only contracts in the Edgeworth box are feasible.[2] Putting together the results of this Section and of Section 6.3.1 we conclude that when the Principal is risk averse and the Agent is risk neutral, the set of Pareto efficient contracts is given by the union of the 45° line out of the origin for the Principal and the portion of the top side of the Edgeworth box from the point of intersection with the 45° line out of the origin for the Principal to the origin for the Agent, as shown in Figure 6.13.

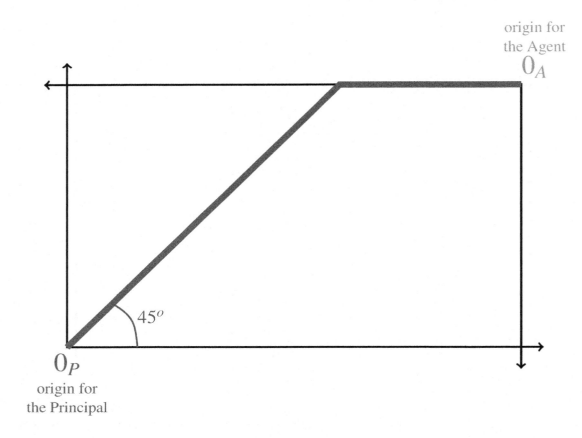

Figure 6.13: The set of Pareto efficient contracts when the Principal is risk averse and the Agent is risk neutral is given by the thick line (the union of the 45° line out of the origin for the Principal and the portion of the top side of the Edgeworth box from the origin for the Agent to the point of intersection with the 45° line out of the origin for the Principal).

6.4.2 Risk neutral Principal and risk averse Agent

Now let us revisit the case of Section 6.3.2, where the Principal is risk neutral (so that his indifference curves are straight lines) while the Agent is risk averse (so that her indifference

---

[2] A contract (w^g, w^b) in the shaded area in Figure 6.12 is such that $w^b < 0$ (while $0 \leq w^g < X^g$) and thus it would imply a payment from the Agent to the Principal in the bad state (so that the Principal would receive an amount greater than X^b). Such a payment is feasible only if the Agent has independent funds from which to draw if the state is bad. Since we assumed that neither the Principal nor the Agent have independent funds at their disposal, contracts outside the Edgeworth box are not feasible. The case where the parties do have independent funds will be discussed in Section 6.5.

6.4 Pareto efficient contracts on the sides of the Edgeworth box

curves are convex towards the origin for the Agent). The analysis in this case is symmetric to that of the previous section.

Consider a point, such as point D in Figure 6.14, on the bottom side of the Edgeworth box to the left of the point at which the $45°$ line out of the origin for the Agent intersects that side. From (6.5) (page 178) we know that at such a point the indifference curve of the Principal is steeper than the indifference curve for the Agent, as shown in Figure 6.14. Thus there would potentially be contracts that are Pareto superior to contract D (all those in the shaded area in Figure 6.14, that is, all those that lie between the two indifference curves). However, such contracts are not feasible, because they lie outside the Edgeworth box. Thus there are no contracts *in the Edgeworth box* that are Pareto superior to D; in other words, contract D satisfies Pareto efficiency subject to the constraint that only contracts in the Edgeworth box are feasible.[3]

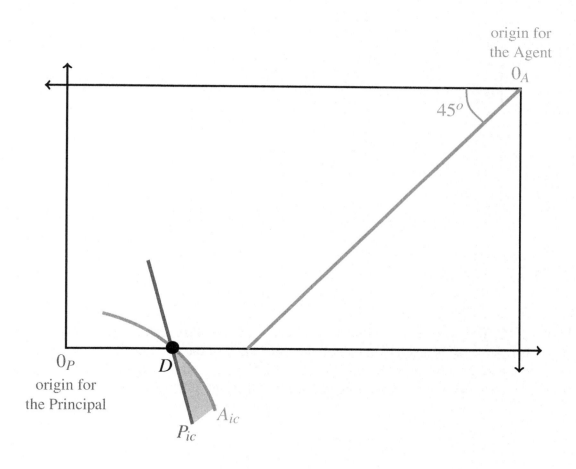

Figure 6.14: Contract D satisfies Pareto efficiency subject to the constraint that only contracts in the Edgeworth box are feasible. A_{ic} stands for "indifference curve of the Agent" and P_{ic} stands for "indifference curve of the Principal".

---

[3] A contract (w^g, w^b) in the shaded area in Figure 6.14 is such that $w^b > X^b$ (while $0 < w^g \leq X^g$) and thus it would imply a payment from the Principal to the Agent in the bad state. Such a payment is feasible only if the Principal has independent funds from which to draw if the state is bad. Since we assumed that neither the Principal nor the Agent have independent funds at their disposal, contracts outside the Edgeworth box are not feasible. The case where the parties do have independent funds will be discussed in Section 6.5.

Putting together the results of this Section and of Section 6.3.2 we conclude that when the Principal is risk neutral and the Agent is risk averse, the set of Pareto efficient contracts is given by the union of the 45° line out of the origin for the Agent and the portion of the bottom side of the Edgeworth box from the origin for the Principal to the point of intersection with the 45° line out of the origin for the Agent, as shown in Figure 6.15.

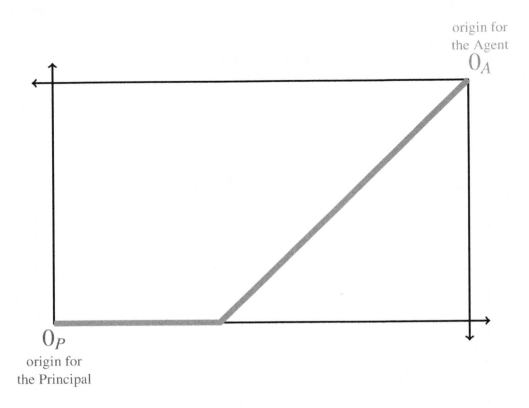

Figure 6.15: The set of Pareto efficient contracts when the Principal is risk neutral and the Agent is risk averse is given by the thick line (the union of the 45° line out of the origin for the Agent and the portion of the bottom side of the Edgeworth box from the origin for the Principal to the point of intersection with the 45° line out of the origin for the Agent).

6.4.3 Both parties risk averse

The same logic applies to the case where both the Principal and the Agent are risk averse: points on the top side of the Edgeworth box where the Principal's indifference curve is less steep than the Agent's indifference curve and points on the bottom side of the Edgeworth box where the Principal's indifference curve is steeper than the Agent's indifference curve correspond to Pareto efficient contracts (subject to the constraint that only contracts in the Edgeworth box are feasible).

The thick curve in Figure 6.16 shows the set of Pareto efficient contracts for a situation where both the Principal and the Agent are risk averse.

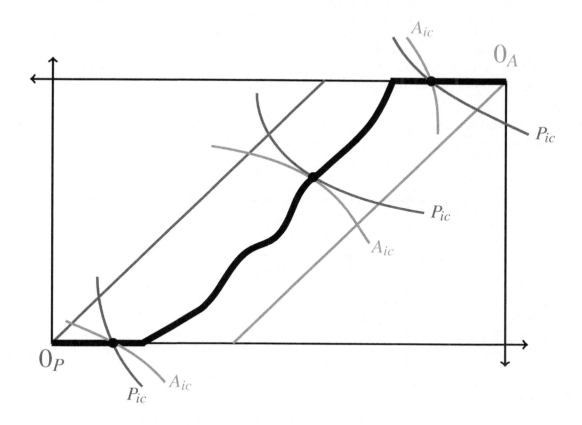

Figure 6.16: The set of Pareto efficient contracts when both the Principal and the Agent are risk averse is shown as a thick curve. A_{ic} stands for "indifference curve of the Agent" and P_{ic} stands for "indifference curve of the Principal".

> Test your understanding of the concepts introduced in this section, by going through the exercises in Section 6.7.4 at the end of this chapter.

6.5 The Edgeworth box when the parties have positive initial wealth

So far we have assumed that only contracts inside the Edgeworth box are feasible or, equivalently, that both the Principal and the Agent have zero initial wealth. If, on the other hand, one or both parties have a positive initial wealth then, as shown in Figure 6.2 on page 169, it is feasible for the parties to agree on a contract that lies outside the Edgeworth box.

As before, let the surplus in the good state be X^g and the surplus in the bad state X^b. Let $\overline{W}_P \geq 0$ be the initial wealth of the Principal and $\overline{W}_A \geq 0$ the initial wealth of the Agent. Construct an extended Edgeworth box as follows: the length of the horizontal side is $X^g + \overline{W}_P + \overline{W}_A$ and the length of the vertical side is $X^b + \overline{W}_P + \overline{W}_A$.

Whereas before we represented a contract as a pair (w^g, w^b), where w^g was the portion, given to the Agent, of the surplus X^g generated in the good state (thus $0 \leq w^g \leq X^g$) and w^b was the portion, given to the Agent, of the surplus X^b generated in the bad state (thus $0 \leq w^b \leq X^b$), we now need to represent a contract differently in order to allow for the possibility of payments from one party to the other. Thus in this more general setting we represent a contract as a pair (z^g, z^b) where z^g is the *wealth* of the Agent in the good state (thus $0 \leq z^g \leq X^g + \overline{W}_P + \overline{W}_A$) and z^b is the *wealth* of the Agent in the bad state (thus $0 \leq z^b \leq +X^b + +\overline{W}_P + \overline{W}_A$).[4]

Figure 6.17 shows the extended Edgeworth box. The dashed box inside the extended box is the Edgeworth box that would apply if the parties had zero initial wealth.

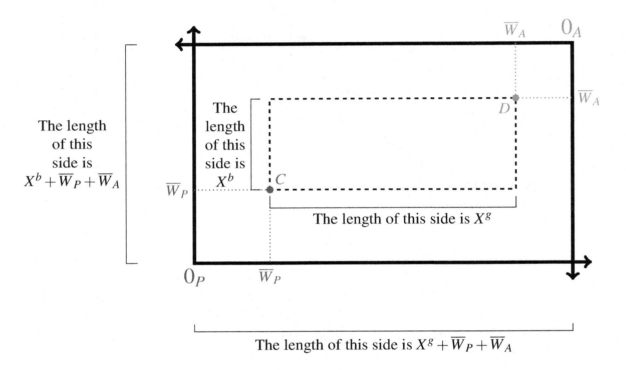

Figure 6.17: The extended Edgeworth box. The dashed box inside the extended box is the Edgeworth box that would apply if the parties had zero wealth.

Point C in Figure 6.17 represents a contract where the Agent gets all the surplus in each state and the Principal retains his initial wealth of $\overline{W}_P$. Note that a wealth of $\overline{W}_P$ for sure is an outside option for the Principal: he can guarantee himself such a wealth by refusing to enter into an agreement with the Agent. Thus the indifference curve of the Principal that goes through point C represents a *reservation level of utility* for the Principal: if the Principal is rational, he will not agree to any contract that gives him an expected utility less than $U_P(\overline{W}_P)$.

---

[4] For example, if $X^g = \$1,500$, $X^b = \$900$ and the parties agree that the Agent will get one third of the surplus in each state (thus $\$500$ in the good state and $\$300$ in the bad state) then we represent this contract not as the pair $(500, 300)$ but as the pair $(z^g = 500 + \overline{W}_A, z^b = 300 + \overline{W}_A)$, where $\overline{W}_A$ is the Agent's initial wealth. Hence, from the Principal's point of view, this contract will yield him a wealth of $1,000 + \overline{W}_P$ in the good state and $600 + \overline{W}_P$ in the bad state, where $\overline{W}_P$ is the Principal's initial wealth.

6.5 The Edgeworth box when the parties have positive initial wealth

Similarly, point D in Figure 6.17 represents a contract where the Principal gets all the surplus in each state and the Agent retains her initial wealth of $\overline{W}_A$. A wealth of $\overline{W}_A$ for sure constitutes an outside option for the Agent: she can guarantee herself such a wealth by refusing to enter into an agreement with the Principal. Thus the indifference curve of the Agent that goes through point D represents a *reservation level of utility* for the Agent: if the Agent is rational, she will not agree to any contract that gives her an expected utility less than $U_A(\overline{W}_A)$.

We call a contract that gives each party at least his/her reservation utility *individually rational*. Thus the set of individually rational contracts is the set of points in the extended Edgeworth box that lie between the two *reservation indifference curves*: the indifference curve of the Principal that goes through point $(\overline{W}_P, \overline{W}_P)$ (measured from the origin for the Principal) and the indifference curve of the Agent that goes through the point $(\overline{W}_A, \overline{W}_A)$ (if measured from the origin for the Agent, or $(X^g + \overline{W}_P, X^b + \overline{W}_P)$ if measured from the origin for the Principal).

Figure 6.18 shows the reservation indifference curve of a of a risk-averse Principal and the reservation indifference curve of a risk-neutral Agent. The area between the two curves consist of the set of individually rational contracts.

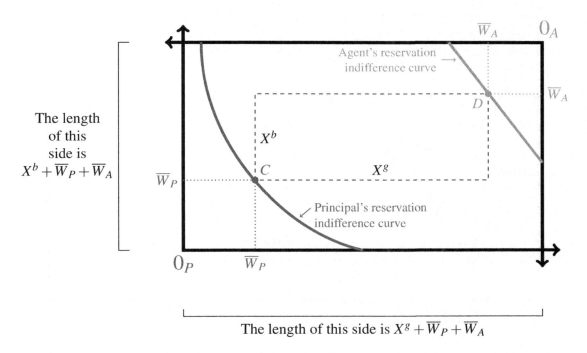

Figure 6.18: The reservation indifference curves of a risk-averse Principal and a risk-neutral Agent.

To find the Pareto efficient contracts we proceed as in the previous sections. The only difference is that rationality of the parties now requires not only Pareto efficiency but also individual rationality. Thus we want to identify the *set of contracts that are both Pareto efficient and individually rational*; let us call it the *set of rational contracts*. It is given by the intersection of the set of Pareto efficient contracts and the set of individually rational contracts.

1. For the case where *the Principal is risk averse and the Agent is risk neutral*, the set of rational contracts consists of the portion of the 45° line out of the origin for the Principal from the point $(\overline{W}_P, \overline{W}_P)$ to the top side of the extended Edgeworth box, followed by the portion of the top side of the extended Edgeworth box from the intersection with the 45° line to the point of intersection with the reservation indifference curve of the Agent. The set of rational (i.e. Pareto efficient and individually rational) contracts is shown as a thick line in Figure 6.19.

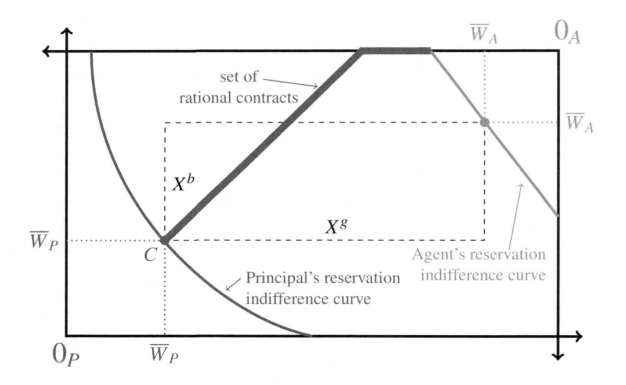

Figure 6.19: The thick line shows the set of rational (i.e. Pareto efficient and individually rational) contracts when the Principal is risk averse and the Agent is risk neutral.

2. For the case where *the Principal is risk neutral and the Agent is risk averse*, the set of rational contracts consists of the portion of the 45° line out of the origin for the Agent from the point $(\overline{W}_A, \overline{W}_A)$ to the bottom side of the extended Edgeworth box, followed by the portion of the bottom side of the extended Edgeworth box from the intersection with the 45° line to the point of intersection with the reservation indifference curve of the Principal. The set of rational (i.e. Pareto efficient and individually rational) contracts is shown as a thick line in Figure 6.20.

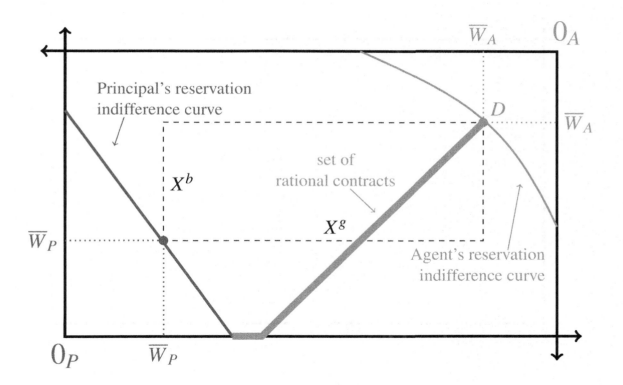

Figure 6.20: The thick line shows the set of rational (i.e. Pareto efficient and individually rational) contracts when the Principal is risk neutral and the Agent is risk averse.

3. For the case where *both the Principal and the Agent are risk neutral*, the set of rational contracts coincides with the set of individually rational contracts (since every contract is Pareto efficient). It is shown as the shaded area between the two reservation indifference curves in Figure 6.21.

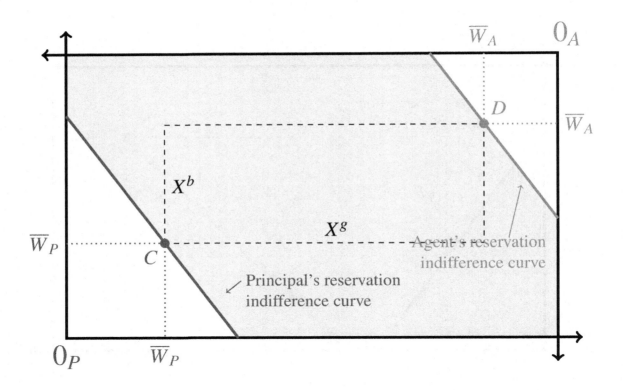

Figure 6.21: The shaded area between the two reservation indifference curves is the set of rational contracts when both parties are risk neutral.

4. For the case where *both the Principal and the Agent are risk averse*, the set of rational contracts is a curve between the two 45° lines together with some segments of the top and bottom sides of the extended Edgeworth box. It is shown as a thick curve in Figure 6.22.

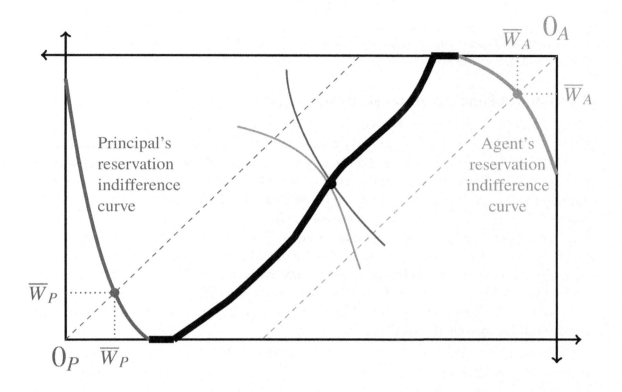

Figure 6.22: The thick curve shows the set of rational (i.e. Pareto efficient and individually rational) contracts when both the Principal and the Agent are risk averse.

> Test your understanding of the concepts introduced in this section, by going through the exercises in Section 6.7.5 at the end of this chapter.

6.6 More than two outcomes

In the previous sections the analysis was restricted to the case of two outcomes (two states) in order to be able to illustrate with diagrams (Edgeworth boxes). In this section we briefly discuss the general case where there are n outcomes, with $n \geq 2$. For simplicity we assume that the initial wealth of both parties is zero.[5]

---

[5]The case of positive initial wealth is dealt with in a manner similar to the analysis of Section 6.5. Let $\overline{W}_P$ be the initial wealth of the Principal and $\overline{W}_A$ be the initial wealth of the Agent. If X_i is the monetary outcome in state i, let $\overline{X}_i = X_i + \overline{W}_P + \overline{W}_A$. Then proceed as explained in this section but replacing X_i with $\overline{X}_i$. The only difference is that each party now has a reservation utility level given by the outside option of keeping his/her wealth and not reaching an agreement and, as a consequence, neither party will accept a contract that gives him/her a level of utility less than the reservation level; that is, to the requirement of **Pareto efficiency** we add the requirement of **individual rationality**.

Let there be n states ($n \geq 2$) and let \$$X_i$ be the outcome in state $i \in \{1,\ldots,n\}$, which occurs with probability p_i ($0 < p_i < 1$, for every $i \in \{1,\ldots,n\}$, and $p_1 + p_2 + \cdots + p_n = 1$). We order the outcomes in such a way that

$$X_1 < X_2 < \cdots < X_n. \tag{6.9}$$

A contract is an n-tuple $(w_1, w_2, \ldots, w_n)$ where w_i is what the Agent gets in state i (with $0 \leq w_i \leq X_i$).

6.6.1 Risk-neutral Principal and risk-averse Agent

The general principle that if one party is risk averse and the other is risk neutral then, for Pareto efficiency, the risk-neutral party should bear all the risk applies in this case too.

Consider first the case where the Principal is risk neutral and the Agent is risk averse. It is easy to see that a contract of the form $\tilde{C} = (\tilde{w}, \tilde{w}, \ldots, \tilde{w})$ (where the risk-averse party, namely the Agent, is guaranteed a fixed income of $\tilde{w}$) is Pareto efficient. Take any other contract $D = (w_1, w_2, \ldots, w_n) \neq \tilde{C}$ that the Principal considers to be at least as good as $\tilde{C}$; then the expected value of D is less than or equal to the expected value of $\tilde{C}$ (which is $\tilde{w}$), that is, $p_1 w_1 + p_2 w_2 + \cdots + p_n w_n \leq \tilde{w}$.[6] On the other hand, the Agent prefers contract $\tilde{C}$ to D: if $\mathbb{E}[D] = \tilde{w}$ then $\tilde{C} \succ_A D$ by definition of risk aversion and if $\mathbb{E}[D] < \tilde{w}$ then the Agent prefers \$$\tilde{w}$ to \$$\mathbb{E}[D]$, because she prefers more money to less, and she considers \$$\mathbb{E}[D]$ for sure to be at least as good as D (better, if D is non-degenerate), by definition of risk aversion; thus, by transitivity, $\tilde{C} \succ_A D$.

However, as in the case where $n = 2$, a guaranteed fixed income for the risk-averse party is only sufficient for Pareto efficiency: it is not necessary. There are contracts on the edges of the "Edgeworth hypercube" that are Pareto efficient. The following proposition helps identifying those contracts.

Proposition 6.6.1 Let the Principal be risk neutral and the Agent risk averse. Let $i, j \in \{1, 2, \ldots, n\}$ with $i < j$ (so that, by (6.9), $X_i < X_j$) and consider a contract $C = (w_1, w_2, \ldots, w_n)$ with $w_i \neq w_j$. If C is Pareto efficient then

(A) $w_j > w_i$, and

(B) $w_i = X_i$.

---

[6] Since the Principal is risk neutral we can take the identity function as his utility-of-money function so that the expected utility of contract $\tilde{C}$ is

$$\sum_{i=1}^n p_i (X_i - \tilde{w}) = \sum_{i=1}^n p_i X_i - \tilde{w}$$

and the expected utility of contract D is

$$\sum_{i=1}^n p_i (X_i - w_i) = \sum_{i=1}^n p_i X_i - \sum_{i=1}^n p_i w_i.$$

The Principal considers D to be at least as good as $\tilde{C}$ if and only if

$$\sum_{i=1}^n p_i X_i - \sum_{i=1}^n p_i w_i \geq \sum_{i=1}^n p_i X_i - \tilde{w}, \text{ that is, if and only if } \sum_{i=1}^n p_i w_i \leq \tilde{w}.$$

6.6 More than two outcomes

Proof. **(A)** Suppose that $w_j < w_i$ (recall that $X_i < X_j$) and let

$$\hat{w} = \frac{p_i}{p_i + p_j} w_i + \frac{p_j}{p_i + p_j} w_j. \tag{6.10}$$

Then $w_j < \hat{w} < w_i$.[7] Modify contract C by replacing both w_i and w_j with $\hat{w}$ and leaving the other coordinates unchanged. Call D the resulting contract. Then the expected value of D is equal to the expected value of C.[8] Hence the Principal is indifferent between contract C and contract D.[9] On the other hand, the Agent prefers contract D to contract C, since C is a mean-preserving spread of D (see Chapter 4, Section 4.4.2). Thus D Pareto dominates C and therefore C is not **Pareto efficient**.

(B) Because of Part (A) we can assume that $w_i < w_j$ (by hypothesis, $w_i \neq w_j$). Suppose that $w_i < X_i$; we want to show that C is not **Pareto efficient**. We need to consider two cases.

Case B.1: $\hat{w} \leq X_i$ where $\hat{w}$ is defined in (6.10) (and thus $w_i < \hat{w} < w_j$). Consider the contract obtained from C by replacing both w_i and w_j with $\hat{w}$. Then, repeating the argument developed in Part (A), the Principal is indifferent between C and D, because $\mathbb{E}[C] = \mathbb{E}[D]$, while the Agent prefers D to C because C is a mean-preserving spread of D. Hence D Pareto dominates C and therefore C is not **Pareto efficient**.

Case B.2: $\hat{w} > X_i$ (where $\hat{w}$ is defined in (6.10); note that this implies that $w_j > X_i$). Construct a new contract, call it D, obtained from C by replacing w_i with X_i and w_j with $\tilde{\tilde{w}}$ where

$$\tilde{\tilde{w}} = w_j - \frac{p_i}{p_j}(X_i - w_i). \tag{6.11}$$

Note that, since - by hypothesis - $w_i < X_i$, $\frac{p_i}{p_j}(X_i - w_i) > 0$ and thus $\tilde{\tilde{w}} < w_j$. Furthermore, $\tilde{\tilde{w}} > X_i$ since

$$w_j - \frac{p_i}{p_j}(X_i - w_i) > X_i \text{ if and only if } p_j w_j - p_i X_i + p_i w_i > p_j X_i$$

$$\text{if and only if } p_i w_i + p_j w_j > (p_i + p_j) X_i$$

$$\text{if and only if } \frac{p_i}{p_i + p_j} w_i + \frac{p_j}{p_i + p_j} w_j > X_i$$

$$\text{if and only if (by (6.10)) } \hat{w} > X_i$$

which is our hypothesis.

---

[7] Since p_i and p_j are strictly between 0 and 1, so are $\frac{p_i}{p_i+p_j}$ and $\frac{p_j}{p_i+p_j}$ and their sum is equal to 1; hence $\hat{w}$ is a convex combination of w_i and w_j, that is, a point strictly between w_i and w_j.

[8] Let $a = \sum_{k=1}^{n} p_k w_k - p_i w_i - p_j w_j$. Then $\mathbb{E}[C] = a + p_i w_i + p_j w_j$ and $\mathbb{E}[D] = a + (p_i + p_j)\hat{w}$. Since $(p_i + p_j)\hat{w} = p_i w_i + p_j w_j$, $\mathbb{E}[C] = \mathbb{E}[D]$.

[9] For the Principal (who, by hypothesis, is risk neutral) the expected utility of contract C is

$$\sum_{k=1}^{n} p_k (X_k - w_k) = \sum_{k=1}^{n} p_k X_k - \sum_{k=1}^{n} p_k w_k = \sum_{k=1}^{n} p_k X_k - \mathbb{E}[C]$$

and, similarly, the expected utility of contract D is $\sum_{k=1}^{n} p_k X_k - \mathbb{E}[D]$.

First we show that $\mathbb{E}[C] = \mathbb{E}[D]$, so that the Principal is indifferent between C and D. Clearly, $\mathbb{E}[C] = \mathbb{E}[D]$ if and only if $p_i X_i + p_j \tilde{\tilde{w}} = p_i w_i + p_j w_j$, which is true since

$$p_i X_i + p_j \tilde{\tilde{w}} = p_i X_i + p_j \left(w_j - \frac{p_i}{p_j}(X_i - w_i) \right) = p_i X_i + p_j w_j - p_i X_i + p_i w_i = p_i w_i + p_j w_j.$$

Next we show that the Agent prefers D to C, so that D Pareto dominates C and therefore C is not Pareto efficient. The Agent prefers D to C because D dominates C in the sense of second-order stochastic dominance (see Chapter 4, Definition 4.4.3); indeed the lottery corresponding to contract C can be obtained from the lottery corresponding to contract D by a sequence of two mean-preserving spreads. To see this, consider the following lotteries where the dots stand for entries of the form $\begin{pmatrix} w_k \\ p_k \end{pmatrix}$ for $k \in \{1, 2, \ldots, n\} \setminus \{i, j\}$.

$$L_C = \begin{pmatrix} \ldots & w_i & X_i & \ldots & \tilde{\tilde{w}} & w_j & \ldots \\ \ldots & p_i & 0 & \ldots & 0 & p_j & \ldots \end{pmatrix} \quad (6.12)$$

$$L_D = \begin{pmatrix} \ldots & w_i & X_i & \ldots & \tilde{\tilde{w}} & w_j & \ldots \\ \ldots & 0 & p_i & \ldots & p_j & 0 & \ldots \end{pmatrix} \quad (6.13)$$

$$L_E = \begin{pmatrix} \ldots & w_i & X_i & \ldots & \tilde{\tilde{w}} & w_j & \ldots \\ \ldots & \alpha p_i & 0 & \ldots & p_j & (1-\alpha)p_i & \ldots \end{pmatrix} \quad (6.14)$$

$$L_F = \begin{pmatrix} \ldots & w_i & X_i & \ldots & \tilde{\tilde{w}} & w_j & \ldots \\ \ldots & \alpha p_i + \beta p_j & 0 & \ldots & 0 & (1-\alpha)p_i + (1-\beta)p_j & \ldots \end{pmatrix} \quad (6.15)$$

$$(6.16)$$

where

$$\alpha = \frac{w_j - X_i}{w_j - w_i} \quad \text{and} \quad \beta = \frac{w_j - \tilde{\tilde{w}}}{w_j - w_i} \quad (6.17)$$

L_C is the lottery (for the Agent) corresponding to contract C and L_D is the lottery (for the Agent) corresponding to contract D. We want to show that L_E is a mean-preserving spread of L_D, L_F is a mean-preserving spread of L_E and $L_F = L_C$.

- L_E is a mean-preserving spread of L_D because (1) $w_i < X_i$ (by hypothesis), (2) $w_j > \tilde{\tilde{w}}$ (as shown above) and (3) $\alpha p_i w_i + (1-\alpha) p_i w_j = p_i X_i$ (so that the expected value of E equals the expected value of D).[10]

---

[10] In fact,

$$\alpha p_i w_i + (1-\alpha) p_i w_j = \frac{w_j - X_i}{w_j - w_i} p_i w_i + \frac{X_i - w_i}{w_j - w_i} p_i w_j = \left(\frac{w_i w_j - w_i X_i + w_j X_i - w_i w_j}{w_j - w_i} \right) p_i =$$

$$= \frac{w_j - w_i}{w_j - w_i} p_i X_i = p_i X_i.$$

- L_F is a mean-preserving spread of L_E because (1) $w_i < \tilde{\tilde{w}}$ (since, by hypothesis, $w_i < X_i$ and, as shown above, $X_i < \tilde{\tilde{w}}$), (2) $w_j > \tilde{\tilde{w}}$ (as shown above) and (3) $\beta p_j w_i + (1-\beta) p_j w_j = p_j \tilde{\tilde{w}}$ (so that the expected value of F equals the expected value of E).[11]

- Finally, $L_F = L_C$ since $\alpha p_i + \beta p_j = p_i$ and $(1-\alpha)p_i + (1-\beta)p_j = p_j$.[12]

∎

6.6.2 Risk-averse Principal and risk-neutral Agent

The case where the Principal is risk-averse and the Agent is risk neutral is symmetric to the case considered in the previous section. Thus we will merely state, without proof, the counterpart to Proposition 6.6.1.

Proposition 6.6.2 Let the Principal be risk averse and the Agent risk neutral. Let $i, j \in \{1, 2, \ldots, n\}$ with $i < j$ (so that, by (6.9), $X_i < X_j$) and consider a contract $C = (w_1, w_2, \ldots, w_n)$ with $w_i \neq w_j$. If C is Pareto efficient then

(A) $X_j - w_j > X_i - w_i$, and

(B) $w_i = 0$.

6.6.3 Both parties risk neutral

As in the case of two outcomes, if both parties are risk neutral then every contract is Pareto efficient. This is because if one party prefers a contract, say D, to another contract, say C, then the expected value of the lottery - for that party - corresponding to contract D is *higher* than the expected value of the lottery - for that party - corresponding to contract C, which implies that the expected value of the lottery - for the other party - corresponding to contract D is *lower* than the expected value of the lottery - for the other party - corresponding to contract C; hence the other party prefers C to D.

---

[11] In fact,

$$\beta p_j w_i + (1-\beta) p_j w_j = \frac{w_j - \tilde{\tilde{w}}}{w_j - w_i} p_j w_i + \frac{\tilde{\tilde{w}} - w_i}{w_j - w_i} p_j w_j = \frac{w_j - w_i}{w_j - w_i} p_j \tilde{\tilde{w}} = p_j \tilde{\tilde{w}}.$$

[12] In fact,

$$\alpha p_i + \beta p_j = \frac{w_j - X_i}{w_j - w_i} p_i + \frac{w_j - \tilde{\tilde{w}}}{w_j - w_i} p_j = \frac{(w_j - X_i) p_i + \left[w_j - \left(w_j - \left(\frac{p_i}{p_j}(X_i - w_i)\right)\right)\right] p_j}{w_j - w_i}$$

$$= \frac{(w_j - X_i) p_i + (X_i - w_i) p_i}{w_j - w_i} = \frac{w_j - w_i}{w_j - w_i} p_i = p_i$$

and

$$(1-\alpha) p_i + (1-\beta) p_j = \left(1 - \frac{w_j - X_i}{w_j - w_i}\right) p_i + \left(1 - \frac{w_j - \tilde{\tilde{w}}}{w_j - w_i}\right) p_j = \frac{X_i - w_i}{w_j - w_i} p_i + \frac{\tilde{\tilde{w}} - w_i}{w_j - w_i} p_j$$

$$= \frac{X_i - w_i}{w_j - w_i} p_i + \frac{w_j p_j - (X_i - w_i) p_i - w_i p_j}{w_j - w_i} = \frac{w_j - w_i}{w_j - w_i} p_j = p_j.$$

6.6.4 Both parties risk averse

In the case of only two outcomes we saw that a contract in the interior of the Edgeworth box is Pareto efficient only if the indifference curves of the two parties through that point are tangent. This requirement, expressed as equation (6.6) (page 180) extends to the case of more than two outcomes as follows.

As before, let there be n states ($n \geq 2$) and let $\$X_i$ be the outcome in state $i \in \{1,\ldots,n\}$, which occurs with probability p_i ($0 < p_i < 1$, for every $i \in \{1,\ldots,n\}$, and $p_1 + p_2 + \cdots + p_n = 1$). We order the outcomes in such a way that

$$X_1 < X_2 < \cdots < X_n.$$

Let $C = (w_1, w_2, \ldots, w_n)$ be an interior contract, that is, a contract such that, for every $i = 1, 2, \ldots, n$, $0 < w_i < X_i$. If C is Pareto efficient then[13]

$$\frac{U'_P(X_1 - w_1)}{U'_P(X_2 - w_2)} = \frac{U'_A(w_1)}{U'_A(w_2)},$$

$$\frac{U'_P(X_2 - w_2)}{U'_P(X_3 - w_3)} = \frac{U'_A(w_2)}{U'_A(w_3)}$$

$$\cdots$$

$$\frac{U'_P(X_{n-1} - w_{n-1})}{U'_P(X_n - w_n)} = \frac{U'_A(w_{n-1})}{U'_A(w_n)}.$$

As in the case of two outcomes, there are also Pareto efficient contracts that are not interior contracts, that is, contracts where, in some states, one of the parties gets the entire surplus. We will omit a discussion of necessary conditions for Pareto efficiency for such contracts.

> Test your understanding of the concepts introduced in this section, by going through the exercises in Section 6.7.6 at the end of this chapter.

---

[13] Note that if the $n-1$ equations below are satisfied, then, for every $i, j = 1,\ldots,n$ with $i \neq j$, $\frac{U'_P(X_i - w_i)}{U'_P(X_j - w_j)} = \frac{U'_A(w_i)}{U'_A(w_j)}$. For example, one can get $\frac{U'_P(X_1 - w_1)}{U'_P(X_3 - w_3)} = \frac{U'_A(w_1)}{U'_A(w_3)}$ by multiplying the equation $\frac{U'_P(X_1 - w_1)}{U'_P(X_2 - w_2)} = \frac{U'_A(w_1)}{U'_A(w_2)}$ by the equation $\frac{U'_P(X_2 - w_2)}{U'_P(X_3 - w_3)} = \frac{U'_A(w_2)}{U'_A(w_3)}$.

6.7 Exercises

The solutions to the following exercises are given in Section 6.8 at the end of this chapter.

6.7.1 Exercises for Section 6.1: Sharing an uncertain surplus

Exercise 6.1 A Principal wants to hire an Agent to run his firm. The Principal's utility-of-money function is $U_P(m) = ln(m)$, while the Agent's utility-of-money function is $U_A(m) = 2m + 2$. There are three possible profit levels: $X_1 = \$2,400, X_2 = \$1,600$ and $X_3 = \$900$. The corresponding probabilities are $p_1 = \frac{1}{5}$, $p_2 = \frac{2}{5}$ and $p_3 = \frac{2}{5}$. Let w_1 be the payment to the Agent if the outcome is X_1 and similarly for w_2 and w_3. Show that contract $A = (w_1 = 700, w_2 = 700, w_3 = 700)$ is Pareto dominated by contract $B = (w_1 = 1,200, w_2 = 1,000, w_3 = 200)$.

Exercise 6.2 John's von Neumann-Morgenstern utility-of-money function is $U(m) = \sqrt{m}$. He owns a firm and is thinking of hiring Joanne to run the firm for him. Joanne's von Neumann-Morgenstern utility-of-money function is $V(m) = 2m$. In the past there were good times when the firm's yearly profits were \$4,000 and bad times when the firm's yearly profits were \$1,600. About $\frac{2}{3}$ of the time it was a good year and $\frac{1}{3}$ of the time it was a bad year. John offered Joanne a contract, call it A, that pays her a fixed salary of \$1,000 per year.

(a) What is John's attitude to risk?

(b) What is Joanne's attitude to risk?

(c) Show that the alternative contract, call it B, that pays Joanne \$1,500 if the profit turns out to be \$4,000 and pays her nothing if the profit turns out to be \$1,600, is as good as contract A for Joanne but gives John a higher expected utility. That is, contract B Pareto dominates contract A.

6.7.2 Exercises for Section 6.2: The Edgeworth box

Exercise 6.3 Let the surplus in the good state be $X^g = \$200$ and the surplus in the bad state be $X^b = \$120$. Consider the following contracts, where the first coordinate is the amount of money that the Agent receives in the good state and the second coordinate is the amount of money that the Agent receives in the bad state: $C = (60, 80)$ and $D = (100, 60)$. The probability of the good state is 25% (so that the probability of the bad state is 75%).

(a) Represent the two contracts as points in an Edgeworth box.

(b) If the Principal is risk neutral, how does he rank the two contracts?

(c) If the Agent is risk neutral, how does she rank the two contracts?

Exercise 6.4 Consider the contracts shown in Figure 6.23.

(a) What is the Principal's attitude to risk?
(b) What is the Agent's attitude to risk?
(c) How does the Principal rank the five contracts A, B, C, D and E?
(d) How does the Agent rank the five contracts A, B, C, D and E?
(e) Among the five contracts A, B, C, D and E find all the pairs of contracts such that one Pareto dominates the other.

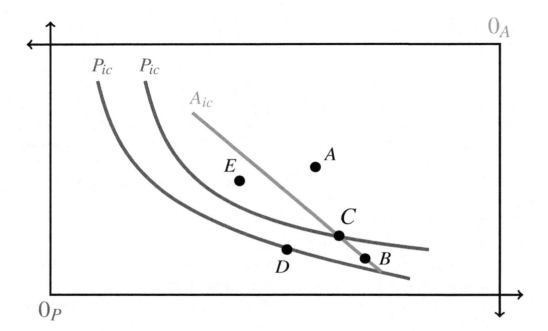

Figure 6.23: The Edgeworth box for Exercise 6.4. P_{ic} stands for "indifference curve of the Principal" and A_{ic} for "indifference curve of the Agent".

Exercise 6.5 Let the surplus in the good state be $X^g = \$200$ and the surplus in the bad state be $X^b = \$120$. Consider the following contracts, where the first coordinate is the amount of money that the Agent receives in the good state and the second coordinate is the amount of money that the Agent receives in the bad state: $C = (60, 80)$ and $D = (100, 60)$. The probability of the good state is 25% (so that the probability of the bad state is 75%). The Principal's von Neumann-Morgenstern utility-of-money function is $U_P(m) = \sqrt{m}$ and the Agent's von Neumann-Morgenstern utility-of-money function is $U_A(m) = \ln(m)$. Does one of the two contracts Pareto dominate the other?

6.7 Exercises

6.7.3 Exercises for Section 6.3: Points of tangency

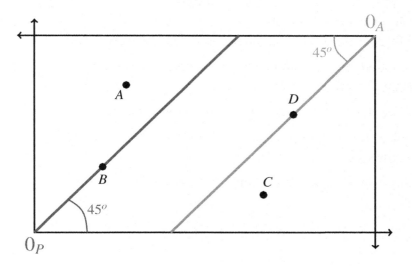

Figure 6.24: The Edgeworth box for Exercise 6.6.

Exercise 6.6 Consider the Edgeworth box of Figure 6.24.
(a) Suppose that the Principal is risk neutral and the Agent is risk averse. Of the four contracts A, B, C and D, which (if any) is Pareto efficient?
(b) Suppose that the Principal is risk averse and the Agent is risk neutral. Of the four contracts A, B, C and D, which (if any) is Pareto efficient?
(c) Suppose that both the Principal and the Agent are risk averse. Of the four contracts A, B, C and D, which (if any) is Pareto efficient?
(d) Suppose that both the Principal and the Agent are risk neutral. Of the four contracts A, B, C and D, which (if any) is Pareto efficient?

Exercise 6.7 Let the surplus in the good state be $X^g = \$800$ and the surplus in the bad state be $X^b = \$400$. The Principal's von Neumann-Morgenstern utility-of-money function is $U_P(m) = 82 - \left(10 - \frac{m}{100}\right)^2$ while the Agent's von Neumann-Morgenstern utility-of-money function is $U_A(m) = 2m + 4$. Consider the following contract (where, as usual, the first coordinate is the amount of money that the Agent receives in the good state and the second coordinate is the amount of money that the Agent receives in the bad state): $C = (400, 200)$.
(a) Is contract C Pareto efficient? Explain.
(b) Represent contract C as a point in an Edgeworth box and sketch the indifference curves of Principal and Agent that go through that point.
(c) In the Edgeworth box show a contract D such that $D \succ_P C$ and $D \sim_A C$ (that is, the Principal prefers D to C and the Agent finds D to be just as good as C).

Exercise 6.8 Let the surplus in the good state be $X^g = \$1,206$ and the surplus in the bad state be $X^b = \$676$. The probability of the good state is 25%. The Principal's von Neumann-Morgenstern utility-of-money function is $U_P(m) = m$ while the Agent's von Neumann-Morgenstern utility-of-money function is $U_A(m) = \sqrt{m}$.

(a) Find a Pareto efficient contract in the interior of the Edgeworth box at which the Principal's expected utility is 232.5.

(b) Calculate the Agent's expected utility at the contract of Part (a).

(c) Find a Pareto efficient contract on one of the sides of the Edgeworth box at which the Agent's expected utility is 27.

(d) Calculate the Principal's expected utility at the contract of Part (c).

Exercise 6.9 The owner of a firm (the Principal) hires a manager (the Agent) to run the firm. The Principal's utility-of-money function is $U(m) = \ln(m)$, while the Agent's utility-of-money function is $V(m) = 100\left[1 - e^{-\left(\frac{x}{100}\right)}\right]$ (where e is the number $2.71828...$). The profit of the firm is affected by random events and can turn out to be $X^g = \$1,000$ (this is expected to happen with probability $\frac{1}{4}$) or $X^b = \$600$ (with probability $\frac{3}{4}$). The Principal offers the following contract to the Agent: if the profit turns out to be \$1,000, I will pay you $w^g = \$400$, otherwise I will pay you $w^b = \$200$.

(a) What is the attitude to risk of the Principal?

(b) What is the attitude to risk of the Agent?

(c) Is the proposed contract Pareto efficient? Explain.

(d) If you were to propose a contract that both Principal and Agent prefer to the one considered above, which of the following suggestions would you make? Explain your answer by making use of an Edgeworth box.

   1. Increase both w^g and w^b.
   2. Decrease both w^g and w^b.
   3. Increase w^g and decrease w^b.
   4. Decrease w^g and increase w^b.

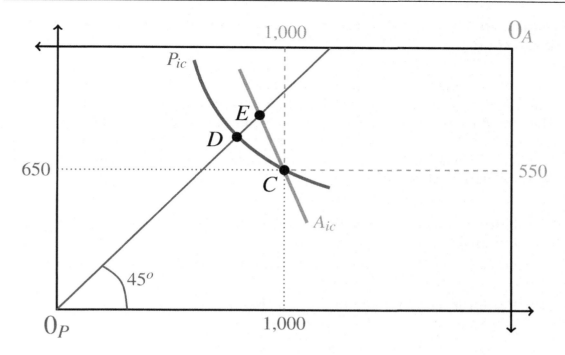

Figure 6.25: The Edgeworth box for Exercise 6.10.

Exercise 6.10 Consider the Edgeworth box of Figure 6.25. Clearly, the Agent is risk neutral while the Principal is risk averse. The Principal's von Neumann-Morgenstern utility-of-money function is $U_P(m) = \sqrt{m}$. The probability of the good state is $\frac{2}{5}$.
  (a) What is the value of X^g, the surplus in the good state?
  (b) What is the value of X^b, the surplus in the bad state?
  (c) Calculate the expected utility of both parties at contract C.
  (d) Find the coordinates of contract D and calculate the expected utility of both parties at that contract.
  (e) Find the coordinates of contract E and calculate the expected utility of both parties at that contract.
  (f) Find three contracts that Pareto dominate contract C.

Exercise 6.11 Let the surplus in the good state be $X^g = \$1,000$ and the surplus in the bad state be $X^b = \$400$. The Principal's von Neumann-Morgenstern utility-of-money function is $U_P(m) = \sqrt{m}$ while the Agent's von Neumann-Morgenstern utility-of-money function is $U_A(m) = \ln(m)$. Is contract $C = (600, 300)$ (where, as usual, the first coordinate is what the Agent gets in the good state and the second coordinate is what the Agent gets in the bad state) Pareto efficient?

6.7.4 Exercises for Section 6.4: Pareto efficient contracts on the sides of the Edgeworth box

Exercise 6.12 Let the surplus in the good state be $X^g = \$1,000$ and the surplus in the bad state be $X^b = \$600$. The probability of the good state is $\frac{2}{3}$. The Agent is risk neutral, while the Principal is risk averse with von Neumann-Morgenstern utility-of-money function $U_P(m) = \ln(m)$. Consider contract $C = (250, 150)$ (where, as usual, the first coordinate is what the Agent gets in the good state and the second coordinate is what the Agent gets in the bad state).

(a) Is contract C Pareto efficient?

(b) Represent contract C in an Edgeworth box and sketch the indifference curves of Principal and Agent through point C.

(c) Find a *Pareto efficient* contract, call it D, such that the Agent is indifferent between C and D while the Principal prefers D to C.

(d) Represent contract D in the Edgeworth box of Part (b).

Exercise 6.13 Let the surplus in the good state be $X^g = \$2,000$ and the surplus in the bad state be $X^b = \$1,200$. The probability of the good state is $\frac{7}{9}$. The Principal is risk neutral, while the Agent is risk averse with von Neumann-Morgenstern utility-of-money function $U_A(m) = \sqrt{m}$. Consider contract $C = (1559, 1004)$ (where, as usual, the first coordinate is what the Agent gets in the good state and the second coordinate is what the Agent gets in the bad state).

(a) Is contract C Pareto efficient?

(b) Represent contract C in an Edgeworth box and sketch the indifference curves of Principal and Agent through point C.

(c) Find a *Pareto efficient* contract, call it D, such that the Agent is indifferent between C and D while the Principal prefers D to C.

(d) Represent contract D in the Edgeworth box of Part (b).

Exercise 6.14 As in Exercise 6.13, let the surplus in the good state be $X^g = \$2,000$ and the surplus in the bad state be $X^b = \$1,200$. The probability of the good state is $\frac{7}{9}$. However, consider now the case where both the Principal and the Agent are risk averse with the same von Neumann-Morgenstern utility-of-money function: $U_P(m) = \sqrt{m}$ and $U_A(m) = \sqrt{m}$. Consider again contracts $C = (1559, 1004)$ and $D = (1493.04, 1200)$ of Exercise 6.13.

(a) Is contract C Pareto efficient?

(b) How does the Principal rank the two contracts C and D?

(c) How does the Agent rank the two contracts C and D?

(d) Is contract D Pareto efficient?

6.7 Exercises

Exercise 6.15 Let the surplus in the good state be $X^g = \$3,000$ and the surplus in the bad state be $X^b = \$1,800$. Both the Principal and the Agent are risk averse with the same von Neumann-Morgenstern utility-of-money function:

$$U_P(m) = \ln\left(1 + \frac{m}{1,000}\right) \quad \text{and} \quad U_A(m) = \ln\left(1 + \frac{m}{1,000}\right).$$

(a) Find the range of values of w^g for which contracts of the form $(w^g, 0)$ with $0 \leq w^g \leq X^g$ are Pareto efficient. [Hint: refer to Figure 6.15 on page 186.]

(b) Find the range of values of w^g for which contracts of the form $(w^g, 1800)$ with $0 \leq w^g \leq X^g$ are Pareto efficient.

Exercise 6.16 Mr. P wants to hire Ms. A to run his firm. If Ms. A works for Mr. P, one of two outcomes will occur: the profit of the firm will be $520 (this occurs with probability $\frac{45}{98}$) or it will be $200 (with probability $\frac{53}{98}$). Mr. P's von Neumann-Morgenstern utility-of-money function is $U(m) = \sqrt{m}$, while Ms. A is risk neutral. Consider the following contract, call it C: Ms. A will get $144 if the profit of the firm turns out to be $520, and she will get $90 if the profit of the firm turns out to be $200.

(a) What is Mr. P's expected utility from this contract?

(b) What is Ms. A's expected utility from this contract?

(c) Find a Pareto efficient contract in the Edgeworth box, call it D, that Mr. P considers to be just as good as C and Ms. A prefers to C.

(d) Find a a Pareto efficient contract in the Edgeworth box, call it E, that Mr. P prefers to C and Ms. A considers to be just as good as C.

(e) How does Mr. P rank the three contracts, C, D and E?

(f) How does Ms. A rank the three contracts, C, D and E?

6.7.5 Exercises for Section 6.5: The Edgeworth box when the parties have positive initial wealth

Exercise 6.17 The Principal, whose initial wealth is $\overline{W}_P = \$1,000$, is risk averse with utility-of-money function $U_P(m) = \sqrt{m+1} - 1$. The Agent, whose initial wealth is $\overline{W}_A = \$800$, is risk neutral. If they agree on a contract then the surplus in the good state will be $X^g = \$2,000$ and the surplus in the bad state will be $X^b = \$1,000$. The probability of the good state is $p^g = 15\%$.

Consider the following possible contracts:

1. Contract C: in each state the surplus is split equally between the Principal and the Agent.
2. Contract D: in the good state the entire surplus goes to the Principal and, furthermore, the Agent gives $200 to the Principal, while in the bad state the Agent gets the entire surplus (and there are no further payments by either party).

(a) What are the coordinates of point C in the extended Edgeworth box?
(b) Is contract C individually rational?
(c) Is contract C Pareto efficient?
(d) What are the coordinates of point D in the extended Edgeworth box?
(e) Is contract D individually rational?
(f) Is contract D Pareto efficient?
(g) Find a contract that is individually rational and leaves the Principal with zero wealth in the good state.
(h) Is the contract of Part (g) Pareto efficient?

Exercise 6.18 The Principal, whose initial wealth is $\overline{W}_P = \$200$, is risk averse with utility-of-money function $U_P(m) = \sqrt{m+1}$. The Agent, whose initial wealth is $\overline{W}_A = \$100$, is risk averse with utility-of-money function $U_A(m) = \ln\left(\frac{m}{100} + 1\right)$. If they agree on a contract then the surplus in the good state will be $X^g = \$700$ and the surplus in the bad state will be $X^b = \$300$. The two states are equally likely.

Consider the following contracts (where the first coordinate is the Agent's wealth in the good state and the second coordinate is the Agent's wealth in the bad state): $C = (350, 0)$, $D = (500, 300)$, $E = (700, 600)$.

(a) Represent the three contracts as points in an extended Edgeworth box.
(b) Is contract C individually rational?
(c) Is contract C Pareto efficient?
(d) Is contract D individually rational?
(e) Is contract D Pareto efficient?
(f) Is contract E individually rational?
(g) Is contract E Pareto efficient?
(h) In the extended Edgeworth box, sketch the indifference curves of Principal and Agent through the three contracts C, D and E.

6.7.6 Exercises for Section 6.6: More than two outcomes

Exercise 6.19 Suppose that there are three possible outcomes as shown in the following table:

$$\text{outcome:} \quad X_1 = \$500 \quad X_2 = \$600 \quad X_3 = \$800$$
$$\text{probability:} \quad \tfrac{1}{16} \quad \tfrac{3}{16} \quad \tfrac{12}{16}$$

The Principal is risk averse with von Neumann-Morgenstern utility-of-money function $U_P(m) = \sqrt{m}$, while the Agent is risk neutral. Consider the contract, call it C, where the Agent is given \$400 no matter what the outcome.

(a) Calculate the expected utility from contract C for the two parties.

(b) Find a contract, call it D, that (1) Pareto dominates C and (2) is **Pareto efficient**.

Exercise 6.20 Suppose that there are five possible outcomes:

$$\text{outcome:} \quad X_1 = \$141 \quad X_2 = \$164 \quad X_3 = \$461 \quad X_4 = \$645 \quad X_5 = \$749$$
$$\text{probability:} \quad \tfrac{1}{5} \quad \tfrac{1}{5} \quad \tfrac{1}{5} \quad \tfrac{1}{5} \quad \tfrac{1}{5}$$

The Principal is risk averse with von Neumann-Morgenstern utility-of-money function $U_P(m) = \sqrt{m}$, while the Agent is risk neutral. Suppose that the Principal offers the following contract, call it C, to the Agent: the Agent will be paid \$20 no matter what the outcome.

(a) What is the Principal's expected utility from contract C? What is the Agent's expected utility?

(b) Consider an alternative contract, call it D: the Agent will be paid nothing is the outcome is \$141 or \$164 or \$461, while she will be paid \$60 if the outcome is either \$645 or \$749. Is contract D Pareto superior to contact C?

For Exercises 6.21 and 6.22 make use of Propositions 6.6.1 and 6.6.2 and the logic used in the proof of Proposition 6.22.

Exercise 6.21 Suppose that there are four possible outcomes:

$$\text{outcome:} \quad X_1 = \$141 \quad X_2 = \$164 \quad X_3 = \$461 \quad X_4 = \$645$$
$$\text{probability:} \quad \tfrac{1}{10} \quad \tfrac{3}{10} \quad \tfrac{3}{10} \quad \tfrac{3}{10}$$

The Principal is risk neutral while the Agent is risk averse with von Neumann-Morgenstern utility-of-money function $U_P(m) = \ln\left(\tfrac{m}{100}\right)$. Consider the following contract (where the first coordinate is what the Agent gets if the the outcome is \$141, the second coordinate is what she gets if the outcome is \$164, etc.): $C = (141, 164, 400, 500)$.

Is contract C Pareto efficient? If your answer is 'Yes', then explain why, if your answer is 'No' then find a contract that Pareto dominates C.

Exercise 6.22 Suppose that there are three possible outcomes:

$$\text{outcome}: \quad X_1 = \$164 \quad X_2 = \$461 \quad X_3 = \$645$$
$$\text{probability}: \quad \tfrac{3}{10} \quad \tfrac{3}{10} \quad \tfrac{4}{10}$$

The Agent is risk neutral while the Principal is risk averse with von Neumann-Morgenstern utility-of-money function $U_A(m) = \sqrt{m}$. Consider the following contracts (where the first coordinate is what the Agent gets if the the outcome is $164, the second coordinate is what she gets if the outcome is $461, etc.): $C = (144, 100, 500)$, $D = (0, 80, 200)$.

(a) Is contract C Pareto efficient? If your answer is 'Yes', then explain why, if your answer is 'No' then find a contract that Pareto dominates C.

(b) Is contract D Pareto efficient? If your answer is 'Yes', then explain why, if your answer is 'No' then find a contract that Pareto dominates D.

Exercise 6.23 Suppose that there are three possible outcomes:

$$\text{outcome}: \quad X_1 = \$264 \quad X_2 = \$561 \quad X_3 = \$745$$
$$\text{probability}: \quad \tfrac{5}{10} \quad \tfrac{3}{10} \quad \tfrac{2}{10}$$

The Principal is risk averse with von Neumann-Morgenstern utility-of-money function $U_P(m) = \sqrt{m}$ and the Agent is risk averse with von Neumann-Morgenstern utility-of-money function $U_A(m) = \ln\left(\tfrac{m}{100}\right)$. Consider the following contracts: $C = (w_1 = 100, w_2 = 100, w_3 = 100)$, $D = (w_1 = 164, w_2 = 336, w_3 = 450)$.

(a) Is contract C Pareto efficient?

(b) Is contract D Pareto efficient?

Exercise 6.24 Suppose that there are three possible outcomes:

$$\text{outcome}: \quad X_1 = \$400 \quad X_2 = \$900 \quad X_3 = \$1,600$$
$$\text{probability}: \quad p \quad q \quad 1-p-q$$

with $0 < p+q < 1$.

The Principal and the Agent are risk neutral. Consider the following contract: $C = (w_1 = 400, w_2 = 0, w_3 = 800)$. For what values of p and q is contract C Pareto efficient?

6.8 Solutions to Exercises

Solution to Exercise 6.1.

Contract A gives rise to the following money lottery for the Agent: $\begin{pmatrix} \$700 \\ 1 \end{pmatrix}$ and therefore an expected utility of $U_A(700) = 2(700) + 2 = 1402$. The corresponding money lottery for the Principal is

$$\begin{pmatrix} \$(2,400-700) & \$(1,600-700) & \$(900-700) \\ \frac{1}{5} & \frac{2}{5} & \frac{2}{5} \end{pmatrix} = \begin{pmatrix} \$1,700 & \$900 & \$200 \\ \frac{1}{5} & \frac{2}{5} & \frac{2}{5} \end{pmatrix}$$

with corresponding expected utility of $\frac{1}{5}\ln(1,700) + \frac{2}{5}\ln(900) + \frac{2}{5}\ln(200) = 6.328$.

Contract B gives rise to the following lottery for the Agent:

$$\begin{pmatrix} \$1,200 & \$1,000 & \$200 \\ \frac{1}{5} & \frac{2}{5} & \frac{2}{5} \end{pmatrix}$$

with an expected utility of $\frac{1}{5}(2(1,200)+2) + \frac{2}{5}(2(1,000)+2) + \frac{2}{5}(2(200)+2) = 1,442$. The corresponding lottery for the Principal is

$$\begin{pmatrix} \$(2,400-1,200) & \$(1,600-1,000) & \$(900-200) \\ \frac{1}{5} & \frac{2}{5} & \frac{2}{5} \end{pmatrix} = \begin{pmatrix} \$1,200 & \$600 & \$700 \\ \frac{1}{5} & \frac{2}{5} & \frac{2}{5} \end{pmatrix}$$

with corresponding expected utility of $\frac{1}{5}\ln(1,200) + \frac{2}{5}\ln(600) + \frac{2}{5}\ln(700) = 6.597$.

Thus both Principal and Agent prefer contract B to contract A, that is, contract A is Pareto dominated by contract B. □

Solution to Exercise 6.2.

(a) Since $U''(m) = -\frac{1}{4\sqrt{m^3}} < 0$, John is risk averse.

(b) Since $V''(m) = 0$, Joanne is risk neutral.

(c) Contract A gives rise to the following lottery for John:

$$\begin{pmatrix} \$(4,000-1,000) = \$3,000 & \$(1,600-1,000) = \$600 \\ \frac{2}{3} & \frac{1}{3} \end{pmatrix}$$

with corresponding expected utility of $\frac{2}{3}\sqrt{3,000} + \frac{1}{3}\sqrt{600} = 44.68$. Joanne's utility from contract A is $V(1,000) = 2(1,000) = 2,000$. Contract B gives rise to the following lottery for John: $\begin{pmatrix} \$(4,000-1,500) = \$2,500 & \$1,600 \\ \frac{2}{3} & \frac{1}{3} \end{pmatrix}$ with corresponding expected utility of $\frac{2}{3}\sqrt{2,500} + \frac{1}{3}\sqrt{1,600} = 46.67$. Thus John prefers contract B to contract A. For Joanne contract B gives rise to the following lottery

$$\begin{pmatrix} 1,500 & 0 \\ \frac{2}{3} & \frac{1}{3} \end{pmatrix}$$

with corresponding expected utility of $\frac{2}{3}V(2,500) + \frac{1}{3}V(0) = \frac{2}{3}2(1,500) + \frac{1}{3}2(0) = 2,000$. Thus Joanne is indifferent between the two contracts. □

Solution to Exercise 6.3.

(a) The Edgeworth box is shown in Figure 6.26.

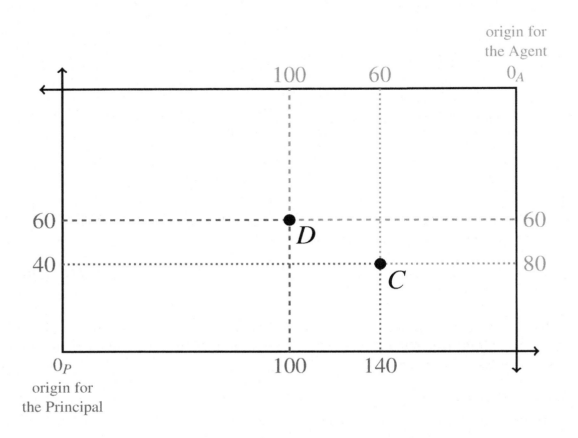

Figure 6.26: The Edgeworth box for Exercise 6.3.

(b) From the point of view of the Principal, contract C corresponds to the money lottery $\begin{pmatrix} \$140 & \$40 \\ \frac{1}{4} & \frac{3}{4} \end{pmatrix}$ and contract D corresponds to the money lottery $\begin{pmatrix} \$100 & \$60 \\ \frac{1}{4} & \frac{3}{4} \end{pmatrix}$. The expected value of C is $\frac{1}{4}140 + \frac{3}{4}40 = 65$ and the expected value of D is $\frac{1}{4}100 + \frac{3}{4}60 = 70$. Thus a risk-neutral Principal prefers contract D to contract C.

(c) From the point of view of the Agent, contract C corresponds to the money lottery $\begin{pmatrix} \$60 & \$80 \\ \frac{1}{4} & \frac{3}{4} \end{pmatrix}$ and contract D corresponds to the money lottery $\begin{pmatrix} \$100 & \$60 \\ \frac{1}{4} & \frac{3}{4} \end{pmatrix}$. The expected value of C is $\frac{1}{4}60 + \frac{3}{4}80 = 75$ and the expected value of D is $\frac{1}{4}100 + \frac{3}{4}60 = 70$. Thus a risk-neutral Agent prefers contract C to contract D. □

6.8 Solutions to Exercises

Solution to Exercise 6.4.

(a) The Principal is risk averse.

(b) The Agent is risk neutral.

(c) The Principal's ranking is as follows:

$$A \succ_P E \succ_P C \succ_P B \succ_P D.$$

(d) The Agent's ranking is as follows:

$$D \succ_A E \succ_A C \sim_A B \succ_A A.$$

(e) The following pairs:

- C Pareto dominates B (since $C \succ_P B$ and $C \sim_A B$).
- E Pareto dominates B (since $E \succ_P B$ and $E \succ_A B$).
- E Pareto dominates C (since $E \succ_P C$ and $E \succ_A C$). □

Solution to Exercise 6.5.

For the Principal the expected utility of contract C is
$\mathbb{E}[U_P(C)] = \frac{1}{4}\sqrt{140} + \frac{3}{4}\sqrt{40} = 7.7$ and the expected utility of contract D is
$\mathbb{E}[U_P(D)] = \frac{1}{4}\sqrt{100} + \frac{3}{4}\sqrt{60} = 8.31$. Thus the Principal prefers D to C.

For the Agent the expected utility of contract C is $\mathbb{E}[U_A(C)] = \frac{1}{4}\ln(60) + \frac{3}{4}\ln(80) = 4.31$ and the expected utility of contract D is $\mathbb{E}[U_A(D)] = \frac{1}{4}\ln(100) + \frac{3}{4}\ln(60) = 4.22$. Thus the Agent prefers C to D.

Hence it is neither the case that C Pareto dominates D nor the case that D Pareto dominates C. □

Solution to Exercise 6.6.

(a) Only contract D.

(b) Only contract B.

(c) None of them.

(d) All of them. □

Solution to Exercise 6.7.

(a) The Principal is risk averse ($U_P''(m) = -\frac{1}{5,000} < 0$) and the Agent is risk neutral ($U_A''(m) = 0$). Thus, since contract C is in the interior of the Edgeworth box (that is, $0 < w_C^g < X^g$ and $0 < w_C^b < X^b$), Pareto efficiency requires that the contract lie on the 45° line out of the Principal's origin, which is not the case with contract C since $X^g - w_C^g = 800 - 400 = 400 \neq 200 = 400 - 200 = X^b - w_C^b$. Hence contract C is not Pareto efficient.

(b) See Figure 6.27.

(c) One such contract is contract D shown in Figure 6.27. There are many more: any contract on the portion of the straight-line indifference curve of the Agent which lies above the indifference curve of the Principal. Of all those contracts, contract D is the only one that is Pareto efficient. □

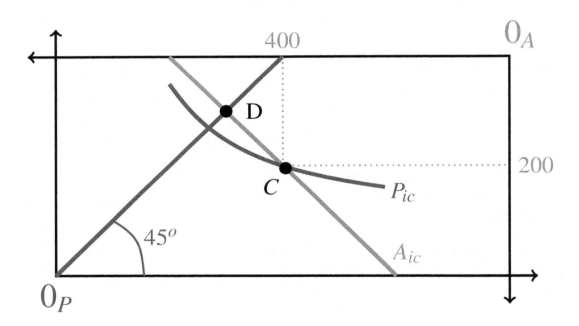

Figure 6.27: The Edgeworth box for Exercise 6.7. P_{ic} stands for "indifference curve of the Principal" and A_{ic} for "indifference curve of the Agent".

6.8 Solutions to Exercises

Solution to Exercise 6.8.

(a) Since the Principal is risk neutral and the Agent is risk averse, a Pareto efficient contract in the interior of the Edgeworth box must be on the 45° line out of the origin for the Agent, that is, it must be a contract that guarantees a fixed amount w to the Agent. Thus w is the solution to

$$\frac{1}{4}(1,206-w)+\frac{3}{4}(676-w)=232.5$$

which is $w = 576$.

(b) The Agent's expected utility is $\sqrt{576} = 24$.

(c) It must be a contract of the form $C = (w^g, 676)$ with $\frac{1}{4}\sqrt{w^g} + \frac{3}{4}\sqrt{676} = 27$. The solution is $w^g = 900$. Thus the contract is $C = (900, 676)$.

(d) At contract $C = (900, 676)$ the Principal's expected utility is $\frac{1}{4}(1,206 - 900) + \frac{3}{4}(0) = 76.5$. □

Solution to Exercise 6.9.

(a) The Principal is risk-averse, since $U''(m) = -\frac{1}{m^2} < 0$.

(b) The Agent is also risk-averse, since $V''(m) = -\frac{1}{100}e^{-\frac{m}{100}} < 0$ (recall that $\frac{d}{dx}e^x = e^x$).

(c) Since the proposed contract is in the interior of the Edgeworth box, Pareto efficiency requires that $\frac{U'(X^g-w^g)}{U'(X^b-w^b)} = \frac{V'(w^g)}{V'(w^b)}$. Since $U'(m) = \frac{1}{m}$ and $V'(m) = e^{-\frac{x}{100}}$,

$$\frac{U'(X^g - w^g)}{U'(X^b - w^b)} = \frac{U'(600)}{U'(400)} = \frac{\frac{1}{600}}{\frac{1}{400}} = \frac{400}{600} = \frac{2}{3} = 0.67$$

and

$$\frac{V'(w^g)}{V'(w^b)} = \frac{V'(400)}{V'(200)} = \frac{e^{-4}}{e^{-2}} = e^{-2} = 0.135.$$

Thus the contract is not Pareto efficient.

(d) From the above calculations we see that the Principal's indifference curve through the proposed contract is steeper than the Agent's indifference curve. Thus any contract in the shaded region in Figure 6.28 is Pareto superior to the given contract. Hence w^g should be decreased and w^b should be increased. □

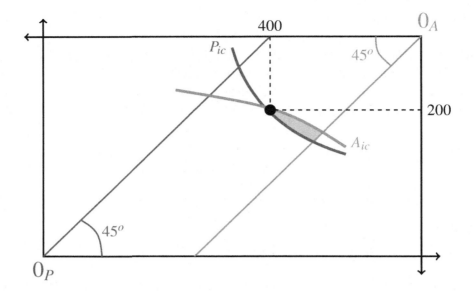

Figure 6.28: The Edgeworth box for Exercise 6.9.

Solution to Exercise 6.10.

(a) $X^g = 1,000 + 1,000 = 2,000$.

(b) $X^b = 650 + 550 = 1,200$.

(c) Since the Agent is risk neutral, we can take the identity function as her utility function: $U_A(m) = m$. Thus $\mathbb{E}[U_A(C)] = \frac{2}{5}(1,000) + \frac{3}{5}(550) = 730$. The expected utility for the Principal is $\mathbb{E}[U_P(C)] = \frac{2}{5}\sqrt{1,000} + \frac{3}{5}\sqrt{650} = 27.9462$.

(d) Contract $D = (w_D^g, w_D^b)$ is such that $2,000 - w_D^g = 1,200 - w_D^b$ (since it is on the 45° line out of the origin for the Principal) and $\sqrt{2,000 - w_D^g} = 27.9462$ (since it is on the Principal's indifference curve through point C). From the latter equation we get $w_D^g = 1,219.01$ and thus, from the first equation we get $w_D^b = 419.01$. At contract D the Principal's expected utility is the same as at C, namely 27.9462, while the Agent's expected utility is $\mathbb{E}[U_A(D)] = \frac{2}{5}(1,219.01) + \frac{3}{5}(419.01) = 739.01$. Thus contract D Pareto dominates contract C.

(e) Contract $E = (w_E^g, w_E^b)$ is such that $2,000 - w_E^g = 1,200 - w_E^b$ (since it is on the 45° line out of the origin for the Principal) and $\frac{2}{5}(w_E^g) + \frac{3}{5}(w_E^b) = 730$ (since it is on the Agent's indifference curve through point C). Solving this system of two equations we get $w_E^g = 1,210$ and $w_E^b = 410$. At contract E the Agent's expected utility is the same as at C, namely 730, while the Principal's expected utility is $\sqrt{2,000 - 1,210} = 28.1069$. Thus contract E Pareto dominates contract C.

(f) In Parts (d) and (e) we already found two contracts that Pareto dominate contract C, namely contracts $D = (1219.01, 419.01)$ and $E = (1210, 410)$. To find a third one we can take the mid point between D and E on the 45° line out of the origin for the Principal, call it point F; then $F = \left(\frac{1,219.01+1,210}{2}, \frac{419.01+410}{2}\right) = (1214.51, 414.51)$. Of course, any other point between the two indifference curves would have been a possible choice. □

6.8 Solutions to Exercises

Solution to Exercise 6.11.

Since contract $C = (600, 300)$ is such that $0 < w^g < X^g$ and $0 < w^b < X^b$ (that is, it is in the interior of the Edgeworth box) a necessary and sufficient condition for it to be Pareto efficient is

$$\frac{U'_P(X^g - w^g)}{U'_P(X^b - w^b)} = \frac{U'_A(w^g)}{U'_A(w^b)} \text{ that is, } \frac{U'_P(400)}{U'_P(100)} = \frac{U'_A(600)}{U'_A(300)}.$$

Indeed, $\quad \dfrac{U'_P(400)}{U'_P(100)} = \dfrac{\sqrt{100}}{\sqrt{400}} = \dfrac{1}{2} \quad$ and $\quad \dfrac{U'_A(600)}{U'_A(300)} = \dfrac{300}{600} = \dfrac{1}{2}.$

Thus the contract is Pareto efficient. □

Solution to Exercise 6.12.

(a) Contract C is not Pareto efficient, because it is in the interior of the Edgeworth box and yet does not lie on the 45° line out of the Principal's origin.

(b) See Figure 6.29.

(c) For the Agent we can take as utility-of-money function the identity function: $U_A(m) = m$. Thus the Agent's expected utility from contract C is its expected value, namely $\frac{2}{3} 250 + \frac{1}{3} 150 = \frac{650}{3} = 216.667$. Inside the Edgeworth box there is no point on the 45° line out of the Principal's origin that has the same expected value as point C. In fact it would have to be a point (w^g, w^b) such that (1) $1,000 - w^g = 600 - w^b$ and (2) $\frac{2}{3} w^g + \frac{1}{3} w^b = \frac{650}{3}$ and the only point that satisfies these two inequalities is the point $(w^g = 350, w^b = -50)$ which lies outside the Edgeworth box. Thus the point we are seeking must be on the top side of the Edgeworth box, that is it must be a point $D = (w^g, 0)$ such that $\frac{2}{3} w^g = \frac{650}{3}$; hence $D = (325, 0)$.

(d) See Figure 6.29. □

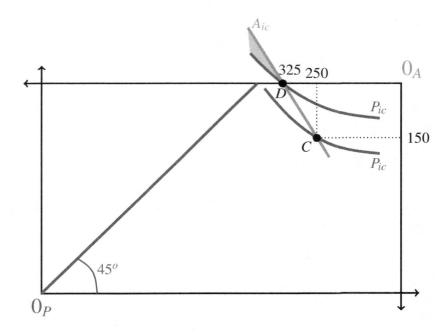

Figure 6.29: The Edgeworth box for Exercise 6.12.

Solution to Exercise 6.13.

(a) Contract C is not Pareto efficient, because it is in the interior of the Edgeworth box and yet does not lie on the 45° line out of the Agent's origin.

(b) See Figure 6.30.

(c) For the Agent the expected utility from contract C is $\frac{7}{9}\sqrt{1,559} + \frac{2}{9}\sqrt{1,004} = 37.7512$. There is no point inside the Edgeworth and on the 45° line out of the Agent's origin that has the same expected utility as point C. In fact it would have to be a point (w^g, w^b) such that (1) $w^g = w^b$ and (2) $\frac{7}{9}\sqrt{w^g} + \frac{2}{9}\sqrt{w^b} = 37.7512$ and the only point that satisfies these two inequalities is the point $(w^g = 1425.16, w^b = 1425.16)$ which lies outside the Edgeworth box (since $w^b = 1425.16 > X^b = 1,200$). Thus the point we are seeking must be on the bottom side of the Edgeworth box, that is it must be a point $D = (w^g, 1200)$ such that $\frac{7}{9}\sqrt{w^g} + \frac{2}{9}\sqrt{1200} = 37.7512$; hence $D = (1493.04, 1200)$.

(d) See Figure 6.30. □

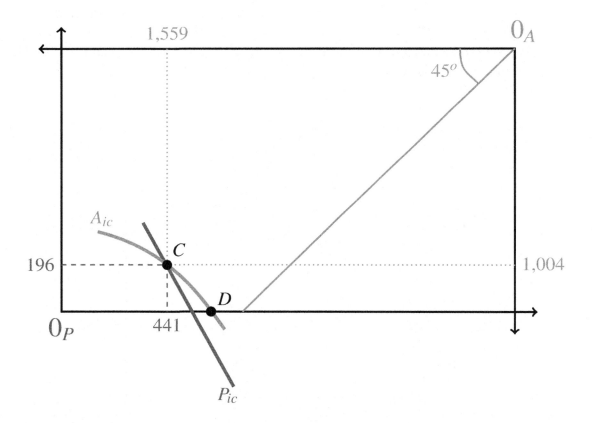

Figure 6.30: The Edgeworth box for Exercise 6.13.

6.8 Solutions to Exercises

Solution to Exercise 6.14.

(a) Contract C is not Pareto efficient, because it is in the interior of the Edgeworth box and the indifference curves of Principal and Agent are not tangent at that point:

$$\frac{U_P'(441)}{U_P'(196)} = \frac{\sqrt{196}}{\sqrt{441}} = \frac{2}{3} = 0.667$$

while

$$\frac{U_A'(1,559)}{U_A'(1,004)} = \frac{\sqrt{1,004}}{\sqrt{1,559}} = 0.8025.$$

(b) For the Principal the expected utility of contract C is $\frac{7}{9}\sqrt{441} + \frac{2}{9}\sqrt{196} = \frac{175}{9} = 19.4444$ and the expected utility of contract D is $\frac{7}{9}\sqrt{2,000-1,493.04} + \frac{2}{9}\sqrt{0} = 17.5123$. Thus the Principal prefers contract C to contract D.

(c) As calculated in Exercise 6.13, the Agent is indifferent between contract C and contract D.

(d) It follows from Parts (b) and (c) that contract C Pareto dominates contract D; hence contract D is not Pareto efficient. □

Solution to Exercise 6.15.

(a) A contract of the form $(w^g, 0)$ lies on the top side of the Edgeworth box and thus is Pareto efficient if and only if the Principal's indifference curve at that point is as steep as, or less steep than, the Agent's indifference curve (see Figure 6.15 on page 186), that is, if and only if

$$\frac{U_P'(3,000-w^g)}{U_P'(1,800)} \leq \frac{U_A'(w^g)}{U_A'(0)} \quad \text{that is} \quad \frac{2,800}{4,000-w^g} \leq \frac{1,000}{w^g+1,000}.$$

The solution is $w^g \leq \frac{6,000}{19} = 315.7895$.

(b) A contract of the form $(w^g, 1800)$ lies on the bottom side of the Edgeworth box and thus is Pareto efficient if and only if the Principal's indifference curve at that point is as steep as, or steeper than, the Agent's indifference curve (see Figure 6.15 on page 186), that is, if and only if

$$\frac{U_P'(3,000-w^g)}{U_P'(0)} \geq \frac{U_A'(w^g)}{U_A'(1,800)} \quad \text{that is} \quad \frac{1,000}{4,000-w^g} \geq \frac{2,800}{w^g+1,000}.$$

The solution is $w^g \geq \frac{51,000}{19} = 2,684.2105$. □

Solution to Exercise 6.16.

(a) Mr. P's expected utility from contract C is: $\frac{45}{98}\sqrt{520-144} + \frac{53}{98}\sqrt{200-90} = 14.576$.

(b) For Ms. A we can take as utility function the identity function, so that the expected utility of a contract coincides with its expected value. The expected value of contract C is: $\frac{45}{98}144 + \frac{53}{98}90 = 114.796$.

(c) Since P is risk-averse and A is risk neutral, the Pareto efficient contracts in the interior of the Edgeworth box must lie on the 45° out of the origin for the Principal. Let us see if there is such a contract which, furthermore, is as good as contract C for the Principal. Then it must be a contract (w^g, w^b) such that (1) $520 - w^g = 200 - w^b$ and (2) $\sqrt{520 - w^g} = 14.576$. From (2) we get that $w^g = 307.54$ and from this and (1) we get that $w^b = -12.46$. This contract is not feasible, because it does not lie inside the Edgeworth box. Thus we need to find a contract on the top side of the Edgeworth box, that is, a contract of the form $D = (w_D^g, 0)$ such that $\frac{45}{98}\sqrt{520 - w_D^g} + \frac{45}{98}\sqrt{200} = 14.576$. The solution is $w_D^g = 292.38$. Hence $D = (292.38, 0)$. Ms. A indeed prefers contract D to contract C since the expected value of D is $\frac{45}{98}292.38 = 134.256$.

(d) A similar reasoning would lead us to look for a point on the 45° out of the origin for the Principal which lies on the straight-line indifference curve of Ms. A that goes through point C, that is a point (w^g, w^b) such that (1) $520 - w^g = 200 - w^b$ and (2) $\frac{45}{98}w^g + \frac{53}{98}w^b = 114.796$. However, such a point lies outside the Edgeworth box (it is the point $(287.86, -32.14)$). Hence we need to find a point on the top side of the Edgeworth box that Ms. A finds just as good as C. Call this point $E = (w_E^g, 0)$. Then it must be that $\frac{45}{98}w_E^g = 114.796$. The solution is $w_E^g = 250$, that is, $E = (250, 0)$.

(e) Mr. P's ranking is $E \succ_P C \sim_P D$ since $\mathbb{E}[U_P(E)] = \frac{45}{98}\sqrt{520 - 250} + \frac{53}{98}\sqrt{200} = 15.1935 > 14.576 = \mathbb{E}[U_P(C)] = \mathbb{E}[U_P(D)]$.

(f) From the previous calculations it is clear that $D \succ_A C \sim_A E$ ($\mathbb{E}[D] = 134.256 > \mathbb{E}[C] = \mathbb{E}[E] = 114.796$). □

Solution to Exercise 6.17.

(a) $C = (1800, 1300)$ (the first coordinate is the Agent's wealth in the good state and the second coordinate is her wealth in the bad state).

(b) Yes, contract C is individually rational. The expected utility of contract C for the Principal is $\frac{15}{100}\left(\sqrt{2,000+1} - 1\right) + \frac{85}{100}\left(\sqrt{1,500+1} - 1\right) = 38.641$ which is greater than the utility from his initial wealth $\sqrt{1,000+1} - 1 = 30.639$. For the Agent we can take as utility function the identity function so that the expected utility of contract C is $\frac{15}{100}1800 + \frac{85}{100}1300 = 1,375$ which is greater than the utility from her initial wealth, namely 800.

(c) Contract C is not Pareto efficient because it is in the interior of the extended Edgeworth box and not on the 45° line out of the origin for the Principal (who is the only risk-averse party).

(d) $D = (600, 1800)$ (again, the first coordinate is the Agent's wealth in the good state and the second coordinate her wealth in the bad state).

6.8 Solutions to Exercises

(e) The expected utility of contract D for the Principal is $\frac{15}{100}\left(\sqrt{3,200+1}-1\right) + \frac{85}{100}\left(\sqrt{1,000+1}-1\right) = 34.379$ which is greater than the utility from his initial wealth $\sqrt{1,000+1}-1 = 30.639$. For the Agent the expected utility of contract D is $\frac{15}{100}600 + \frac{85}{100}1800 = 1,620$ which is greater than the utility from her initial wealth, namely 800. Thus contract D is individually rational.

(f) Like contract C, contract D is not Pareto efficient because it is in the interior of the extended Edgeworth box and not on the 45° line out of the origin for the Principal (the only risk-averse party).

(g) Let us see if there is a contract of the form $(3800,x)$ (again, the first coordinate is the Agent's wealth in the good state and the second coordinate her wealth in the bad state) that the Principal considers to be at least as good as keeping his initial wealth with no agreement, that is, such that $\frac{15}{100}\left(\sqrt{1}-1\right) + \frac{85}{100}\left(\sqrt{2,800-x+1}-1\right) \geq \sqrt{1,000+1}-1 = 34.379$; then it must be that $x \leq 1,428.64$.
Let us try contract $E = (3800, 1428)$. The Principal then prefers contract E to keeping his initial wealth with no agreement. For the Agent the expected utility of contract E is $\frac{15}{100}3800 + \frac{85}{100}1428 = 1,783.8$, greater than her reservation utility of 800. Thus E is individually rational.
(Any other contract of the form $(3800,x)$ with $270.59 \leq x \leq 1,428.64$ is also individually rational.)

(h) Since contract E lies on the left side of the extended Edgeworth box it is not Pareto efficient. In fact, at that point the slope of the Principal's indifference curve is, in absolute value, greater than $\frac{\frac{15}{100}}{\frac{85}{100}} = \frac{3}{17}$ (because point E lies above the 45° line for the Principal), which is the absolute value of the slope of the straight-line indifference curve of the Agent. Hence there are contracts inside the extended Edgeworth box that lie between the two indifference curves through point E and such contracts Pareto dominate contract E. □

Solution to Exercise 6.18.

(a) See Figure 6.31

(b) It is clear that the Principal prefers contract C to keeping his wealth of \$200 with no agreement. Thus we only need to check if the Agent views contract C to be at least as good as keeping her wealth of \$100 with no agreement. $U_A(100) = \ln(2) = 0.693$; the Agent's expected utility from contract C is $\frac{1}{2}\ln(4.5) + \frac{1}{2}\ln(1) = 0.752$. Thus the Agent prefers contract C to keeping her wealth. Hence contract C is individually rational.

(c) Contract C is Pareto efficient if and only if the indifference curve of the Principal at point C is less steep than, or as steep as, the indifference curve of the Agent at that point (see Figure 6.16 on page 187), that is, if and only if

$$\frac{U'_P(650)}{U'_P(600)} \leq \frac{U'_A(350)}{U'_A(0)}, \quad \text{that is,} \quad \frac{\frac{1}{2\sqrt{651}}}{\frac{1}{2\sqrt{601}}} \leq \frac{\frac{1}{450}}{\frac{1}{100}}$$

which is not the case since $\frac{\frac{1}{2\sqrt{651}}}{\frac{1}{2\sqrt{601}}} = 0.961$ and $\frac{\frac{1}{450}}{\frac{1}{100}} = 0.222$. Thus contract C is not

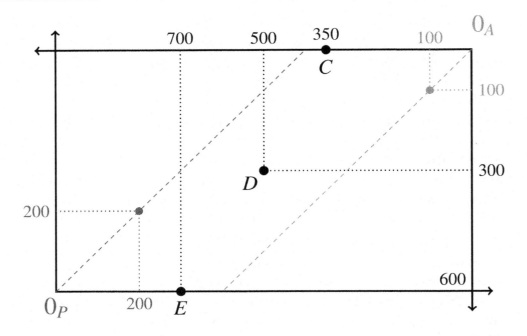

Figure 6.31: The Edgeworth box for Part (a) of Exercise 6.18.

Pareto efficient.

(d) For the Principal the expected utility of contract D is $\frac{1}{2}\sqrt{501}+\frac{1}{2}\sqrt{301}=19.866$ which is greater than $\sqrt{201}=14.177$ (the utility of his initial wealth), hence the Principal prefers contract D to keeping his initial wealth. For the Agent the expected utility of contract D is $\frac{1}{2}\ln(6)+\frac{1}{2}\ln(4)=1.589$ which is greater than $\ln(2)=0.693$ (the utility of her initial wealth), hence the Agent prefers contract D to keeping her initial wealth. Hence contract D is individually rational.

(e) Contract D is Pareto efficient if and only if the indifference curve of the Principal at point D has the same slope as the indifference curve of the Agent at that point, that is, if and only if

$$\frac{U'_P(500)}{U'_P(300)}=\frac{U'_A(500)}{U'_A(300)}, \quad \text{that is,} \quad \frac{\frac{1}{2\sqrt{501}}}{\frac{1}{2\sqrt{301}}}=\frac{\frac{1}{600}}{\frac{1}{400}}$$

which is not the case since $\frac{\frac{1}{2\sqrt{501}}}{\frac{1}{2\sqrt{301}}}=0.775$ while $\frac{\frac{1}{600}}{\frac{1}{400}}=0.667$. Thus contract D is not Pareto efficient.

(f) For the Principal the expected utility of contract E is $\frac{1}{2}\sqrt{301}+\frac{1}{2}\sqrt{1}=9.175$ which is less than $\sqrt{201}=14.177$ (the utility of his initial wealth), hence the Principal prefers keeping his initial wealth to contract E, so that contract E is not individually rational.

(g) Contract E is Pareto efficient if and only if the indifference curve of the Principal is steeper than, or as steep as, the indifference curve of the Agent at that point (see

Figure 6.16 on page 187), that is, if and only if

$$\frac{U'_P(300)}{U'_P(0)} \geq \frac{U'_A(700)}{U'_A(600)}, \quad \text{that is,} \quad \frac{\frac{1}{2\sqrt{301}}}{\frac{1}{2\sqrt{1}}} \geq \frac{\frac{1}{800}}{\frac{1}{700}}$$

which is not the case since $\frac{\frac{1}{2\sqrt{301}}}{\frac{1}{2\sqrt{1}}} = 0.058$ and $\frac{\frac{1}{800}}{\frac{1}{700}} = 0.875$. Thus contract E is not Pareto efficient.

(h) See Figure 6.32. □

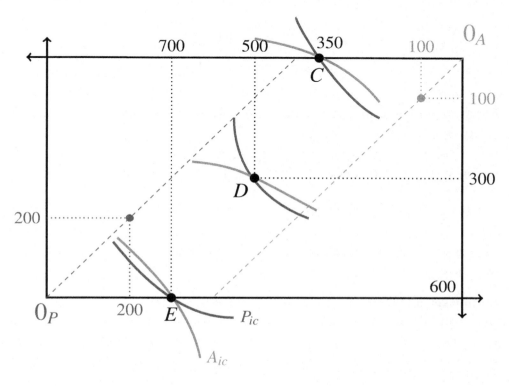

Figure 6.32: The Edgeworth box for Part (h) of Exercise 6.18.

Solution to Exercise 6.19.

(a) Expected for the Principal is

$$\frac{1}{16}\sqrt{500-400} + \frac{3}{16}\sqrt{600-400} + \frac{12}{16}\sqrt{800-400} = 18.277.$$

For the Agent we can take the identity function as her utility function and thus her utility from contract C is 400.

(b) Since the Principal is risk averse and the Agent is risk neutral, Pareto efficiency requires that the Agent bear all the risk (i.e. the Principal must be guaranteed a fixed income). There are many contracts that are Pareto efficient and Pareto dominate contract C. One example is that fixed-income (for the Principal) contract, call it D, that the Principal considers to be just as good as contract C; to find such a contract solve the equation $\sqrt{x} = 18.277$ to obtain $x = 334.05$. Then $D = (500 - 334.05, 600 - 334.05, 800 - 334.05) = (165.95, 265.95, 465.95)$ and the Agent prefers D to C since for her the expected utility from contract D is

$$\frac{1}{16}165.95 + \frac{3}{16}265.95 + \frac{12}{16}465.95 = 409.7$$

□

Solution to Exercise 6.20.

(a) The Principal's expected utility from contract C is

$$\frac{1}{5}\sqrt{141-20} + \frac{1}{5}\sqrt{164-20} + \frac{1}{5}\sqrt{461-20} + \frac{1}{5}\sqrt{645-20} + \frac{1}{5}\sqrt{749-20}$$
$$= \frac{1}{5}(11+12+21+25+27) = 19.2$$

For the Agent we can take the identity function as her utility function and thus her utility from contract C is 20.

(b) Under contract D the Agent's expected utility is $\frac{3}{5}0 + \frac{2}{5}60 = 24$ and thus the Agent prefers contract D to contract C. Under contract D the Principal's expected utility is:

$$\frac{1}{5}\left(\sqrt{141} + \sqrt{164} + \sqrt{461} + \sqrt{645-60} + \sqrt{749-60}\right) = 19.3174.$$

Thus also the Principal prefers contract D to contract C. Hence contract D Pareto dominates contract C. □

Solution to Exercise 6.21.

It follows from Proposition 6.6.1 that contract C is not Pareto efficient, because $w_3 = 400 < w_4 = 500$ and yet $w_3 \neq X_3 = 461$. To find a contract that Pareto dominates contract C, let us use the method employed in the proof of Proposition 6.6.1: replace w_3 and w_4 with $\hat{w} = \frac{p_3}{p_3+p_4}w_3 + \frac{p_4}{p_3+p_4}w_4 = \frac{1}{2}400 + \frac{1}{2}500 = 450$; that is, consider the contract $B = (141, 164, 450, 450)$. For the Agent

$$\mathbb{E}[U_A(B)] = \frac{1}{10}\ln(1.41) + \frac{3}{10}\ln(1.64) + \frac{6}{10}\ln(4.5) = 1.0852$$

$$\mathbb{E}[U_A(C)] = \frac{1}{10}\ln(1.41) + \frac{3}{10}\ln(1.64) + \frac{3}{10}\ln(4) + \frac{3}{10}\ln(5) = 1.0815.$$

Thus the Agent prefers B to C. For the Principal we can take the identity function as his utility-of-money function so that

$$\mathbb{E}[U_P(B)] = \frac{1}{10}0 + \frac{3}{10}0 + \frac{3}{10}(461-450) + \frac{3}{10}(645-450) = 61.8$$

$$\mathbb{E}[U_P(C)] = \frac{1}{10}0 + \frac{3}{10}0 + \frac{3}{10}(461-400) + \frac{3}{10}(645-500) = 61.8$$

Thus the Principal is indifferent between B and C and therefore contract B Pareto dominates contract C. □

6.8 Solutions to Exercises

Solution to Exercise 6.22.

(a) Contract C is not Pareto efficient because, contrary to Proposition 6.6.2, $X_2 - w_2 = 361 > X_3 - w_3 = 145$. From the point of view of the Principal, contract C corresponds to the money lottery

$$\begin{pmatrix} \$20 & \$361 & \$145 \\ \frac{3}{10} & \frac{3}{10} & \frac{4}{10} \end{pmatrix}.$$

Let us create a new lottery for the Principal, call it E, where we replace outcomes $\$361$ and $\$145$ with an amount x such that the Principal is indifferent between the new lottery and the lottery corresponding to contract C. Since for the Principal

$$\mathbb{E}[U_P(C)] = \frac{3}{10}\sqrt{20} + \frac{3}{10}\sqrt{361} + \frac{4}{10}\sqrt{145} = 11.858,$$

we want x to be such that

$$\mathbb{E}[U_P(E)] = \frac{3}{10}\sqrt{20} + \frac{7}{10}\sqrt{x} = 11.858.$$

Thus $x = 225.70$. It remains to show that the Agent prefers contract E to contract C. E is the contract $(w_1 = 144, w_2 = 461 - 225.70, w_3 = 645 - 225.70) = (144, 235.3, 419.3)$. Since the Agent is risk neutral, she ranks contracts according to their expected value:

$$\mathbb{E}[C] = \frac{3}{10}144 + \frac{3}{10}100 + \frac{4}{10}500 = 273.2 \text{ and}$$

$$\mathbb{E}[E] = \frac{3}{10}144 + \frac{3}{10}235.3 + \frac{4}{10}419.3 = 281.51.$$

Thus the Agent prefers E to C and hence E Pareto dominates C.

(b) Contract D is not Pareto efficient because, contrary to Proposition 6.6.2, although $X_1 - w_1 = 164 < X_2 - w_2 = 461 - 80 = 381 < X_3 - w_3 = 645 - 200 = 445$, it is not the case that $w_2 = 0$. Let us find an alternative contract, call it F, that the Principal considers just as good as contract D and gives the Principal the same income is states 2 and 3. Since

$$\mathbb{E}[U_P(D)] = \frac{3}{10}\sqrt{164} + \frac{3}{10}\sqrt{381} + \frac{4}{10}\sqrt{445} = 18.1357,$$

we need to solve the equation

$$\frac{3}{10}\sqrt{164} + \frac{7}{10}\sqrt{x} = 18.1357.$$

The solution is $x = 416.966$. Thus $F = (0, 461 - 416.966, 645 - 416.966) = (0, 44.034, 228.034)$ Since the Agent is risk neutral, she ranks contracts according to their expected value: $\mathbb{E}[D] = \frac{3}{10}80 + \frac{4}{10}200 = 104$ and $\mathbb{E}[F] = \frac{3}{10}44.034 + \frac{4}{10}228.034 = 104.424$. Thus the Agent prefers contract F to contract D, so that D is Pareto dominated by F.

□

Solution to Exercise 6.23.

(a) Contract $C = (100, 100, 100)$ is not Pareto efficient because

$$\frac{U'_P(X_1 - w_1)}{U'_P(X_2 - w_2)} = \frac{U'_P(164)}{U'_P(461)} = \frac{\sqrt{461}}{\sqrt{164}} = 1.6766 \neq \frac{U'_A(w_1)}{U'_A(w_2)} = \frac{U'_A(100)}{U'_A(100)} = 1.$$

(b) Contract $D = (164, 336, 450)$ is not Pareto efficient because

$$\frac{U'_P(X_1 - w_1)}{U'_P(X_2 - w_2)} = \frac{U'_P(100)}{U'_P(225)} = \frac{\sqrt{225}}{\sqrt{100}} = 1.5 \neq \frac{U'_A(w_1)}{U'_A(w_2)} = \frac{U'_A(164)}{U'_A(336)} = 2.0488.$$

□

Solution to Exercise 6.24.

When both parties are risk neutral, every contract is Pareto efficient, no matter what the probabilities are. Thus the answer is: for all (meaningful) values of p and q. □

III Asymmetric Information: Adverse Selection

7 Adverse Selection 227
- 7.1 Adverse selection or hidden type
- 7.2 Conditional probability and belief updating
- 7.3 The market for used cars
- 7.4 Exercises
- 7.5 Solutions to Exercises

8 Adverse Selection in Insurance 253
- 8.1 Adverse selection in insurance markets
- 8.2 Two types of customers
- 8.3 The monopolist under asymmetric information
- 8.4 A perfectly competitive insurance industry
- 8.5 Exercises
- 8.6 Solutions to Exercises

7. Adverse Selection

7.1 Adverse selection or hidden type

The expression 'adverse selection', or 'hidden type', refers to situations in which one party to a contract (e.g. a buyer) possesses information relevant to the contract that is not available to the opposing party (e.g. a seller). Thus it is a situation of *asymmetric information*.

For example, in the context of health insurance, the insurance company (the seller of insurance) is typically aware of the fact that there are individuals who – because of their family history – are at a higher risk of developing a condition that requires extensive medical services, while other individuals represent a lower risk. If the insurance company offers a contract that would, on average, be profitable *if everybody (high-risk and low-risk individuals) were to purchase that contract*, it might discover that its costs are much higher than expected, because only (or mostly) the high-risk individuals ended up purchasing the contract.[1] In a situation of adverse selection the uninformed party realizes that *the terms of a proposed contract determine the composition of the pool of individuals who will find that contract acceptable* and a change in the contract that would be beneficial to the uninformed party, if everybody found the contract acceptable, might have undesirable consequences because of an adverse change in the proportion of "bad types" within the pool of applicants. Adverse selection in insurance markets will be discussed in the next chapter. In this chapter we will discuss how adverse selection arises in other markets and what its consequences are.

---

[1] This was the rationale behind the original provision of the Affordable Care Act that established a mandate for individuals to purchase health insurance.

The phenomenon of adverse selection was brought to the attention of economists by George Akerlof in 1970.[2] Akerlof analyzed the market for second-hand cars, which will be discussed in Section 7.3. Here we begin with a simple illustration of the phenomenon of adverse selection in a different context.

Suppose that you have just opened an all-you-can-eat buffet restaurant in a small facility that can accommodate up to a maximum of 50 customers. Since this is your first business venture, you are uncertain as to how much to charge and decide to start with a low price of $6. On the first day you notice that, at this price, there is excess demand: your restaurant is full (all 50 seats are taken) and you had to turn away some potential customers. At the end of the first day you calculate that, on average, each customer consumed an amount of food that cost you $4.50, so that you made a profit of $1.50 per customer, for a total profit of $(1.50 \times 50) = \$75$. Having recently graduate with a degree in economics you remember that when there is excess demand the price should be increased. The potential downside of increasing the price is that the higher price might drive away too many customers and you might end up not being able to fill your restaurant; so you decide to first try a modest price increase: from $6 to $7. To your delight, on the second day - with the higher price of $7 - there is again excess demand: all the 50 seats are taken and, again, some people had to be turned away. At the end of the second day, you calculate your total profit for the day, expecting it to be $(7 \times 50 - 4.5 \times 50) = \$125$ but to your dismay you realize that it is only $50, less than on the first day when your price was lower! What happened?

The reduction in profit is not due to a drop in demand, because you still served the same number of customers, namely 50. In fact, your revenue did increase: from $(6 \times 50) = \$300$ to $(7 \times 50) = \$350$; hence the adverse effect of the price increase occurred on the cost side of the equation: your total costs increased from $225 to $300. How could this happen? A simple explanation is as follows. There are two types of potential customers: the light eaters, denoted by L, and the heavy eaters, denoted by H. Each L-type consumes a small amount of food that costs $3, while each H-type consumes a large amount of food that costs $6. Because of their moderate consumption, the L-types are not willing to pay more than $6 for a buffet, while the H-types are willing to pay up to $7 (or even more). There are as many L-types as H-types in the population and their arrival at your restaurant is random, so that the probability of each *served* customer being of one type or the other is the same, namely 50%, *provided that both types are in fact willing to enter your restaurant*: this is the case if the price is $6 but not if the price is $7. In other words, if you charge only $6, admitting a customer corresponds to playing a lottery where, with probability $\frac{1}{2}$ the cost of serving that customer will be $3 and with probability $\frac{1}{2}$ the cost of serving that customer will be $6, so that the expected cost of serving any one customer is $4.50 and thus the expected profit from any one customer is $(6 - 4.50) = \$1.50$. On the other hand, if you charge a price of $7, then only the H-types will enter your restaurant and thus admitting a customer corresponds to playing a lottery where, with probability 1, the cost of serving that customer will be $6, with a corresponding profit of $(7 - 6) = \$1$ per customer. In other words, increasing the price from $6 to $7 changed the composition of

---

[2] In "The market for 'lemons': qualitative uncertainty and the price mechanism", *Quarterly Journal of Economics*, 1970, Vol. 84, pp. 488-500. The Nobel Memorial Prize in Economics was awarded in 2001 to George Akerlof, Michael Spence and Joseph Stiglitz "for their analyses of markets with asymmetric information".

your 50 customers

$$\text{from} \quad \begin{pmatrix} \text{Type } L & \text{Type } H \\ 50\% & 50\% \end{pmatrix} \quad \text{to} \quad \begin{pmatrix} \text{Type } H \\ 100\% \end{pmatrix}.$$

This simple example illustrates the logic of the adverse selection phenomenon.

In order to be able to develop a more general analysis, we need to take a side tour into the topic of conditional probability and belief updating. To illustrate the reason for this, consider te following, slightly more complex, version of the above example, where instead of two types there are three: L, M and H. The types are characterized as follows (where 'reservation price' is the maximum price that the individual is willing to pay for a buffet):

type:	L	M	H
fraction of total population:	$\frac{2}{6}$	$\frac{3}{6}$	$\frac{1}{6}$
reservation price:	$6	$6.50	$7
cost of food consumed:	$3	$6	$9

If you charge $6 for the buffet then all types will be willing to enter your restaurant. Thus (assuming that the probability of any given customer being of a particular type is equal to the fraction of that type in the population) from the point of view of cost admitting a customer correspond to playing the following lottery:

$$\begin{pmatrix} \text{cost of serving the customer:} & \$3 & \$6 & \$9 \\ \text{probability:} & \frac{2}{6} & \frac{3}{6} & \frac{1}{6} \end{pmatrix}$$

so that the expected cost of serving each customer is $\frac{2}{6}3 + \frac{3}{6}6 + \frac{1}{6}9 = \$5.50$. On the other hand, if you charge \$6.50 then the L-types will not enter your restaurant and thus, from the from point of view of cost, admitting a customer correspond to facing the following lottery:

$$\begin{pmatrix} \text{cost of serving the customer:} & \$6 & \$9 \\ \text{probability:} & p & 1-p \end{pmatrix}$$

What is the value of p? This question is answered in the following section.

7.2 Conditional probability and belief updating

So far we have been focussing on money lotteries representing uncertainty concerning possible levels of wealth or possible levels of profit or cost, etc. More generally, we can use lotteries to represent uncertainty about anything. Let as call a possible item of uncertainty a "state of the world". Then an individual's uncertainty can be represented by a set, listing all the states of the world that the individual considers possible.

Consider, for example, the state of uncertainty of a doctor who, after listening to her patient's symptoms, reaches the conclusion that there are only five possible causes: (1) a bacterial infection (call this state a), (2) a viral infection (state b), (3) an allergic reaction to a drug (state c), (4) an allergic reaction to food (state d) and (5) environmental

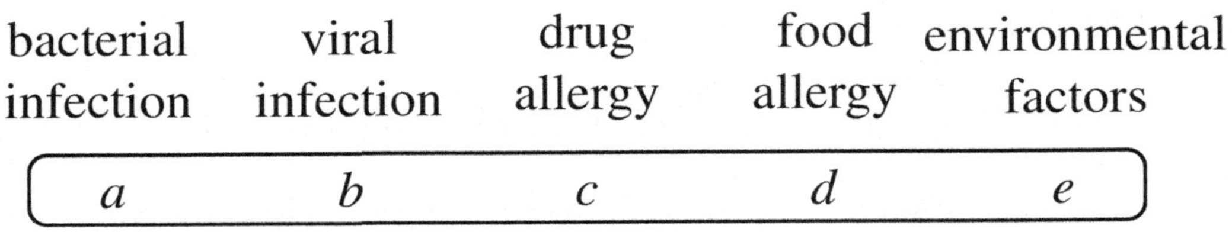

bacterial infection	viral infection	drug allergy	food allergy	environmental factors
a	b	c	d	e

Figure 7.1: The doctor's initial state of uncertainty

factors (state e). Then we can represent the doctor's state of uncertainty by the set $\{a,b,c,d,e\}$, as shown in Figure 7.1.

Of all the states that are possible, the individual might consider some to be more likely than others and might even dismiss some states as "extremely unlikely" or "implausible". To represent the individual's probabilistic beliefs we use a probability distribution over the set of states.

Continuing the doctor's example, suppose that - based upon her past experience with similar cases - she considers a bacterial infection (state a) to be twice as likely as a viral infection (state b), she considers a food allergy (state d) to be three times as likely as a drug allergy (state c), which - in turn - she considers to be as likely as environmental factors (state e); that is, she has the following beliefs:

$$\begin{pmatrix} \text{state:} & a & b & c & d & e \\ \text{probability:} & \frac{4}{11} & \frac{2}{11} & \frac{1}{11} & \frac{3}{11} & \frac{1}{11} \end{pmatrix}.$$

Suppose that the doctor can acquire further information by ordering a blood test. How should she revise her beliefs when she learns the result of the blood test? In order to answer this question we need to introduce the notion of conditional probability and be more precise about what we mean by information.

7.2.1 Conditional probability

Let us frame the issue of uncertainty in general terms. Let U ('U' stands for 'universal set') be a finite set of possibilities. An element $s \in U$ is called a *state* and any subset E of U ($E \subseteq U$) is called an *event*. A *probability distribution* P on U is a function $P \to [0,1]$ that assigns to every state $s \in U$ a number $P(s)$, called the *probability of state s*, such that $0 \leq P(s) \leq 1$. It is required that the probabilities add up to 1: $\sum_{s \in U} P(s) = 1$. Given an event $E \subseteq U$, we denote by $P(E)$ the *probability of event E* and define it as the sum of the probabilities of the states in E: $P(E) = \sum_{s \in E} P(s)$. Denote the empty set (which is a subset of U) by $\varnothing$; then we set, by definition, $P(\varnothing) = 0$.

Let $s \in U$ be a state and $E \subseteq U$ an event. While $P(s)$ is the *unconditional* probability of state s, we can also define the probability of s *conditional on event* E, denoted by $P(s|E)$. It is meant to capture the new probability that one should assign to state s if informed that the "true state" is an element of E and it is defined as follows:

$$\text{if} \quad P(E) > 0 \quad \text{then} \quad P(s|E) = \begin{cases} 0 & \text{if } s \notin E \\ \frac{P(s)}{P(E)} & \text{if } s \in E \end{cases}. \tag{7.1}$$

7.2 Conditional probability and belief updating

Note that the probability conditional on an event E is defined only if $P(E) > 0$, that is, if E is an event that has positive unconditional probability.

Conditional probability can also be extended to events, as follows. Let D and E be events with $P(E) > 0$. Then the probability of D conditional on E, denoted by $P(D|E)$ is defined as[3]

$$P(D|E) = \sum_{s \in D} P(s|E). \tag{7.2}$$

7.2.2 Belief updating

Sometimes uncertainty can be reduced by acquiring information. Indeed, information can be thought of as "reduction of uncertainty". Continuing the example of the doctor, whose initial beliefs are represented by the probability distribution

$$\begin{pmatrix} \text{state:} & a & b & c & d & e \\ \text{probability:} & \frac{4}{11} & \frac{2}{11} & \frac{1}{11} & \frac{3}{11} & \frac{1}{11} \end{pmatrix},$$

suppose that the doctor can order a blood test: a positive blood test will reveal that there is an infection and rule out states c, d and e, while a negative blood test will reveal that there is no infection, thus ruling out states a and b. We can represent the information obtained from a blood test as a set of states (an event): the set $\{a, b\}$ represents the information conveyed by a positive blood test, while the set $\{c, d, e\}$ represents the information conveyed by a negative blood test.

Suppose that the doctor orders the blood test and it comes back positive. How should she revise her beliefs in light of this piece of information?

The issue of how to "rationally" modify one's initial beliefs - expressed as a probability distribution P on a finite set U - after receiving an item of information (represented by a subset F of U) has been studied extensively by philosophers and logicians. Two different situations may arise:

- In one case, the item of information F was not ruled out by the initial beliefs, in the sense that event F was assigned positive probability ($P(F) > 0$). Information might still be somewhat surprising, in case $P(F)$ is small (close to zero), but it is not completely unexpected. We call this case *belief updating*.

- The other case is where the item of information was initially dismissed, in the sense that it was assigned zero probability ($P(F) = 0$). In this case the information received is completely surprising or completely unexpected. We call this case *belief revision*.

In this book we will only address the issue of belief updating.[4]

It is generally agreed that the rational way to update one's beliefs is by conditioning the initial beliefs on the information received, that is, by using the conditional probability formula (7.1).

---

[3] Typically, conditional probability is defined directly for events as follows: if $D, E \subseteq U$ and $P(E) > 0$ then $P(D|E) = \frac{P(D \cap E)}{P(E)}$ where $D \cap E$ is the intersection of D and E, that is, the set of states that belong to both D and E. The reader should convince himself/herself that the conjunction of (7.1) and 7.2 is equivalent to this definition (interpreting $P(s|E)$ as $P(\{s\}|E)$ and recalling that $P(\varnothing) = 0$).

[4] The issue of belief revision is discussed in my book *Decision Making* (see http://faculty.econ.ucdavis.edu/faculty/bonanno/).

Definition 7.2.1 We use the expression *belief updating* or *Bayesian updating* to refer to the modification of initial beliefs (expressed by an initial probability distribution P) obtained by applying the conditional probability rule; this assumes that the belief change is prompted by the arrival of new information, represented by an event F such that $P(F) > 0$.

Thus, when receiving a piece of information $F \subseteq U$ such that $P(F) > 0$, one would change one's initial probability distribution P into a new probability distribution P_{new} by

- reducing the probability of every state in $U \setminus F$ (the complement of F) to zero (this captures the notion that the information represented by F is trusted to be correct), and
- setting $P_{new}(s) = P(s|F)$ for every state $s \in F$.

Thus, for every state $s \in U$,

$$P_{new}(s) = P(s|F) = \begin{cases} 0 & \text{if } s \notin F \\ \frac{P(s)}{P(F)} & \text{if } s \in F \end{cases} \quad (7.3)$$

(recall the assumption that $P(F) > 0$). Thus, for every event $E \subseteq U$, $P_{new}(E) = \sum_{s \in E} P_{new}(s) = \sum_{s \in E} P(s|F) = P(E|F)$.

For instance, in the doctor's example, belief updating requires the following. Recall that the doctor's initial beliefs are:

$$\begin{pmatrix} \text{state:} & a & b & c & d & e \\ \text{probability:} & \frac{4}{11} & \frac{2}{11} & \frac{1}{11} & \frac{3}{11} & \frac{1}{11} \end{pmatrix}.$$

Let $+$ be the event that the blood test is positive (that is, $+ = \{a,b\}$ and thus $P(+) = \frac{6}{11}$). Let $-$ be the event that the blood test is negative (that is, $- = \{c,d,e\}$ and thus $P(-) = \frac{5}{11}$). Then

state	a	b	c	d	e
initial beliefs	$\frac{4}{11}$	$\frac{2}{11}$	$\frac{1}{11}$	$\frac{3}{11}$	$\frac{1}{11}$
beliefs updated on information $+$	$\frac{4/11}{6/11} = \frac{2}{3}$	$\frac{2/11}{6/11} = \frac{1}{3}$	0	0	0
beliefs updated on information $-$	0	0	$\frac{1/11}{5/11} = \frac{1}{5}$	$\frac{3/11}{5/11} = \frac{3}{5}$	$\frac{1/11}{5/11} = \frac{1}{5}$

7.2 Conditional probability and belief updating

As a further example, suppose that there are only three students in a class: Ann, Bob and Carla. The professor tells them that in the last exam one of them got 95 points (out of 100), another 78 and the third 54.

We can think of a state as a triple (a,b,c), where a is Ann's score, b is Bob's score and c is Carla's score. Then, based on the information given by the professor, the set of possible states is:

$$U = \{(95,78,54),(95,54,78),(78,95,54),(78,54,95),(54,95,78),(54,78,95)\}.$$

Suppose that in all the previous exams Ann and Bob always obtained a higher score than Carla and often Ann outperformed Bob. Then Ann might consider states (95,78,54) and (78,95,54) much more likely than (78,54,95) and (54,78,95).

For example, suppose that Ann's beliefs are as follows:

$$\begin{pmatrix} (95,78,54) & (95,54,78) & (78,95,54) & (54,95,78) & (78,54,95) & (54,78,95) \\ \frac{16}{32} & \frac{8}{32} & \frac{4}{32} & \frac{2}{32} & \frac{1}{32} & \frac{1}{32} \end{pmatrix}.$$

Suppose that, before distributing the exams, the professor says "I was surprised to see that, this time, Ann did not get the highest score". Based on this information, how should Ann revise her beliefs? The information is that Ann did not receive the highest score, which is represented by the event

$$F = \{(78,95,54),(54,95,78),(78,54,95),(54,78,95)\}.$$

Conditioning on this event yields the following updated beliefs:

$$\begin{pmatrix} (95,78,54) & (95,54,78) & (78,95,54) & (54,95,78) & (78,54,95) & (54,78,95) \\ 0 & 0 & \frac{4}{8} & \frac{2}{8} & \frac{1}{8} & \frac{1}{8} \end{pmatrix}. \quad (7.4)$$

These updated beliefs can be represented more succinctly as follows, by not listing the states that are ruled out by information F (that is, the states in the complement of F, which are zero-probability states in the updated beliefs):

$$\begin{pmatrix} (78,95,54) & (54,95,78) & (78,54,95) & (54,78,95) \\ \frac{4}{8} & \frac{2}{8} & \frac{1}{8} & \frac{1}{8} \end{pmatrix}. \quad (7.5)$$

The belief updating rule can also be applied sequentially if one first receives information F (with $P(F) > 0$) and later receives a further piece of information E (with $E \subseteq F$ and $P(E|F) > 0$ or, equivalently, $P(E \cap F) > 0$). For instance, in the above example, suppose that the professor first informs the students that Ann did not get the highest score and later tells them that Carla received a higher score than Bob. Call F the first piece of information and E the second piece of information. Then, as we saw above, F is the set of states where it is in fact true that Ann did not get the highest score:

$$F = \{(78,95,54),(54,95,78),(78,54,95),(54,78,95)\}.$$

On the other hand, E is the set of states where it is in fact true that Carla received a higher score than Bob:
$$E = \{(95,54,78),(78,54,95),(54,78,95)\}.$$

Ann's updated beliefs after learning information F are given above in (7.4). Updating those beliefs by conditioning on E yields

$$\begin{pmatrix} (95,78,54) & (95,54,78) & (78,95,54) & (54,95,78) & (78,54,95) & (54,78,95) \\ 0 & 0 & 0 & 0 & \frac{1}{2} & \frac{1}{2} \end{pmatrix}$$

Clearly, this is the same as conditioning the initial beliefs on
$$E \cap F = \{(78,54,95),(54,78,95)\}.$$

Expressing all of this more succinctly, we have that the updated beliefs after learning F are as given in (7.5) above, namely

$$\begin{pmatrix} (78,95,54) & (54,95,78) & (78,54,95) & (54,78,95) \\ \frac{4}{8} & \frac{2}{8} & \frac{1}{8} & \frac{1}{8} \end{pmatrix}$$

and the final beliefs are obtained by conditioning these beliefs on E or, equivalently, by conditioning the initial beliefs on $E \cap F$:

$$\begin{pmatrix} (78,54,95) & (54,78,95) \\ \frac{1}{2} & \frac{1}{2} \end{pmatrix}.$$

> Test your understanding of the concepts introduced in this section, by going through the exercises in Section 7.4.1 at the end of this chapter.

7.3 The market for used cars

Akerlof's seminal paper studied the role of adverse selection in the market for used cars and showed that it can lead to considerable market inefficiencies. We will also take the market for used cars as our starting point. The model described in this section is a much simplified version of Akerlof's model: its purpose is to illustrate the phenomenon as simply as possible and it is not intended to be realistic.

Suppose that there are two groups of individuals in the population: Group S ('S' stands for potential 'seller') and Group B ('B' stands for potential 'buyer'). The number of individuals in Group B is at least as large as the number of individuals in Group S. Each Group-S individual owns a car, while no Group-B individual owns a car.

7.3 The market for used cars

Cars are of different qualities. Let there be n possible quality levels: $q_1, q_2, \ldots, q_n$ with q_i denoting a lower quality level than q_{i+1}, for every $i = 1, 2, \ldots, n-1$. We express this as follows:

$$q_1 \prec q_2 \prec \cdots \prec q_n. \tag{7.6}$$

We assume that each current owner of a car of quality q_i (a Group-S individual) considers owning that car to be just as good as having $\$S_{q_i}$; thus we can think of S_{q_i} as her reservation price for the car, in the sense that she would be happy to sell her car at any price $P > S_{q_i}$.[5] We call S_{q_i} *the value of a car of quality q_i to its initial owner*. Given the assumed ranking of possible qualities (see (7.6)), it is natural to postulate that higher-quality cars have a higher value to their owners than lower-quality cars, that is,

$$S_{q_1} < S_{q_2} < \cdots < S_{q_n}. \tag{7.7}$$

On the other side of the market, we assume that each individual within Group B considers becoming the owner of a car of quality q_i to be just as good as having $\$B_{q_i}$; thus we can think of B_{q_i} as his reservation price for such a car, in the sense that he would be happy to buy a car of quality q_i at any price $P < B_{q_i}$.[6] We call B_{q_i} *the value of a car of quality q_i to a Group-B individual*. Given the assumed ranking of possible qualities (see (7.6)), it is natural to postulate that higher-quality cars have a higher value to potential buyers than lower-quality cars, that is,

$$B_{q_1} < B_{q_2} < \cdots < B_{q_n}. \tag{7.8}$$

Now we introduce two crucial assumptions:

- For every quality level q_i ($i = 1, 2, \ldots, n$),

$$B_{q_i} > S_{q_i}. \tag{7.9}$$

This means that, for every car, there are potential gains from trade, in the sense that for a car of quality q_i there is a price P such that (1) an individual in Group B would be willing to pay $\$P$ for that car and (2) the owner of such a car (a Group-S individual) would be happy to sell at price P and (3) the trade would make each party better off (indeed this would be true for every P such that $S_{q_i} < P < B_{q_i}$).

---

[5] For example, the utility-of-money function of the owner of a car of quality q_i could be
$$U^S_{q_i}(m) = \begin{cases} m + S_{q_i} & \text{if she has a car of quality } q_i \\ m & \text{if she has no car} \end{cases}.$$ Let $\overline{m}$ be her initial endowment of money; then, since she owns a car of quality q_i her current utility is $\overline{m} + S_{q_i}$, while if she sells her car for $\$P$ then her utility is $\overline{m} + P$. Thus she is better off selling her car if and only if $P > S_{q_i}$ (and she is indifferent if $P = S_{q_i}$).

[6] For example, his utility-of-money function could be
$$U^B_{q_i}(m) = \begin{cases} m + B_{q_i} & \text{if he has a car of quality } q_i \\ m & \text{if he has no car} \end{cases}.$$ Let $\overline{m}$ be his initial endowment of money; then, since he currently does not own a car, his current utility is $\overline{m}$, while if he buys a car of quality q_i at price $\$P$ then his utility is $\overline{m} - P + B_{q_i}$. Thus he is better off buying such a car if and only if $P < B_{q_i}$ (and he is indifferent if $P = B_{q_i}$).

- Information about quality is asymmetric: each car-owner knows the quality of her own car (because she has had extensive experience with it and knows how well she took care of it), while a potential buyer is not able to determine the quality of a car by mere inspection.[7] Of course, a potential buyer can ask the owner what the quality of her car is, but the owner would have an incentive to claim that it is higher than it actually is, hoping to sell the car for a higher price.

By (7.9) the initial situation (where cars are currently in the hands of Group-S individuals) is *Pareto inefficient*: it would be a Pareto improvement to have each car sold to a Group-B individual (at an appropriate price). We now show that the postulated asymmetric information prevents the potential gains from trade from being realized, in the sense that some cars will remain in the "wrong hands", that is, in the hands of Group-S individuals.

The crucial observation is that, although Group-B individuals have different reservation prices for different quality levels, *there cannot be different prices on the market for cars of different qualities*, because buyers are unable to determine the quality of the cars that are offered for sale and thus would not know if they should pay a high price or a low price; furthermore, they realize that the owners of low-quality cars would have an incentive to claim that their cars are of high quality in order to obtain a higher price and thus any claims made by the sellers would have to be discarded as not credible. Hence *there can only be one price for all second-hand cars*.

Finally, we make two additional assumptions:

- The potential buyers (Group-B individuals) are risk neutral.[8]

- The potential buyers know, for every quality q_i, the fraction of cars of that quality within the total population of second-hand cars.[9] Denote that fraction by p_i (thus $0 < p_i < 1$). Hence, if a buyer were to be able to pick a second-hand car at random, the probability that he would end up with a car of quality q_i is p_i.

Let us begin with an example. Let there be six quality levels. For each quality level, the fraction of cars of that quality and the value of a car of that quality to its current owner and to a potential buyer is shown in the following table:

quality:	q_1	q_2	q_3	q_4	q_5	q_6
proportion:	$\frac{1}{12}$	$\frac{3}{12}$	$\frac{4}{12}$	$\frac{1}{12}$	$\frac{2}{12}$	$\frac{1}{12}$
value to current owner S_{q_i}:	\$900	\$1,800	\$2,700	\$3,600	\$4,500	\$5,400
value to potential buyer B_{q_i}:	\$1,000	\$2,000	\$3,000	\$4,000	\$5,000	\$6,000

---

[7] Some features of a car, such as mileage, exterior damage, etc., can be ascertained by a potential buyer upon inspection. Other features cannot: for example, whether it was driven with care, whether the car was affected by a flood or involved in an accident, etc. These are *hidden* features and it is natural to assume that they are known to the current owner, but cannot be ascertained by a potential buyer.

[8] We make this assumption in order to show that the inefficiencies that arise have nothing to do with the buyers being risk averse. An example where the buyers are risk averse is given in Exercise 7.10.

[9] Without this information, the potential buyers would find themselves in an even worse position.

7.3 The market for used cars

A naïve potential buyer would reason as follows (recall the assumption of risk neutrality):

"For me, picking a car at random corresponds to facing the money lottery

$$\begin{pmatrix} \$1{,}000 & \$2{,}000 & \$3{,}000 & \$4{,}000 & \$5{,}000 & \$6{,}000 \\ \frac{1}{12} & \frac{3}{12} & \frac{4}{12} & \frac{1}{12} & \frac{2}{12} & \frac{1}{12} \end{pmatrix} \qquad (7.10)$$

whose expected value is

$$\tfrac{1}{12}1000 + \tfrac{3}{12}2000 + \tfrac{4}{12}3000 + \tfrac{1}{12}4000 + \tfrac{2}{12}5000 + \tfrac{1}{12}6000 = 3{,}250.$$

Thus, as long as the price P of a second-hand car is less than \$3,250, I expect to make a positive net gain by buying a car."

Suppose that, in fact, the price of a second-hand car is \$3,000. Should the potential buyer decide to buy a car that is offered for sale at that price, expecting a gain of $\$(3{,}250 - 3{,}000) = \$250$? The answer is negative, because when the price is \$3,000 not every car will be offered for sale: the owners of cars of qualities q_4, q_5 and q_6 will not be willing to sell.[10] Thus only cars of qualities q_1, q_2 and q_3 will be offered for sale when the price is \$3,000, so that buying a car at that price means facing the following lottery, where the probabilities are obtained from (7.10) by conditioning on the event $\{q_1, q_2, q_3\}$:

$$\begin{pmatrix} \$1{,}000 & \$2{,}000 & \$3{,}000 \\ \frac{1}{8} & \frac{3}{8} & \frac{4}{8} \end{pmatrix} \qquad (7.11)$$

whose expected value is

$$\tfrac{1}{8}1000 + \tfrac{3}{8}2000 + \tfrac{4}{8}3000 = 2{,}375.$$

Thus the buyer would be paying \$3,000 expecting a benefit of only \$2,375! That is, buying a car for \$3,000 means facing an expected loss of \$625.

Might paying a price somewhat below \$2,375 be a good idea? For example, should the buyer be willing to pay \$2,000 for a second-hand car? The answer is again negative: when the price is \$2,000 the owners of cars of quality q_3 will drop out of the market (because they value their cars at \$2,700: more than the price) and thus buying a car for \$2,000 means facing the lottery[11]

$$\begin{pmatrix} \$1{,}000 & \$2{,}000 \\ \frac{1}{4} & \frac{3}{4} \end{pmatrix} \qquad (7.12)$$

whose expected value is

$$\tfrac{1}{4}1000 + \tfrac{3}{4}2000 = 1{,}750.$$

---

[10] Since, for $i = 3, 4, 5$, $S_{q_i} > 3{,}000$. That is, the owners have a reservation price that exceeds the market price and thus selling at that price would make them worse off.

[11] The probabilities are obtained from (7.10) by conditioning on the event $\{q_1, q_2\}$ or, equivalently, from (7.12) by conditioning on the event $\{q_1, q_2\}$.

Thus the buyer would be paying $2,000 expecting a benefit of only $1,750! That is, buying a car for $2,000 means facing an expected loss of $250.

It is only when the price P is in the range between $900 and $1,000, that buying a car at that price is rational for the buyer: when $900 < P < 1,000$ then only cars of the lowest quality, namely q_1, are offered for sale and the buyer knows this (such cars are referred to as "lemons"; hence the expression 'the market for lemons' used by Akerlof in his seminal paper). Thus in this example we have an extreme inefficiency: of all the used cars in existence, only the lowest-quality cars are being traded in the market, despite the fact that for every car that is not traded there is a potential buyer who would be willing to pay a price that exceeds the reservation price of the owner of that car.

We can now define what an equilibrium price in the market for used cars is in the presence of adverse selection.

> **Definition 7.3.1** A price P for used cars is an *equilibrium price* if there is an $m \in \{1, 2, \ldots, n\}$ such that
>
> 1. $S_{q_m} < P < S_{q_{m+1}}$.
>
> 2. $\mathbb{E}[L] > P$, where L is the money lottery

$$L = \begin{pmatrix} \$B_{q_1} & \cdots & \$B_{q_m} \\ \frac{p_1}{\sum_{i=1}^{m} p_i} & \cdots & \frac{p_m}{\sum_{i=1}^{m} p_i} \end{pmatrix}. \quad (7.13)$$

The first condition in Definition 7.3.1 says that at price P all the qualities $q_1, \ldots, q_m$ are offered for sale and none of the qualities above q_m are offered for sale.[12] Thus, conditioning on the fact that the qualities offered for sale are precisely $\{q_1, \ldots, q_m\}$ the buyer realizes that buying a used car at price P means facing the following money lottery in terms of potential net gain:

$$\begin{pmatrix} \$(B_{q_1} - P) & \cdots & \$(B_{q_m} - P) \\ \frac{p_1}{\sum_{i=1}^{m} p_i} & \cdots & \frac{p_m}{\sum_{i=1}^{m} p_i} \end{pmatrix} \quad (7.14)$$

whose expected value is $\mathbb{E}[L] - P$ where L is given by (7.13). Thus, condition 2 of Definition 7.3.1 says that every potential buyer expects to gain from purchasing a car that is offered for sale.

---

[12] Note that, by (7.7), (1) $S_{q_m} < P$ implies that, for every $i = 1, \ldots, m-1$, $S_{q_i} < P$ and (2) $S_{q_{m+1}} > P$ implies that, for every $i = m+2, \ldots, n$, $S_{q_i} > P$.

7.3 The market for used cars

The example analyzed above illustrates the logic of the adverse selection phenomenon, which is as follows. In order for all the used cars to be put up for sale, the price P must exceed the value of the top-quality car for the owner of such a car, that is, it must be that $P > S_{q_n}$. When all the used cars are offered for sale, a potential buyer faces the following lottery in terms of potential net gain:

$$\begin{pmatrix} \$(B_{q_1} - P) & \cdots & \$(B_{q_n} - P) \\ p_1 & \cdots & p_n \end{pmatrix} \tag{7.15}$$

whose expected value is $\left(p_1 B_{q_1} + \cdots + p_n B_{q_n}\right) - P$. Note that

$$\left(p_1 B_{q_1} + \cdots + p_n B_{q_n}\right) < B_{q_n}$$

(since it is a convex combination of all the values B_{q_i}, of which B_{q_n} is the largest). Our hypothesis is that $B_{q_n} > S_{q_n}$ and thus it is, in principle, possible that $\left(p_1 B_{q_1} + \cdots + p_m B_{q_n}\right) > S_{q_n}$, in which case one can find a price P such that

$$S_{q_n} < P < \left(p_1 B_{q_1} + \cdots + p_n B_{q_n}\right).$$

If that is the case, then at such a price all the cars would be traded and thus Pareto efficiency would be achieved. In the above example, on the other hand, we had that

$$\left(p_1 B_{q_1} + \cdots + p_n B_{q_n}\right) < S_{q_n} \tag{7.16}$$

and thus at any price P that would induce all the car-owners to offer their cars for sale (that is, at any P such that $P > S_{q_m}$) no potential buyer would be willing to buy, so that the highest-quality cars would not be traded, leading to a Pareto inefficient situation.

Then the reasoning can repeated for the case of all qualities but the top one being offered for sale. This would require a price P such that $S_{q_{n-1}} < P < S_{q_n}$. Then the lottery faced by a potential buyer contemplating buying a used car offered for sale would be

$$\begin{pmatrix} \$(B_{q_1} - P) & \cdots & \$(B_{q_{n-1}} - P) \\ p_1 & \cdots & p_{n-1} \end{pmatrix} \tag{7.17}$$

whose expected value is $\left(p_1 B_{q_1} + \cdots + p_{n-1} B_{q_{n-1}}\right) - P$. Again, the important observation is that $\left(p_1 B_{q_1} + \cdots + p_{n-1} B_{q_{n-1}}\right) < B_{q_{n-1}}$. Given our assumption that $B_{q_{n-1}} > S_{q_{n-1}}$ it is, in principle, possible that $\left(p_1 B_{q_1} + \cdots + p_{n-1} B_{q_{n-1}}\right) > S_{q_{n-1}}$, in which case one can find a price P such that $S_{q_{n-1}} < P < \left(p_1 B_{q_1} + \cdots + p_{n-1} B_{q_{n-1}}\right)$, in which case all the qualities except for the top one would be traded. However, it is also possible - as in our example above - that $\left(p_1 B_{q_1} + \cdots + p_{n-1} B_{q_{n-1}}\right) < S_{q_{n-1}}$, in which case there cannot be a price at which all the qualities up to q_{n-1} are traded. This argument can be repeated for every quality level. In the extreme case - as in our example above - the only possible equilibrium is one where only the lowest-quality cars are traded. Note that, given our assumptions (namely (7.9), in particular $S_{q_1} < B_{q_1}$), an equilibrium where only the lowest-quality cars are traded always exists: any price P such that $S_{q_1} < P < \min\{B_{q_1}, S_{q_2}\}$ would give rise to such an equilibrium.

Depending on the difference between the seller's value and the buyer's value of each quality many possibilities arise:

- If the difference is small - as in our example above - then it may be that the only possible equilibrium is one where only the lowest quality cars are traded. Thus this is a situation where the bad-quality cars drive the good-quality cars out of the market and the lack of trading for good-quality cars gives rise to a Pareto inefficiency.
- If the difference is somewhat large then there may be several possible equilibria that can be "Pareto ranked" in terms of efficiency (this is illustrated in the example below).
- If the difference is substantially large then among the possible equilibria there is also the most efficient one where all the cars are traded.

The following is an example of the second possibility listed above. Let there be three qualities: L (for 'low'), M (for 'medium') and H (for 'high'). The corresponding proportions and valuations are as shown in the following table:

quality:	L	M	H
fraction:	$\frac{1}{5}$	$\frac{3}{5}$	$\frac{1}{5}$
value to current owner:	$\$10,000$	$\$14,000$	$\$16,000$
value to potential buyer:	$\$12,000$	$\$15,000$	$\$18,000$

Let us see what values of P (the market price of a used car) give rise to an equilibrium.[13]

1. If $P > 16,000$ then all the cars will be offered for sale. A potential buyer then faces the following net-gain lottery if he buys a car:

$$\begin{pmatrix} \$(12,000-P) & \$(15,000-P) & \$(18,000-P) \\ \frac{1}{5} & \frac{3}{5} & \frac{1}{5} \end{pmatrix}$$

whose expected value is $15,000 - P < 0$. Thus there is no equilibrium at any such price.

2. If $14,000 < P \leq 16,000$ then only cars of qualities L and M are offered for sale. A potential buyer then faces the following net-gain lottery if he buys a car:

$$\begin{pmatrix} \$(12,000-P) & \$(15,000-P) \\ \frac{1}{4} & \frac{3}{4} \end{pmatrix}$$

whose expected value is $14,250 - P$. This is positive if and only if $P < 14,250$. Thus
- If $14,250 \leq P \leq 16,000$ there is no equilibrium at such price.
- If $14,000 < P < 14,250$ then, for every such price there is an equilibrium where all the L-quality and all the M-quality cars are traded, while the H-quality cars are not.

---

[13] We assume that, if indifferent between offering her car for sale and not offering it, the owner chooses *not* to offer it and, if indifferent between buying and not buying, the potential buyer chooses *not* to buy.

7.3 The market for used cars

3. If $10,000 < P \leq 14,000$ then only the L-cars are offered for sale, so that a potential buyer realizes that he would buy a car worth \$12,000 to him. Thus
   - If $12,000 \leq P \leq 14,000$ there is no equilibrium at such price.
   - If $10,000 < P < 12,000$ then, for every such price there is an equilibrium where all and only the L-quality cars are traded.

4. If $P \leq 10,000$ then no cars are offered for sale and thus there is no trading.

Clearly, the equilibria under Point 2 are Pareto superior to the equilibria under Point 3, since more cars are traded. None of them, however, is Pareto efficient, since the H-quality cars are not traded and remain "in the wrong hands".

7.3.1 Possible remedies

The root cause of the market inefficiency highlighted in the previous section is the asymmetric information between the seller (who is informed) and the buyer (who lacks information). Are there any solutions to this problem?

The owner of a good-quality car finds herself unable to sell her car because of the presence of low-quality cars in the market. Claiming (truthfully) that her car deserves a higher price because it is is of high quality is pointless, because every seller would want to imitate that claim (if seen to be successful). So any claims made by the seller have to be *credible*, not just "cheap talk". Is there a way to make the claim credible? The answer is affirmative and involves the notion of signalling, which will be covered in Chapter 9. Thus we postpone this discussion to Chapter 9, where we will consider warranties as signals of high quality.

While a seller's claims should be discarded as not credible, perhaps a knowledgeable third party, such as a mechanic, could be consulted to ascertain the quality of a car offered for sale. This solution, however, is problematic for a number of reasons. First of all, there is a moral hazard problem (the notion of moral hazard will be discussed in Chapter 10): would the mechanic have an incentive to do due diligence, that is, to thoroughly inspect the car? If the mechanic is paid a fixed fee then he might decide to save time and perform only a cursory inspection. Secondly, who would pay the mechanic's fee? If the fee is paid by the potential buyer, then sellers will not face any costs in claiming that their cars are of high quality and will thus have no disincentive to lie. On the other hand, if the fee is paid by the seller, then it could play the role of a signal (see Chapter 9) and be effective in separating high-quality cars from lower-quality ones. However, the buyer might be suspicious of a high-quality certification provided by a mechanic chosen by the seller, since there might be collusion between the two. On the other hand, the seller might be reluctant to let the buyer choose the mechanic, because the latter might be in cahoots with the former (the mechanic might certify the car to be of low quality, thus giving an excuse to the buyer not to buy, and then share the fee with the buyer).

7.3.2 Further remarks

One might wonder whether the phenomenon pointed out in this section, namely that "low-quality cars drive high-quality cars out of the market" applies also to *new* cars. The answer is negative: a dealership does not acquire, by use, knowledge of the quality of any given car (and thus cannot keep the better cars supplied by the manufacturers for itself and offer for sale the lower-quality ones); in other words, in the market for new cars there is no asymmetric information between buyer and seller. When buying a new car a buyer is just as likely to obtain an above-average-quality car as a below-average-quality car; hence new cars sell for a market price that reflects the average quality of all new cars: there is no adverse selection in the market for new cars.

One could object to the analysis of this section by pointing out that there are observable characteristics of used cars, such as mileage and age, that are easily verified by the buyer and can be the basis for price differences: typically, a 2014 Toyota Corolla will sell for a lower price than a 2018 Toyota Corolla, or a 2014 Toyota Corolla with 30,000 miles will sell for a higher price than a 2014 Toyota Corolla with 85,000 miles. The answer to this objection is that, indeed, observable differences can be associated with different prices, but within each category of car, e.g. a 2014 Toyota Corolla with approximately 80,000 miles, there typically are better cars and worse cars and information about the car's quality is asymmetric: the seller has that information, the buyer does not. Thus the "lemons problem" arises within each well-defined category of used car.

The adverse selection problem arises in many different markets. In this chapter we considered the market for used car, or - more generally - the market for durable goods. In the next chapter we will analyze adverse selection in the market for insurance. Stglitz and Weiss[14] suggested that adverse selection could be the cause of credit rationing in the market for unsecured loans, that is, loans for which the borrower cannot offer a collateral. Consider, for example, a bank that offers loans not knowing the credit worthiness of the borrowers: some borrowers are "good quality" in that they are low risk, either because they only borrow if they expect to be able to repay the loan and/or they plan to invest in a low-return but reasonably safe project, while other borrowers are "low quality" in that they are high risk, either because they borrow without worrying about defaulting and/or they plan to invest in high-return but high-risk projects. The low-risk types are more sensitive to increases in the rate of interest and drop out of the market when the rate of interest is high, while the high-risk types are less sensitive to increases in the rate of interest and continue to borrow even if the rate is high. In this case lenders might prefer to keep the rate of interest low, so as to have a better mix of "good" and "bad" types, even if at that low rate there is excess demand for loans. That is, if the bank faces excess demand for loans, it might prefer not to raise its interest rate to clear the market, because by doing so it would drive away some low-risk borrowers and increase the proportion of high-risk borrowers in the pool of applicants, thus facing a higher probability of defaulting borrowers.

> Test your understanding of the concepts introduced in this section, by going through the exercises in Section 7.4.2 at the end of this chapter.

---

[14] Stiglitz, Joseph and Andrew Weiss, "Credit rationing in markets with imperfect information", *The American Economic Review*, 1981, Vol. 71, pp. 393-410.

7.4 Exercises

The solutions to the following exercises are given in Section 7.5 at the end of this chapter.

7.4.1 Exercises for Section 7.2.2: Conditional probability and belief updating

Exercise 7.1 Consider the following probability distribution:

$$\begin{pmatrix} z_1 & z_2 & z_3 & z_4 & z_5 & z_6 & z_7 \\ \frac{3}{12} & \frac{1}{12} & 0 & \frac{3}{12} & \frac{2}{12} & 0 & \frac{3}{12} \end{pmatrix}.$$

What is the probability of the event $\{z_2, z_3, z_5, z_6, z_7\}$?

Exercise 7.2 Let the universal set be $U = \{z_1, z_2, z_3, z_4, z_5, z_6, z_7, z_8\}$.
Let $A = \{z_2, z_4, z_5, z_7\}$, $B = \{z_3, z_6, z_8\}$, $C = \{z_2, z_6\}$, $D = \{z_3, z_4\}$ and $E = \{z_7, z_8\}$.
You are given the following data: $P(A \cup B) = \frac{21}{24}$, $P(A \cap C) = \frac{5}{24}$, $P(B \cap C) = \frac{3}{24}$, $P(A \cap D) = \frac{2}{24}$, $P(B \cap D) = \frac{3}{24}$, $P(B) = \frac{7}{24}$ and $P(E) = \frac{2}{24}$.

(a) Find the probability $P(z_i)$ for each $i = 1, \ldots, 8$.

(b) Calculate $P((A \cup B) \cap (C \cup D))$.

Exercise 7.3 Let $U = \{a, b, c, d, e, f, g, h, i\}$ and consider the following probability distribution:

$$\begin{pmatrix} a & b & c & d & e & f & g & h & i \\ \frac{11}{60} & 0 & \frac{7}{60} & \frac{9}{60} & \frac{16}{60} & \frac{5}{60} & \frac{4}{60} & \frac{8}{60} & 0 \end{pmatrix}.$$

(a) Let $E = \{a, f, g, h, i\}$. What is the probability of E?

(b) List all the events that have probability 1.

Exercise 7.4 There is an urn with 40 balls: 4 red, 16 white, 10 blue and 10 black. You close your eyes and pick a ball at random. Let E be the event "the selected ball is either red or white".

(a) What is the probability of E?

(b) Now somebody tells you: "the ball in your hand is not black". How likely is it now that you picked either a red or a white ball?

Exercise 7.5 Suppose there are 3 individuals. It is known that one of them has a virus. A blood test can be performed to test for the virus. If an individual does have the virus, then the result of the test will be positive. However, the test will be positive also for an individual who does not have the virus but has a particular defective gene.

It is known that exactly one of the three individuals has this defective gene: it could be the same person who has the virus or somebody who does not have the virus. A positive test result will come up if and only if either the patient has the virus or the defective gene (or both).

Suppose that Individual 1 takes the blood test and the result is positive. Assuming that all the states are equally likely, what is the probability that he has the virus? [Hint: think of the universal set (or sample space) U as a list of states and each state tells you which individual has the virus and which individual has the defective gene.]

Exercise 7.6 In a remote rural clinic with limited resources, a patient arrives complaining of low-abdomen pain. Based on all the information available, the doctor thinks that there are only four possible causes: a bacterial infection (b), a viral infection (v), cancer (c), internal bleeding (i). Of the four, only the bacterial infection and internal bleeding are treatable at the clinic. In the past the doctor has seen 600 similar cases and they eventually turned out to be as follows:

b : bacterial infection	v : viral infection	c : cancer	i : internal bleeding
140	110	90	260

The doctor's probabilistic estimates are based on those past cases.

(a) What is the probability that the patient has a treatable disease?

There are two possible ways of gathering more information: a blood test and an ultrasound. A positive blood test will reveal that there is an infection, however it could be either bacterial or viral; a negative blood test rules out an infection and thus leaves cancer and internal bleeding as the only possibilities. The ultrasound, on the other hand, will reveal if there is internal bleeding.

(b) Suppose that the patient gets an ultrasound and it turns out that there is no internal bleeding. What is the probability that he does **not** have a treatable disease? What is the probability that he has cancer?

(c) If instead of getting the ultrasound he had taken the blood test and it had been positive, what would the probability that he had a treatable disease have been?

(d) Now let us go back to the hypothesis that the patient only gets the ultrasound and it turns out that there is no internal bleeding. He then asks the doctor: "if I were to take the blood test too (that is, in addition to the ultrasound), how likely is it that it would be positive?". What should the doctor's answer be?

(e) Finally, suppose that the patient gets both the ultrasound and the blood test and the ultrasound reveals that there is no internal bleeding, while the blood test is positive. How likely is it that he has a treatable disease?

7.4 Exercises

7.4.2 Exercises for Section 7.3: The market for used cars

Exercise 7.7 There are 200 cars in total. Cars are of different quality. Quality is measured in terms of the expected number of years of residual life of the car. Make use of the following information:

Quality:	4	8	10	16
Fraction of total number:	$\frac{1}{8}$	$\frac{3}{8}$	$\frac{2}{8}$	$\frac{2}{8}$
Value of car to current owner:	$2,000	$3,000	$4,000	$5,000

Fill in the following table:

If the price is:	Number of cars offered for sale	Average quality of cars offered for sale
$2,500		
$3,100		
$4,600		
$5,225		
$6,100		

Exercise 7.8 There are two groups of individuals. Group 1 individuals own cars, while Group 2 do not. There are four possible quality levels of cars as shown in the following table, together with the total number of cars of each quality.

Quality:	A	B	C	D
Number of cars:	1,000	2,000	1,000	4,000

The value that a Group-1 individual attaches to a car of a given quality is lower than the value of the same quality car to a Group-2 individual, as shown in the following table:

Quality:	A	B	C	D
Value to Group 1 individuals:	$5,400	$4,500	$3,600	$2,700
Value to Group 2 individuals:	$6,000	$5,000	$4,000	$3,000

The quality of a car is known to the owner but not to the prospective buyer. All individuals are risk-neutral.
  (a) Write the lottery for a Group-2 individual that corresponds to picking a car at random from the entire pool of cars and calculate the expected value.
  (b) Suppose that the price of a second-hand car is $3,800. Should a Group-2 individual be willing to buy a car at that price? Explain your answer.
  (c) Let P be the price at which second-hand cars are traded. What are the possible values of P such that, at that price, 4,000 cars are traded?

Exercise 7.9 Making use of the information in Exercise 7.8, for every positive price P determine if there is trading of second-hand cars at that price. Assume that, if indifferent between selling and not selling, a Group-1 individual would decide to sell and, if indifferent between buying and not buying, a Group-2 individual would decide to buy. ■

Exercise 7.10 Let the quality of a second-hand motorcycle be denoted by $\theta \in \{1,2,3\}$, where θ is the number of comprehensive tune-ups that the motorcycle received in the past. The owner knows the value of θ but a potential buyer does not. The value of a motorcycle of quality θ to the seller is $\$800\theta$. Each potential buyer has an initial wealth of $\$9,025$ and the utility of purchasing a motorcycle of quality θ at price P is $\sqrt{9,025-P+1,000\theta}$, while the utility of not buying is $\sqrt{9,025} = 95$. Let the proportion of motorcycles of each quality be as follows (where q is a number strictly between 0 and $\frac{1}{3}$):

$$\begin{pmatrix} \theta: & 1 & 2 & 3 \\ \text{proportion:} & q & \frac{2}{3}-q & \frac{1}{3} \end{pmatrix}.$$

Suppose that the price of a second-hand motorcycle is $P = \$1,744$. [In the following assume that, if indifferent between selling and not selling, the owner of a motorcycle would sell and, if indifferent between buying and not buying, a potential buyer would buy.]

(a) Are there values of q such that ALL motorcycles are traded?

(b) Are there values of q such that all motorcycles of quality $\theta = 1$ and $\theta = 2$ are traded?

(c) Are there values of q such that only motorcycles of quality $\theta = 1$ are traded?

■

Exercise 7.11 Suppose that you have just opened an all-you-can-eat buffet restaurant. The capacity of your restaurant is 50, that is, you can accommodate at most 50 customers. Suppose it costs $\$2$ to provide one serving of food (e.g. a standard-size plate). Assume that you are risk neutral. Each potential customer can be described by a pair (r,c) where r is the reservation price (the customer will come to your restaurant if and only if the admission price p is less than or equal to r) and c is the number of servings of food he/she consumes. There is a total of 240 potential customers. Their types and corresponding numbers are given in the following table:

Customer type:	($6,1)	($6,1.5)	($6.50,1.5)	($6.50,2.2)	($7,2.2)	($7,3.5)
Number:	20	20	40	60	40	60

What price should you charge if you want to maximize your profits? ■

7.5 Solutions to Exercises

Solution to Exercise 7.1.

$$P(\{z_2, z_3, z_5, z_6, z_7\}) = \sum_{i \in \{2,3,5,6,7\}} P(z_i) = \frac{1}{12} + 0 + \frac{2}{12} + 0 + \frac{3}{12} = \frac{1}{2}.$$

$\square$

Solution to Exercise 7.2.

(a) Since $\{z_1\}$ is the complement of $A \cup B$, $P(z_1) = 1 - \frac{21}{24} = \frac{3}{24}$.

Since $\{z_2\} = A \cap C$, $P(z_2) = \frac{5}{24}$.

Similarly, $P(z_6) = P(B \cap C) = \frac{3}{24}$, $P(z_3) = P(B \cap D) = \frac{3}{24}$ and $P(z_4) = P(A \cap D) = \frac{2}{24}$.

Thus, $P(z_8) = P(B) - P(z_3) - P(z_6) = \frac{7}{24} - \frac{3}{24} - \frac{3}{24} = \frac{1}{24}$.

Hence, $P(z_7) = P(E) - P(z_8) = \frac{2}{24} - \frac{1}{24} = \frac{1}{24}$.

Finally, $P(z_5) = 1 - \sum_{i \neq 5} P(z_i) = \frac{6}{24}$. Thus, the probability distribution is:

$$\begin{pmatrix} z_1 & z_2 & z_3 & z_4 & z_5 & z_6 & z_7 & z_8 \\ \frac{3}{24} & \frac{5}{24} & \frac{3}{24} & \frac{2}{24} & \frac{6}{24} & \frac{3}{24} & \frac{1}{24} & \frac{1}{24} \end{pmatrix}$$

(b) $A \cup B = \{z_2, z_3, z_4, z_5, z_6, z_7, z_8\}$, $C \cup D = \{z_2, z_3, z_4, z_6\}$.

Hence, $(A \cup B) \cap (C \cup D) = C \cup D = \{z_2, z_3, z_4, z_6\}$

so $P((A \cup B) \cap (C \cup D)) = P(z_2) + P(z_3) + P(z_4) + P(z_6) = \frac{5}{24} + \frac{3}{24} + \frac{2}{24} + \frac{3}{24} = \frac{13}{24}$.

$\square$

Solution to Exercise 7.3.

The probability distribution is:

$$\begin{pmatrix} a & b & c & d & e & f & g & h & i \\ \frac{11}{60} & 0 & \frac{7}{60} & \frac{9}{60} & \frac{16}{60} & \frac{5}{60} & \frac{4}{60} & \frac{8}{60} & 0 \end{pmatrix}.$$

(a) Let $E = \{a, f, g, h, i\}$.

Then $P(E) = P(a) + P(f) + P(g) + P(h) + P(i) = \frac{11}{60} + \frac{5}{60} + \frac{4}{60} + \frac{8}{60} + 0 = \frac{28}{60} = \frac{7}{15}$.

(b) The probability-1 events are: $\{a, c, d, e, f, g, h\} = U \setminus \{b, i\}$, $\{a, b, c, d, e, f, g, h\} = U \setminus \{i\}$, $\{a, c, d, e, f, g, h, i\} = U \setminus \{b\}$ and $\{a, b, c, d, e, f, g, h, i\} = U$.

$\square$

Solution to Exercise 7.4.

(a) $P(E) = \frac{4+16}{40} = \frac{1}{2}$.

(b) Let F be the event "the selected ball is not black". Then, initially, $P(F) = \frac{30}{40} = \frac{3}{4}$. Furthermore, $E \cap F = E$. Thus, $P(E|F) = \frac{P(E \cap F)}{P(F)} = \frac{P(E)}{P(F)} = \frac{\frac{1}{2}}{\frac{3}{4}} = \frac{2}{3}$. □

Solution to Exercise 7.5.

First we list the possible states. A state is a complete description of the external facts that are relevant: it tells you who has the virus and who has the gene. Let us represent a state as a pair (x, y) interpreted as follows: individual x has the virus and individual y has the defective gene.

Then $U = \{a = (1,1), b = (1,2), c = (1,3), d = (2,1), e = (2,2),$
$f = (2,3), g = (3,1), h = (3,2), i = (3,3)\}$.

Let V_1 be the event "Individual 1 has the virus". Then $V_1 = \{a, b, c\}$.

Let G_1 be the event "Individual 1 has the defective gene". Then $G_1 = \{a, d, g\}$.

Since every state is assumed to have probability $\frac{1}{9}$, $P(V_1) = P(G_1) = \frac{1}{9} + \frac{1}{9} + \frac{1}{9} = \frac{1}{3}$. Let 1_+ be the event that a blood test administered to Individual 1 comes up positive. Then $1_+ = \{a, b, c, d, g\}$ and $P(1_+) = \frac{5}{9}$.

We can now compute the requested conditional probability (note that $V_1 \cap 1_+ = V_1$):

$$P(V_1|1_+) = \frac{P(V_1 \cap 1_+)}{P(1_+)} = \frac{P(V_1)}{P(1_+)} = \frac{\frac{1}{3}}{\frac{5}{9}} = \frac{3}{5} = 60\%.$$

□

Solution to Exercise 7.6. The probabilities are as follows:

b	v	c	i
$\frac{140}{600} = \frac{14}{60}$	$\frac{110}{600} = \frac{11}{60}$	$\frac{90}{600} = \frac{9}{60}$	$\frac{260}{600} = \frac{26}{60}$

(a) The event that the patient has a treatable disease is $\{b, i\}$.
$P(\{b,i\}) = P(b) + P(i) = \frac{14}{60} + \frac{26}{60} = \frac{2}{3}$.

(b) A negative result of the ultrasound is represented by the event $\{b, v, c\}$. A non-treatable disease is the event $\{v, c\}$. Thus,

$$P(\{v,c\}|\{b,v,c\}) = \frac{P(\{v,c\} \cap \{b,v,c\})}{P(\{b,v,c\})} = \frac{P(\{v,c\})}{P(\{b,v,c\})} = \frac{\frac{11}{60} + \frac{9}{60}}{\frac{14}{60} + \frac{11}{60} + \frac{9}{60}} = \frac{10}{17} = 58.82\%.$$

$$P(c|\{b,v,c\}) = \frac{P(c)}{P(\{b,v,c\})} = \frac{\frac{9}{60}}{\frac{14}{60} + \frac{11}{60} + \frac{9}{60}} = \frac{9}{34} = 26.47\%.$$

(c) A positive blood test is represented by the event $\{b, v\}$. A treatable disease is the event $\{b, i\}$. Thus,

$$P(\{b,i\}|\{b,v\}) = \frac{P(\{b,i\} \cap \{b,v\})}{P(\{b,v\})} = \frac{P(b)}{P(\{b,v\})} = \frac{\frac{14}{60}}{\frac{14}{60} + \frac{11}{60}} = \frac{14}{25} = 56\%.$$

7.5 Solutions to Exercises

(d) Here we want

$$P(\{b,v\}|\{b,v,c\}) = \frac{P(\{b,v\})}{P(\{b,v,c\})} = \frac{\frac{14}{60} + \frac{11}{60}}{\frac{14}{60} + \frac{11}{60} + \frac{9}{60}} = \frac{25}{34} = 73.53\%.$$

(e) We are conditioning on $\{b,v\} \cap \{b,v,c\} = \{b,v\}$; thus, we want $P(\{b,i\}|\{b,v\})$ which was calculated in Part (c) as $\frac{14}{25} = 56\%$. □

Solution to Exercise 7.7.

If the price is:	Number of cars offered for sale	Average quality of cars offered for sale
$2,500	$\frac{1}{8}200 = 25$	4
$3,100	$\frac{4}{8}200 = 100$	$\frac{1}{4}4 + \frac{3}{4}8 = 7$
$4,600	$\frac{6}{8}200 = 150$	$\frac{1}{6}4 + \frac{3}{6}8 + \frac{2}{6}10 = 8$
$5,225	200	$\frac{1}{8}4 + \frac{3}{8}8 + \frac{2}{8}10 + \frac{2}{8}16 = 10$
$6,100	200	$\frac{1}{8}4 + \frac{3}{8}8 + \frac{2}{8}10 + \frac{2}{8}16 = 10$

□

Solution to Exercise 7.8.

(a) The lottery is $\begin{pmatrix} \$6,000 & \$5,000 & \$4,000 & \$3,000 \\ \frac{1}{8} & \frac{2}{8} & \frac{1}{8} & \frac{4}{8} \end{pmatrix}$. The expected value is 4,000.

(b) No, because if the price is $3,800, only owners of cars of quality C and D will offer their cars for sale and thus buying a car means facing the lottery $\begin{pmatrix} \$4,000 & \$3,000 \\ \frac{1}{5} & \frac{4}{5} \end{pmatrix}$, whose expected value is $3,200, less than the price of $3,800.

(c) Any price P such that $\$2,700 < P < \$3,000$ would lead to all and only cars of quality D being traded and thus 4,000 cars. □

Solution to Exercise 7.9.

- If $P \geq 5,400$ then every car will be offered for sale, but then - as calculated in Part (a) of Exercise 7.8 - a potential buyer would be facing a lottery whose expected value is less than the price (namely $4,000) and thus would not be willing to buy. Thus if $P \geq 5,400$ there is no trading.

- If $4,500 \leq P < 5,400$ then only cars of qualities B, C and D will be offered for sale. Thus a potential buyer would be facing the lottery $\begin{pmatrix} \$5,000 & \$4,000 & \$3,000 \\ \frac{2}{7} & \frac{1}{7} & \frac{4}{7} \end{pmatrix}$, whose expected value is $3,714.29, less than the price, and thus would not be willing to buy. Hence if $4,500 \leq P < 5,400$ there is no trading.

- If $3,600 \leq P < 4,500$ then only cars of qualities C and D will be offered for sale. Thus a potential buyer would be facing the lottery $\begin{pmatrix} \$4,000 & \$3,000 \\ \frac{1}{5} & \frac{4}{5} \end{pmatrix}$, whose expected value is \$3,200, less than the price. Thus if $3,600 \leq P < 4,500$ there is no trading.

- If $2,700 \leq P < 3,600$ then only cars of qualities D will be offered for sale and thus a potential buyer realizes that she would be buying a car worth \$3,000 to her. Hence
    - If $3,000 < P < 3,600$ then potential buyers are not willing to buy and thus there is no trading.
    - If $2,700 \leq P \leq 3,000$ then all (and only) the cars of quality D are traded.

- If $P < 2,700$ no cars will be offered for sale and thus there is no trading. □

Solution to Exercise 7.10.

(a) Since the owner of a motorcycle of quality $\theta = 3$ values the motorcycle at \$2,400, when $P = \$1,744$ she will not be willing to sell. Hence the answer is No.

(b) The owner of a motorcycle of quality $\theta = 1$ values it at \$800 and the owner of a motorcycle of quality $\theta = 2$ values it at \$1,600; hence both qualities will be offered for sale when the price is \$1,744 (but not those of quality $\theta = 3$). Thus, in terms of quality, the buyer faces the following lottery:[15]

$$\begin{pmatrix} \theta = 1 & \theta = 2 \\ \frac{3}{2}q & 1 - \frac{3}{2}q \end{pmatrix}$$

which corresponds to the money lottery

$$\begin{pmatrix} \$(9,025 - 1,744 + 1,000) & \$(9,025 - 1,744 + 2,000) \\ \frac{3}{2}q & 1 - \frac{3}{2}q \end{pmatrix}$$

whose expected utility is:

$$\tfrac{3}{2}q\sqrt{8,281} + \left(1 - \tfrac{3}{2}q\right)\sqrt{9,281} = 136.5q + 96.34 - 144.51q = 96.34 - 8.01q.$$

The buyer will be willing to buy if $96.34 - 8.01q \geq \sqrt{9025} = 95$, that is, if $q \leq 0.1965$. So the answer is: Yes all the values of $q \leq 0.1673$.

(c) No. If $q \leq 0.1673$ then both qualities $\theta = 1$ and $\theta = 2$ are traded and if $q > 0.1673$ then both qualities $\theta = 1$ and $\theta = 2$ are offered for sale, but buyers are not willing to buy.

---

[15] By the conditional probability rule, $P(\theta = 1 | \{\theta = 1, \theta = 2\}) = \frac{q}{q + \frac{2}{3} - q} = \frac{3}{2}q$ and $P(\theta = 2 | \{\theta = 1, \theta = 2\}) = \frac{\frac{2}{3} - q}{q + \frac{2}{3} - q} = 1 - \frac{3}{2}q$.

7.5 Solutions to Exercises

Solution to Exercise 7.11. First of all, let us convert numbers into proportions:

Customer type:	($6, 1)	($6, 1.5)	($6.50, 1.5)	($6.50, 2.2)	($7, 2.2)	($7, 3.5)
Proportion:	$\frac{1}{12}$	$\frac{1}{12}$	$\frac{2}{12}$	$\frac{3}{12}$	$\frac{2}{12}$	$\frac{3}{12}$

Secondly, note that it cannot be profit maximizing to charge a price different from either $6 or $6.50 or $7.[16]

- If you charge $6 then all the 240 people are interested in eating at your restaurant. You will only be able to accommodate 50 of them. Assuming that the order of arrival is random, the probability that a served customer is of any given type coincides with the fraction of that type in the population. Thus letting in any one customer corresponds to playing the following "consumption" lottery:

consumption:	1	1.5	2.2	3.5
probability:	$\frac{1}{12}$	$\frac{1}{12}+\frac{2}{12}=\frac{3}{12}$	$\frac{3}{12}+\frac{2}{12}=\frac{5}{12}$	$\frac{3}{12}$

whose expected value is $\frac{1}{12}1 + \frac{3}{12}(1.5) + \frac{5}{12}(2.2) + \frac{3}{12}(3.5) = 2.25$. Hence the expected cost of a single customer is $(2 \times 2.25) = \$4.50$ so that the expected profit from a single customer is $(6 - 4.50) = \$1.50$. Hence your total expected profit is $(1.50 \times 50) = \boxed{\$75}$.

- If you charge $6.50 then only $\frac{10}{12}$ of the potential customers are interested in eating at your restaurant, for a total of $\frac{10}{12}240 = 200$: still more than you can accommodate. Assuming, again, that the order of arrival is random, the probability that a served customer is of any given type coincides with the fraction of that type in the population *of interested customers*. Applying the conditional probability rule, their types and (updated) proportions are:

Customer type:	(6.50, 1.5)	(6.50, 2.2)	(7, 2.2)	(7, 3.5)
Fraction:	$\frac{2}{10}$	$\frac{3}{10}$	$\frac{2}{10}$	$\frac{3}{10}$

Thus, letting in any one customer corresponds to playing the following consumption lottery:

consumption:	1.5	2.2	3.5
probability	$\frac{2}{10}$	$\frac{3}{10}+\frac{2}{10}=\frac{5}{10}$	$\frac{3}{10}$

whose expected value is 2.45. Hence the expected cost of a single customer is $(2 \times 2.45) = \$4.90$ so that the expected profit from a single customer is $(6.50 - 4.90) = \$1.60$. Hence your total expected profit is $(1.60 \times 50) = \boxed{\$80}$.

---

[16] For example, if you charge $5.50 then your revenue will be $(5.50 \times 50) = \$275$ and if you increase your price to $6 then it will still be the case that at least 50 customers want to enter your restaurant and your revenue will increase to $(6 \times 50) = \$300$.

- If you charge $7 then only $\frac{5}{12}$ of the potential customers are interested in eating at your restaurant, for a total of $\frac{5}{12}240 = 100$: still more than you can accommodate. Applying the conditional probability rule, their types and (updated) proportions are:

$$\begin{array}{c|cc} \text{Customer type:} & (7, 2.2) & (7, 3.5) \\ \text{Fraction:} & \frac{2}{5} & \frac{3}{5} \end{array}$$

Thus, letting in any one customer corresponds to playing the following consumption lottery:

$$\begin{array}{cc} \text{consumption:} & 2.2 \quad 3.5 \\ \text{probability:} & \frac{2}{5} \quad \frac{3}{5} \end{array}$$

whose expected value is 2.98. Hence the expected cost of a single customer is $\$(2 \times 2.98) = \$5.96$ so that the expected profit from a single customer is $\$(7 - 5.96) = \$1.04$. Hence your total expected profit is $\$(1.04 \times 50) = \boxed{\$52}$.

Thus the profit-maximizing price is $6.50. □

8. Adverse Selection in Insurance

8.1 Adverse selection in insurance markets

As we noted in the previous chapter, the phenomenon of adverse selection arises naturally in the context of insurance: the insurance company (the seller of insurance) is typically aware of the fact that there are individuals who – because of their family history – are at a higher risk of developing a condition that requires extensive medical services, while other individuals represent a lower risk. If the insurance company offers a contract that would, on average, cover its expected costs *if everybody (high-risk and low-risk individuals) were to purchase that contract*, it might discover that its costs are much higher than expected, because only the high-risk individuals ended up purchasing the contract.

In Chapter 5 we considered the case of only one type of individual, with a constant probability of loss. In Chapter 10 we will consider the case where the probability of loss is affected by the individual's behavior: a situation referred to as "moral hazard". In this chapter we will continue to assume that the probability of loss is *constant*, that is, not affected by the individual's behavior, but we will consider the case where there are *different types of individuals*, each type with a different probability of loss. In the case of two types, one type has a higher probability of loss and will be called the high-risk type and the other will be called the low-risk type. There is uncertainty on the part of the insurance company due to do *the insurance company's inability to tell high-risk from low-risk individuals apart* (while being fully aware that it faces two different types of potential customers).

8.2 Two types of customers

Suppose that there are two types of individuals. They are all identical in terms of initial wealth, denoted by W_0, and in terms of the potential loss that they face, denoted by ℓ (with $0 < \ell \leq W_0$). They also have the same vNM utility-of-money function $U(m)$. What they differ in is the probability of loss: it is p_H for type-H (= high-risk) individuals and p_L for type-L (= low-risk) individuals, with

$$0 < p_L < p_H < 1.$$

It follows that type-H individuals have steeper indifference curves than type-L individuals, as shown in Figure 8.1. In fact, fix an arbitrary point $C = (W_1^C, W_2^C)$ in the wealth plane. The slope of the indifference curve going through this point is

$$-\frac{p_H}{1-p_H}\frac{U'(W_1^C)}{U'(W_2^C)} \quad \text{for type-H individuals}$$

and

$$-\frac{p_L}{1-p_L}\frac{U'(W_1^C)}{U'(W_2^C)} \quad \text{for type-L individuals.}$$

Since $p_L < p_H$,

$$\frac{p_L}{1-p_L} < \frac{p_H}{1-p_H}.$$

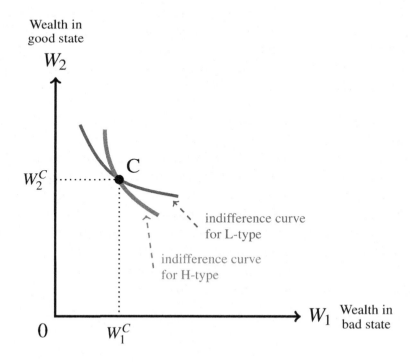

Figure 8.1: The indifference curve through point C for type-H is steeper than the indifference curve through point C for type-L.

8.2 Two types of customers

Since the H-type indifference curve is steeper than the L-type indifference curve at any point, this must be true also at the no-insurance point, that is, the reservation indifference curve for the H-type is steeper than the reservation indifference curve for the L-type, as shown in Figure 8.2.[1]

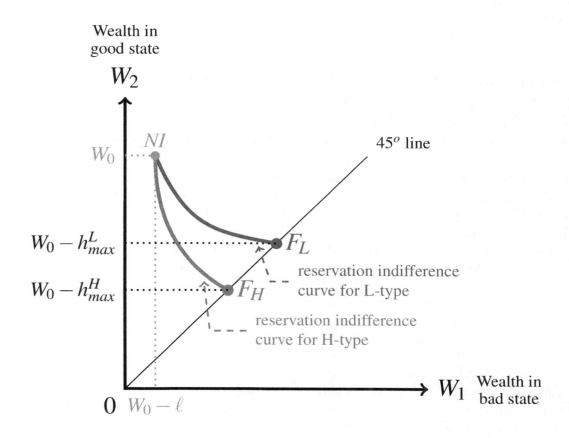

Figure 8.2: The reservation indifference curve of an H-type is steeper than the reservation indifference curve of an L-type.

It follows that the maximum premium that the L-type individuals are willing to pay for full insurance, denoted by h^L_{max}, is smaller than the maximum premium that the H-type individuals are willing to pay for full insurance, denoted by h^H_{max}: $h^L_{max} < h^H_{max}$, as shown in Figure 8.2. Letting F_L be the full-insurance contract that the L-type individuals consider to be just as good as no insurance and F_H the full-insurance contract that the H-type individuals consider to be just as good as no insurance, we have that $F_L = \left(W_0 - h^L_{max}, W_0 - h^L_{max}\right)$ and $F_H = \left(W_0 - h^H_{max}, W_0 - h^H_{max}\right)$, with $W_0 - h^L_{max} > W_0 - h^H_{max}$.

---

[1] Recall that the reservation indifference curve is defined to be the indifference curve that goes through the no-insurance point NI.

Let $N_H > 0$ be the number of H-type individuals in the population and $N_L > 0$ be the number of L-type individuals and define

$$q_H = \frac{N_H}{N_H + N_L} \quad \text{so that} \quad 1 - q_H = \frac{N_L}{N_H + N_L}. \tag{8.1}$$

Then $0 < q_H < 1$ and $0 < 1 - q_H < 1$.

8.2.1 The contracts offered by a monopolist who can tell individuals apart

As a benchmark, we shall first consider the case of a monopolist who is able to tell whether an individual who applies for insurance is an H-type or and L-type. For example, a health insurance company might be legally allowed to require applicants to submit to a DNA test that reveals whether a defective gene is present, in which case the individual is more likely to develop a particular disease requiring extensive medical care.

In the perfect-information case, from the point of view of the monopolist there are effectively two separate insurance markets: one for the H-types and one for the L-types. Then we can apply the analysis of Chapter 5 (Section 5.2.1) and conclude that the monopolist would offer the full-insurance contract F_L to type-L individuals and the full-insurance contract F_H to type-H individuals so that its expected profits would be[2]

$$\text{total profits:} \quad \left(h_{max}^H - p_H \ell\right) N_H + \left(h_{max}^L - p_L \ell\right) N_L \tag{8.2}$$

$$\text{profit per customer:} \quad \left(h_{max}^H - p_H \ell\right) q_H + \left(h_{max}^L - p_L \ell\right) (1 - q_H). \tag{8.3}$$

Which type of individual is "better" for the insurance company, that is, which type yields higher profits? The H-type is better in that she is willing to pay a higher premium for full insurance, but on the other hand she will submit a claim with higher probability, that is, the H-type yields higher revenue but also higher cost. Thus, in principle, either type could be more profitable. The answer depends on the specific values of the parameters.

For example, suppose that initial wealth is $W_0 = 3,600$, potential loss is $\ell = 2,000$ and the utility-of-money function is $U(m) = \sqrt{m}$.

- Let $p_L = \frac{1}{10}$ and $p_H = \frac{4}{10}$. To find h_{max}^L solve the equation

$$\frac{1}{10}\sqrt{1,600} + \frac{9}{10}\sqrt{3,600} = \sqrt{W}.$$

The solution is $W = 3,364$ so that $h_{max}^L = 3,600 - 3,364 = \$236$ and thus the expected profit from an L-type is

$$236 - \frac{1}{10}(2,000) = \$36.$$

To find h_{max}^H solve the equation

$$\frac{4}{10}\sqrt{1,600} + \frac{6}{10}\sqrt{3,600} = \sqrt{W}.$$

---

[2] To obtain profit per customer from total profits, divide by $(N_H + N_L)$ and use (8.1).

The solution is $W = 2,704$ so that $h^H_{max} = 3,600 - 2,704 = \$896$ and thus the expected profit from an H-type is

$$896 - \frac{4}{10}(2,000) = \$96.$$

Thus in this case insuring an H-type is more profitable than insuring an L-type.

- Let $p_L = \frac{3}{10}$ and $p_H = \frac{8}{10}$. To find h^L_{max} solve the equation

$$\frac{3}{10}\sqrt{1,600} + \frac{7}{10}\sqrt{3,600} = \sqrt{W}.$$

The solution is $W = 2,916$ so that $h^L_{max} = 3,600 - 2,916 = \$684$ and thus the expected profit from an L-type is

$$684 - \frac{3}{10}(2,000) = \$84.$$

To find h^H_{max} solve the equation

$$\frac{8}{10}\sqrt{1,600} + \frac{2}{10}\sqrt{3,600} = \sqrt{W}.$$

The solution is $W = 1,936$ so that $h^H_{max} = 3,600 - 1,936 = \$1,664$ and thus the expected profit from an H-type is

$$1,664 - \frac{8}{10}(2,000) = \$64.$$

Thus in this case insuring an L-type is more profitable than insuring an H-type.

Test your understanding of the concepts introduced in this section, by going through the exercises in Section 8.5.1 at the end of this chapter.

8.3 The monopolist under asymmetric information

We now turn to the case of asymmetric information, where each individual knows her own probability of loss, but the monopolist only knows that there are N_H high-risk individuals with probability of loss p_H and N_L low-risk individuals with probability of loss p_L.

We will consider three options for the monopolist:

Option 1. Cater only to the high-risk individuals by offering one insurance contract, designed in such a way that only the H-type will purchase it.

Option 2. Cater to both types of individuals, by offering one insurance contract that is attractive to both the L-type and the H-type.

Option 3. Offer a menu of two contracts: one – call it C_H – targeted to the H-type and the other – call it C_L – targeted to the L-type.

The shaded area in left pane of Figure 8.3 shows the set of insurance contracts that are attractive to the H-type, in that they yield at least the reservation utility to this type of individuals, while the shaded area in right pane shows the set of insurance contracts that are attractive to the L-type, in that they yield at least the reservation utility to this type of individuals. It is clear from Figure 8.3 that if an insurance contract is attractive to an L-type then it is also attractive to an H-type.

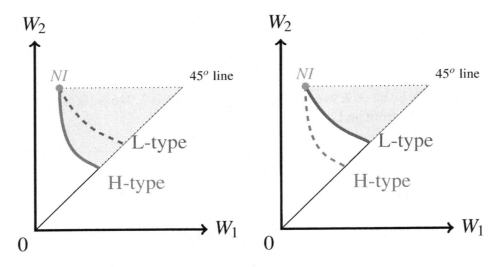

Figure 8.3: The shaded area in the left pane shows the set of insurance contracts that are acceptable to the H-type; the shaded area in the right pane shows the set of insurance contracts that are acceptable to the L-type.

8.3.1 The monopolist's profit under Option 1

If the monopolist chooses Option 1 then it will offer a contract that lies in the shaded area shown in Figure 8.4: the area between the two reservation indifference curves.

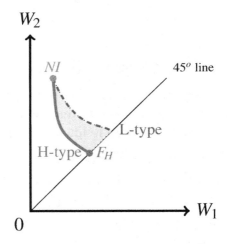

Figure 8.4: Contracts in the shaded area are acceptable to the H-type but not to the L-type.

8.3 The monopolist under asymmetric information

Under Option 1, the monopolist caters only to one type of individuals, namely the H-type, and thus we can use the analysis of Chapter 5 (Section 5.2.1) and conclude that, in order to maximize its profits, it will offer the full-insurance contract that leaves the H-type indifferent between insuring and not insuring (shown as point F_H in Figure 8.4). Let h_{max}^H be the premium of this contract. Then the monopolist's total profits under Option 1, denoted by π_1, will be

$$\pi_1 = N_H \left(h_{max}^H - p_H \ell \right). \tag{8.4}$$

For example, if the individuals' initial wealth is $W_0 = 3,600$, the potential loss is $\ell = 2,000$, the utility-of-money function is $U(m) = \sqrt{m}$ and $p_H = \frac{8}{10}$, then, as calculated at the end of the previous section, $h_{max}^H = \$1,664$ and the expected profit from a single contract would be $1,664 - \frac{8}{10}(2,000) = \$64$, so that total profits would be $\$64 N_H$.

8.3.2 The monopolist's profit under Option 2

If the monopolist chooses Option 2 then it will offer a contract that lies in the shaded area shown in the right pane of Figure 8.3: the area on and above the reservation indifference curve of the L-type. Which of these contracts maximizes the monopolist's profits?

One might be tempted to infer from the analysis of Chapter 5 that the monopolist would offer the full-insurance contract at the intersection of the reservation indifference curve of the L-type and the 45° line. However this conclusion is not correct: the monopolist – under Option 2 – would prefer to offer (to everybody) a *partial*-insurance contract.

To see this, recall the reasoning developed in Chapter 5: the crucial step in that reasoning was to note that, at any point *not* on the 45° line, the reservation indifference curve of the L-type is steeper than the isoprofit line with slope $-\frac{p_L}{1-p_L}$, so that there are points to the right of the point under consideration which represent contracts that are acceptable to the L-type and yield higher profit to the insurer *if sold only to the L-types*. In other words, the line with slope $-\frac{p_L}{1-p_L}$ is a relevant isoprofit line only under the assumption that the insurer is dealing only with L-type individuals. However, as remarked above, *any contract that is acceptable to an L-type is also acceptable to an H-type* and thus offering such a contract implies that the expected profit from this contract is **not** $[h - p_L(\ell - d)]$ (where h is the premium and d the deductible), because the probability of receiving a claim from a customer should reflect the fact that some customers are L-types and others are H-types.

This is the essence of the notion of adverse selection: the contract that is offered determines the composition of the pool of applicants: if the insurer offers the full insurance contract with premium h_{max}^H determined in Section 8.3.1, then the pool of applicants will consist entirely of H-types, while if the insurer offers a contract that is acceptable to the L-types then the pool of applicants will consist of all the individuals, L-types and H-types.

What is the probability of receiving a claim from a customer if the insurance contract is purchased by both types? Recall that q_H is the fraction of individuals in the population who are H-types (and $(1-q_H)$ is the fraction of L-types; see (8.1) on page 256). Thus we can take q_H as the probability that any particular customer taken from the set of customers who submit a claim is an H-type (and $(1-q_H)$ as the probability that she is an L-type). Thus the expected profit from a contract with premium h and deductible d which is purchased by both types is:

$$h - [q_H p_H(\ell-d) + (1-q_H)p_L(\ell-d)] = h - [q_H p_H + (1-q_H)p_L](\ell-d). \quad (8.5)$$

We call the number $[q_H p_H + (1-q_H)p_L]$ the *average probability of loss* and denote it by $\bar{p}$:

$$\text{average probability of loss:} \quad \bar{p} = q_H p_H + (1-q_H)p_L. \quad (8.6)$$

Note that, since $p_L < p_H$ and $0 < q_H < 1$,

$$p_L < \bar{p} < p_H. \quad (8.7)$$

Thus when both types are insured with the same contract, the relevant isoprofit line is a straight line with slope $-\frac{\bar{p}}{1-\bar{p}}$; we call isoprofit lines with this slope *average isoprofit lines*. It follows from (8.7) that

$$\frac{p_L}{1-p_L} < \frac{\bar{p}}{1-\bar{p}} < \frac{p_H}{1-p_H}. \quad (8.8)$$

Of course, it is still true that at a point on the 45° line the slope of the L-type indifference curve is $-\frac{p_L}{1-p_L}$; however the straight line with this slope is no longer a relevant isoprofit line: the relevant isoprofit line has a slope of $-\frac{\bar{p}}{1-\bar{p}}$ and is thus steeper than the L-type indifference curve at that point. Figure 8.5 shows this for the reservation indifference curve of the L-type.

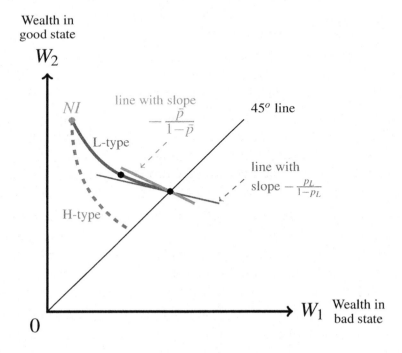

Figure 8.5: The reservation indifference curve of the L-type is less steep, at a point on the 45° line, than the average isoprofit line, whose slope is $-\frac{\bar{p}}{1-\bar{p}}$.

8.3 The monopolist under asymmetric information

Given the relative slope of the L-type reservation indifference curve and the average isoprofit line at a full-insurance contract, such a contract cannot be profit-maximizing under Option 2: there will be contracts to the left of it (thus partial-insurance contracts) that are acceptable to the L-type (and thus to both types) and are below that average isoprofit line (and thus yield higher expected profits). Of course, this argument applies to any contract where the average isoprofit line is steeper than the L-type reservation indifference curve. Hence, the profit-maximizing choice for the monopolist under Option 2 is that contract on the L-type reservation indifference curve where there is a tangency between the indifference curve and the average isoprofit line, as shown in Figure 8.6.

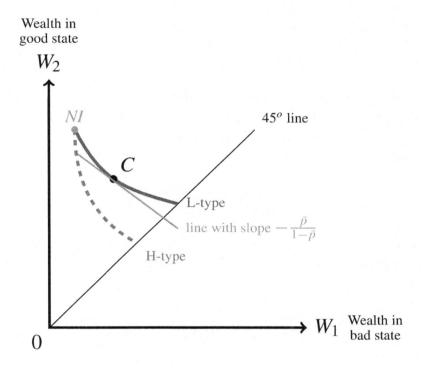

Figure 8.6: C is the profit-maximizing contract for the monopolist under Option 2.

The existence of such a contract is guaranteed if and only if the slope of the L-type reservation indifference curve at the no-insurance point is, in absolute value, greater than $\frac{\bar{p}}{1-\bar{p}}$.[3] On the other hand, if the slope of the L-type reservation indifference curve at the no-insurance point is, in absolute value, less than $\frac{\bar{p}}{1-\bar{p}}$, then Option 2 cannot yield positive profits. The reason for this is that the average isoprofit line that goes through the no-insurance point is the zero-profit line and thus every contract that is acceptable to the L-types will be above the zero profit line, which means that it would yield negative profits.

---

[3] If this condition is satisfied, then at NI the slope of the indifference curve is larger than $\frac{\bar{p}}{1-\bar{p}}$ and at a point on the 45° line it is smaller than $\frac{\bar{p}}{1-\bar{p}}$; thus, by the Intermediate Value Theorem, there must be a point along the curve where it is equal.

If Option 2 is profitable, the profit-maximizing contract under this option, let us denote it by $C = (W_1^C, W_2^C)$, is given by the solution to the following equations:

$$p_L U(W_1^C) + (1 - p_L) U(W_2^C) = p_L U(W_0 - \ell) + (1 - p_L) U(W_0) \tag{8.9}$$

$$\frac{p_L}{1 - p_L} \left(\frac{U'(W_1^C)}{U'(W_2^C)} \right) = \frac{\bar{p}}{1 - \bar{p}}. \tag{8.10}$$

Equation (8.9) states that an L-type individual is indifferent between contract C and no insurance, that is, contract C lies on the reservation indifference curve for the L-type; equation (8.10) states that, at point C, the reservation indifference curve of the L-type is tangent to (has the same slope as) the average isoprofit line.

As an example, let us revisit the case considered at the end of Section 8.2.1 where the individuals' initial wealth is $W_0 = 3,600$, potential loss is $\ell = 2,000$, the utility-of-money function is $U(m) = \sqrt{m}$, $p_L = \frac{3}{10}$ and $p_H = \frac{8}{10}$; furthermore, let $N_H = 2,400$ and $N_L = 3,900$, so that $q_H = \frac{8}{21}$. Thus the average probability of loss is

$$\bar{p} = \frac{8}{21} \left(\frac{8}{10} \right) + \frac{13}{21} \left(\frac{3}{10} \right) = \frac{103}{210}.$$

To see if Option 2 is profitable, we check if the L-type reservation indifference curve is steeper, at the no-insurance point $NI = (1600, 3600)$, than the average isoprofit line; that is, we check if

$$\frac{p_L}{1 - p_L} \left(\frac{U'(1,600)}{U'(3,600)} \right) > \frac{\bar{p}}{1 - \bar{p}}. \tag{8.11}$$

Since

$$\frac{p_L}{1 - p_L} \left(\frac{U'(1,600)}{U'(3,600)} \right) = \frac{\frac{3}{10}}{\frac{7}{10}} \left(\frac{\frac{1}{80}}{\frac{1}{120}} \right) = \frac{9}{14} = 0.6429$$

and

$$\frac{\bar{p}}{1 - \bar{p}} = \frac{\frac{103}{210}}{\frac{107}{210}} = 0.9626,$$

inequality (8.11) is not satisfied and thus Option 2 is **not** profitable.

Let us now change the value of N_L from 3,900 to 44,000: $N_L = 44,000$ (while everything else remains as above). Then $q_H = \frac{2,400}{2,400 + 44,000} = \frac{3}{58}$; thus

$$\bar{p} = \frac{3}{58} \left(\frac{8}{10} \right) + \frac{55}{58} \left(\frac{3}{10} \right) = \frac{189}{580} \quad \text{so that} \quad \frac{\bar{p}}{1 - \bar{p}} = \frac{189}{391} = 0.483$$

and thus inequality (8.11) is satisfied and Option 2 is profitable. The profit-maximizing contract under Option 2, denoted by $C = (W_1^C, W_2^C)$, is given by the solution to the following equations (which correspond to equations (8.9) and (8.10)):

8.3 The monopolist under asymmetric information

$$\frac{3}{10}\sqrt{W_1^C} + \frac{7}{10}\sqrt{W_2^C} = \frac{3}{10}\sqrt{1,600} + \frac{7}{10}\sqrt{3,600}$$

$$\frac{\frac{3}{10}\left(\frac{1}{2\sqrt{W_1^C}}\right)}{\frac{7}{10}\left(\frac{1}{2\sqrt{W_2^C}}\right)} = \frac{\frac{189}{580}}{\frac{391}{580}}.$$

The solution is $W_1^C = 2,456.53$ and $W_2^C = 3,124.97$, that is, $C = (2456.53, 3124.97)$; the corresponding premium is $3,600 - 3,124.97 = \$475.03$ and the deductible is $3,124.97 - 2,456.53 = \$668.44$ so that the expected profit from a single contract is

$$475.03 - \bar{p}(2,000 - 668.44) = 475.03 - \frac{189}{580}(1,331.56) = \$41.13$$

and total expected profits are

$$41.13\,(N_L + N_H) = 41.13(2,400 + 44,000) = \$1,908,432.$$

8.3.3 The monopolist's profit under Option 3

If the monopolist chooses Option 3 then it will offer two contracts: one contract– call it C_H – targeted to the H-type and the other contract – call it C_L – targeted to the L-type. Let us express these contracts in terms of premium and deductible and denote them by

$$C_H = (h_H, d_H) \qquad \text{and} \qquad C_L = (h_L, d_L).$$

We shall use the following abbreviations:

$\mathbb{E}_H[U(NI)]$	H-type's expected utility from no insurance
$\mathbb{E}_L[U(NI)]$	L-type's expected utility from no insurance
$\mathbb{E}_H[U(C_H)]$	H-type's expected utility from contract C_H
$\mathbb{E}_L[U(C_H)]$	L-type's expected utility from contract C_H
$\mathbb{E}_H[U(C_L)]$	H-type's expected utility from contract C_L
$\mathbb{E}_L[U(C_L)]$	L-type's expected utility from contract C_L.

Thus

$$\begin{aligned}
\mathbb{E}_H[U(NI)] &= p_H U(W_0 - \ell) + (1 - p_H) U(W_0) \\
\mathbb{E}_L[U(NI)] &= p_L U(W_0 - \ell) + (1 - p_L) U(W_0) \\
\mathbb{E}_H[U(C_H)] &= p_H U(W_0 - h_H - d_H) + (1 - p_H) U(W_0 - h_H) \\
\mathbb{E}_L[U(C_H)] &= p_L U(W_0 - h_H - d_H) + (1 - p_L) U(W_0 - h_H) \\
\mathbb{E}_H[U(C_L)] &= p_H U(W_0 - h_L - d_L) + (1 - p_H) U(W_0 - h_L) \\
\mathbb{E}_L[U(C_L)] &= p_L U(W_0 - h_L - d_L) + (1 - p_L) U(W_0 - h_L).
\end{aligned}$$

In order for contract C_H to be chosen by H-type individuals two conditions must be satisfied:

$$\mathbb{E}_H[U(C_H)] \geq \mathbb{E}_H[U(NI)] \qquad (IR_H)$$

$$\mathbb{E}_H[U(C_H)] \geq \mathbb{E}_H[U(C_L)] \qquad (IC_H)$$

The first condition, (IR_H), is called the *Individual Rationality constraint for type H* and says that the H-types must consider the contract targeted to them to be at least as good as no insurance. The second condition, (IC_H), is called the *Incentive Compatibility constraint for type H* and says that the H-types must consider the contract targeted to them to be at least as good as the other contract that is offered (namely C_L).

Similarly, in order for contract C_L to be chosen by L-type individuals two conditions must be satisfied:

$$\mathbb{E}_L[U(C_L)] \geq \mathbb{E}_L[U(NI)] \tag{IR_L}$$

$$\mathbb{E}_L[U(C_L)] \geq \mathbb{E}_L[U(C_H)] \tag{IC_L}$$

The first condition, (IR_L), is the *Individual Rationality constraint for type L*: it says that the L-types must consider the contract targeted to them to be at least as good as no insurance. The second condition, (IC_L), is he *Incentive Compatibility constraint for type L*: it says that the L-types must consider the contract targeted to them to be at least as good as the other contract that is offered (namely C_H).

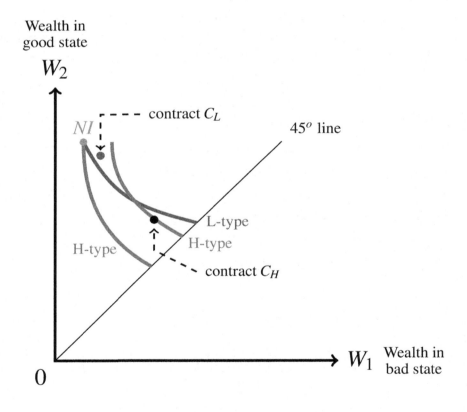

Figure 8.7: Two contracts that satisfy the four constraints.

Figure 8.7 shows a pair of contracts that satisfy all four constraints as strict inequalities: (1) contract C_H is strictly above the H-type reservation indifference curve and thus (IR_H) is satisfied as a strict inequality, (2) contract C_L is to the left of the H-type indifference curve that goes through contract C_H and thus (IC_H) is satisfied as a strict inequality, (3) contract C_L is strictly above the L-type reservation indifference curve and thus (IR_L) is

8.3 The monopolist under asymmetric information

satisfied as a strict inequality and (4) contract C_H is worse than contract C_L for the L-type (indeed, it is even worse than no insurance).

On the other hand, Figure 8.8 shows a pair of contracts where the (IC_H) and (IR_L) constraints are satisfied as equalities while the other two constraints are satisfied as strict inequalities.

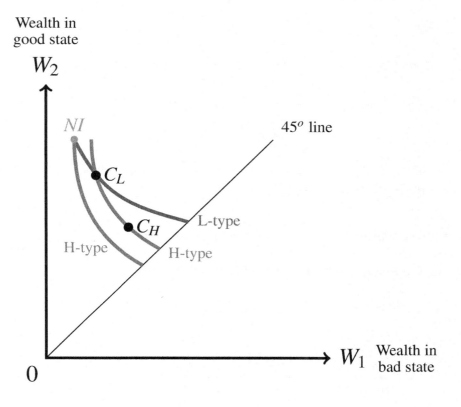

Figure 8.8: Another pair of contracts that satisfy the four constraints.

From now on, *we will assume that, if indifferent between contract C_H and contract C_L the H-types will choose contract C_H*. Furthermore, we will continue to assume that, if indifferent between insuring and not insuring, each individual will choose to insure.

If the monopolist offers a menu of two contracts, C_H and C_L, that satisfy the four constraints, then the H-types will purchase contract $C_H = (h_H, d_H)$ and the L-types will purchase contract $C_L = (h_L, d_L)$ and thus the monopolist's expected total profits will be

$$\pi_3 = N_H \left[h_H - p_H \left(\ell - d_H \right) \right] + N_L \left[h_L - p_L \left(\ell - d_L \right) \right].$$

Thus the monopolist, under Option 3, faces the following maximization problem:

$$\underset{h_H, d_H, h_L, d_L}{Max} \pi_3 = N_H \left[h_H - p_H \left(\ell - d_H \right) \right] + N_L \left[h_L - p_L \left(\ell - d_L \right) \right]$$

subject to

$(IR_H) \quad \mathbb{E}_H[U(C_H)] \geq \mathbb{E}_H[U(NI)]$
$(IC_H) \quad \mathbb{E}_H[U(C_H)] \geq \mathbb{E}_H[U(C_L)]$
$(IR_L) \quad \mathbb{E}_L[U(C_L)] \geq \mathbb{E}_L[U(NI)]$
$(IC_L) \quad \mathbb{E}_L[U(C_L)] \geq \mathbb{E}_L[U(C_H)]$

Let us study this maximization problem.

We showed at the beginning of this section (see Figure 8.3) that, if an insurance contract is acceptable to the L-type (in that it lies on or above the L-type's reservation indifference curve), then it is acceptable to the H-type too (that is, it lies on or above the H-type's reservation indifference curve); thus

$$\mathbb{E}_L[U(C_L)] \geq \mathbb{E}_L[U(NI)] \quad \text{implies that} \quad \mathbb{E}_H[U(C_L)] \geq \mathbb{E}_H[U(NI)]. \quad (8.12)$$

It follows that the (IR_H) constraint can be derived from the (IR_L) and (IC_H) constraints:

- by (IR_L), $\mathbb{E}_L[U(C_L)] \geq \mathbb{E}_L[U(NI)]$, which, by (8.12) implies

$$\mathbb{E}_H[U(C_L)] \geq \mathbb{E}_H[U(NI)]; \quad (8.13)$$

- by (IC_H), $\mathbb{E}_H[U(C_H)] \geq \mathbb{E}_H[U(C_L)]$ and this, together with (8.13) yields the (IR_H) constraint: $\mathbb{E}_H[U(C_H)] \geq \mathbb{E}_H[U(NI)]$.

Thus:

♦ **First observation:** the (IR_H) constraint is redundant.

Hence the monopolist's maximization problem can be simplified to:

$$\underset{h_H, d_H, h_L, d_L}{\text{Max}} \pi_3 = N_H \left[h_H - p_H (\ell - d_H) \right] + N_L \left[h_L - p_L (\ell - d_L) \right]$$

subject to:

(IC_H) $\overbrace{p_H U(W_0 - h_H - d_H) + (1 - p_H) U(W_0 - h_H)}^{\mathbb{E}_H[U(C_H)]}$

$\geq \underbrace{p_H U(W_0 - h_L - d_L) + (1 - p_H) U(W_0 - h_L)}_{\mathbb{E}_H[U(C_L)]}$

(IR_L) $\overbrace{p_L U(W_0 - h_L - d_L) + (1 - p_L) U(W_0 - h_L)}^{\mathbb{E}_L[U(C_L)]}$ (8.14)

$\geq \underbrace{p_L U(W_0 - \ell) + (1 - p_L) U(W_0)}_{\mathbb{E}_L[U(NI)]}$

(IC_L) $\overbrace{p_L U(W_0 - h_L - d_L) + (1 - p_L) U(W_0 - h_L)}^{\mathbb{E}_L[U(C_L)]}$

$\geq \underbrace{p_L U(W_0 - h_H - d_H) + (1 - p_L) U(W_0 - h_H)}_{\mathbb{E}_L[U(C_H)]}$

♦ **Second observation:** at a solution of the above maximization problem, the (IC_H) constraint must be satisfied as an equality, that is, contracts C_H and C_L must be on the same indifference curve for the H-type (as illustrated in Figure 8.8 on page 265).

8.3 The monopolist under asymmetric information

To see this, start with two contracts (C_H) and (C_L) that satisfy the above three constraints and suppose that $\mathbb{E}_H[U(C_H)] > \mathbb{E}_H[U(C_L)]$. Modify contract C_H by increasing the premium h_H up to the point where (IC_H) is satisfied as an equality, that is, up to the point where $\mathbb{E}_H[U(C_H)] = \mathbb{E}_H[U(C_L)]$.[4] Then profits will increase, since π_3 is increasing in h_H, and thus the initial pair $\{C_H, C_L\}$ could not have been a solution to the maximization problem.[5]

So far we have concluded that the solution to the initial constrained optimization problem requires that the two contracts C_H and C_L must be on the same indifference curve for the H-type.

- ♦ **Third observation:** at a solution of the maximization problem (8.14), contract C_L – which, by the second observation, must be on the same H-type indifference curve as contract C_H – must be above contract C_H.

To see this, suppose that contract C_H were above contract C_L, as shown in Figure 8.9.

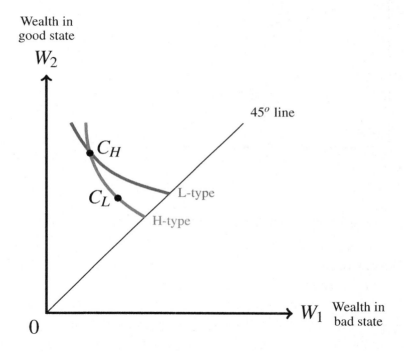

Figure 8.9: Contract C_H – which, by the second observation, must be on the same H-type indifference curve as contract C_L – cannot be above contract C_L.

Then we can draw the indifference curve of the L-type that goes through contract C_H: it will be less steep than the indifference curve of the H-type and thus contract C_L will be below this L-type indifference curve, implying the the L-type would strictly prefer contract C_H to contact C_L, contradicting the incentive compatibility constraint for the L-type, (IC_L).

---

[4]The right-hand side of (IC_H) is independent of h_H while the left-hand side is decreasing in h_H.

[5]Note that an increase in h_H does not affect the (IR_L) constraint (both sides of it are independent of h_H), while it reinforces the (IC_L) constraint, since the left-hand side of (IC_L) is independent of h_H, while the right-hand side is decreasing in h_H; thus if the (IC_L) constraint was satisfied to start with, then it will continue to be satisfied after the increase in h_H.

Thus, by the second and third observation, the two contracts C_H and C_L must be on the same H-type indifference curve, with C_L above C_H, as shown in Figure 8.10.[6]

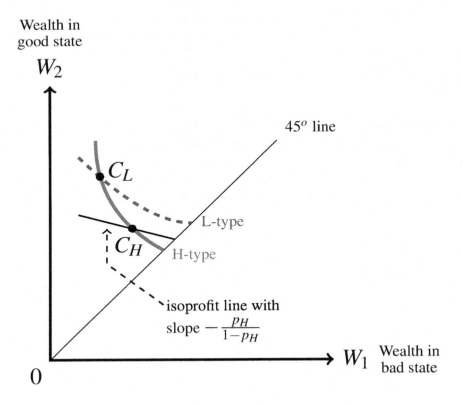

Figure 8.10: Contract C_H cannot be above the 45° line.

♦ **Fourth observation:** at a solution of the maximization problem (8.14), contract C_H must be a full-insurance contract.

To see this, suppose that C_H is not a full-insurance contract, that is, suppose that it lies above the 45° line. Then, as we know from Chapter 5, the H-type indifference curve is steeper at point C_H than the isoprofit line with slope $-\frac{p_H}{1-p_H}$, as shown in Figure 8.10. This is indeed a relevant isoprofit line, because – by the (IC_L) constraint – contract C_H will be purchased only by the H-types. Hence there are points below contract C_H, on the H-type indifference curve, that will yield higher profits to the monopolist, since any such contract would still be bought only by the H-types.[7]

---

[6]To reach this conclusion one also needs to rule out the possibility that $C_H = C_L$. This is a consequence of the fourth observation below: starting from $C_H = C_L$ above the 45° line, the monopolist could increase its profits by separating C_H from C_L and moving it, along the H-type indifference curve, towards the 45° line; on the other hand, if – to start with – $C_H = C_L$ is already on the 45° line, then, by the (IC_L) constraint it must be on or above the reservation indifference curve for the L-type and we know from the analysis of Option 2 that this is not a profit-maximizing configuration.

[7]Moving contract C_H towards the 45° line, along the H-type indifference curve, will not alter the (IR_L) constraint (which is independent of h_H and d_H) and will make contract C_H even less attractive than contract C_L for the L-type, that is, the (IC_L) constraint will still hold.

8.3 The monopolist under asymmetric information

♦ **Fifth observation:** at a solution of the maximization problem (8.14), the (IR_L) constraint must be satisfied as an equality, that is, contract C_L must be on the reservation indifference curve of the L-type.

To see this, consider the situation depicted in Figure 8.11 where contract C_L is above the reservation indifference curve of the L-type (and – in accordance with the previous observations – C_L and C_H lie on the same indifference curve of the H-type; furthermore, C_H is a full-insurance contract, that is, it lies on the 45° line). Draw the isoprofit line with slope $-\frac{p_L}{1-p_L}$ that goes through contract C_L. We know from Chapter 5 that the H-type indifference curve at point C_L is steeper than the line with slope $-\frac{p_H}{1-p_H}$ which, in turn, is steeper than the line with slope $-\frac{p_L}{1-p_L}$. Thus there are points on the H-type indifference curve (to which both C_L and C_H belong) that are below this isoprofit line. Modify contract C_L by moving it along the H-type indifference curve up to the point where it intersects the reservation indifference curve of the L-type, that is, until the (IR_L) constraint is satisfied as an equality. Then the (IC_H) constraint is not affected (it is still satisfied as an equality) and the (IC_L) constraint is also not affected, since contract C_H is still worse, for the L-type, than the modified contract C_L. Thus the new C_L contract is still purchased only by the L-types and hence yields higher profits to the monopolist than the original C_L contract (since the new contract is below the isoprofit line with slope $-\frac{p_L}{1-p_L}$ that goes through the original contract).

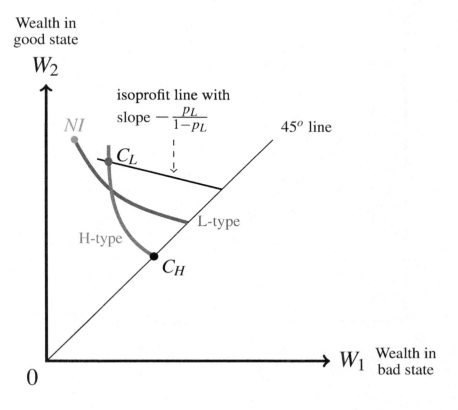

Figure 8.11: Contract C_L cannot be above the L-type reservation indifference curve.

We conclude from the above five observations that

> The pair of contracts (C_H, C_L)
> is a solution of the maximization problem (8.14) only if
> - C_H is on the 45° line and
> - C_L lies at the intersection of
>   (1) the indifference curve of the H-type that goes through C_H and
>   (2) the indifference curve of the L-type that goes through NI.

Fix an arbitrary premium h_H for the full-insurance contract C_H (thus $d_H = 0$), such that C_H lies on the segment of the 45° line between F_H and F_L, where F_H is the point of intersection of the reservation indifference curve of the H-type and the 45° line and F_L is the point of intersection of the reservation indifference curve of the L-type and the 45° line: see Figure 8.12. Then the contract C_L at the intersection of the reservation indifference curve of the L-type and the indifference curve of the H-type that goes through contract C_H is uniquely determined; hence we can think of this contract C_L as a function of h_H:

$$C_L(h_H) = (h_L(h_H), d_L(h_H)). \tag{8.15}$$

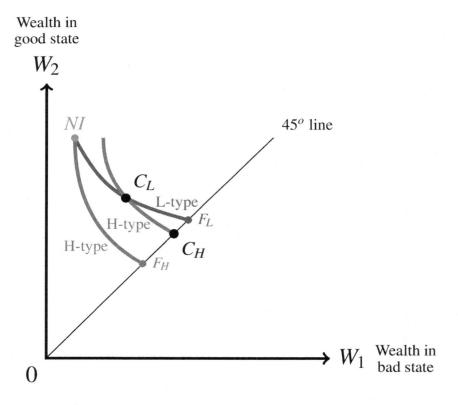

Figure 8.12: Contract C_L is uniquely determined by the choice of contract C_H on the segment of the 45° line between points F_H and F_L.

8.3 The monopolist under asymmetric information

Then the constrained maximization problem (8.14) can be reduced to the following unconstrained maximization problem:

$$\underset{h_H \in [h_{max}^L, h_{max}^H]}{Max} \pi_3(h_H) = N_H(h_H - p_H \ell) + N_L[h_L(h_H) - p_L(\ell - d_L(h_H))] \quad (8.16)$$

where h_{max}^L is the maximum premium that the L-type is willing to pay for full insurance (the premium of contract F_L in Figure 8.12) and h_{max}^H is the maximum premium that the H-type is willing to pay for full insurance (the premium of contract F_H in Figure 8.12).

(R) Note that one possible choice under Option 3 is to set $h_H = h_{max}^H$, that is, to choose $C_H = F_H$ (see Figure 8.12), in which case the corresponding contract for the L-type is the trivial contract with $h_L = 0$ and $d_L = \ell$, that is, $C_L = NI$. This amounts to insuring only the H-types, with the full-insurance contract that was obtained as the profit-maximizing contract under Option 1. Thus *Option 1 is a special case of Option 3*.

Before we discuss the solution to (8.16) in general, let us consider a numerical example.

Let the following be common to all individuals: initial wealth $W_0 = 1,600$, potential loss $\ell = 700$ and vNM utility-of-money function $U(m) = \sqrt{m}$. The H-types face a probability of loss $p_H = \frac{1}{5}$ while the L-types face a probability of loss $p_L = \frac{1}{10}$.

- To find h_{max}^L solve the equation

$$\frac{1}{10}\sqrt{900} + \frac{9}{10}\sqrt{1,600} = \sqrt{1,600 - h}.$$

The solution is $h_{max}^L = 79$.

- To find h_{max}^H solve the equation

$$\frac{1}{5}\sqrt{900} + \frac{4}{5}\sqrt{1,600} = \sqrt{1,600 - h}.$$

The solution is $h_{max}^H = 156$.

Given $h_H \in [79, 156]$, contract C_L is given by the solution to the following pair of equations:

$$\frac{1}{10}\sqrt{900} + \frac{9}{10}\sqrt{1,600} = \frac{1}{10}\sqrt{1,600 - h_L - d_L} + \frac{9}{10}\sqrt{1,600 - h_L}$$

(8.17)

$$\frac{1}{5}\sqrt{1,600 - h_L - d_L} + \frac{4}{5}\sqrt{1,600 - h_L} = \sqrt{1,600 - h_H}.$$

The first equation states that C_L lies on the reservation indifference curve of the L-type and the second equation states that C_L lies on the indifference curve of the H-type that goes through the full-insurance contract C_H with premium h_H. The solution to (8.17) is

$$h_L(h_H) = h_H + 156\sqrt{1,600 - h_H} - 6,084 \quad (8.18)$$

$$d_L(h_H) = 80 h_H + 5,460\sqrt{1,600 - h_H} - 219,260. \quad (8.19)$$

Let there be a total of N individuals and let q_H be the fraction of type-H individuals (thus $N_H = q_H N$), so that $(1 - q_H)$ is the fraction of type-L individuals (thus $N_L = (1 - q_H)N$). Then the monopolist's objective is to choose that value of $h_H \in [79, 156]$ that maximizes the function

$$\pi_3(h_H) = N\left[q_H\left(h_H - p_H\, 700\right) + (1 - q_H)\left[h_L(h_H) - p_L(700 - d_L(h_H))\right]\right] \quad (8.20)$$

where $h_L(h_H)$ and $d_L(h_H)$ are given by (8.18) and (8.19), respectively. The solution of this maximization problem depends on the value of q_H, that is, on how many H-types there are relative to the L-types.

For example, if $q_H = \frac{1}{20}$ then the graph of the profit function (8.20) is shown in Figure 8.13. The profit-maximizing value of h_H is an interior point of the interval $[79, 156]$, namely 96.64. Replacing this value in (8.18) and (8.19) we obtain $h_L = 61.26$ and $d_L = 172.80$. Thus the monopolist offers a full-insurance contract $C_H = (h_H = 96.64, d_H = 0)$ and a partial-insurance contract $C_L = (h_L = 61.26, d_L = 172.80)$ and the H-types purchase contract C_H while the L-types purchase contract C_L. We call such a situation a *separating equilibrium*, since the monopolist – through the menu of contracts it offers – is able to induce a separation of the types: all the individuals of one type purchase one contract and all the individuals of the other type purchase the other contract.

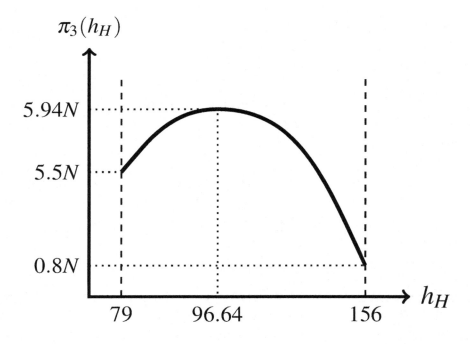

Figure 8.13: The graph of the profit function (8.20) when $q_H = \frac{1}{20}$.

8.3 The monopolist under asymmetric information

Now consider the case where $q_H = \frac{1}{5}$. For this case the graph of the profit function (8.20) is shown in Figure 8.14. It is clear from the graph that in this case the solution of the **profit-maximizing problem is a corner solution** at $h_H = h_{max}^H = 156$ and only the H-types insure (the contract targeted to the L-types is the trivial contract with $h_L = 0$ and $d_L = 700$: see the remark on page 271).

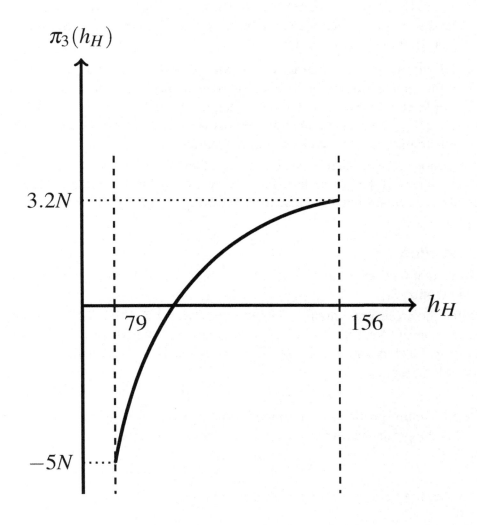

Figure 8.14: The graph of the profit function (8.20) when $q_H = \frac{1}{5}$.

The above example illustrates a general feature of the profit-maximization under Option 3:

- When q_H is "sufficiently close to 1" (that is, when the number of H-types is large relative to the entire population of potential customers), the monopolist will choose to insure only the H-types by offering the full-insurance contract with premium h_{max}^H (that is, the solution to the profit maximization problem (8.16) given on page 271 is the corner solution, as illustrated in Figure 8.14). As a consequence, the (IR_H) constraint is satisfied as an equality.

- Otherwise the monopolist will offer two contracts:

  (1) a full-insurance contract C_H with premium $h_H < h_{max}^H$, which will be purchased by the H-types, who therefore enjoy a surplus (that is, they are strictly better off than with no insurance or, in other words, the (IR_H) constraint is satisfied as a strict inequality), and

  (2) a partial-insurance contract which will be purchased by the L-types, located at the intersection of the reservation indifference curve of the L-types and the indifference curve of the H-types that goes through contract C_H (thus the (IR_L) and (IC_H) constraints are satisfied as equalities while the (IR_H) and (IC_L) constraints are satisfied as strict inequalities).

The expression "q_H sufficiently close to 1" is rather vague: its exact meaning depends on the specific values of the parameters. For instance, it can be shown that, in the example considered above, "q_H sufficiently close to 1" means $q_H \geq \frac{9}{47} = 0.1915$.[8]

8.3.4 Option 2 revisited

We saw above that Option 1 can be viewed as a subcase of Option 3. Now we compare Option 2 and Option 3.

Recall that the profit-maximizing contract under Option 2 (if it exists) is that contract on the reservation indifference curve of the L-type where the slope of the indifference curve is equal to the slope of the average profit line, which is $-\frac{\bar{p}}{1-\bar{p}}$, where $\bar{p}$ is the average probability of loss, that is,

$$\bar{p} = q_H p_H + (1 - p_H) p_L.$$

Denote the maximum profits that the monopolist can make under Option 2 by π_2^*. If $B = (h_B, d_B)$ is the profit-maximizing contract under Option 2 then

$$\pi_2^* = (N_H + N_L)[h_B - \bar{p}(\ell - d_B)],$$

where N_H is the number of individuals of type H and N_L is the number of individuals of type L.

---

[8]Thus, in that example, if $q_H \geq \frac{9}{47}$ then the monopolist will choose to insure only the H-types, while if $q_H < \frac{9}{47}$ then the monopolist will implement a separating two-contract solution. To find this critical value of q_H, first calculate the derivative of the function $\pi_3(h_H)$ given in (8.20) and evaluate it at the corner point $h_H = 156$; this will give an expression in terms of q_H and then set this expression equal to zero and solve for q_H. In this case the solution is $q_H = \frac{9}{47}$; hence if $q_H \geq \frac{9}{47}$ then the function $\pi_3(h_H)$ is increasing or constant at $h_H = 156$ and thus the function is maximized at $h_H = 156$, while if $q_H < \frac{9}{47}$ then the function $\pi_3(h_H)$ is decreasing at $h_H = 156$ and thus the function is maximized at a point to the left of $h_H = 156$.

8.3 The monopolist under asymmetric information

We want to show that $\pi_2^* < \pi_3^*$, where π_3^* is the maximum profit that the monopolist can make under Option 3.

Figure 8.15 shows the contract, denoted by B, that maximizes profits under Option 2. If the monopolist offers only this contract, then both types of individuals will purchase it. Suppose that the monopolist switches from a one-contract menu containing only contract B to a two-contract menu $\{B, F\}$ obtained by adding to contract B also the full-insurance contract F given by the intersection of the H-type indifference curve that goes through B and the 45° line, as shown in Figure 8.15. Then the L-types will continue to buy contract B (since it is strictly better for them that the newly added contract F), while the H-types will switch to contract F.[9] Thus profits from the L-types will not change, but profits from the H-types will increase.[10] The pair of contracts $\{B, F\}$ satisfies all the constraints considered under Option 3 (namely, IR_H, IC_H, IR_L, IC_L) and yields profits that are larger than π_2^*; thus π_3^* (which may be even larger) is greater than π_2^*.

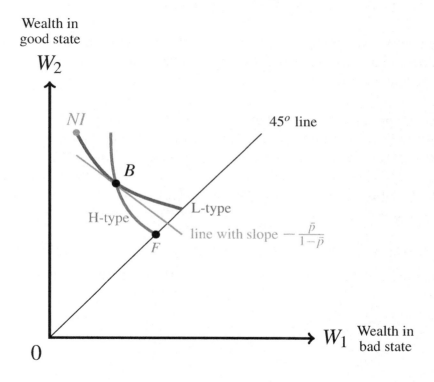

Figure 8.15: Option 2 is inferior to Option 3.

> Test your understanding of the concepts introduced in this section, by going through the exercises in Section 8.5.2 at the end of this chapter.

---

[9] As usual, we assume that, if indifferent, the H-types will choose the contract targeted to them. Otherwise the newly offered contract would have to be slightly above contract F on the 45° line.

[10] Because of the usual argument that at a point above the 45° line, such as point B in Figure 8.15, the H-type indifference curve is steeper than the isoprofit line with slope $-\frac{p_H}{1-p_H}$, which is the relevant isoprofit line if we consider contracts on the portion of the H-type indifference curve between point B and point F, since those contracts would be purchased only by the H-types.

8.4 A perfectly competitive insurance industry

In Chapters 2 and 5 (Sections 2.6.4 and 5.2.2) we studied the equilibrium in a perfectly competitive insurance industry with free entry when there is only one type of potential customer. Now we extend the analysis to the case of asymmetric information with two types of individuals. We continue to assume that all the individuals are identical in terms of initial wealth W_0 and potential loss ℓ (with $0 < \ell \leq W_0$); furthermore, they also have the same vNM utility-of-money function $U(m)$. What they differ in is the probability of loss: it is p_H for type-H (= high-risk) individuals and p_L for type-L (= low-risk) individuals, with $0 < p_L < p_H < 1$.

Recall that a free-entry competitive equilibrium is defined as a situation where

1. each firm in the industry makes zero profits, and

2. there is no unexploited profit opportunity in the industry, that is, there is no currently not offered contract that would yield positive profits to a (existing or new) firm that offered that contract.

In the one-type case we saw that at the free-entry competitive equilibrium every firm offers the full-insurance contract that lies at the intersection of the zero-profit line and the 45° line. Recall that the no-insurance point NI can be thought of as a trivial contract with zero premium and deductible equal to the full loss ℓ: such a "contract" obviously yields zero profits; thus the zero-profit line goes through point NI. In the two-type context the situation is complicated by the fact that there are **three** zero-profit lines:

- a "low-risk" line (through NI) with slope $-\frac{p_L}{1-p_L}$, which is a relevant isoprofit line if and only if the contracts on this line are sold only to the low-risk individuals,

- an "average-risk" line (through NI) with slope $-\frac{\bar{p}}{1-\bar{p}}$, where

$$\bar{p} = q_H p_H + (1-q_H) p_L,$$

which is a relevant isoprofit line if and only if the contracts on this line are sold to both types of individuals,

- a "high- risk" line (through NI) with slope $-\frac{p_H}{1-p_H}$, which is a relevant isoprofit line if and only if the contracts on this line are sold only to the hight-risk individuals.

Since $0 < p_L < p_H < 1$ and $0 < q_H < 1$, $p_L < \bar{p} < p_H$ and thus

$$\frac{p_L}{1-p_L} < \frac{\bar{p}}{1-\bar{p}} < \frac{p_H}{1-p_H}. \tag{8.21}$$

Hence the low-risk zero-profit line is less steep that the average risk zero-profit line, which, in turn, is less steep than the high-risk zero-profit line.

Figure 8.16 shows the three zero-profit lines.

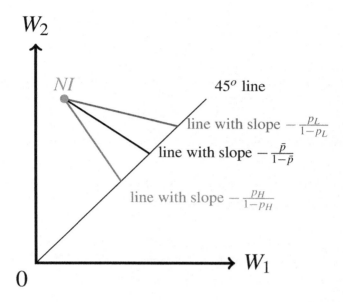

Figure 8.16: Three zero-profit lines in the two-type case.

We also note that, at any insurance contract, the slope of the H-type indifference curve is – in absolute value – greater than or equal to $\frac{p_H}{1-p_H}$ and thus, by (8.21), it is greater than the absolute value of the slope of the average isoprofit line through that point, as shown in Figure 8.17.

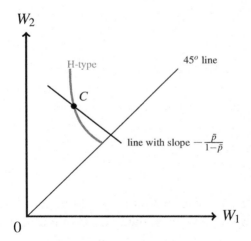

Figure 8.17: At any (full- or partial-) insurance contract the H-type indifference curve is steeper than the average isoprofit line.

In what follows we shall assume that the reservation indifference curve of the L-type is steeper, at the no-insurance point, than the average zero-profit line, that is,

$$\frac{p_L}{1-p_L}\left(\frac{U'(W_0-\ell)}{U'(W_0)}\right) > \frac{\bar{p}}{1-\bar{p}}. \tag{8.22}$$

Inequality (8.22) ensures that it is possible to make positive profits by insuring both types of individuals with the same contract.[11]

In principle, a free-entry competitive equilibrium could be one of two types:

- a *pooling equilibrium* where all the firms in the industry offer the same contract, which is bought by both types of individuals, or

- a *separating equilibrium* where two contracts are offered in the industry: one contract, denoted by C_H, which is purchased only by the H-types and the other contract, denoted by C_L, which is purchased only by the L-types.

Let us begin by considering the possibility of a pooling equilibrium. We want to show that such an equilibrium is *not* possible. By Condition 1 of the definition of free-entry competitive equilibrium, the contract in question, call it $B = (h_B, d_B)$ (with $0 \leq d_B < \ell$), must be on the average zero profit line, that is,

$$h_B - \bar{p}(\ell - d_B) = 0. \tag{8.23}$$

Consider the function $\pi_L(h,d) = h - p_L(\ell - d)$ that gives, for every insurance contract (h,d) the expected profit from that contract *if it is bought only by the low-risk individuals*, that is, only by the L-types. Since $p_L < \bar{p}$, $p_L(\ell - d_B) < \bar{p}(\ell - d_B)$ and thus it follows from (8.23) that

$$\pi_L(h_B, d_B) = h_B - p_L(\ell - d_B) > 0. \tag{8.24}$$

Since the function $\pi_L(h,d)$ is a continuous function, it follows from (8.24) that, for every insurance contract $A = (h_A, d_A)$,

if A is sufficiently close to B then $\pi_L(h_A, d_A) = h_A - p_L(\ell - d_A) > 0$. (8.25)

Thus, if we can find a contract, close to B, that would be considered better than B by the L-types, but worse than B by the H-types, then any firm that introduced contract A would attract only the L-types and thus, by (8.25), it would make positive profits, contradicting the second requirement of the definition of a free-entry competitive equilibrium. Does such a contract exist?

---

[11] By (8.22) there are contracts that are above the reservation indifference curve of the L-type (and thus attractive to both types) and below the average zero-profit line (and thus yielding positive profits if purchased by both types).

8.4 A perfectly competitive insurance industry

The answer is affirmative, as shown in Figure 8.18: draw the indifference curves of the two types that go through contract B. The L-type indifference curve is less steep than the H-type indifference curve and thus there are contracts, such as contract A in Figure 8.18, which are below the H-type indifference curve through B and above the L-type indifference curve through B. Thus if such a contract A were to be introduced, the L-types would switch from the original contract B to the new contract A while the H-types would stay with contract B. Hence, by (8.25), the firm that introduced contract A would make positive profits, contradicting the second requirement of the definition of free-entry competitive equilibrium.

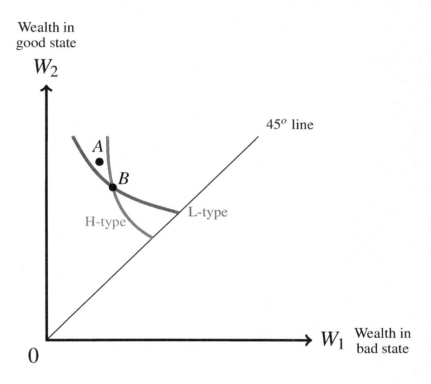

Figure 8.18: If, initially, both types purchase contract B and then contract A is added as an option, then the H-types will not switch to A while the L-types will.

Thus we conclude that, if there is a free-entry competitive equilibrium, then it must be a two-contract separating equilibrium. We now turn to the question of whether a two-contract $\{C_H, C_L\}$ equilibrium exists with all H-types purchasing contract C_H and all L-type purchasing contract C_L.

- By the zero-profit condition (the first requirement of a free-entry competitive equilibrium), contract C_H must be on the high-risk zero-profit line (the line through NI with slope $-\frac{p_H}{1-p_H}$) and contract C_L must be on the low-risk zero-profit line (the line through NI with slope $-\frac{p_L}{1-p_L}$).

- Furthermore, contract C_H must be the full-insurance contract on the high-risk zero-profit line because, if it were above the 45° line, then – by the usual argument based on the observation that at such a point the H-type indifference curve is steeper than the high-risk zero-profit line – there would be contracts below that zero profit line and above that indifference curve that would yield positive profits to a firm that introduced such a contract (which would induce the H-types to switch to it), contradicting the second requirement of a free-entry competitive equilibrium.

It remains to determine where on the low-risk zero-profit line contract C_L should be. Draw the indifference curve of the H-type that goes through contract C_H and call the point at the intersection of this indifference curve and the low-risk zero-profit line contract C, as shown in Figure 8.19.

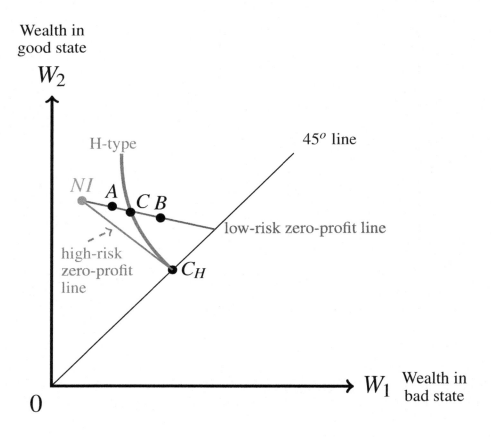

Figure 8.19: Where on the low-risk zero-profit line could contract C_L be?

- Suppose that contract C_L is on the low-risk zero-profit line to the right of point C, such as point B in Figure 8.19. Then such a contract B would be preferred to C_H by both types,[12] giving rise to a situation where all types purchase the same contract, which – as we saw above – cannot be a free-entry competitive equilibrium.

---

[12] B is preferred to C_H by type H because B is to the right of the H-type indifference curve through C_H and B is preferred to C_H by type L because C_H is below the L-type indifference curve through B: this indifference curve is not shown in Figure 8.19, but it is less steep than the indifference curve of the H-type through B (also not shown); hence, since C_H is below the latter, it is also below the former.

8.4 A perfectly competitive insurance industry

- Suppose that contract C_L is on the low-risk zero-profit line to the left of point C, such as point A in Figure 8.19. Then – by the usual argument based on the observation that at such a point the L-type indifference curve is steeper than the low-risk zero-profit line – there would be contracts below that zero profit line and above the indifference curve of the L-type that goes through A that would attract the L-types, and only the L-types, and yield positive profits, contradicting the first requirement of a free-entry competitive equilibrium.

Thus we conclude that contract C_L must be at the intersection of the low-risk zero-profit line and the indifference curve of the H-type that goes through contract C_H, that is, it must coincide with point C in Figure 8.19.

We have determined that necessary conditions for a pair of contracts $\{C_H, C_L\}$ to be a free-entry competitive equilibrium are:

(1) C_H is at the intersection of the high-risk zero-profit line and the 45° line, and

(2) C_L is at the intersection of the low-risk zero-profit line and the H-type indifference curve through C_H.

While necessary, the above two conditions are not sufficient for a free-entry competitive equilibrium. To see this, consider the situation depicted in Figure 8.20.

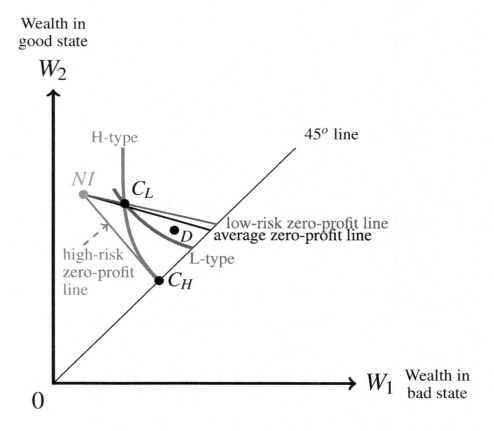

Figure 8.20: A case where the pair of contracts $\{C_H, C_L\}$ is not a free-entry competitive equilibrium because of the existence of contracts like D.

Suppose that the contracts currently offered in the industry are C_H and C_L and one of the existing firms, or a new firm, introduces contract D. The H-types will switch to contract D, since it is better than the contract that they are currently purchasing, namely C_H (D is to the right of the H-type indifference curve through C_H) and the L-types will also switch to D, since it is better than the contract that they are currently purchasing, namely C_L (D is to the right of the L-type indifference curve through C_L). Then, for the firm that introduced contract D, the relevant isoprofit lines are the average isoprofit lines; since contract D is below the average zero-profit line, it yields positive profits to the firm, contradicting the second requirement of a free-entry competitive equilibrium.

Thus, in order for the two-contract configuration $\{C_H, C_L\}$ described above to be a free-entry competitive equilibrium, it is also necessary that there be no contracts such as contract D described above, that is, it must **not** be the case that the average zero-profit line crosses the L-type indifference curve that goes through contract C_L. In other words, the average zero-profit line must be entirely below the L-type indifference curve through C_L, as shown in Figure 8.21.

Since the higher the value of q_H (that is, the larger the number of H-types in the population relative to the number of L-types), the closer the average zero-profit line will be to the high-risk zero-profit line, this additional requirement for the existence of a free-entry competitive equilibrium can be understood in terms of q_H being "sufficiently large".

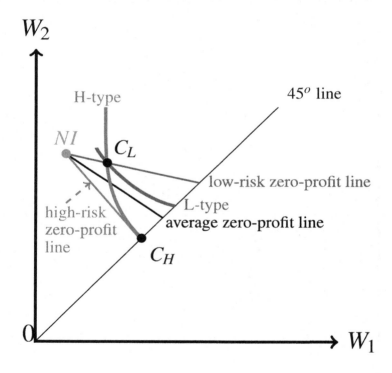

Figure 8.21: The pair of contracts $\{C_H, C_L\}$ is a free-entry competitive equilibrium.

Test your understanding of the concepts introduced in this section, by going through the exercises in Section 8.5.3 at the end of this chapter.

8.5 Exercises

The solutions to the following exercises are given in Section 8.6 at the end of this chapter.

8.5.1 Exercises for Section 8.2: Two types of customers

Exercise 8.1 Sara and Mary have the same initial wealth of $400 and face the same potential loss of $280. They also have the same vNM utility-of-money function $U(m) = \ln(m)$. They differ, however, in the probability of loss, which is $p_S = \frac{1}{2}$ for Sara and $p_M = \frac{1}{5}$ for Mary.

(a) Calculate the slope of Sara's reservation indifference curve at the no-insurance point.

(b) Calculate the slope of Mary's reservation indifference curve at the no-insurance point.

(c) Find the maximum premium that Sara would be willing to pay for full insurance and calculate the insurance company's expected profit from selling that full-insurance contract to Sara.

(d) Find the maximum premium that Mary would be willing to pay for full insurance and calculate the insurance company's expected profit from selling that full-insurance contract to Mary.

Exercise 8.2 Diana and Fran have the same initial wealth of $4,096 and face the same potential loss of $2,800. They also have the same vNM utility-of-money function $U(m) = \sqrt{m}$. They differ, however, in the probability of loss, which is $p_D = \frac{1}{4}$ for Diana and $p_F = \frac{1}{16}$ for Fran.

Consider a monopolist seller of insurance who knows all of the above information about Diana and Fran.

(a) What insurance contract would the monopolist offer to Diana?

(b) What insurance contract would the monopolist offer to Fran?

(c) Assume that, when indifferent between not insuring and insuring, both Diana and Fran will choose to insure. Calculate the monopolist's expected profit from selling insurance to Diana and Fran.

8.5.2 Exercises for Section 8.3: The monopolist under asymmetric information

Exercise 8.3 There are 16,000 individuals, all identical in terms of initial wealth $W_0 = \$4,000$, potential loss $\ell = \$2,500$ and vNM utility-of-money function $U(m) = 10\ln\left(\frac{m}{1,000}\right)$. Of these individuals, 12,000 have a high probability of loss $p_H = \frac{1}{5}$ and 4,000 have a low probability of loss $p_L = \frac{1}{15}$. A monopolist seller of insurance is considering using Option 1 (Section 8.3.1). What will its expected total profits be? [As usual, assume that – if indifferent between insuring and not insuring – individuals will choose to insure.]

Exercise 8.4 Consider again the case described in Exercise 8.3: there are 16,000 individuals, all identical in terms of initial wealth $W_0 = \$4,000$, potential loss $\ell = \$2,500$ and vNM utility-of-money function $U(m) = 10\ln\left(\frac{m}{1,000}\right)$; of these individuals, 12,000 have a high probability of loss $p_H = \frac{1}{5}$ and 4,000 have a low probability of loss $p_L = \frac{1}{15}$.

(a) Show that, for a monopolist seller of insurance, Option 2 (Section 8.3.2) is not profitable.

(b) Calculate what the monopolist's total expected profits would be if it offered a full-insurance contract that makes the L-type indifferent between insuring and not insuring. [As usual, assume that – if indifferent between insuring and not insuring – individuals will choose to insure.]

Exercise 8.5 Consider again the case described in Exercise 8.3, but reduce the number of high-risk individuals from 12,000 to 6,000; thus there are 10,000 individuals, all identical in terms of initial wealth $W_0 = \$4,000$, potential loss $\ell = \$2,500$ and vNM utility-of-money function $U(m) = 10\ln\left(\frac{m}{1,000}\right)$; of these individuals, 6,000 have a high probability of loss $p_H = \frac{1}{5}$ and 4,000 have a low probability of loss $p_L = \frac{1}{15}$.

(a) Show that, for a monopolist seller of insurance, Option 2 (Section 8.3.2) is profitable, by calculating the slopes of the relevant curves at the no-insurance point.

(b) Write two equations, whose solution gives the contract that maximizes the monopolist's profits under Option 2. If you are able to, compute the solution and determine the monopolist's expected total profits if it offers that contract. [As usual, assume that – if indifferent between insuring and not insuring – individuals will choose to insure.]

8.5 Exercises

Exercise 8.6 There are 6,000 individuals, all with the same initial wealth $W_0 = 16,000$, facing the same potential loss $\ell = 7,000$ and with the same vNM utility-of-money function $U(m) = \sqrt{m}$. Of these 6,000 individuals, 1,000 are high-risk with a probability of loss $p_H = \frac{2}{10}$ while the remaining 5,000 are low-risk with a probability of loss $p_L = \frac{1}{10}$.

(a) Calculate the monopolist's total expected profits if it decides to pursue Option 1.

(b) Calculate the average probability of loss $\bar{p}$.

(c) Write two equations whose solution gives the profit-maximizing contract under Option 2.

(d) Suppose that, under Option 3, the monopolist decides to offer a full-insurance contract with premium \$1,400. Write a pair of equations whose solution gives the other contract that the monopolist will offer.

(e) The solution of the pair of equations in Part (d) is the following contract, expressed in term of wealth levels: $C = (10169.41, 15832.48)$. Calculate the monopolist's profits if it offers the two contracts of Part (d).

∎

Exercise 8.7 There are 8,000 individuals, all with the same initial wealth $W_0 = 10,000$, facing the same potential loss $\ell = 6,000$ and with the same vNM utility-of-money function $U(m) = \ln(m)$. Of these 8,000 individuals, 1,500 are high-risk with a probability of loss $p_H = \frac{1}{4}$ while the remaining 6,500 are low-risk with a probability of loss $p_L = \frac{1}{16}$.

(a) Calculate the monopolist's total expected profits if it decides to pursue Option 1.

(b) Calculate the average probability of loss $\bar{p}$.

(c) Write two equations whose solution gives the profit-maximizing contract under Option 2.

(d) Suppose that, under Option 3, the monopolist decides to offer a full-insurance contract with premium \$2,000. Write a pair of equations whose solution gives the other contract that the monopolist will offer.

(e) The solution of the pair of equations in Part (d) is the following contract, expressed in term of wealth levels: $C = (4120.36, 9980.26)$. Calculate the monopolist's profits if it offers the two contracts of Part (d).

∎

8.5.3 Exercises for Section 8.4: A perfectly competitive insurance industry

Exercise 8.8 Consider again the information given in Exercise 8.6: there are 6,000 individuals, all with the same initial wealth $W_0 = 16,000$, facing the same potential loss $\ell = 7,000$ and with the same vNM utility-of-money function $U(m) = \sqrt{m}$; of these 6,000 individuals, 1,000 are high-risk with probability of loss $p_H = \frac{2}{10}$ while the remaining 5,000 are low-risk with probability of loss $p_L = \frac{1}{10}$.

(a) Find the pair of contracts that is the only candidate for a free-entry perfectly competitive equilibrium.

(b) Calculate the average probability of loss $\bar{p}$.

(c) Write a pair of equations such that: (1) if it has a solution then the pair of contracts of Part (a) is **not** a free-entry perfectly competitive equilibrium and (2) if it does not have a solution then the pair of contracts of Part (a) **is** a free-entry perfectly competitive equilibrium.

Exercise 8.9 Consider again the information given in Exercise 8.7: there are 8,000 individuals, all with the same initial wealth $W_0 = 10,000$, facing the same potential loss $\ell = 6,000$ and with the same vNM utility-of-money function $U(m) = \ln(m)$; of these 8,000 individuals, 1,500 are high-risk with probability of loss $p_H = \frac{1}{4}$ while the remaining 6,500 are low-risk with probability of loss $p_L = \frac{1}{16}$.

(a) Find the pair of contracts that is the only candidate for a free-entry perfectly competitive equilibrium.

(b) Calculate the average probability of loss $\bar{p}$.

(c) Write a pair of equations such that: (1) if it has a solution then the pair of contracts of Part (a) is **not** a free-entry perfectly competitive equilibrium and (2) if it does not have a solution then the pair of contracts of Part (a) **is** a free-entry perfectly competitive equilibrium.

8.6 Solutions to Exercises

Solution to Exercise 8.1

(a) The slope of Sara's reservation indifference curve at $NI = (120, 400)$ is

$$-\frac{p_S}{1-p_S}\left(\frac{U'(120)}{U'(400)}\right) = -\frac{\frac{1}{2}}{1-\frac{1}{2}}\left(\frac{\frac{1}{120}}{\frac{1}{400}}\right) = -\frac{10}{3} = -3.33.$$

(b) The slope of Mary's reservation indifference curve at $NI = (120, 400)$ is

$$-\frac{p_M}{1-p_M}\left(\frac{U'(120)}{U'(400)}\right) = -\frac{\frac{1}{5}}{1-\frac{1}{5}}\left(\frac{\frac{1}{120}}{\frac{1}{400}}\right) = -\frac{5}{6} = -0.83.$$

(c) To find the full-insurance contract that makes Sara indifferent between insuring and not insuring we need to solve the equation $\ln(W) = \frac{1}{2}\ln(120) + \frac{1}{2}\ln(400)$. The solution is $W = 219.09$, so that the maximum premium that Sara is willing to pay for full insurance is $400 - 219.09 = \$180.91$. If Sara purchases this full-insurance contract then the insurance company's expected profit is $180.91 - \frac{1}{2}(280) = \$40.91$.

(d) To find the full-insurance contract that makes Mary indifferent between insuring and not insuring we need to solve the equation $\ln(W) = \frac{1}{5}\ln(120) + \frac{4}{5}\ln(400)$. The solution is $W = 314.40$, so that the maximum premium that Mary is willing to pay for full insurance is $400 - 314.40 = \$85.60$. If Mary purchases this full-insurance contract then the insurance company's expected profit is $85.60 - \frac{1}{5}(280) = \$29.60$. □

Solution to Exercise 8.2

(a) The monopolist will offer Diana the full-insurance contract that makes her indifferent between insuring and not insuring, which is determined by the solution to $\sqrt{W} = \frac{1}{4}\sqrt{1,296} + \frac{3}{4}\sqrt{4,096}$. The solution is $W = 3,249$, so that the premium of the full-insurance contract is $4,096 - 3,249 = \$847$. If Diana purchases this full-insurance contract then the insurance company's expected profit from this contract is $847 - \frac{1}{4}(2,800) = \$147$.

(b) The monopolist will offer Fran the full-insurance contract that makes her indifferent between insuring and not insuring, which is determined by the solution to $\sqrt{W} = \frac{1}{16}\sqrt{1,296} + \frac{15}{16}\sqrt{4,096}$. The solution is $W = 3,875.06$, so that the premium of the full-insurance contract is $4,096 - 3,875.06 = \$220.94$. If Fran purchases this full-insurance contract then the insurance company's expected profit is $220.94 - \frac{1}{16}(2,800) = \$45.94$.

(c) The monopolist's expected profit from insuring Diana and Fran is $147 + 45.94 = \$192.94$. □

Solution to Exercise 8.3

The monopolist would offer the full-insurance contract that makes the H-types indifferent between insuring and not insuring. To find that contract, solve the equation $U(W) = p_H U(W_0 - \ell) + (1 - p_H)U(W_0)$, that is,

$$10\ln\left(\frac{W}{1,000}\right) = \frac{1}{5}10\ln(1.5) + \frac{4}{5}10\ln(4).$$

The solution is $W = 3,287.50$. Thus the offered full-insurance contract has a premium of $4,000 - 3,287.50 = \$712.50$. This contract will be purchased only by the H-types (the L-types are better off without insurance). Thus the monopolist's expected total profits are

$$12,000\left[712.50 - \frac{1}{5}(2,500)\right] = \$2,550,000.$$

□

Solution to Exercise 8.4

(a) We need to show that the L-type reservation indifference curve is less steep at the no-insurance point, than the average isoprofit line, that is,

$$\frac{p_L}{1-p_L}\left(\frac{U'(W_0-\ell)}{U'(W_0)}\right) \leq \frac{\bar{p}}{1-\bar{p}} \qquad (8.26)$$

First we compute the average probability of loss $\bar{p}$. Since $q_H = \frac{12,000}{16,000} = \frac{3}{4}$,

$$\bar{p} = \frac{3}{4}\left(\frac{1}{5}\right) + \frac{1}{4}\left(\frac{1}{15}\right) = \frac{1}{6}.$$

Thus

$$\frac{\bar{p}}{1-\bar{p}} = \frac{1}{5} = 0.2.$$

On the other hand,

$$\frac{p_L}{1-p_L}\left(\frac{U'(W_0-\ell)}{U'(W_0)}\right) = \frac{1}{14}\frac{\frac{10}{1,500}}{\frac{10}{4,000}} = \frac{4}{21} = 0.1905.$$

Thus inequality (8.26) is indeed satisfied.

(b) To find that contract, solve the equation $U(W) = p_L U(W_0 - \ell) + (1 - p_L)U(W_0)$, that is,

$$10\ln\left(\frac{W}{1,000}\right) = \frac{1}{15}10\ln(1.5) + \frac{14}{15}10\ln(4).$$

The solution is $W = 3,746.81$. Thus the offered full-insurance contract has a premium of $4,000 - 3,746.81 = \$253.19$. This contract would be purchased by both types. Thus the monopolist's expected total profits would be $N(253.19 - \bar{p}\ell)$:

$$16,000\left[253.19 - \frac{1}{6}(2,500)\right] = \$-2,615,626.67,$$

that is, a loss.

□

8.6 Solutions to Exercises

Solution to Exercise 8.5

(a) We need to show that the L-type reservation indifference curve is steeper, at the no-insurance point, than the average isoprofit line, that is,

$$\frac{p_L}{1-p_L}\left(\frac{U'(W_0-\ell)}{U'(W_0)}\right) > \frac{\bar{p}}{1-\bar{p}} \qquad (8.27)$$

First we compute the average probability of loss $\bar{p}$. Since $q_H = \frac{6{,}000}{10{,}000} = \frac{3}{5}$,

$$\bar{p} = \frac{3}{5}\left(\frac{1}{5}\right) + \frac{2}{5}\left(\frac{1}{15}\right) = \frac{11}{75}.$$

Thus

$$\frac{\bar{p}}{1-\bar{p}} = \frac{11}{64} = 0.1719.$$

On the other hand,

$$\frac{p_L}{1-p_L}\left(\frac{U'(W_0-\ell)}{U'(W_0)}\right) = \frac{1}{14}\frac{\frac{10}{1{,}500}}{\frac{10}{4{,}000}} = \frac{4}{21} = 0.1905.$$

Thus inequality (8.27) is indeed satisfied.

(b) The equations are as follows (see (8.9) and (8.10) on page 262):

$$p_L U(W_1) + (1-p_L)U(W_2) = p_L U(W_0 - \ell) + (1-p_L)U(W_0)$$

$$\frac{p_L}{1-p_L}\left(\frac{U'(W_1)}{U'(W_2)}\right) = \frac{\bar{p}}{1-\bar{p}}.$$

that is,

$$\frac{1}{15}10\ln\left(\frac{W_1}{1{,}000}\right) + \frac{14}{15}10\ln\left(\frac{W_1}{1{,}000}\right) = \frac{1}{15}10\ln(1.5) + \frac{14}{15}10\ln(4)$$

$$\frac{\frac{1}{15}\left(\frac{10}{W_1}\right)}{\frac{14}{15}\left(\frac{10}{W_2}\right)} = \frac{\frac{11}{75}}{\frac{64}{75}}.$$

The solution is $W_1 = 1{,}650.99$ and $W_2 = 3{,}972.69$. Thus the premium of the offered contract is $4{,}000 - 3{,}972.69 = \$27.31$ and the deductible is $3{,}972.69 - 1{,}650.99 = \$2{,}321.70$. Both types purchase this contract. Thus the monopolist's expected total profits are:

$$10{,}000\left[27.31 - \frac{11}{75}(2{,}500 - 2{,}321.70)\right] = \$11{,}593.33.$$

□

Solution to Exercise 8.6

(a) First calculate the maximum premium that the H-types are willing to pay for full insurance by solving

$$\frac{2}{10}\sqrt{9,000} + \frac{8}{10}\sqrt{16,000} = \sqrt{16,000 - h}.$$

The solution is $h_{max}^H = \$1,560$. Thus under Option 1 the monopolist would only offer full insurance at a premium of $\$1,560$, attracting only the H-types; its total expected profits would be

$$1,000\left(1,560 - \frac{2}{10}7,000\right) = \$160,000.$$

(b) The average probability of loss is

$$\bar{p} = q_H p_H + (1 - q_H) p_L = \frac{1}{6}\left(\frac{2}{10}\right) + \frac{5}{6}\left(\frac{1}{10}\right) = \frac{7}{60}.$$

(c) The equations whose solution gives the profit-maximizing contract under Option 2 are:

$$p_L U(W_0 - \ell) + (1 - p_L) U(W_0) = p_L U(W_0 - h - d) + (1 - p_L) U(W_0 - h)$$

$$\frac{p_L}{1 - p_L}\left(\frac{U'(W_0 - h - d)}{U'(W_0 - h)}\right) = \frac{\bar{p}}{1 - \bar{p}}, \quad \text{that is,}$$

$$\frac{1}{10}\sqrt{9,000} + \frac{9}{10}\sqrt{16,000} = \frac{1}{10}\sqrt{16,000 - h - d} + \frac{9}{10}\sqrt{16,000 - h}$$

$$\frac{\frac{1}{10}\left(\frac{1}{2\sqrt{16,000-h-d}}\right)}{\frac{9}{10}\left(\frac{1}{2\sqrt{16,000-h}}\right)} = \frac{\frac{7}{60}}{\frac{53}{60}}.$$

(d) The assumption is that $C_H = (h_H = 1400, d_H = 0)$. To find contract $C_L = (h_L, d_L)$ solve the following equations:

$$\frac{2}{10}\sqrt{16,000 - h - d} + \frac{8}{10}\sqrt{16,000 - h} = \sqrt{16,000 - 1,400}$$

$$\frac{1}{10}\sqrt{16,000 - h - d} + \frac{9}{10}\sqrt{16,000 - h} = \frac{1}{10}\sqrt{9,000} + \frac{9}{10}\sqrt{16,000}$$

(e) The two contracts are: $C_H = (h_H = 1400, d_H = 0)$, which will be bought by the H-types, and $C_L = (h_L = 167.52, d_L = 5663.07)$, which will be bought by the L-types.[13] Thus the monopolist's expected total profits will be

$$1,000\left(1,400 - \frac{2}{10}7,000\right) + 5,000\left[167.52 - \frac{1}{10}(7,000 - 5,663.07)\right] = \$169,135. \square$$

---

[13] The contract was given in terms of wealth levels as $(10169.41, 15832.48)$, from which we obtain the premium as $16,000 - 15,832.48 = 167.52$ and the deductible as $15,832.48 - 10,169.41 = 5,663.07$.

8.6 Solutions to Exercises

Solution to Exercise 8.7

(a) First calculate the maximum premium that the H-types are willing to pay for full insurance by solving

$$\frac{1}{4}\ln(4,000) + \frac{3}{4}\ln(10,000) = \ln(10,000 - h).$$

The solution is $h_{max}^H = \$2,047.29$. Thus under Option 1 the monopolist would only offer full insurance at a premium of $\$2,047.29$, attracting only the H-types; its total expected profits would be

$$1,500\left(2,047.29 - \frac{1}{4}(6,000)\right) = \$820,935.$$

(b) The average probability of loss is

$$\bar{p} = q_H p_H + (1 - q_H)p_L = \frac{3}{16}\left(\frac{1}{4}\right) + \frac{13}{16}\left(\frac{1}{16}\right) = \frac{25}{256}.$$

(c) The equations whose solution gives the profit-maximizing contract under Option 2 are:

$$p_L U(W_0 - \ell) + (1 - p_L)U(W_0) = p_L U(W_0 - h - d) + (1 - p_L)U(W_0 - h)$$

$$\frac{p_L}{1 - p_L}\left(\frac{U'(W_0 - h - d)}{U'(W_0 - h)}\right) = \frac{\bar{p}}{1 - \bar{p}}$$

that is,

$$\frac{1}{16}\ln(4,000) + \frac{15}{16}\ln(10,000) = \frac{1}{16}\ln(10,000 - h - d) + \frac{15}{16}\ln(10,000 - h)$$

$$\frac{\frac{1}{16}}{\frac{15}{16}}\left(\frac{\frac{1}{10,000-h-d}}{\frac{1}{10,000-h}}\right) = \frac{\frac{25}{256}}{\frac{231}{256}}.$$

(d) The assumption is that $C_H = (h_H = 2000, d_H = 0)$. To find contract $C_L = (h_L, d_L)$ solve the following equations:

$$\frac{1}{4}\ln(10,000 - h - d) + \frac{3}{4}\ln(10,000 - h) = \ln(10,000 - 2,000)$$

$$\frac{1}{16}\ln(10,000 - h - d) + \frac{15}{16}\ln(10,000 - h) = \frac{1}{16}\ln(4,000) + \frac{15}{16}\ln(10,000)$$

(e) The two contracts are: $C_H = (h_H = 2000, d_H = 0)$, which will be bought by the H-types, and $C_L = (h_L = 19.74, d_L = 5859.9)$, which will be bought by the L-types.[14] Thus the monopolist's expected total profits will be

$$1,500\left(2,000 - \frac{1}{4}6,000\right) + 6,500\left[19.74 - \frac{1}{16}(6,000 - 5,859.9)\right] = \$821,394.38. \square$$

---

[14]The contract was given in terms of wealth levels as $(4120.36, 9980.26)$, from which we obtain the premium as $10,000 - 9,980.26 = 19.74$ and the deductible as $9,980.26 - 4,120.36 = 5,859.9$.

Solution to Exercise 8.8

(a) Contract C_H is the full-insurance contract that yields zero profits if bought only by the H-types. Thus its premium is given by the solution to $h_H - p_H \ell = 0$, that is, $h_H = \frac{2}{10}(7,000) = \$1,400$. Contract C_L is given by the intersection of the H-type indifference curve through C_H and the low-risk zero-profit line; thus it is given by the solution to

$$\sqrt{16,000 - 1,400} = \frac{2}{10}\sqrt{16,000 - h - d} + \frac{8}{10}\sqrt{16,000 - h}$$

$$h - \frac{1}{10}(7,000 - d) = 0$$

which is $C_L = (h_L = 109.32, d_L = 5906.81)$.

(b) The average probability of loss is

$$\bar{p} = q_H p_H + (1 - q_H) p_L = \frac{1}{6}\left(\frac{2}{10}\right) + \frac{5}{6}\left(\frac{1}{10}\right) = \frac{7}{60}.$$

(c) We need to express the fact that there is a contract at which the average zero-profit line intersects the L-type indifference curve through contract $C_L = (h_L = 109.32, d_L = 5906.81)$:

$$h - \frac{7}{60}(7,000 - d) = 0$$

$$\frac{1}{10}\sqrt{16,000 - 109.32 - 5,906.81} + \frac{9}{10}\sqrt{16,000 - 109.32}$$
$$= \frac{1}{10}\sqrt{16,000 - h - d} + \frac{9}{10}\sqrt{16,000 - h}.$$

□

Solution to Exercise 8.9

(a) Contract C_H is the full-insurance contract that yields zero profits if bought only by the H-types. Thus its premium is given by the solution to $h_H - p_H \ell = 0$, that is, $h_H = \frac{1}{4}(6,000) = \$1,500$. Contract C_L is given by the intersection of the H-type indifference curve through C_H and the low-risk zero-profit line; thus it is given by the solution to

$$\ln(10,000 - 1,500) = \frac{1}{4}\ln(10,000 - h - d) + \frac{3}{4}\ln(10,000 - h)$$

$$h - \frac{1}{16}(6,000 - d) = 0$$

which is $C_L = (h_L = 90.98, d_L = 4544.31)$.

8.6 Solutions to Exercises

(b) The average probability of loss is

$$\bar{p} = q_H p_H + (1 - q_H) p_L = \frac{3}{16}\left(\frac{1}{4}\right) + \frac{13}{16}\left(\frac{1}{16}\right) = \frac{25}{256}.$$

(c) We need to express the fact that there is a contract at which the average zero-profit line intersects the L-type indifference curve through contract $C_L = (h_L = 90.98, d_L = 4544.31)$:

$$h - \frac{25}{256}(6,000 - d) = 0$$

$$\frac{1}{16}\ln(10,000 - 90.98 - 4,544.31) + \frac{15}{16}\ln(10,000 - 90.98)$$
$$= \frac{1}{16}\ln(10,000 - h - d) + \frac{15}{16}\ln(10,000 - h).$$

□

IV Asymmetric Information: Signaling

9 Signaling 297
    9.1   Earnings and education
    9.2   Signaling in the job market
    9.3   Indices versus signals
    9.4   More than two types
    9.5   A more general analysis
    9.6   Signaling in other markets
    9.7   Exercises
    9.8   Solutions to Exercises

9. Signaling

9.1 Earnings and education

It is well-known that education can be viewed as an investment, since - typically - higher levels of education are associated with higher earnings. Table 9.1 shows the relationship between level of education and median annual income for the year 2018.[1]

Table 9.1: Median annual earnings by level of education, 2018.

Educational attainment	Median annual earnings
Less than a high school diploma	$28,756
High school diploma	$37,960
Some college, no degree	$41,704
Associate's degree	$44,824
Bachelor's degree	$62,296
Master's degree	$74,568
Doctoral degree	$94,900
Professional degree	$97,968

Thus, for example, in 2018 a worker with a Bachelor's degree had an annual income

---

[1] The data in Table 9.1 refers to persons of age 25 and over, who are full-time wage and salary workers. Source: Current Population Survey, U.S. Department of Labor, U.S. Bureau of Labor Statistics, https://www.bls.gov/emp/tables/unemployment-earnings-education.htm. We have converted the data from weekly to annual figures.

that was 64% higher than the income of a worker with only a High-school diploma, and a Master's degree translated into a further 20% increase in income. Given the positive correlation between level of education and earnings, it is natural to ask the following questions:

1. Why do some people choose lower levels of education than others?
2. Why do employers reward higher levels of education with higher salaries?
3. Does the availability of educational institutions make society better off?

The answer to the first question is that, while education offers clear benefits in terms of earnings, it also involves direct and opportunity costs. The opportunity cost of pursuing a college degree, for example, is the income that one foregoes during the four years of college. The direct cost of a college degree is the amount of money that one spends during those four years in tuition, books, etc., as well as the subsequent interest cost on loans taken during the college years. For some individuals those costs are lower than for others: for example, children of more affluent parents do not need to borrow in order to pay tuition costs or are able to obtain zero-interest loans from family members. Furthermore, there are also differential psychological costs associated with college life: some find studying more difficult and more burdensome than others. Thus, for some, a cost-benefit calculation leads to the decision to acquire a lower level of education, while others pursue higher levels of education.

The answer to the second question seems obvious too: employers pay more educated workers more, because those workers have become more productive and more valuable to the employer as a consequence of the additional education. In other words, *employers recognize that there is an objective, causal relationship between education and productivity: the more education you acquire, the more productive you become.* But is there truly such a causal relationship between education and productivity? Is it at all possible that employers are objectively wrong in postulating such a relationship between education and productivity? What if a person's productivity was determined at birth by his/her genetic makeup and education had no effect at all on productivity? Could this be possible?

Before the 1974 seminal contribution of Michael Spence,[2] an economist would have denied such a possibility by arguing as follows. It is certainly possible that employers might start with some incorrect hypothesis about the relationship between education and productivity, but then their experience would reveal that, sometimes, highly educated employees turn out to be less productive than, or as productive as, less educated employees. The employers would then adjust their beliefs, so that, with sufficient time and experience, they would discover that their initial hypothesis was wrong and would therefore no longer automatically offer higher salaries to more educated job applicants. Spence's contribution was to show the possibility *self-confirming beliefs*: the employers' (objectively wrong) beliefs induce them to make education-dependent wage offers, which - in turn - induce prospective employees to make choices of education levels which then confirm the employers' beliefs, thus generating an equilibrium where nobody has any reason to change his/her actions and beliefs. Such a situation is called a *signaling equilibrium* and is the object of the next section.

---

[2] Michael Spence, *Market signaling: Informational transfer in hiring and related screening processes*, Harvard University Press, 1974.

9.2 Signaling in the job market

9.2.1 Signaling equilibrium

Let us begin with a simple example. In Table 9.2 we measure the possible levels of education of a job applicant in terms of the number of years spent in school, denoted by y, and associated educational certificate:

Table 9.2: Possible levels of education and corresponding certificates.

Years of schooling	Corresponding education certificate
$y = 6$	Elementary school
$y = 12$	High school diploma
$y = 16$	Bachelor's degree
$y = 18$	Master's degree
$y = 21$	Ph.D. degree

Suppose that employers believe that education increases productivity, so that the more educated a candidate is, the more valuable he/she is to the employer. These beliefs are manifested through a wage schedule that associates higher salaries with higher levels of education, as shown in the following table:

Table 9.3: Offered wage as a function of education.

Education	Wage offered
$y = 6$	\$6,000
$y = 12$	\$20,000
$y = 16$	\$25,000
$y = 18$	\$30,000
$y = 21$	\$32,000

Thus, for example, a job candidate who only has a High-school diploma will be offered a salary of \$20,000, while a job candidate with a Bachelor's degree will be offered a higher salary, namely \$25,000.

Now the reader is asked to *imagine a world where education has no effect on a person's productivity*. In particular, in this hypothetical world there are only two types of individuals: Type H whose productivity is worth \$30,000 to potential employers (and is unaffected by education), and type L whose productivity is worth \$20,000 to potential employers (and is also unaffected by education). The proportion of individuals of type H in the population is p_H, with $0 < p_H < 1$, so that the proportion of type L is $(1 - p_H)$. We assume that each individual knows her own type, while a potential employer is unable to determine the type of a job applicant. Thus we are in a situation of *asymmetric information*. One last assumption is that the two types have different monetary costs of acquiring education, which are as follows:

$$\text{For type } H: \quad C_H(y) = \begin{cases} 0 & \text{if } y \leq 6 \\ 1{,}000(y-6) & \text{if } y > 6 \end{cases}$$

$$\text{For type } L: \quad C_L(y) = \begin{cases} 0 & \text{if } y \leq 6 \\ 2{,}000(y-6) & \text{if } y > 6 \end{cases}$$

Thus every year of schooling beyond 6th grade costs \$1,000 to an H-type and \$2,000 to an L-type.

Each type will choose that level of education that yields the largest net income. The cost-benefit analysis for a type-H person is shown in Table 9.4.

Table 9.4: The cost-benefit analysis of a type-H person.

y years in school	w gross wage	C_H cost	$w - C_H$ net wage
$y = 6$	\$6,000	\$0	\$6,000
$y = 12$	\$20,000	\$6,000	\$14,000
$y = 16$	\$25,000	\$10,000	\$15,000
$\boxed{y = 18}$	\$30,000	\$12,000	$\boxed{\$18{,}000}$
$y = 21$	\$32,000	\$15,000	\$17,000

Thus an H-type will maximize her net income by pursuing a Master's degree (corresponding to 18 years of schooling).

On the other hand, a type-L person faces the cost-benefit calculations shown in Table 9.5.

Table 9.5: The cost-benefit analysis of a type-L person.

y years in school	w gross wage	C_L cost	$w - C_L$ net wage
$y = 6$	\$6,000	\$0	\$6,000
$\boxed{y = 12}$	\$20,000	\$12,000	$\boxed{\$8{,}000}$
$y = 16$	\$25,000	\$20,000	\$5,000
$y = 18$	\$30,000	\$24,000	\$6,000
$y = 21$	\$32,000	\$30,000	\$2,000

Hence a type-L person will maximize his net income by obtaining a High-school diploma (corresponding to 12 years of schooling).

In this hypothetical world type-L individuals, whose productivity is $20,000, will present themselves at a job interview with a High-school diploma and, according to the employers' wage schedule (Table 9.3), they will be offered a wage of $20,000 which matches their true productivity. On the other hand, type-H individuals, whose productivity is $30,000, will present themselves at a job interview with a Master's degree and, according to the employers' wage schedule, they will be offered a wage of $30,000 which matches their true productivity. After hiring candidates according to the wage schedule shown in Table 9.3 - which reflects their initial beliefs that more education causes higher productivity - employers will observe that, indeed, those with a Master's degree turn out to be more productive than those who only have a High-school diploma, thus confirming their initial (wrong) beliefs; furthermore, every employee is paid an amount that matches her/his true productivity. Hence employers have no reason to change their beliefs and their hiring practices. Since the wage schedule remains the same, both types have no reason to change their education choices. Thus we have a situation of equilibrium. Following Spence, we call such a situation a *signaling equilibrium*.

9.2.2 Pareto inefficiency

In the previous section we asked the question: "Does the availability of educational institutions make society better off?". Let us continue to analyse the hypothetical world described in the previous section and ask whether it is possible that, were the government to ban all institutions of higher education, everybody would be at least as well off as before the government intervention and some individuals would be better off. That is, we ask whether closing down educational institutions beyond High school would lead to a *Pareto improvement*.

Suppose that, in the new world, every individual were *required* to obtain a High-school diploma, but no further education were available. Furthermore, suppose that employers were instructed to pay each job applicant a wage equal to the average wage that they were paying in the pre-intervention world.[3] Let N be the number of workers hired by an employer. Before the government intervention, since the fraction p_H of the population is of type H, the employer would have employed $p_H N$ people of type H at a salary of $30,000 (those who had a Master's degree) and $(1-p_H)N$ people of type L at a salary of $20,000 (those who had a High-school diploma), for a total wage bill of $p_H N 30,000 + (1-p_H)N 20,000 = [p_H 30,000 + (1-p_H)20,000]N$ and thus a wage of $[p_H 30,000 + (1-p_H)20,000]$ per worker. If the employer were required to pay this amount to each job applicant in the post-intervention world, then the employer would be as well off as before.

In the post-intervention world each type-L worker would be better off, since $[p_H 30,000 + (1-p_H)20,000] > 20,000$, that is, for these individuals, the new-world wage is higher than the old-world wage (and the education level, and associated cost, are the same). What about the type-H workers? A type-H individual will be better off if her net income is higher; in the old world her net income was $18,000 (equal to a wage of $30,000 minus the cost of acquiring a Master's degree, which is $12,000), while in the new world her net

---

[3] This could be the initial wage, which can then be adjusted, up or down, later when the employer discovers the true productivity of each employee.

income is $[p_H 30,000 + (1-p_H)20,000] - 6,000$ (where \$6,000 is her cost of obtaining a High-school diploma). Thus, a type-H individual is made better off by the government intervention if and only if

$$[p_H 30,000 + (1-p_H)20,000] - 6,000 > 18,000,$$

that is, if and only if $p_H > \frac{2}{5}$. That is, if type-H individuals constitute at least 40% of the population, then eliminating all the institutions of higher education would lead to a Pareto improvement![4]

9.2.3 Alternative interpretation of a signaling equilibrium

In Section 9.2.1 we interpreted a signaling equilibrium as a situation where the employers' objectively wrong beliefs become self confirming: employers manifest their beliefs in education-dependent wage offers, which induce different types of prospective employees to make different choices of education, which in turn leads to employers getting information that confirms their initial beliefs, so that the situation is self-sustaining and there is no reason for anybody to change his/her beliefs and choices.

An alternative interpretation of a signaling equilibrium is not based on the assumption that employers hold wrong beliefs. Employers may be fully aware that education has no effect on productivity, but they are also aware of the fact that in the population there are different types of individuals with different productivity. As in Section 9.2.1 suppose that there are only two types of individuals: type H with high productivity and type L with low productivity; furthermore, employers cannot tell individuals apart, while each prospective employee knows her own type. Then high-productivity individuals face the problem of how to credibly convey to employers that they are of type H, in order to be paid a higher wage. Simply claiming to be a high-productivity type would not work, because every individual would make such a claim and thus it would not be credible. What is needed is a *costly signal* that is too costly for a type-L individual to use but not too costly for a type-H individual, so that only the latter avail themselves of it. Such a signal would allow the better types to *separate themselves* from the worse types. A signaling equilibrium is then a *separating equilibrium* in which the H types send the costly signal, while the L types do not and thus employers can distinguish between job applicants on the basis of the presence or absence of such a signal. In the job market education can be such a signal.

We shall now give a more precise definition of a signaling equilibrium in the more general case where education can potentially affect productivity. For the moment we continue to assume that there are only two types in the population: type H and type L, with proportions p_H and $(1-p_H)$, respectively. Suppose that productivity is a (possibly constant) function of the amount of education y, as follows:

$$\text{For type } H: \quad a + s_H y \qquad (9.1)$$
$$\text{For type } L: \quad b + s_L y \qquad (9.2)$$

with $0 \leq b \leq a$, $0 \leq s_L \leq s_H$ and either $b < a$ or $s_L < s_H$ (or both). Thus, if $b < a$ and $s_L = s_H = 0$, then we are in the world considered in Section 9.2.1 where education has

---

[4]If also High schools were to be eliminated, then every worker would be even better off, since workers would now choose $y = 6$ and a type-L individual would save \$12,000 in education costs, while a type-H individual would save an additional \$6,000 relative to obtaining a High-school diploma. Indeed, in this case for a Pareto improvement it is sufficient to have $p_H 30,000 + (1-p_H)20,000 > 18,000$, that is, $p_H > \frac{1}{5}$.

9.2 Signaling in the job market

no effect on productivity, while if $s_H > s_L$ then more education translates into higher productivity (for both types if $s_L > 0$ or only for the H type if $s_L = 0$).[5]

As in Section 9.2.1, the additional crucial assumption is that education is more costly for individuals of type L than for individuals of type H. Let the monetary cost of education be:

$$\text{For type } H: \quad c_H\, y \qquad (9.3)$$

$$\text{For type } L: \quad c_L\, y \qquad (9.4)$$

with $0 < c_H < c_L$, $c_L > s_L$ and $c_H > s_H$; the last two inequalities mean that, for each type, the cost of an extra unit of education exceeds the benefit in terms of the extra productivity gained.

We assume that employers know the relationship between education and productivity given by (9.1) and (9.2) and thus are willing to offer higher wages to more educated job applicants. However, if a job applicant has level of education $\hat{y}$, then the employer would not know whether to offer a wage equal to $a + s_H \hat{y}$ or a wage equal to $b + s_L \hat{y}$, because the employer does not know if the applicant is of type H or of type L. Suppose, therefore, that employers choose an arbitrary threshold level of education y^* and announce that anybody who applies with education level $y \geq y^*$ will be presumed to be of type H and offered a wage equal to $a + s_H y$ and anybody with education level $y < y^*$ will be presumed to be of type L and offered a wage equal to $b + s_L y$.

> **Definition 9.2.1** A *separating signaling equilibrium* is a triple (y^*, y_H, y_L) where y^* is the threshold level set by employers, y_H is the education level chosen by every individual of type H and y_L is the education level chosen by every individual of type L, such that:
>
> 1. $y_H \geq y^* > y_L$, so that a type H is paid a wage equal to $a + s_H y_H$ and a type L is paid a wage equal to $b + s_L y_L$,
>
> 2. the net income of a type H is maximized when she chooses education level y_H,
>
> 3. the net income of a type L is maximized when he chooses education level y_L.

The term 'separating' means that the two types make difference choices of education.

> (R) Note that, since $c_L > s_L$, at a signaling equilibrium it must be that $y_L = 0$, because if $y_L > 0$ then the net income of a type L is $b + s_L y_L - c_L y_L = b + (s_L - c_L) y_L < b$, violating Point 3 of Definition 9.2.1: a type L would get a higher net income, namely b, if he were to choose $y = 0$.
>
> Similarly, since $c_H > s_H$, at a signaling equilibrium it must be that $y_H = y^*$, because if $y_H > y^*$ then the net income of a type H is $a + s_H y_H - c_H y_H = a + (s_H - c_H) y_H < a + (s_H - c_H) y^*$, violating Point 2 of Definition 9.2.1: a type H would get a higher net income, namely $a + (s_H - c_H) y^*$, is she were to switch from y_H to y^*.
>
> The same argument shows that every individual - whatever her type - will only consider choosing either $y = 0$ or $y = y^*$: any choice strictly between 0 and y^* is worse than 0 and any choice greater than y^* is worse than y^*.

---

[5] The initial example considered by Spence is one where $a = 2$, $b = 1$ and $s_L = s_H = 0$.

Thus (y^*, y_H, y_L) is a separating signaling equilibrium (given the employers' wage schedule, according to which a candidate with $y \geq y^*$ is classified as type H and everybody else is classified as type L) if and only if:[6]

1.
$$a + s_H y^* - c_H y^* \geq b \quad (9.5)$$

(this inequality says that a type H prefers to choose $y = y^*$ and be classified correctly as type H, rather than choosing $y = 0$ and be classified incorrectly as type L, where 'prefers' means 'obtains a higher net income'),

2.
$$b \geq a + s_H y^* - c_L y^* \quad (9.6)$$

(this inequality says that a type L prefers to choose $y = 0$ and be classified correctly as type L, rather than choosing $y = y^*$ and be classified incorrectly as a type H, in which case he would be paid a wage equal to $a + s_H y^*$).

It should be noted that there may be a *multiplicity of separating signaling equilibria* (indeed, even a continuum). For example, let us consider the case where $a = 2$, $b = 1$, $s_H = s_L = 0$, $c_H = \frac{1}{2}$ and $c_H = 1$ (thus, in this case, productivity is not affected by education). Then inequalities (9.5) and (9.6) become:

$$2 - \tfrac{1}{2} y^* \geq 1$$
$$1 \geq 2 - y^*$$

which are equivalent to $1 \leq y^* \leq 2$. Thus, for every $y^* \in [1, 2]$, the triple $(y^*, y_H = y^*, y_L = 0)$ is a separating signaling equilibrium. These equilibria are *Pareto ranked*: the lower the value of y^* the better off individuals of type H are (since their net income is $2 - \tfrac{1}{2} y^*$); on the other hand, the L types are indifferent among all the equilibria, since their net income is always 1 and the employers are also indifferent because their total wage bill is the same at each of those equilibria, namely $2 p_H N + (1 - p_H) N$ (where, as before, p_H is the proportion of type H in the population and N is the number of people employed), which, in turn is equal to total productivity.

To reiterate the point made in Section 9.2.2, we show that also in this example it is possible for a signaling equilibrium to be Pareto inefficient. Consider the alternative situation where

(1) the possibility of signaling through education is removed, so that every individual is forced to choose $y = 0$ and

(2) everybody is paid a wage equal to the average productivity of the population, which is

---
[6] Whether we use weak or strict inequalities depends on what we assume in case an individual is indifferent. Since we use weak inequalities, our implicit assumption is that, when indifferent between $y = 0$ and $y = y^*$, a type H would choose $y = y^*$ while a type L would choose $y = 0$.

$2p_H + (1 - p_H) = 1 + p_H.$

Then employers are as well off in the new situation and type L individuals are better off (their wage is now $1 + p_H$ whereas in the previous situation it was 1). Type H individuals are better off in the new situation if and only if $1 + p_H > 2 - \frac{1}{2}y^*$, which is possible: for example if $y^* = 1.5$ and $p_H > \frac{1}{4}$.

> Test your understanding of the concepts introduced in this section, by going through the exercises in Section 9.7.1 at the end of this chapter.

9.3 Indices versus signals

A signal is an observable characteristic that can be modified by the agents concerned and is available to every type of individual. Examples of signals are: education, hair style, the way one dresses, whether one wears make-up or not, etc. If employers indicate that they take a particular signal as a sign of higher productivity - by offering a higher salary to those who display that signal - then in principle every individual can choose that signal and qualify for a higher wage. For example, if employers believed that people with short hair were more productive, then everybody could choose to cut their hair short and obtain a higher wage. The reason why some people do choose a particular signal (e.g. a sufficiently high level of education) and others do not is that the former face a lower cost of acquiring the signal.

There are also other characteristics that *cannot* be modified (or are prohibitively expensive to modify) by the individual, such as race, gender, height, skin color, etc. Any such characteristic is called an *index* (the plural is 'indices'). If employers believed that taller people were more productive, and thus offered a higher salary to those whose height was above a certain threshold, then there would be nothing that short people could do to qualify for the higher salary.

At the beginning of the previous section we offered an interpretation of a signaling equilibrium in the job market in terms of self-confirming - although objectively wrong - beliefs (in that context the wrong beliefs were about the causal relationship between education and productivity). It seems that this phenomenon cannot happen when the wrong beliefs involve an index rather than a signal. To continue the example of height, if there is no objective correlation between height and productivity and yet employers believed that taller people were more productive, then initially they would offer taller people higher salaries, but over time they would observe that shorter employees, on average, were as productive as taller employees and the evidence would force them to change their beliefs.

Spence, however, showed that this intuition is wrong: the possibility of objectively wrong beliefs concerning an index can be self-confirming if the index is combined with a signal.

We will show this by continuing the example analyzed in Section 9.2.1. We consider a world where education has no effect on a person's productivity. In particular, in this hypothetical world there are only two types of individuals: type H whose productivity is worth $30,000 to potential employers (and is unaffected by education), and type L whose productivity is worth $20,000 to potential employers (and is also unaffected by education). The proportion of individuals of type H in the population is p_H, with $0 < p_H < 1$ and the proportion of type L is thus $(1 - p_H)$. We also assume that, within each group, men and women are equinumerous, that is, 50% of type H are men and 50% are women and, similarly, 50% of type L are men and 50% are women. We also assume that employers hold beliefs that are *doubly wrong*: they believe that

1. education increases productivity, and
2. women are less able to learn and thus require more education than their male counterpart in order to achieve a higher level of productivity.

Employers manifest their beliefs by offering different wage schedules to men and women: there is no difference up to High-school diploma, but then certificates of higher education are remunerated differently across men and women. The wage schedules are as shown in Table 9.6 (note that, for men, the wage schedule coincides with Table 9.3 in Section 9.2.1).

Table 9.6: Offered wage as a function of education and gender.

Education	Wage offered to men	Wage offered to women
Elementary school ($y = 6$)	$6,000	$6,000
High-school diploma ($y = 12$)	$20,000	$20,000
College degree ($y = 16$)	$25,000	$23,000
Master's degree ($y = 18$)	$30,000	$26,000
Ph.D. degree ($y = 21$)	$32,000	$30,000

Thus employers' beliefs embody a wrong view of the effect of education on productivity (recall that productivity is assumed to be constant and thus independent of the amount of education) as well as a prejudice against women (women are thought to be innately less able to convert education into productivity).

We continue to assume, as in Section 9.2.1, that the two types of individuals have different monetary costs of acquiring education:

For type H (man or woman): $C_H(y) = \begin{cases} 0 & \text{if } y \leq 6 \\ 1,000(y-6) & \text{if } y > 6 \end{cases}$

For type L (man or woman): $C_L(y) = \begin{cases} 0 & \text{if } y \leq 6 \\ 2,000(y-6) & \text{if } y > 6 \end{cases}$

Thus every year of schooling beyond 6th grade costs $1,000 to an H-type, whether it is a man or a woman, and $2,000 to an L-type, whether it is a man or a woman.

9.3 Indices versus signals

The cost-benefit analysis for a *man* of type L is the same as in Table 9.5 in Section 9.2.1, with the conclusion that a man of type L would choose $y = 12$.

A *woman* of type-L faces the cost-benefit calculations shown in Table 9.7.

Table 9.7: The cost-benefit analysis of a type-L woman.

y years in school	w gross wage	C_L cost	$w - C_L$ net wage
$y = 6$	\$6,000	\$0	\$6,000
$\boxed{y = 12}$	\$20,000	\$12,000	$\boxed{\$8,000}$
$y = 16$	\$23,000	\$20,000	\$3,000
$y = 18$	\$26,000	\$24,000	\$2,000
$y = 21$	\$30,000	\$30,000	\$0

Thus also a woman of type L would choose $y = 12$.

The cost-benefit analysis for a *man* of type H is the same as in Table 9.4 in Section 9.2.1, with the conclusion that a man of type H would choose $y = 18$.

Finally, for a *woman* of type H the cost-benefit calculations are shown in Table 9.8.

Table 9.8: The cost-benefit analysis of a type-H woman.

y years in school	w gross wage	C_L cost	$w - C_L$ net wage
$y = 6$	\$6,000	\$0	\$6,000
$y = 12$	\$20,000	\$6,000	\$14,000
$y = 16$	\$23,000	\$10,000	\$13,000
$y = 18$	\$26,000	\$12,000	\$14,000
$\boxed{y = 21}$	\$30,000	\$15,000	$\boxed{\$15,000}$

Thus a type-H woman would choose $y = 21$.

Hence we have a separating equilibrium where all type-L individuals (men and women) choose to stop at a High-school diploma and are hired at a salary of \$20,000, which corresponds to their true productivity; type-H men choose to obtain a Master's degree and are hired at a salary of \$30,000, which corresponds to their true productivity; type-H women choose to obtain a Ph.D. degree and are hired at a salary of \$30,000, which corresponds to their true productivity. At this equilibrium employers never observe men and women with the same graduate degree: if they did, they would realize that their beliefs concerning women's abilities were wrong and would revise those beliefs, thereby abandoning their prejudices. What they do observe is that those whose productivity is $30,000 are either men with 18 years of schooling or women with 21 years of schooling and would thus find confirmation of their beliefs that "women need to spend more time in school in order to achieve the higher level of productivity". In other words, the employers' doubly wrong beliefs are self-confirming at a separating equilibrium.

To sum up, the question that the presence of indices gives rise to is the following: can the informational structure of the market bring about persistent and consistent discrimination between objectively identical individuals? We considered the case where the unchangeable attribute (index) is gender. We supposed that within each gender there were both low-productivity and high-productivity individuals. Signaling costs (in our example, costs of acquiring education) were different for low-productivity and high-productivity people, but individuals with the same level of productivity had the same signaling costs, no matter whether they were men or women. We also assumed that people (both men and women) with the same productivity had the same preferences and the same objective: to maximize their income net of education costs. Therefore the index (gender) should be absolutely irrelevant: in principle, people with the same opportunities and the same preferences ought to make similar decisions and end up in similar situations. The informational structure of the market, however, can destroy this principle. If employers believe that gender (besides education) is correlated with productivity, they might offer a wage schedule that is differentiated on the basis of education *and* gender, thus presenting otherwise identical individuals with different opportunity sets. As a consequence, the employer's beliefs may force high-productivity women to invest in education more than their male counterpart (that is, more than high-productivity men). The reason why this situation can persist is that employers will interpret the incoming data separately for the two groups of men and women. If different levels of education were associated with the same observed level of productivity *within the same group*, employers would be forced to revise their beliefs. For example, if within the group of men different levels of education were accompanied by the same observed productivity, then employers would conclude that, at least above a certain level, education no longer increases productivity (at least for men). But since men and women are judged separately and independently (data on men is not used to classify women and *vice versa*), employers can consistently think that women need to acquire more education than their male counterpart in order to compensate for a "genetic" handicap. The employers' beliefs induce women to invest more in education than men, thereby confirming the prejudice that women require more education in order to achieve the same level of productivity as men (despite the fact that those beliefs have no objective grounds: they constitute, indeed, a prejudice). As a consequence, women end up being over-qualified for their jobs as compared to men.

> Test your understanding of the concepts introduced in this section, by going through the exercises in Section 9.7.2 at the end of this chapter.

9.4 More than two types

In the previous sections we restricted attention to the case where there are only two types of individuals. However, the reasoning developed in those sections applies also to the case of more than two types. Let us consider a simple example with three types.

Suppose that education has no effect on productivity and that the are three types of individuals: Type 1 with productivity 4, Type 2 with productivity 5 and Type 3 with productivity 6. As in the previous sections, the crucial assumption is that the cost of education is inversely related to productivity: the higher the (innate) productivity of an individual, the lower the cost of education. Let us suppose that the cost of education is as follows:

Type	Productivity	Cost of education
1	4	$C_1(y) = 3y$
2	5	$C_2(y) = 2y$
3	6	$C_3(y) = y$

Suppose that employers set two threshold levels of education, y_1^* and y_2^*, and announce that wage offers will depend on the level of education y of the applicant, as follows:

Level of eduction y	Wage offered
$y < y_1^*$	4
$y_1^* \leq y < y_2^*$	5
$y \geq y_2^*$	6

That is, applicants with $y < y_1^*$ are presumed to be of type 1, applicants with $y_1^* \leq y < y_2^*$ are presumed to be of type 2 and applicants with $y \geq y_2^*$ are presumed to be of type 3.

For what values of y_1^* and y_2^* do we have a separating signaling equilibrium?

Since - except for the threshold values - increasing y increases the cost of education but leaves the wage constant, each individual will only consider choosing either $y = 0$ or $y = y_1^*$ or $y = y_2^*$. At a separating equilibrium, type-1 individuals must choose $y = 0$ in order to be paid a wage equal to their true productivity, type-2 individuals must choose $y = y_1^*$ and type-3 individuals must choose $y = y_2^*$; furthermore, it must be in their interest to do so. Thus we need two inequalities to be satisfied for each type.

Let us begin with Type 1. The following table shows the net wage for a type-1 individual for each of the three choices of education.

Type 1

choice	wage	cost	net wage
$y = 0$	4	0	4
$y = y_1^*$	5	$3y_1^*$	$5 - 3y_1^*$
$y = y_2^*$	6	$3y_2^*$	$6 - 3y_2^*$

- In order for $y=0$ to be better than[7] $y=y_1^*$ we need

$$4 \geq 5 - 3y_1^*, \quad \text{that is,} \quad y_1^* \geq \tfrac{1}{3}. \tag{9.7}$$

- In order for $y=0$ to be better than $y=y_2^*$ we need

$$4 \geq 6 - 3y_2^*, \quad \text{that is,} \quad y_2^* \geq \tfrac{2}{3}. \tag{9.8}$$

The following table shows the net wage for Type 2 for each of the three choices of education.

Type 2

choice	wage	cost	net wage
$y=0$	4	0	4
$y=y_1^*$	5	$2y_1^*$	$5-2y_1^*$
$y=y_2^*$	6	$2y_2^*$	$6-2y_2^*$

- In order for $y=y_1^*$ to be better than $y=0$ we need

$$5 - 2y_1^* \geq 4, \quad \text{that is,} \quad y_1^* \leq \tfrac{1}{2}. \tag{9.9}$$

- In order for $y=y_1^*$ to be better than $y=y_2^*$ we need

$$5 - 2y_1^* \geq 6 - 2y_2^*, \quad \text{that is,} \quad y_2^* \geq \tfrac{1}{2} + y_1^*. \tag{9.10}$$

The following table shows the net wage for Type 3 for each of the three choices of education.

Type 3

choice	wage	cost	net wage
$y=0$	4	0	4
$y=y_1^*$	5	y_1^*	$5-y_1^*$
$y=y_2^*$	6	y_2^*	$6-y_2^*$

- In order for $y=y_2^*$ to be better than $y=0$ we need

$$6 - y_2^* \geq 4 \quad \text{that is,} \quad y_2^* \leq 2. \tag{9.11}$$

- In order for $y=y_2^*$ to be better than $y=y_1^*$ we need

$$6 - y_2^* \geq 5 - y_1^* \quad \text{that is,} \quad y_2^* \leq 1 + y_1^*. \tag{9.12}$$

---

[7] As in the previous sections, we assume that, if indifferent between two levels of education, a Type 1 would choose the lower level.

From (9.7) and (9.9) we get that

$$\tfrac{1}{3} \leq y_1^* \leq \tfrac{1}{2}. \tag{9.13}$$

It follows from (9.13) that
(1) $1 + y_1^* < 2$ so that if (9.12) is satisfied then (9.11) is also satisfied, and
(2) $\tfrac{1}{2} + y_1^* > \tfrac{2}{3}$ so that if (9.10) is satisfied then (9.8) is also satisfied.
Thus from (9.10) and (9.12) we get that

$$\tfrac{1}{2} + y_1^* \leq y_2^* \leq 1 + y_1^*. \tag{9.14}$$

Whenever inequalities (9.13) and (9.14) are satisfied we have a separating signaling equilibrium. For example, both inequalities are satisfied if $y_1^* = \tfrac{5}{12}$ and $y_2^* = 1$.

In general, if there are n types then, for each type, $(n-1)$ inequalities need to be satisfied, for a total of $n(n-1)$ inequalities. In Exercise 9.9 the reader is asked to find the relevant inequalities for the case where $n = 4$.

> Test your understanding of the concepts introduced in this section, by going through the exercises in Section 9.7.3 at the end of this chapter.

9.5 A more general analysis

In the previous four sections we assumed that individuals were facing a monetary cost of education and that their objective was to choose that level of education that maximized their net income. A crucial assumption was that lower-productivity people faced higher monetary costs of acquiring education. Although we indicated some reasons why this might be the case, it would be preferable to carry out the analysis assuming that, while the monetary cost of education is essentially the same for everybody, it is the psychological cost of education that differs across different types of individuals. In other words, different types have different preferences over pairs of income and education levels.

We assume that every individual has a utility function $U(m, y)$ over income, denoted by m, and education, denoted by y. Individuals prefer more money to less, that is, for every level of education y and any two levels of income m_1 and m_2, with $m_1 < m_2$, $U(m_2, y) > U(m_1, y)$. In other words, utility is an *increasing* function of income; this can be expressed by saying that the partial derivative of U with respect to m is positive:

$$\text{for all } (m, y), \quad \frac{\partial U}{\partial m}(m, y) > 0. \tag{9.15}$$

The second assumption is that acquiring education involves effort and thus a psychological cost, so that - at any level of income m - the individual prefers less education to more education, that is, if $y_1 < y_2$ then $U(m, y_1) > U(m, y_2)$. In other words, utility is a *decreasing* function of education; this can be expressed by saying that the partial derivative of U with respect to y is negative:

$$\text{for all } (m, y), \quad \frac{\partial U}{\partial y}(m, y) < 0. \tag{9.16}$$

It follows from (9.15) and (9.16) that indifference curves in the (y, m) plane must be increasing: starting from a point $(\hat{y}, \hat{m})$ if another point (y, m) with $y > \hat{y}$ is to give the same utility as $(\hat{y}, \hat{m})$ (that is, is to be on the indifference curve that goes through $(\hat{y}, \hat{m})$) it must be that $m > \hat{m}$. We shall consider the case where indifference curves are convex, as shown in Figure 9.1.[8]

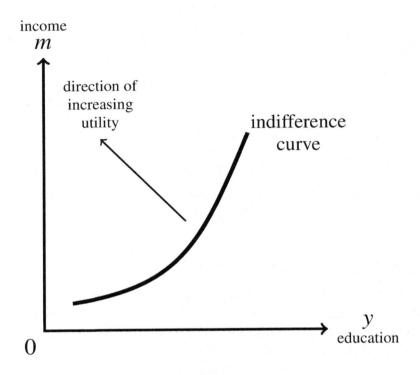

Figure 9.1: An indifference curve in the (y, m) plane.

Indifference curves can be used to obtain the monetary equivalent of the psychological cost (or "disutility") associated with an increase in the amount of education. Starting from an education-income pair $(\hat{y}, \hat{m})$ (which lies on the indifference curve corresponding to some level of utility $\bar{u}$), if education is increased by one unit and income is kept constant, then utility goes down, that is, the individual is worse off. One can thus ask: How much extra income should the individual be given to compensate for the reduction in utility due to the increase in y? In other words, what is the amount by which income has to be increased in order to keep the individual on the same indifference curve?

---

[8] For example, if $U(y, m) = \sqrt{m} - y$ then the equation of the indifference curve corresponding to utility level $\bar{u}$ is $m = (\bar{u} + y)^2$, which is increasing and convex in y.

9.5 A more general analysis

This is shown in Figure 9.2: starting from the education-income pair $(\hat{y}, \hat{m})$, if education is increased by one unit to $\hat{y} + 1$ then the individual requires an additional amount of income equal to $(m_1 - \hat{m})$ in order to remain on the same indifference curve; if education is then increased by one more unit, from $\hat{y} + 1$ to $\hat{y} + 2$, then the individual requires an additional income compensation equal to $(m_2 - m_1)$. Note that, since the indifference curve is convex, $(m_2 - m_1) > (m_1 - \hat{m})$, that is, every additional unit of education requires a larger compensation in terms of income.

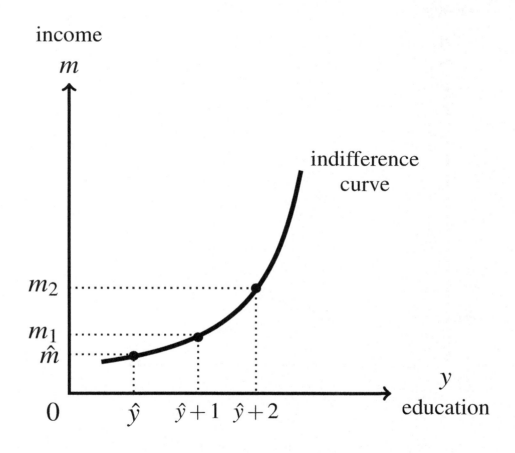

Figure 9.2: The monetary equivalent of the psychological cost of education.

Recall that the crucial assumption in the analysis of the previous sections was that higher-productivity people had a lower monetary cost of education. We can now express this difference in education costs in terms of preferences, as follows. Let us focus on the simple case where there are only two types of individuals: Type H and Type L; the latter are the less productive ones. We want to capture, using indifference curves, the fact that education is more "psychologically costly" for type-L individuals than for type-H individuals: for any given increase in education, the income compensation required by an L-type is larger than the income compensation required by an H-type. This will be the case if and only if the indifference of an L-type that goes through a given education-income pair $(\hat{y}, \hat{m})$ is *steeper* than the indifference curve of an H-type through $(\hat{y}, \hat{m})$.

This is shown in Figure 9.3: at income level $\hat{m}$, increasing education from $\hat{y}$ to $\hat{y}+1$ makes every type worse off; in order to restore a type-L individual to the original utility level (that is, in order to keep him on the L-type indifference curve through $(\hat{y},\hat{m})$) an increase in income equal to $(m_L - \hat{m})$ is required, while for a type-H individual the required increase in income is $(m_H - \hat{m})$. As shown in Figure 9.3, $(m_L - \hat{m}) > (m_H - \hat{m})$.

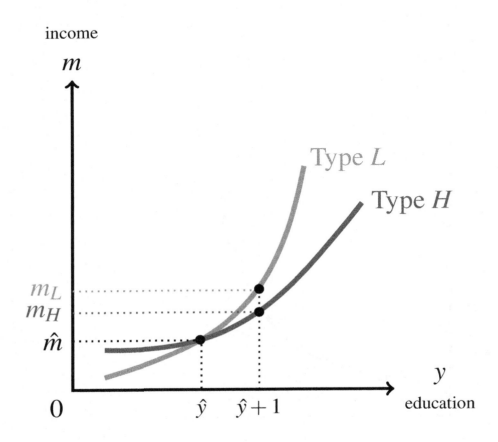

Figure 9.3: The monetary compensation for an extra unit of education required by an L-type is larger than that required by an H-type.

Let us assume that education does increase productivity, but at different rates for the two types. Specifically, we assume that productivity, denoted by Π, is as follows, with $0 < k_L < k_H$:

$$\text{Type } L: \quad \Pi_L(y) = k_L y$$
$$\text{Type } H: \quad \Pi_H(y) = k_H y.$$

9.5 A more general analysis

The productivity functions for the two types are shown in Figure 9.4.

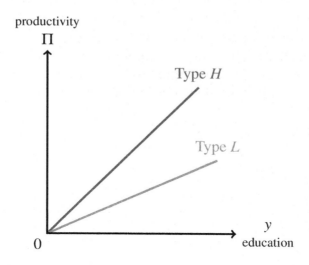

Figure 9.4: Productivity as a function of education.

What education levels would the two types choose in a perfect-information world in which employers were able to determine the type of each job applicant? The answer is illustrated in Figure 9.5.

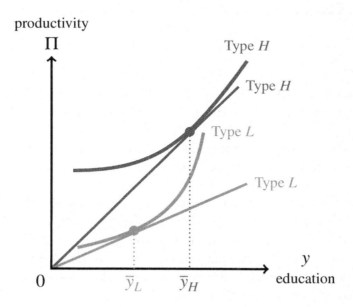

Figure 9.5: The education choices of the two types under perfect information.

In the perfect-information case (where employers can determine the type of a job applicant and offer a wage equal to his/her productivity), the optimal choice of education for a type is given by the horizontal coordinate of the point at which there is a tangency between the productivity line of that type and an indifference curve of that type. Indeed, if an individual chooses a level of education corresponding to a point at which the indifference curve crosses the productivity line, such as point A in Figure 9.6 for type L, then there are points to the left of that point (corresponding to lower levels of education) that lie on a higher indifference curve (and thus are better for the individual).

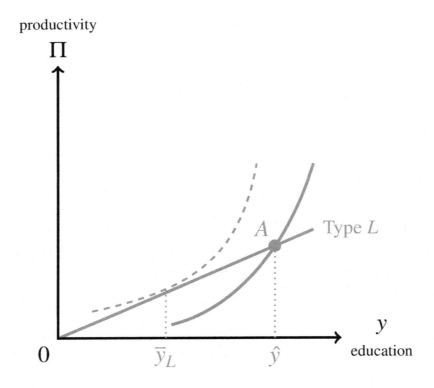

Figure 9.6: An education level, such as $\hat{y}$, at which the indifference curve crosses the wage/productivity line is not optimal (this is shown for a type-L individual).

We denote the perfect-information choice of education for type L by $\bar{y}_L$ and the perfect-information choice of education for type H by $\bar{y}_H$.

Let us now return to the case where employers are *not* able to determine the type of a job applicant. We assume, as in the previous sections, that employers set a threshold level of education, denoted by y^*, and announce that anybody with a level of education less than y^* will be classified as a type-L individual and will be offered a wage equal to $k_L y$ (where y is the level of education he/she has) and anybody with a level of education greater than or equal y^* will be classified as a type-H individual and will be offered a wage equal to $k_H y$.

9.5 A more general analysis

This threshold, education-dependent, wage schedule is shown in Figure 9.7 as the union of the two thick lines.

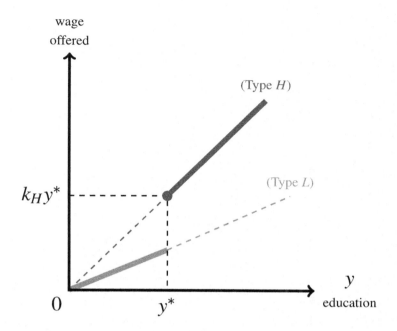

Figure 9.7: The wage offered by employers as a function of education, with a threshold value y^*.

We want to determine under what circumstances a separating signaling equilibrium exists. Let us consider first the case where the threshold value y^* is greater than the level of education that would be chosen by an H-type under perfect information, that is, the case where

$$y^* > \bar{y}_H.$$

Then the indifference curve of an H-type that goes through the point $(y^*, k_H y^*)$ crosses the H-type productivity line at that point, so that points to the right of it are worse choices for the H-type. Hence a type-H individual will only consider either education level y^* (that will have her classified correctly as type H) or a lower education level (that would have her classified incorrectly as type L). Two cases are possible:

1. the indifference curve of the H-type that goes through the point $(y^*, k_H y^*)$ lies entirely above the segment of the wage schedule to the left of that point,

2. the indifference curve of the H type that goes through the point $(y^*, k_H y^*)$ crosses the segment of the wage schedule to the left of that point.

In Case 1, an H-type would choose level of education y^*, while in Case 2 an H-type would choose a level of education less than y^* and thus be classified incorrectly as type-L, with the consequence that there would be no separating signaling equilibrium.

Case 1 is shown in Figure 9.8 while Case 2 is shown in Figure 9.9.

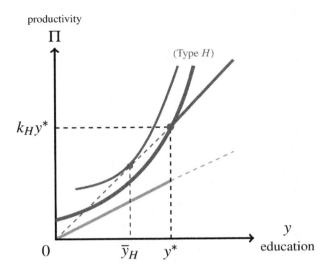

Figure 9.8: Case 1: the optimal choice of education for an H-type is y^*.

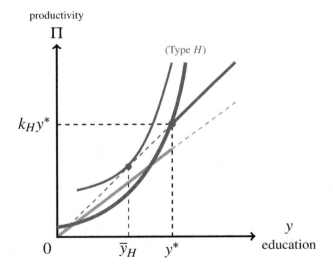

Figure 9.9: Case 2: the optimal choice of education for an H-type is less than y^*.

9.5 A more general analysis

Thus, in order for a separating signaling equilibrium to exist, it is necessary that we are in Case 1 above where the indifference curve of the H-type that goes through the point $(y^*, k_H y^*)$ lies entirely above the segment of the wage schedule to the left of that point. This guarantees that the H-type individuals will choose level of education y^* and will thus be correctly classified as type-H and remunerated according to their true productivity.

The second requirement for the existence of a separating signaling equilibrium is that the L-types choose a level of education less than y^* (so that they will be correctly classified as type-L and remunerated according to their true productivity). The relevant indifference curve for the L-type is the one that goes through the point corresponding to the L-type choice of education under perfect information, namely point $(\bar{y}_L, k_L \bar{y}_L)$.[9]

One possibility, illustrated in Figure 9.10, is that this indifference curve of the L-type cuts the second segment of the wage schedule. In this case the L-type would choose a level of education greater than, or equal to, y^* and thus there is no separating signaling equilibrium.

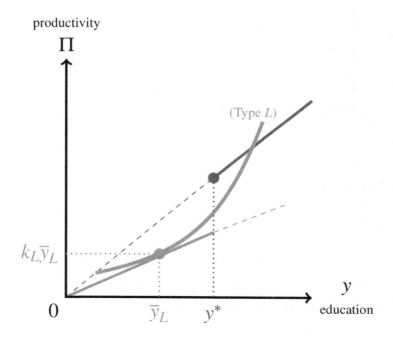

Figure 9.10: The case where the optimal choice of education for an L-type is greater than, or equal to, y^*.

The other possibility is that the indifference curve of the L-type that goes through point $(\bar{y}_L, k_L \bar{y}_L)$ lies entirely above the second segment of the wage schedule, that is, the segment corresponding to levels of education greater than or equal to y^*. In this case the optimal choice of education for the L-type is $\bar{y}_L$, with the consequence that type-L individuals are correctly classified as type L and are paid according to their true productivity.

---

[9] Note that, since we are looking at the case where $\bar{y}_H < y^*$, and $\bar{y}_L < \bar{y}_H$, the point $(\bar{y}_L, k_L \bar{y}_L)$ lies on the first segment of the wage schedule, that is, the segment corresponding to choices of education less than y^*.

The latter case is illustrated in Figure 9.11.

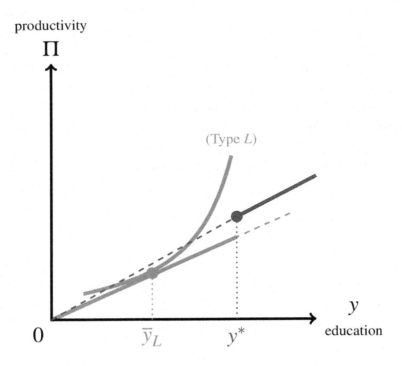

Figure 9.11: The case where the optimal choice of education for an L-type is $\bar{y}_L$.

Putting together the cases illustrated in Figures 9.8 and 9.11 we obtain the conditions that yield the existence of a separating signaling equilibrium:

1. the indifference curve of the H-type that goes through the point $(y^*, k_H y^*)$ lies entirely above the segment of the wage schedule to the left of that point (that is, the segment from $(0,0)$ to $(y^*, k_L y^*)$,

2. the indifference curve of the L-type that goes through point $(\bar{y}_L, k_L \bar{y}_L)$ lies entirely to the left of the second segment of the wage schedule (that is, the segment that starts at the point $(y^*, k_H y^*)$

9.5 A more general analysis

Figure 9.12 illustrates the case where a separating signaling equilibrium exists: all type-H individuals choose level of education y^* and are paid $k_H y^*$, while all type-L individuals choose level of education $\bar{y}_L$ and are paid $k_L \bar{y}_L$.

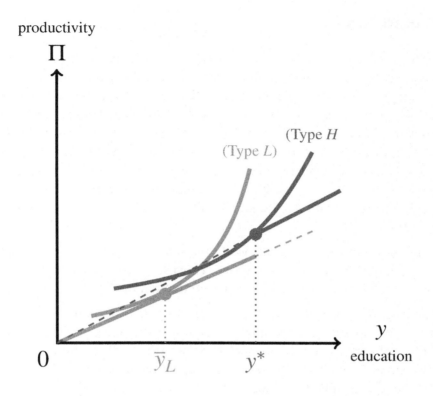

Figure 9.12: The case where a separating signaling equilibrium exists.

Note that, since $y^* > \bar{y}_H$, at the separating signaling equilibrium illustrated in Figure 9.12 there is *over-investment in education*: the H-types invest in education more than they would in a perfect-information world. Thus the asymmetry of information between employers and job applicants involves a cost for society that would not be incurred if there were perfect information.

We considered the case where the threshold value y^* is greater than the level of education that would be chosen by an H-type under perfect information, that is, the case where $y^* > \bar{y}_H$. The remaining two cases, namely $y^* < \bar{y}_L$ and $\bar{y}_L < y^* < \bar{y}_H$ are examined in Exercises 9.10 and 9.11.

Test your understanding of the concepts introduced in this section, by going through the exercises in Section 9.7.4 at the end of this chapter.

9.6 Signaling in other markets

We conclude with a brief discussion of other markets in which signaling can take place.

9.6.1 Market for used cars

We saw in Chapter 7 that, due to adverse selection, it is possible that in the market for second-hand cars some qualities (in the extreme case, all but the lowest quality) cannot be traded, giving rise to an inefficiency if potential buyers value those cars more than the owners. Thus the owner of a good-quality car gets "stuck" with her car, unable to convince a potential buyer that her car is of good quality and thus justifies a higher price than the low market price. Merely claiming that her car is of good quality is "cheap talk" which can be imitated by the owners of cars of inferior quality. Credible communication with potential buyers would require a *costly signal* which other sellers would not find profitable to imitate. What could constitute such a signal? The answer is: *offering a warranty* to cover future repairs.

We shall not develop a formal analysis of this, since - as explained below - this is more of a theoretical possibility than a practical one. However, a formal example is developed in detail in Exercise 9.12, which the reader is urged to attempt.

Presumably, in the case of cars 'high quality' means 'unlikely to break down and require an expensive repair' and 'low quality' means 'likely to require an expensive repair'. Indeed, the buyer of a used car will typically worry that she will end up with a "lemon" into which she will have to sink a lot of money for maintenance. The owner of a good-quality car knows that her car is unlikely to require major repairs and would in principle be willing to offer a warranty against such future repairs, that is, she will be willing to contractually commit herself to paying for the cost of any such repairs (within a specified period of time). This commitment will end up involving a low expected cost for her, because of the low probability of a major breakdown (since the car is, after all, a good-quality car). On the other hand, the owner of a low-quality car would not be willing to undertake such a commitment, because she recognizes that the probability of her having to pay for a major repair in the future is, in fact, quite high. Thus offering to sell with warranty can indeed work as a credible signal of high quality and induce buyers to correspondingly pay a higher price for cars sold with warranty.

However, from a practical point of view there are several factors that work against this form of signaling. First of all, while a warranty offered by an established dealership is perhaps sufficiently credible,[10] a warranty offered by a private individual is less credible: the seller might "disappear" (e.g. move to a different state) and become untraceable when the warranty becomes relevant (due to a needed repair) or the seller might declare personal bankruptcy or become insolvent, etc. There is also an issue of *moral hazard* involving the buyer, which is a source of concern for the seller: if the car is insured against future repairs, the new owner might abuse the car and cause a breakdown that could be avoided with due care. The topic of moral hazard will be discussed in the next chapter.

---

[10] However, even dealerships can go bankrupt, leaving the buyer with a worthless warranty.

9.6.2 Advertising as a signal of quality

Advertising is pervasive in our daily lives: we are exposed to it as we drive on the freeway, as we watch television, while we browse the internet, etc. Why do firms advertise? What is the purpose of advertising? What information, if any, do consumers obtain from advertisements?

It is clear that there cannot be a single answer to the above questions, because advertising falls into several different categories. In terms of content, for example, advertising can be informative or uninformative. The former makes consumers aware of something they did not know, such as the existence of a product, or its properties, or its price, or where it can be obtained. Most advertising, however, does not seem to fall into such category: for example, an ad showing a pop-star or an athlete drinking Coca Cola does not seem to convey to consumers any information that they did not already have (are there many people who do not know what Coca Cola is?); an ad claiming that a particular model of car is "the best" seems to be just "cheap talk", etc.

In this section we focus on "cheap talk" advertising, that is, claims made about a product that are easily imitated by other producers. Does this type of advertising make sense? Should consumers pay attention to it?

Nelson[11] provided an explanation for this type of advertising in terms of what we now call signaling. He observed that the characteristics that differentiate products in a given market can be classified into *search* characteristics and *experience* characteristics.

Search characteristics are those that can be ascertained before purchasing the good (e.g. the style of a dress). Since consumers can verify by themselves what the properties of the good are - before buying it - in this case there is no scope for false or misleading advertising: a false or exaggerated claim by the seller will not induce any purchases and will only damage the seller's reputation.

Experience characteristics, on the other hand, can only be learned through use and therefore after the purchase (e.g. the quality of a stereo system or the taste of a brand of canned tuna fish). In this case there is scope for false or misleading advertising: some consumers might be induced to buy the product by claims that will turn out to be false. However, Nelson argues that high-quality brands will obtain more repeat purchases, *ceteris paribus*, than low-quality brands, because consumers will be satisfied with the product and will buy it again in the future and/or recommend it to their friends. A dollar spent on advertising for a high-quality good generates future revenue that justifies the advertising expense. Producers of low-quality goods, on the other hand, might be able to fool a consumer into buying the first time, but will experience no repeat purchases. In other words, advertising is an expensive signal, which is more costly for the producer of a low-quality product than for the producer of a high-quality product and can thus be used by the latter to separate herself from the competitors who sell inferior goods. Hence advertising *is* informative, *no matter what its content*: the information conveyed by advertising is that the advertiser can afford the cost of advertising because its product is successful due to its high quality: advertising is a signal that the advertised product is of high quality.

---

[11] Phillip Nelson, Advertising as information, *Journal of Political Economy*, 1974, Vol. 82, No. 4, pp. 729-754.

9.6.3 Other markets

There are more markets where the phenomenon of signaling takes place. For example, Spence[12] examines signaling in the market for loans and household credit and Bhattacharya[13] shows that firms may use their dividend policy as a signal of their financial strength. We shall not pursue this topic any further.

> Test your understanding of the concepts introduced in this section, by going through the exercises in Section 9.7.5 at the end of this chapter.

---

[12] Michael Spence, *Market signaling: Informational transfer in hiring and related screening processes*, Harvard University Press, 1974.

[13] Sudipto Bhattacharya, Imperfect information, dividend policy and the "Bird in the Hand" fallacy, *Bell Journal of Economics*, 1979, Vol. 110, pp. 257-70.

9.7 Exercises

The solutions to the following exercises are given in Section 9.8 at the end of this chapter.

9.7.1 Exercises for Section 9.2: Signaling in the job market

Table 9.9: Wage offered as a function of the number of years of schooling.

Education	Wage offered
$y = 6$	$10,000
$y = 12$	$24,000
$y = 16$	$29,000
$y = 18$	$34,000
$y = 21$	$36,000

Exercise 9.1 Suppose that employers offer the wage schedule shown in Table 9.9. There are two types of individuals in the population: type H with productivity $34,000 (independent of education) and type L with productivity $10,000 (also independent of education). Education is costly and the monetary cost of acquiring education for the two types is as follows:

$$\text{For type } H: \quad C_H(y) = \begin{cases} 0 & \text{if } y \leq 6 \\ 1,600(y-6) & \text{if } y > 6 \end{cases}$$

$$\text{For type } L: \quad C_L(y) = \begin{cases} 0 & \text{if } y \leq 6 \\ 2,500(y-6) & \text{if } y > 6 \end{cases}$$

(a) Is there a separating signaling equilibrium?

(b) Let p_H be the proportion of H-types in the population. For what values of p_H would the following situation be Pareto superior to the signaling equilibrium of Part (a)? Institutions of education beyond sixth grade (that is, beyond $y = 6$) are abolished and everybody is hired at a wage equal to the average productivity of the population.

Exercise 9.2 Suppose that there are two groups of individuals: Group L with productivity 2 (independent of education) and Group H with productivity 3 (independent of education). Group H constitutes $\frac{1}{3}$ of the population. Workers of both types are able to buy education, at a cost. The amount of education y is a continuous variable and is fully verifiable (e.g. through a certificate).

Type-L individuals face a higher cost of acquiring education than type-H individuals: $C_L(y) = y$ and $C_H(y) = \frac{y}{2}$.

Employers believe that anybody with a level of education less than y^* has a productivity of 2 (and thus is offered a wage of 2) while anybody with a level of education greater than or equal to y^* has a productivity of 3 (and thus is offered a wage of 3).

(a) What values of y^* give rise to a separating signaling equilibrium?

(b) If the government intervened and forced everybody to choose $y = 0$ and employers to pay the same wage to everybody, equal to the average productivity in the population, would there be a Pareto improvement?

Exercise 9.3 Consider the following situation. Education does increase productivity. There are two groups in the population.

People in Group L have a productivity of $\left(1 + \frac{y}{4}\right)$ (where y is the amount of education) and their cost of acquiring y units of education is $\$y$.

People in Group H have a productivity of $\left(2 + \frac{y}{4}\right)$ and the cost of acquiring y units of education is $\$\frac{y}{2}$

Find all the signaling equilibria, when the employers' beliefs are as follows: if a job applicant has $y < y^*$, then he/she must be from Group L (and thus will be offered a wage of $1 + \frac{y}{4}$), while if he/she has $y \geq y^*$, then he/she must be from Group H (and thus will be offered a wage of $2 + \frac{y}{4}$).

Exercise 9.4 Consider the following situation, where education increases productivity. There are two groups in the population.

People in Group L have a productivity of $(4 + 2y)$ (where y is the amount of education) and their cost of acquiring y units of education is $\$5y$.

People in Group H have a productivity of $(6 + 3y)$ and the cost of acquiring y units of education is $\$4y$

Find all the signaling equilibria, when the employers' beliefs are as follows: if a job applicant has $y < y^*$, then he/she must be from Group L (and thus will be offered a wage of $4 + 2y$), while if he/she has $y \geq y^*$, then he/she must be from Group H (and thus will be offered a wage of $6 + 3y$).

9.7 Exercises

Table 9.10: Wage offered as a function of the number of years of schooling.

Education	Wage offered
$y = 6$	$10,000
$y = 12$	$15,000
$y = 16$	$20,000
$y = 18$	$25,000
$y = 21$	$30,000

Exercise 9.5 Suppose that employers offer the wage schedule shown in Table 9.10. There are two types of individuals in the population: type H with productivity π_H (independent of education) and type L with productivity π_L (also independent of education). Education is costly and the monetary cost of acquiring education for the two types is as follows:

$$\text{For type } H: \quad C_H(y) = \begin{cases} 0 & \text{if } y \leq 6 \\ 900(y-6) & \text{if } y > 6 \end{cases}$$

$$\text{For type } L: \quad C_L(y) = \begin{cases} 0 & \text{if } y \leq 6 \\ 1{,}400(y-6) & \text{if } y > 6 \end{cases}$$

(a) For what values of π_H and π_L is there a separating signaling equilibrium?

(b) Assume the values of π_H and π_L found in Part (a). Let p_H be the proportion of H-types in the population. For what values of p_H would the following situation be Pareto superior to the signaling equilibrium of Part (a)? Institutions of education beyond sixth grade (that is, beyond $y = 6$) are abolished and everybody is hired at a wage equal to the average productivity of the population.

Exercise 9.6 There are two types in the population: type H and type L. Productivity and cost are functions of the amount of education y, as follows:

For type H : productivity: $a + 4y$ cost: $5y$
For type L : productivity: $b + 3y$ cost: $6y$

Employers believe that applicants with $y \geq y^* > 0$ are of type H and are thus offered a wage equal to $a + 4y$ and everybody else is offered a wage equal to $b + 3y$.

For what values of a and b is there a separating signaling equilibrium?

9.7.2 Exercises for Section 9.3: Indices versus signals

Exercise 9.7 Suppose that there are two groups of individuals:

Group L with productivity 1 (independent of education), and

Group H with productivity 2 (independent of education).

Group H constitutes 50% of the population. Workers of both types are able to buy education, at a cost. The amount of education y is a continuous variable and is fully verifiable (e.g. through a certificate).

Type-L individuals face a higher cost of acquiring education than type-H individuals:

$$C_L(y) = y \quad \text{and} \quad C_H(y) = \frac{y}{2}.$$

Within each group there are as many men as women. Thus the composition of the populations is as follows:

Type/gender	percentage of population
men of type H	25%
women of type H	25%
men of type L	25%
women of type L	25%

Note that productivity is innate and is not influenced by either education or gender.

Suppose that employers mistakenly believe, not only that education affects productivity, but also that women are somewhat "genetically handicapped" and therefore need to acquire more education in order to become more productive. Accordingly, the employers offer the following wage schedules, with $y_w^* > y_m^*$.

If applicant is MALE		If applicant is FEMALE	
education	wage	education	wage
$y < y_m^*$	1	$y < y_w^*$	1
$y \geq y_m^*$	2	$y \geq y_w^*$	2

Are there values of y_m^* and y_w^* that give rise to a separating signaling equilibrium where the employers beliefs are confirmed?

9.7.3 Exercises for Section 9.4: More than two types

Exercise 9.8 Let y denote the amount of education. There are three types of potential workers:

those (Group I) with productivity 36 (a constant, thus independent of education),

those (Group II) with productivity $(60 + 3y)$, and

those (Group III) with productivity $(72 + 2y)$.

Each worker knows whether she belongs to Group I or Group II or Group III, while the potential employer does not. The cost of acquiring y units of education is

$24y$ for Group I,

$12y$ for Group II, and

$6y$ for Group III.

Let $0 < a < b$. The potential employer believes that those applicants with education less than a belong to Group I, those with education at least a but less than b belong to Group II and those with education at least b belong to Group III and offers each applicant a wage equal to the applicant's estimated productivity, given the applicant's level of education (the level of education can be verified by the employer during the job interview).

(a) Write a list of inequalities (involving the parameters a and b) that are necessary and sufficient for the existence of a signaling equilibrium.

(b) Explain why $a = 2$ and $b = 2.5$ is not a signaling equilibrium.

(c) Is $a = 2.5$ and $b = 4$ a signaling equilibrium?

Exercise 9.9 Suppose that there are four types in the population with the following productivity and cost of education (y is the amount of education), with $a_1 < a_2 < a_3 < a_4$ and $b_1 > b_2 > b_3 > b_4 > 2$.

	Type 1	Type 2	Type 3	Type 4
productivity	a_1	a_2	$a_3 + y$	$a_4 + 2y$
cost of education	$b_1 y$	$b_2 y$	$b_3 y$	$b_4 y$

Employers set three threshold levels of education, y_1^*, y_2^* and y_3^* and offer the following wages, depending on the level of education y of the job applicant:

Education y	wage
$y < y_1^*$	a_1
$y_1^* \leq y < y_2^*$	a_2
$y_2^* \leq y < y_3^*$	$a_3 + y$
$y \geq y_3^*$	$a_4 + 2y$

Write the inequalities that need to be satisfied in order to have a separating signaling equilibrium (where any two types make different choices of education).

9.7.4 Exercises for Section 9.5: A more general analysis

Exercise 9.10 Continuing the analysis of Section 9.5, consider the case where the threshold value y^* is less than the level of education that would be chosen by an L-type under perfect information, that is, the case where $y^* < \bar{y}_L$.

Draw a diagram showing the wage schedule and the relevant indifference curves of the two types and determine whether there can be a separating signaling equilibrium in this case. ∎

Exercise 9.11 Continuing the analysis of Section 9.5, consider the case where the threshold value y^* is greater than the level of education that would be chosen by an L-type under perfect information, and less than the level of education that would be chosen by an H-type under perfect information that is, the case where $\bar{y}_L < y^* < \bar{y}_H$.

Draw a diagram showing the wage schedule and the relevant indifference curves of the two types and determine whether there can be a separating signaling equilibrium in this case. [Hint: you need to distinguish two cases.] ∎

9.7.5 Exercises for Section 9.6: Signaling in other markets

Exercise 9.12 Consider the market for second-hand cars. There are four possible qualities with the following proportions and values to sellers:

quality of car:	A	B	C	D
proportion:	$\frac{1}{8}$	$\frac{2}{8}$	$\frac{2}{8}$	$\frac{3}{8}$
value to seller:	$15,000	$10,000	$8,000	$6,000.

All sellers and buyers are risk neutral. While each seller knows the quality of his car, each buyer is unable to determine the quality of any car offered for sale.

A car of quality $i \in \{A, B, C, D\}$ has probability q_i of requiring a major repair within the next 5 years with $q_A = \frac{1}{10}$, $q_B = \frac{1}{2}$, $q_C = \frac{4}{5}$, $q_D = \frac{99}{100}$. A major repair costs $15,000. The buyer's valuation b_i of a car of quality i reflects this, in the sense that, for all $i \in \{A, B, C, D\}$, $b_i = \$(24{,}000 - 15{,}000 q_i)$.

(a) Compute the value of each quality to the buyers.

(b) Suppose first that there is only one price for used cars, $p = \$9{,}000$. What cars are traded?

(c) Suppose now that each seller can offer his car for sale either with or without warranty. If a car is sold with warranty, the seller credibly undertakes to pay for the repair himself, should a repair become necessary within the next 5 years. In this new situation, there can be two prices in the market: a price p_N for cars sold *without* warranty and a price p_W for cars sold *with* warranty. A car of quality A sold with warranty is worth $24,000 to the buyer. Suppose that $p_W = \$17{,}000$ and $p_N = \$11{,}000$. What cars are sold with warranty and what cars are sold without warranty?

9.8 Solutions to Exercises

Solution to Exercise 9.1.

(a) The cost-benefit analysis of a type-H person is shown in Table 9.11. Thus a type-H individual will choose $y = 18$ and be paid \$34,000 which is equal to her true productivity.

Table 9.11: The cost-benefit analysis of a type-H person.

y years in school	w gross wage	C_H cost	$w - C_H$ net wage
$y = 6$	\$10,000	\$0	\$10,000
$y = 12$	\$24,000	\$9,600	\$14,400
$y = 16$	\$29,000	\$16,000	\$13,000
$\boxed{y = 18}$	\$34,000	\$19,200	$\boxed{\$14,800}$
$y = 21$	\$36,000	\$24,000	\$12,000

The cost-benefit analysis of a type-L person is shown in Table 9.12. Thus a type-L individual will choose $y = 6$ and be paid \$10,000 which is equal to his true productivity.
Hence we do have a separating signaling equilibrium.

Table 9.12: The cost-benefit analysis of a type-L person.

y years in school	w gross wage	C_L cost	$w - C_L$ net wage
$\boxed{y = 6}$	\$10,000	\$0	$\boxed{\$10,000}$
$y = 12$	\$24,000	\$15,000	\$9,000
$y = 16$	\$29,000	\$25,000	\$4,000
$y = 18$	\$34,000	\$30,000	\$4,000
$y = 21$	\$36,000	\$37,500	\$-1,500

(b) In the world everybody chooses $y = 6$ and faces zero costs of education. The average productivity is $34,000 p_H + 10,000(1 - p_H) = 10,000 + 24,000 p_H$. Type-$L$ individuals will be better off because $10,000 + 24,000 p_H > 10,000$. Type-$H$ individuals will now have a net income of $10,000 + 24,000 p_H$, which is greater than or equal to their net income at the signaling equilibrium of Part (a), namely \$14,800, if and only if $p_H \geq \frac{1}{5}$. Thus we have a Pareto improvement if and only if $p_H \geq \frac{1}{5}$. □

Solution to Exercise 9.2.

(a) Nobody will want to acquire a level of education $y > y^*$ or a level $0 < y < y^*$. Thus every individual will limit herself to choosing between $y = 0$ and $y = y^*$.

For a type-L, $y = 0$ yields a net income of 2 and $y = y^*$ yields a net income of $3 - y^*$. Thus he will choose $y = 0$ if and only if $2 \geq 3 - y^*$, that is, if and only if $\boxed{y^* \geq 1.}$

For a type-H, $y = 0$ yields a net income of 2 and $y = y^*$ yields a net income of $3 - \frac{y^*}{2}$. Thus she will choose $y = y^*$ if and only if $3 - \frac{y^*}{2} \geq 2$, that is, if and only if $\boxed{y^* \leq 2.}$

Hence every $y^* \in [1,2]$, yields a separating signaling equilibrium.

(b) The average productivity is $\frac{1}{3}3 + \frac{2}{3}2 = \frac{7}{3}$. In the new situation employers are as well off as before and type-L individuals are better off. Type-H individuals are not worse off if and only if $\frac{7}{3} \geq 3 - \frac{y^*}{2}$, which is the case if and only if $y^* \geq \frac{4}{3}$. Thus if $y^* \in [\frac{4}{3}, 2]$ then the government intervention leads to a Pareto improvement, while if $y^* \in [1, \frac{4}{3})$, then there is no Pareto improvement because type-H individuals are made worse off by the government intervention. □

Solution to Exercise 9.3.

First of all, note that the only sensible choices are $y = 0$ and $y = y^*$. In fact, if you increase y by 1 unit, you get an extra $0.25 but you pay more than this (you pay an extra $1 if you belong to Group L and an extra $0.50 if you belong to Group H).

Decision for a Group-L person:

education	wage	cost	net income
$y = 0$	$1 + \frac{0}{4} = 1$	0	1
$y = y^*$	$2 + \frac{y^*}{4}$	y^*	$2 - \frac{3}{4}y^*$

Thus a Group-L person will choose $y = 0$ and be paid a wage equal to his true productivity if and only if $1 \geq 2 - \frac{3}{4}y^*$, that is, if and only if $\boxed{y^* \geq \frac{4}{3}}$.

Decision for a Group-H person:

education	wage	cost	net income
$y = 0$	$1 + \frac{0}{4} = 1$	0	1
$y = y^*$	$2 + \frac{y^*}{4}$	$\frac{y^*}{2}$	$2 - \frac{1}{4}y^*$

Thus a Group-H person will choose $y = y^*$ and be paid a wage equal to her true productivity if and only if $2 - \frac{1}{4}y^* \geq 1$, that is, if and only if $\boxed{y^* \leq 4}$.

Thus every $y^* \in [\frac{4}{3}, 4]$ gives rise to a separating signaling equilibrium. □

9.8 Solutions to Exercises

Solution to Exercise 9.4.

As usual, the only sensible choices are $y = 0$ and $y = y^*$.

Decision for a Group-L person:

education	wage	cost	net income
$y = 0$	4	0	4
$y = y^*$	$6 + 3y^*$	$5y^*$	$6 - 2y^*$

Thus a Group-L person will choose $y = 0$ and be paid a wage equal to his true productivity if and only if $4 \geq 6 - 2y^*$, that is, if and only if $\boxed{y^* \geq 1}$.

Decision for a Group-H person:

education	wage	cost	net income
$y = 0$	4	0	4
$y = y^*$	$6 + 3y^*$	$4y^*$	$6 - y^*$

Thus a Group-H person will choose $y = y^*$ and be paid a wage equal to her true productivity if and only if $6 - y^* \geq 4$, that is, if and only if $\boxed{y^* \leq 2}$.

Thus every $y^* \in [1,2]$ gives rise to a separating signaling equilibrium. □

Solution to Exercise 9.5.

(a) The cost-benefit analysis of a type-H person is shown in the following table. Thus a type-H individual will choose $y = 21$ and be paid $30,000.

y	w	C_H	$w - C_H$
$y = 6$	$10,000	$0	$10,000
$y = 12$	$15,000	$5,400	$9,600
$y = 16$	$20,000	$9,000	$11,000
$y = 18$	$25,000	$10,800	$14,200
$\boxed{y = 21}$	$30,000	$13,500	$\boxed{16,500}$

The cost-benefit analysis of a type-L person is shown in the following table. Thus a type-L individual will choose $y = 6$ and be paid $10,000.

Hence in order to have a signaling equilibrium it must be that $\pi_H = 30,000$ and $\pi_L = 10,000$.

y	w	C_L	$w - C_L$
$\boxed{y = 6}$	$10,000	$0	$\boxed{10,000}$
$y = 12$	$15,000	$8,400	$6,600
$y = 16$	$20,000	$14,000	$6,000
$y = 18$	$25,000	$16,800	$8,200
$y = 21$	$30,000	$21,000	$9,000

(b) In the new world everybody chooses $y = 6$ (the only available choice). The average productivity is $30,000 p_H + 10,000(1 - p_H) = 10,000 + 20,000 p_H$. Thus type-L individuals will be better off, since $10,000 + 20,000 p_H > 10,000$. Type-H individuals will now have a net income of $10,000 + 20,000 p_H$; this is greater than, or equal to, their net income at the signaling equilibrium of Part (a), namely $16,500, if and only if $p_H \geq \frac{13}{40}$. Thus we have a Pareto improvement if and only if $p_H \geq \frac{13}{40}$. □

Solution to Exercise 9.6.

As usual, we only need to compare the choices $y = 0$ and $y = y^*$. An H type will choose $y = y^*$ if and only if

$$a + 4y^* - 5y^* \geq b \quad \text{that is,} \quad a - b \geq y^*. \tag{9.17}$$

An L type will choose $y = 0$ if and only if

$$b \geq a + 4y^* - 6y^* \quad \text{that is,} \quad a - b \leq 2y^*. \tag{9.18}$$

Thus any two values of a and b such that $y^* \leq a - b \leq 2y^*$ will give rise to a separating signaling equilibrium. □

Solution to Exercise 9.7.

Let us construct an equilibrium where (1) all type-L individuals (male and female) choose $y = 1$, (2) type-H men choose $y = y_m^*$ and (3) type-H women $y = y_w^*$.

1. For (1) we need $1 \geq 2 - y_m^*$ (for men), that is $y_m^* \geq 1$ and $1 \geq 2 - y_w^*$ (for women), that is $y_w^* \geq 1$. Since $y_w^* > y_m^*$, both conditions are satisfied if

$$1 \leq y_m^*. \tag{9.19}$$

2. For (2) we need $2 - \frac{y_m^*}{2} \geq 1$, that is,

$$y_m^* \leq 2. \tag{9.20}$$

3. For (3) we need $2 - \frac{y_w^*}{2} \geq 1$, that is,

$$y_w^* \leq 2. \tag{9.21}$$

Since $y_w^* > y_m^*$, (9.21) implies (9.20). Thus any pair of values (y_m^*, y_w^*) such that $1 \leq y_m^* < y_w^* \leq 2$ gives rise to a separating equilibrium where employers' beliefs are confirmed in every respect. In particular, they obtain no evidence against their belief that, in order to become more productive, women need to spend more time in school: a man acquires a productivity of 2 by spending y_m^* years in school, while women acquire a productivity of 2 by spending more time in school, namely y_w^* years rather than y_m^*. □

9.8 Solutions to Exercises

Solution to Exercise 9.8.

(a) First of all, since for every group the cost of one extra unit of education exceeds the benefit (in terms of increased salary), everybody will only consider only $y=0$, $y=a$ and $y=b$. The inequalities are as follows.

For Group I:

(1) $36 \geq 60 + 3a - 24a$, that is, $a \geq \frac{8}{7}$.

(2) $36 \geq 72 + 2b - 24b$, that is, $b \geq \frac{18}{11}$.

For Group II:

(3) $60 + 3a - 12a \geq 36$, that is, $a \leq \frac{8}{3}$.

(4) $60 + 3a - 12a \geq 72 + 2b - 12b$, that is, $b \geq \frac{6}{5} + \frac{9}{10}a$.

For Group III:

(5) $72 + 2b - 6b \geq 36$, that is, $b \leq 9$.

(6) $72 + 2b - 6b \geq 60 + 3a - 6a$, that is, $b \leq 3 + \frac{3}{4}a$.

(b) When $a = 2$ and $b = 2.5$, inequality (4) is violated. Thus Group II individuals would be better off pretending to be Group III by choosing $y = b = 2.5$ (instead of $y = a = 2$).

(c) Yes, when $a = 2.5$ and $b = 4$, all the above inequalities are satisfied. □

Solution to Exercise 9.9.

There are 12 inequalities, which are as follows.

For Group 1:

(1) $a_1 \geq a_2 - b_1 y_1^*$.

(2) $a_1 \geq a_3 + y_2^* - b_1 y_2^*$.

(3) $a_1 \geq a_4 + 2y_3^* - b_1 y_3^*$.

For Group 2:

(4) $a_2 - b_2 y_1^* \geq a_1$.

(5) $a_2 - b_2 y_1^* \geq a_3 + y_2^* - b_2 y_2^*$.

(6) $a_2 - b_2 y_1^* \geq a_4 + 2y_3^* - b_2 y_3^*$.

For Group 3:

(7) $a_3 + y_2^* - b_3 y_2^* \geq a_1$.

(8) $a_3 + y_2^* - b_3 y_2^* \geq a_2 - b_3 y_1^*$.

(9) $a_3 + y_2^* - b_3 y_2^* \geq a_4 + 2y_3^* - b_3 y_3^*$.

For Group 4:

(10) $a_4 + 2y_3^* - b_4 y_3^* \geq a_1$.

(11) $a_4 + 2y_3^* - b_4 y_3^* \geq a_2 - b_4 y_1^*$.

(12) $a_4 + 2y_3^* - b_4 y_3^* \geq a_3 + y_2^* - b_4 y_2^*$. □

Solution to Exercise 9.10.

There is no signaling equilibrium in this case, which is illustrated in Figure 9.13.[14] The H-type will choose education level $\bar{y}_H$, because the point $(\bar{y}_H, k_H \bar{y}_H)$ is the best along the productivity line $\Pi = k_H y$ and hence also better than any point on the lower productivity line $\Pi = k_L y$ and thus it is the utility-maximizing point on the wage schedule. Type L individuals will choose an education level $y \geq y^*$ for the following reason: the point $(\bar{y}_L, k_L \bar{y}_L)$ is the best point for the L-type along the productivity line $\Pi = k_L y$ and the point $(\bar{y}_L, k_H \bar{y}_L)$ is even better, because it involves a larger income; it follows that $(\bar{y}_L, k_H \bar{y}_L)$ is better than any point on the productivity line $\Pi = k_L y$, in particular, the segment of it which belongs to the wage schedule. Since $(\bar{y}_L, k_H \bar{y}_L)$ is available (it belongs to the wage schedule) the L-types will not make a choice of education that leads to them being remunerated according to their true productivity. Hence, even if their choice of education is different from the choice made by the H-types, so that we would have a separating outcome, it would not be an *equilibrium*, because employers would discover that they are overpaying some of the employees and would want to change the wage schedule.

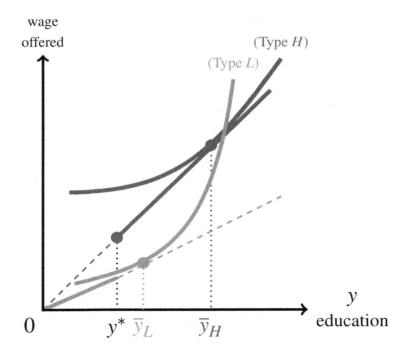

Figure 9.13: Every point on the first segment of the wage schedule is worse for the L-types than some point on the second segment of the wage schedule.

---

[14] We have drawn the case where the point $(\bar{y}_H, k_H \bar{y}_H)$ lies above the L-type indifference curve that goes through the point $(\bar{y}_L, k_L \bar{y}_L)$, but this is not a relevant fact: even if this were not the case, the argument would remain valid.

9.8 Solutions to Exercises

Solution to Exercise 9.11.

Since $y_H > y^*$, the H-types will choose education level y_H and be remunerated according to their true productivity. The issue is what choice the L-types will make. We need to distinguish two cases.

Case 1: The point $(y^*, k_H y^*)$ lies above the L-type indifference curve that goes through the point $(\bar{y}_L, k_L \bar{y}_L)$. This case is illustrated in Figure 9.14.

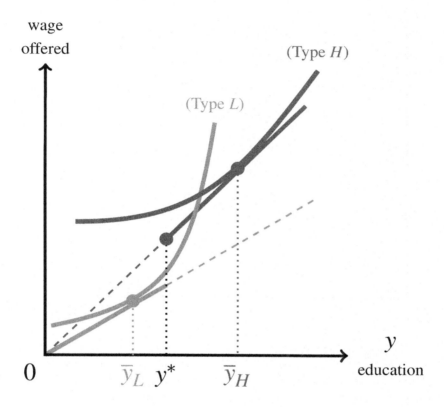

Figure 9.14: The case where the point $(y^*, k_H y^*)$ lies above the L-type indifference curve that goes through the point $(\bar{y}_L, k_L \bar{y}_L)$.

In this case the point $(y^*, k_H y^*)$ - which is on the wage schedule - is better than the point $(\bar{y}_L, k_L \bar{y}_L)$, which is the best point on the first segment of the wage schedule (indeed the best point on the entire line corresponding to the productivity of the L-type: $\Pi = k_L y$). Thus the L-type will **not** choose a level of education less than y^* and thus will not be remunerated according to their true productivity. As remarked in the answer to Exercise 9.10, even if the choice of education of the L-types is different from the choice made by the H-types (namely $\bar{y}_H$) - so that we would have a separating outcome - it would not be an *equilibrium*, because employers would discover that they are overpaying some of the employees and would want to change the wage schedule.

Case 2: The point $(y^*, k_H y^*)$ lies to the right of the L-type indifference curve that goes through the point $(\bar{y}_L, k_L \bar{y}_L)$. This case is illustrated in Figure 9.15.

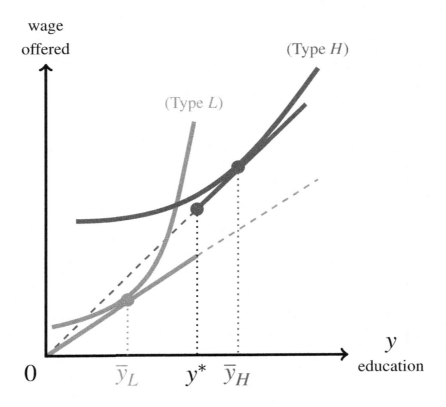

Figure 9.15: The case where the point $(y^*, k_H y^*)$ lies to the right of the L-type indifference curve that goes through the point $(\bar{y}_L, k_L \bar{y}_L)$.

In this case every point on the second segment of the wage schedule (the segment that starts at $(y^*, k_H y^*)$) is worse, for the L-type, than the point $(\bar{y}_L, k_L \bar{y}_L)$, which - in turn - is the best point on the first segment of the wage schedule. Thus the L-types will choose level of education $\bar{y}_L$ and the H-types will choose level of education $\bar{y}_H$ and both types will be remunerated according to their true productivity. Hence in this case we do have a separating signaling equilibrium. Note that it coincides (in terms of education choices and remuneration) with what would happen in the case of perfect information. Thus in this case the asymmetry of information does not have negative consequences; in particular there is no over-investment in education by the H-types (unlike the case where $y^* > \bar{y}_H$ considered in Section 9.5).

Solution to Exercise 9.12.

(a) $b_A = 22,500$, $b_B = 16,500$, $b_C = 12,000$, $b_D = 9,150$.

(b) Since $p = 9,000$, only qualities C and D will be offered for sale. Thus buying a car means facing the lottery
$$\begin{pmatrix} \$12,000 & \$9,150 \\ \frac{2}{5} & \frac{3}{5} \end{pmatrix}$$
whose expected value is $10,290 which is greater than the price of $9,000; hence buyers are willing to buy.[15] Hence only cars of quality C and D are traded.

(c) The owner of a car of quality A is not willing to sell at price $p_N = 11,000$. If he sells at price $p_W = 17,000$ then he faces the lottery
$$\begin{pmatrix} \$17,000 & \$(17,000 - 15,000) \\ \frac{9}{10} & \frac{1}{10} \end{pmatrix}$$
whose expected value is 15,500, greater than the value of the car. Thus he is willing to sell with warranty at price $p_W = 17,000$.

If the owner of a car of quality B sells at price $p_W = 17,000$ then he faces the lottery
$$\begin{pmatrix} \$17,000 & \$(17,000 - 15,000) \\ \frac{1}{2} & \frac{1}{2} \end{pmatrix}$$
whose expected value is 9,500 which is less than the value of the car to him, namely 10,000. Thus he is not willing to sell with warranty.

If the owner of a car of quality C sells at price $p_W = 17,000$ then he faces the lottery
$$\begin{pmatrix} \$17,000 & \$(17,000 - 15,000) \\ \frac{1}{5} & \frac{4}{5} \end{pmatrix}$$
whose expected value is 5,000 which is less than the value of the car to him, namely 8,000. Thus he is not willing to sell with warranty.

If the owner of a car of quality D sells at price $p_W = 17,000$ then he faces the lottery
$$\begin{pmatrix} \$17,000 & \$(17,000 - 15,000) \\ \frac{1}{100} & \frac{99}{100} \end{pmatrix}$$
whose expected value is 2,150 which is less than the value of the car to him, namely 6,000. Thus he is not willing to sell with warranty.

Thus the only cars offered for sale with warranty are the cars of quality A. Since the buyer values a car of quality A sold with warranty at $24,000, he is willing to pay $17,000, realizing a gain equal to $7,000. Thus all cars of quality A will be sold with warranty at price $p_W = 17,000$.

---

[15] Alternatively one could say that the lottery - after paying the price - is
$$\begin{pmatrix} \$3,000 & \$150 \\ \frac{2}{5} & \frac{3}{5} \end{pmatrix}$$
whose expected value is $1,290, hence a positive net benefit from buying.

Now let us look at the market for cars sold without warranty. Since $p_N = 11,000$ the owners of cars of qualities B, C and D are willing to sell (they value their cars less than 11,000). Thus buying a car without warranty means facing the lottery

$$\begin{pmatrix} \$16,500 & \$12,000 & \$9,150 \\ \frac{2}{7} & \frac{2}{7} & \frac{3}{7} \end{pmatrix}$$

which has an expected value of 12,064.29, greater than the price of 11,000. Thus consumers are willing to buy.

In conclusion, cars of quality A will be sold with warranty at a price of \$17,000 and all the other cars will be sold without warranty at a price of \$11,000.

Thus, offering to sell with warranty is a signal used by the owners of the best cars (those of quality A) to credibly convey information to potential buyers about the quality of their cars.

V Moral Hazard

10 Moral Hazard in Insurance 343
    10.1   Moral hazard or hidden action
    10.2   Moral hazard and insurance
    10.3   Exercises
    10.4   Solutions to Exercises

11 Moral Hazard in Principal-Agent 369
    11.1   Moral hazard in Principal-Agent relationships
    11.2   Risk sharing under moral hazard
    11.3   The case with two outcomes and two levels of effort
    11.4   The case with more than two outcomes
    11.5   Exercises
    11.6   Solutions to Exercises

12 Glossary 409

Index 413

10. Moral Hazard in Insurance

10.1 Moral hazard or hidden action

In Chapters 7-9 we analysed the phenomenon of asymmetric information, namely situations where one party to a potential transaction has some relevant characteristics that are known to her but cannot be ascertained (at the time of signing the contract) by the other party. For this reason asymmetric information is also referred to as "hidden type". The expression "moral hazard", on the other hand, refers to situations where the *behavior* of one of the parties to a contract cannot be observed by the other. For this reason it is also called "hidden action".

A parent who hires a babysitter to look after his child while he is at work cares very much about the behavior of the sitter: will she be keeping a constant eye on the child or will she be updating her social media profile? Will she comfort the child if he/she cries or let him/her cry for a long time?

The owner of a store who hires a shopkeeper to take care of business will want the employee to be helpful to customers and do what he can to induce them to make a purchase; but if the owner is not present, she cannot tell whether the employee is working hard or is shirking.

An individual who hires a lawyer to file a lawsuit on her behalf will want the lawyer to spend time and effort studying the case and preparing well-informed briefs. Unfortunately, it is typically the case that the client cannot monitor the lawyer's effort.

What all these cases have in common is the fact that the outcome of the contractual relationship depends on the level of care and effort that one of the two parties puts into the endeavor and monitoring this party's behavior is not possible or too expensive for the other party. Thus, if possible, one has to design the contract in such a way that the un-monitored party has an incentive to behave in a way that is aligned with the interest of the other party.

In this chapter we will examine the role of moral hazard in insurance markets and in the next chapter we will revisit the Principal-Agent environment of Chapter 6 and add the possibility of moral hazard.

10.2 Moral hazard and insurance

In the chapters that dealt with insurance (Chapters 2, 5 and 8) we assumed that the probability of loss was constant and the individual's decision was merely whether or not to insure and which contract to choose from a given menu. When we say that "the probability of loss is constant" we mean that it cannot be affected by the individual's behavior.

In some cases this is a reasonable assumption: for example, there is nothing that a shopkeeper can do to make it less likely that there will be a riot, or an earthquake, or a meteorite strike.

In other cases, however, there is a causal link between the behavior of the insured person and the probability that she will suffer a loss: for example, the probability that her bicycle will be stolen is higher if she leaves it unattended and unlocked, and lower if she locks it to a permanent fixture with a sturdy cable and padlock.

In cases where the probability of loss can be affected by the individual's actions we say that the insurance company faces a situation of *moral hazard* or *hidden action*. Below are a few more examples of possible actions that the individual can take to reduce the probability of loss:

- Install a home security alarm, to make a robbery less likely.
- Always lock the door(s) to one's house, to make a robbery less likely.
- Clear the brush around the house, to make it less likely that a brush fire will reach the building.
- Drive carefully and below the speed limit, to make it less likely that one will be involved in a car accident.
- Exercise regularly and eat healthy food to reduce the probability of vascular or cardiac disease.

As the above examples illustrate, what an individual can do to reduce the probability of loss can be either

- taking an action involving extra effort, or
- incurring an extra expense.

We shall refer to both of the above as *making extra effort*. The crucial element of both is that they involve "disutility", that is, they make the individual worse off, *ceteris paribus*. Because of this, the insurance company realizes that the individual will prefer to avoid the extra effort if she is protected from the consequences of not exerting it. For example, if the individual has full insurance, then she has no incentive to incur extra expenses or exert extra effort in order to reduce the probability of suffering a loss: if the loss occurs, she will be fully reimbursed by the insurance company. On the other hand, the insurance company cares very much about the behavior of its customers, because the more careless they are, the more likely it is that the insurance company will have to cover their losses. In order to incentivize the customer to exert extra effort, the insurance company might want to make it more costly for the insured to suffer a loss, by requiring a substantial deductible.

10.2 Moral hazard and insurance

If the customer's behavior can be observed by the insurance company and verified by a court of law, then the insurance company can specify it in the contract and make any payments conditional on the customer's actions. For example, the insurance company could require the customer to install a security system in her house and make any reimbursements due to theft conditional on proof that the security system was in fact installed. However, in most cases it is impossible, or prohibitively expensive, for the insurer to monitor the behavior of its customers. For example, no insurance company will find it worthwhile to have an insurance agent follow the customer around to make sure that she always locks her bicycle, when left unattended!

We will assume that the customer's behavior cannot be observed by the insurance company; however, the insurance company can try to figure out what the potential customer would do under different insurance contract.

10.2.1 Two levels of unobserved effort

We will limit ourselves to the binary case, where the individual has only two choices in terms of effort: either *exert effort*, denoted by E, or exert *no effort*, denoted by N. The individual's choice affects the probability of loss: it will be lower in she exerts effort, that is, letting p_E be the probability of loss in the case of effort and p_N the probability of loss in the case of no effort,

$$0 < p_E < p_N < 1. \tag{10.1}$$

As in previous chapters, we denote the individual's initial wealth by W_0 and the potential loss by ℓ (with $0 < \ell \leq W_0$). We continue to assume that the individual has vNM preferences; however, the outcomes of the lotteries now include not only wealth levels but also the "inconvenience" or "cost" of exerting effort. Thus we can think of the individual as having two utility-of-money functions: one if she exerts effort, denoted by $U_E(m)$, and the other if she exerts no effort, denoted by $U_N(m)$.[1]

The fact that effort is costly (either in a psychological or in a monetary sense) is captured by the following assumption:

$$U_N(m) > U_E(m), \quad \text{for every } m \geq 0.$$

To simplify the analysis we will consider the following special case: let $U(m)$ be a strictly increasing and concave function then

$$U_N(m) = U(m) \tag{10.2}$$

$$U_E(m) = U(m) - c, \quad \text{with } c > 0. \tag{10.3}$$

Note that, since $p_E < p_N$,[2]

$$\frac{p_E}{1-p_E} < \frac{p_N}{1-p_N}. \tag{10.4}$$

---

[1] Equivalently, the vNM utility function has two arguments: money and level of effort.
[2] This can be seen as follows:
(1) $\frac{p_E}{1-p_E} < \frac{p_N}{1-p_E}$ because the denominator is the same and $p_E < p_N$, and
(2) $\frac{p_N}{1-p_E} < \frac{p_N}{1-p_N}$ because the numerator is the same and $(1-p_E) > (1-p_N)$ (since $p_E < p_N$).

It follows from (10.2) and (10.3) that, for any point (W_1, W_2) in the wealth space,

- with No-effort, the slope of the indifference curve at point (W_1, W_2) is

$$-\frac{p_N}{1-p_N}\left(\frac{U'(W_1)}{U'(W_2)}\right) \tag{10.5}$$

- with Effort, the slope of the indifference curve at point (W_1, W_2) is

$$-\frac{p_E}{1-p_E}\left(\frac{U'(W_1)}{U'(W_2)}\right). \tag{10.6}$$

Thus, for any point $A = (W_1^A, W_2^A)$ in the wealth space, we deduce from (10.4), (10.5) and (10.6) that

> the indifference curve (through point A) corresponding to **Effort**
> is, at point A, **less steep than**,
> the indifference curve (through point A) corresponding to **No-effort**.

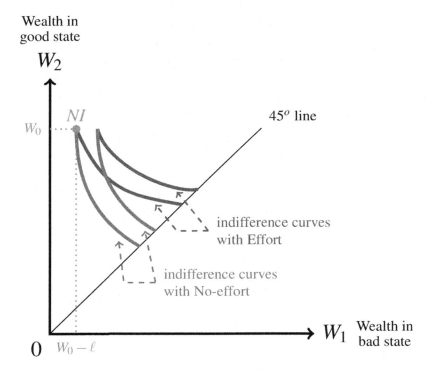

Figure 10.1: Indifference curves corresponding to Effort are less steep than those corresponding to No-effort.

Figure 10.1 shows two sets of indifference curves: one corresponding to Effort (the less steep ones) and one corresponding to No-effort (the steeper ones).

10.2 Moral hazard and insurance

When offered an insurance contract, the individual will have four possible choices:
1. remain uninsured and choose Effort,
2. remain uninsured and choose No-effort,
3. purchase the insurance contract and choose Effort,
4. purchase the insurance contract and choose No-effort,

and she will choose the option that yields the highest expected utility.

In general, the individual's decision problem can be framed as follows:

- first determine the best effort level if uninsured,
- then, for each offered insurance contract, determine the best effort level if that contract is purchased,
- compare the expected utility from the best choice of effort under each option and choose that option that yields the largest expected utility.

For example, consider an individual who has an initial wealth of $50,000 and faces a potential loss of $30,000 with the following probability:

$$\text{probability of loss} = \begin{cases} p_E = \frac{1}{10} & \text{if she chooses Effort} \\ p_N = \frac{1}{5} & \text{if she chooses No-effort.} \end{cases}$$

Her vNM preferences are represented the following vNM utility-of-money function (for $m > 0$):[3]

$$U(m) = \begin{cases} 10 - \frac{10{,}000}{m} & \text{if she chooses Effort} \\ 10.01 - \frac{10{,}000}{m} & \text{if she chooses No-effort.} \end{cases}$$

Suppose that she is offered the following menu of insurance contracts:

	premium	deductible
Contract 1:	$1,000	$5,000
Contract 2:	$500	$8,000
Contract 3:	$100	$12,000

Will she insure and, if so, which contract will she choose?

Step 1. Determine the best effort level in case of no insurance $NI = (20000, 50000)$:

Effort: $\mathbb{E}[U_E(NI)] = \frac{1}{10}\left(10 - \frac{1}{2}\right) + \frac{9}{10}\left(10 - \frac{1}{5}\right) = \boxed{9.77}$.

No-effort: $\mathbb{E}[U_N(NI)] = \frac{1}{5}\left(10.01 - \frac{1}{2}\right) + \frac{4}{5}\left(10.01 - \frac{1}{5}\right) = 9.75$.

Thus, if uninsured, the individual will choose Effort.

---
[3] This is an instance of (10.2) and (10.3) with $c = 0.01$.

Step 2. Determine the best effort level for Contract 1, namely $C_1 = (44000, 49000)$:

Effort: $\mathbb{E}[U_E(C_1)] = \frac{1}{10}\left[10 - \frac{1}{4.4}\right] + \frac{9}{10}\left[10 - \frac{1}{4.9}\right] = 9.7936$.

No-effort: $\mathbb{E}[U_N(C_1)] = \frac{1}{5}\left[10.01 - \frac{1}{4.4}\right] + \frac{4}{5}\left[10.01 - \frac{1}{4.9}\right] = \boxed{9.8013}$.

Thus, under Contract 1, the individual will choose No-effort.

Step 3. Determine the best effort level for Contract 2, namely $C_2 = (41500, 49500)$:

Effort: $\mathbb{E}[U_E(C_2)] = \frac{1}{10}\left[10 - \frac{1}{4.15}\right] + \frac{9}{10}\left[10 - \frac{1}{4.95}\right] = 9.7941$.

No-effort: $\mathbb{E}[U_N(C_2)] = \frac{1}{5}\left[10.01 - \frac{1}{4.15}\right] + \frac{4}{5}\left[10.01 - \frac{1}{4.95}\right] = \boxed{9.8002}$.

Thus, under Contract 2, the individual will choose No-effort.

Step 4. Determine the best effort level for Contract 3, namely $C_3 = (37900, 49900)$:

Effort: $\mathbb{E}[U_E(C_3)] = \frac{1}{10}\left[10 - \frac{1}{3.79}\right] + \frac{9}{10}\left[10 - \frac{1}{4.99}\right] = 9.7933$.

No-effort: $\mathbb{E}[U_N(C_3)] = \frac{1}{5}\left[10.01 - \frac{1}{3.79}\right] + \frac{4}{5}\left[10.01 - \frac{1}{4.99}\right] = \boxed{9.7969}$.

Thus, under Contract 3, the individual will choose No-effort.

Of all these options, the one that gives the highest expected utility is Contract 2 with No-effort. Thus the individual would purchase Contract 2 and choose No-effort. The insurer's expected profit from Contract 2 is thus $h - p_N(\ell - d) = 500 - \frac{1}{5}(30,000 - 8,000) = \$-3,900$: a loss! Hence the insurance company would **not** want to offer Contract 2 (or any of the other two contracts, since they all involve a loss). Before we address the issue of what contract(s) would be offered by an insurer, we need to re-examine the notion of "reservation indifference curve" in the context of moral hazard.

> Test your understanding of the concepts introduced in this section, by going through the exercises in Section 10.3.1 at the end of this chapter.

10.2.2 The reservation utility locus

In previous chapters we defined the reservation indifference curve as the indifference curve that goes through the no-insurance point NI. We can no longer do so in the present context, because, for every point in the wealth space, there are now **two** indifference curves, one corresponding to Effort and the other to No-effort. Since a reservation indifference curve is supposed to contain all the contracts that yield the same expected utility as no insurance, we first need to determine the "reservation utility" of the individual, that is, the maximum utility that she can obtain if she does not insure. Letting $\mathbb{E}[U_E(NI)]$ be the expected utility under no insurance if the individual chooses Effort and $\mathbb{E}[U_N(NI)]$ be the expected utility under no insurance if the individual chooses No-effort, the reservation utility is:

$$EU_{NI} = max\{\mathbb{E}[U_E(NI)], \mathbb{E}[U_N(NI)]\}. \tag{10.7}$$

The interesting case is where under no insurance the individual will choose Effort; it is interesting because insurance might provide an incentive for the individual to switch to

10.2 Moral hazard and insurance

No-effort. Thus in this section and the next we will assume that $\mathbb{E}[U_E(NI)] > \mathbb{E}[U_N(NI)]$ so that, by (10.7),

$$EU_{NI} = \mathbb{E}[U_E(NI)]. \tag{10.8}$$

The individual will reject any contract which, with the best choice of effort, will yield a utility which is less than $\mathbb{E}[U_E(NI)]$, that is, $\mathbb{E}[U_E(NI)]$ provides the *reservation level of utility*. Does this mean that the indifference curve corresponding to Effort that goes through *NI* can be taken to be the reservation indifference curve, that is, the set of contracts that give an expected utility equal to $\mathbb{E}[U_E(NI)]$? The answer is negative, because the fact that the individual prefers to choose Effort if uninsured does not imply that she will continue to choose Effort when insured. For example, *if fully insured then she will be better off by choosing No-effort*.

Figure 10.2 shows the two indifference curves that go through the *NI* point: the less steep one corresponds to Effort and a utility level of $\bar{u} = \mathbb{E}[U_E(NI)]$ and the steeper one to No-effort and a utility level of $\hat{u} = \mathbb{E}[U_N(NI)]$.

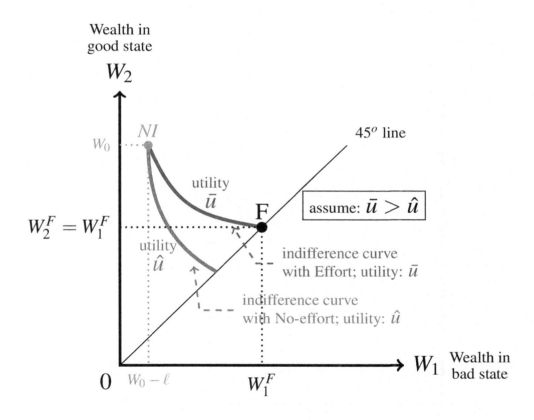

Figure 10.2: The two indifference curves through *NI*.

In accordance with (10.8) we assume that $\bar{u} > \hat{u}$, that is, that when uninsured, the individual chooses Effort. Let $F = (W_1^F, W_1^F)$ be the point at the intersection of the 45° line and the indifference curve corresponding to Effort that goes through *NI*; then $\mathbb{E}[U_E(F)] = U_E(W_1^F)$. By definition of indifference curve, $U_E(W_1^F) = \mathbb{E}[U_E(NI)] = \bar{u}$; however, if offered the full-insurance contract F the individual can achieve a higher level of utility by purchasing the contract and switching to No-effort. In fact, by (10.2) and (10.3),

$$U_N(W_1^F) = U_E(W_1^F) + c = \bar{u} + c > \bar{u}.$$

Let us use the expression *reservation utility locus*[4] to denote the set of points (contracts) in the wealth plane that give an expected utility equal to $\bar{u}$, when the individual makes the best choice of effort; then, while *NI* belongs to it, point *F* does not. *Thus the reservation utility locus does not coincide with the indifference curve corresponding to Effort that goes through NI.*

How do we determine the reservation utility locus?

Continue to denote by $\bar{u}$ the individual's expected utility when uninsured and choosing Effort. We need to consider the expected utility from choosing No-effort. By hypothesis,

$$\mathbb{E}[U_N(NI)] < \bar{u} \quad \text{and, as shown above,} \quad U_N(F) > \bar{u}.$$

Thus, by continuity, there must be a point, call it $A = (W_1^A, W_2^A)$, on the indifference curve corresponding to Effort that goes through *NI*, such that (see Figure 10.3)

$$\mathbb{E}[U_N(A)] = \bar{u}.$$

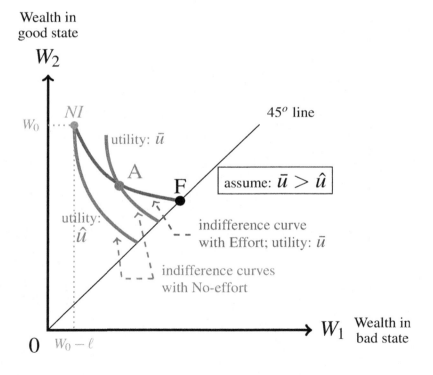

Figure 10.3: Point A is such that $\mathbb{E}[U_N(A)] = \mathbb{E}[U_E(A)] = \bar{u}$.

Thus, since the reservation utility level (that is, the maximum utility that the individual can achieve if not insured) is $\bar{u}$ ($= \mathbb{E}[U_E(NI)]$), the reservation utility locus is a *kinked*

---

[4]Instead of 'reservation indifference curve', since it does not coincide with an indifference curve.

10.2 Moral hazard and insurance

curve consisting of the initial segment from *NI* to point *A* of the indifference curve through *NI* corresponding to Effort and the segment from point *A* to the 45° line of the indifference curve through *A* corresponding to No-effort, where point *A* is such that $\mathbb{E}[U_N(A)] = \mathbb{E}[U_E(A)] = \mathbb{E}[U_E(NI)]$.

The reservation utility locus is shown as a thick continuous kinked curve in Figure 10.4.

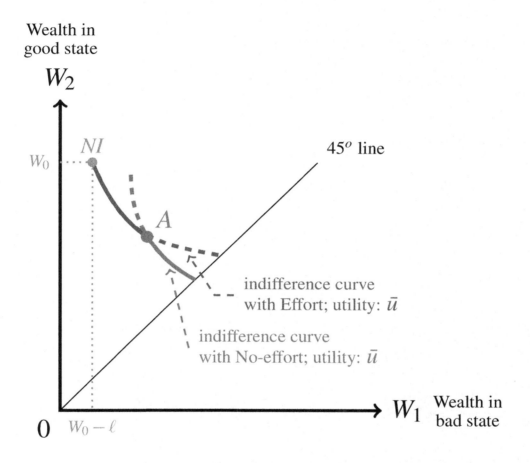

Figure 10.4: The reservation utility locus is the union of the thick continuous curves.

Let us illustrate all of the above in an example.

Consider an individual whose vNM utility-of-money function is

$$\begin{cases} U_N(m) = \sqrt{m} & \text{if she chooses No-effort} \\ U_E(m) = \sqrt{m} - c & \text{if she chooses Effort} \end{cases} \quad \text{with } c > 0.$$

The individual's initial wealth is W_0 and she faces a potential loss of ℓ. The probability of her incurring a loss is p_E if she chooses Effort and p_N if she chooses No-effort, with $0 < p_E < p_N < 1$.

Chapter 10. Moral Hazard in Insurance

♦ Let us first determine for what values of c she will choose Effort when not insured.

Her expected utility if she has no insurance and chooses No-effort is

$$\mathbb{E}[U_N(NI)] = p_N\sqrt{W_0 - \ell} + (1 - p_N)\sqrt{W_0}$$

and her expected utility if she has no insurance and chooses Effort is

$$\mathbb{E}[U_E(NI)] = p_E\left(\sqrt{W_0 - \ell} - c\right) + (1 - p_E)\left(\sqrt{W_0} - c\right)$$
$$= p_E\sqrt{W_0 - \ell} + (1 - p_E)\sqrt{W_0} - c.$$

Then it must be that

$$c < \left(p_E\sqrt{W_0 - \ell} + (1 - p_E)\sqrt{W_0}\right) - \left(p_N\sqrt{W_0 - \ell} + (1 - p_N)\sqrt{W_0}\right),$$

that is,

$$c < (p_N - p_E)\left(\sqrt{W_0} - \sqrt{W_0 - \ell}\right) \tag{10.9}$$

For the rest of this section let us fix the following values of the parameters, which satisfy (10.9):[5]

$$\boxed{W_0 = 2{,}500 \qquad \ell = 1{,}600 \qquad p_E = \frac{1}{20} \qquad p_N = \frac{1}{10} \qquad c = \frac{15}{16}}$$

♦ What is the individual's reservation utility level?

Since (10.9) is satisfied, the individual – if uninsured – will choose Effort and thus her reservation utility is:

$$\mathbb{E}[U_E(NI)] = \frac{1}{20}\sqrt{900} + \frac{19}{20}\sqrt{2{,}500} - \frac{15}{16} = \frac{769}{16} = 48.0625.$$

♦ Let us find the contract, call it A, that would make the individual indifferent between
1. not insuring and choosing Effort,
2. purchasing contract A and choosing Effort,
3. purchasing contract A and choosing No-effort.

---
[5] In fact, with these values, the right-hand side of (10.9) is equal to 1.

10.2 Moral hazard and insurance

Let $A = (W_1^A, W_2^A)$. Then it must be that $\mathbb{E}[U_E(NI)] = \mathbb{E}[U_E(A)]$ and $\mathbb{E}[U_E(A)] = \mathbb{E}[U_N(A)]$, that is,

$$48.0625 = \frac{1}{20}\sqrt{W_1^A} + \frac{19}{20}\sqrt{W_2^A} - \frac{15}{16} \quad \text{and} \tag{10.10}$$

$$\frac{1}{20}\sqrt{W_1^A} + \frac{19}{20}\sqrt{W_2^A} - \frac{15}{16} = \frac{1}{10}\sqrt{W_1^A} + \frac{9}{10}\sqrt{W_2^A}. \tag{10.11}$$

The solution is $W_1^A = 972.66$ and $W_2^A = 2{,}493.75$; thus A is the contract with premium $2{,}500 - 2{,}493.75 = \$6.25$ and deductible $2{,}493.75 - 972.66 = \$1{,}521.09$.

◆ Suppose that the individual is offered contract A and she breaks her indifference by purchasing the contract. What is the insurer's expected profit from this contract?

With contract A the individual is indifferent between Effort and No-effort. Thus expected profit will be
  - $h - p_E(\ell - d) = 6.25 - \frac{1}{20}(1{,}600 - 1{,}521.09) = \$2.31$ if the individual chooses Effort.
  - $h - p_N(\ell - d) = 6.25 - \frac{1}{10}(1{,}600 - 1{,}521.09) = \$-1.641$ if the individual chooses No-effort.

◆ Let us find the full-insurance contract, call it F, that makes the individual indifferent between purchasing the contract and not insuring.

We saw above that, without insurance, the individual can achieve a level of utility of 48.0625 (by opting for Effort). On the other hand, with any full-insurance contract, the individual will maximize her utility by choosing No-effort. Thus we are looking for a level of wealth W such that $\sqrt{W} = 48.0625$. The solution is $W = 2{,}310$. Thus $F = (2310, 2310)$, that is, a contract with premium $2{,}500 - 2{,}310 = \$190$ and zero deductible.

◆ Suppose that the individual is offered contract F and she breaks her indifference by purchasing the contract. What is the insurer's expected profit from this contract?

Expected profit will be $h - p_N \ell = 190 - \frac{1}{10}1600 = \$30$.

◆ What is the reservation utility locus for this individual?

It is the union of the following two curves: (1) the portion of the indifference curve through NI corresponding to Effort, from NI to point A, followed by (2) the portion of the indifference curve through A corresponding to No-effort from point A to point F.

In the above example, an insurer would be better off offering contract F than contract A. We now turn to the issue of what contract(s) would be offered by a monopolist.

> Test your understanding of the concepts introduced in this section, by going through the exercises in Section 10.3.2 at the end of this chapter.

10.2.3 The profit-maximizing contract for a monopolist

In Chapter 5 (Section 5.2.1) we showed that – in the case where the probability of loss p is fixed and thus there is no issue of moral hazard – a monopolist would offer only one contract, namely the full-insurance contract with the maximum premium that the individual is willing to pay for full insurance, namely $h_{max} = p\ell + R_{NI}$, where $p\ell$ is expected loss and R_{NI} is the risk premium associated with the no-insurance lottery. Such contract is determine by the intersection of the reservation indifference curve and the 45° line.

In the case of moral hazard, the situation is more subtle. First of all, there are now two sets of isoprofit lines: one set corresponds to the case where the individual chooses Effort (so that the probability of loss is p_E and the slope of each isoprofit line is $-\frac{p_E}{1-p_E}$) and the other set corresponds to the case where the individual chooses No-effort (so that the probability of loss is p_N and the slope of each isoprofit line is $-\frac{p_N}{1-p_N}$). Since $p_E < p_N$, $\frac{p_E}{1-p_E} < \frac{p_N}{1-p_N}$ and thus the isoprofit lines in the former set are less steep than the ones in the latter set. In order to use the correct isoprofit lines, the monopolist must first figure out what choice of effort the individual will make.

As in the case considered in Chapter 5, the monopolist will want to offer a contract that extracts the maximum surplus from the individual, that is, the contract that leaves the individual just indifferent between insuring and not insuring.

As in the previous section, we will continue to assume that, if uninsured, the individual will choose Effort, that is,
$$\mathbb{E}[U_E(NI)] > \mathbb{E}[U_N(NI)].$$

Then the monopolist's problem is to find that contract on the reservation utility locus that maximizes its profits. Figure 10.5 (which reproduces Figure 10.4) shows the reservation utility locus (it is the union of the two thick, continuous curves).

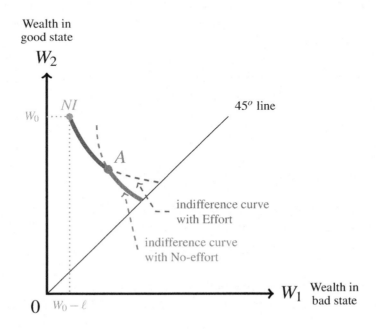

Figure 10.5: The reservation utility locus is the union of the two thick, continuous curves.

10.2 Moral hazard and insurance

Let us begin by considering the first segment of the reservation utility locus, namely the portion of the indifference curve through *NI* corresponding to Effort, from point *NI* to point *A* (where, as before, *A* is the contract that yields the reservation utility no matter whether the individual chooses Effort or No-effort). It is shown in Figure 10.6.

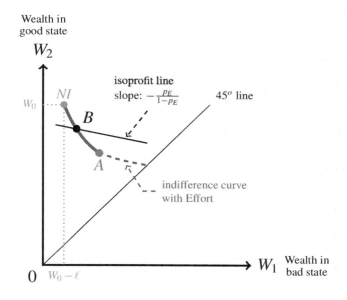

Figure 10.6: Point *A* is such that $\mathbb{E}[U_N(A)] = \mathbb{E}[U_E(A)]$.

If the insurance company wants to offer a contract that
1. leaves the customer with no surplus (that is, her expected utility with the offered contract is her reservation utility, call it $\bar{u}$) and
2. induces the customer to choose Effort,

then the insurance company has to offer a contract on this portion of the reservation utility locus. Note that if the individual purchases a contract that lies on this portion of the reservation utility locus then she will indeed choose Effort. In fact, since contract *A* is such that the individual is indifferent between choosing Effort and No-effort, that is, $\mathbb{E}[U_E(A)] = \mathbb{E}[U_N(A)] = \bar{u}$, any point *B* to the left of point *A* on this portion of the reservation utility locus is such that $\mathbb{E}[U_N(B)] < \bar{u}$ (since it lies on a lower *N*-indifference curve than the *N*-indifference curve that goes through *A*). On the other hand, if offered contract *A* the individual is indifferent between choosing Effort and No-effort; **we will assume that in this case she will choose Effort.**[6]

Since, for any of the contracts being considered, the individual will choose Effort, the relevant probability of loss is p_E and thus the relevant isoprofit lines are those with slope $-\frac{p_E}{1-p_E}$. Figure 10.6 shows one such isoprofit line, namely the one that goes through point *B*. Recall from Chapter 5 (Section 5.1.4) that at any point above the 45° line the Effort-indifference curve through that point is steeper than the p_E-isoprofit-line. Thus

---

[6] Without this assumption, instead of contract *A* the insurance company would offer a contract slightly to the left of point *A* (on the portion of the curve under consideration) in order to provide the customer with an incentive to choose Effort (and thus reduce the probability of loss). To simplify the exposition we assume that, with contract *A*, the individual would choose Effort.

contract B cannot be profit-maximizing for the insurer, since there are points on this portion of the reservation utility locus that lie below the isoprofit line through B and thus yield higher profits than B.

Thus we conclude that, of all the points on the portion of the reservation utility locus considered so far, point A represents the profit-maximizing contract.

Let us now turn to the other portion of the reservation utility locus, namely the segment of the indifference curve through A corresponding to No-effort from point A to the 45° line, shown in Figure 10.7, where the point of intersection between the indifference curve and the 45° line is denoted by F.

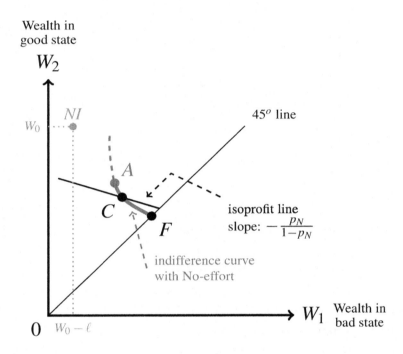

Figure 10.7: Point A is such that $\mathbb{E}[U_N(A)] = \mathbb{E}[U_E(A)]$.

Note that if the individual purchases a contract that lies on this portion of the reservation utility locus then she will choose No-effort. In fact, since contract A lies on the indifference curve corresponding to Effort and utility level $\bar{u} = \mathbb{E}[U_E(NI)]$, any point to the right of A on this portion of the reservation utility locus will be lie on an Effort-indifference curve corresponding to a utility level less than $\bar{u}$ (while it lies on the No-effort-indifference curve corresponding to $\bar{u}$).[7]

Since, for any of the contracts being considered, the individual will choose No-effort, the relevant probability of loss is p_N and thus the relevant isoprofit lines are those with slope $-\frac{p_N}{1-p_N}$. Figure 10.7 shows one such isoprofit line, namely the one that goes through point C. Recall from Chapter 5 (Section 5.1.4) that at any point above the 45° line the No-effort-indifference curve through that point is steeper than the p_N-isoprofit-line. Thus contract C cannot be profit-maximizing for the insurer, since there are points on this portion of the reservation utility locus that lie below the isoprofit line through C and thus yield

---

[7] As for point A we continue to assume that the individual would choose Effort.

10.2 Moral hazard and insurance

higher profits than C.

Thus we conclude that, of all the points on the portion of the reservation utility locus under consideration, point F represents the profit-maximizing contract.

Let $A = \left(W_1^A, W_2^A\right)$ and $F = \left(W^F, W^F\right)$ so that the corresponding premia and deductibles are

	premium	deductible
Contract A :	$h_A = W_0 - W_2^A$	$d_A = W_2^A - W_1^A$
Contract F :	$h_F = W_0 - W^F$	$d_F = 0$

Furthermore, let π_A be the expected profit from contract A and π_F be the expected profit from contract F, that is,

$$\pi_A = h_A - p_E(\ell - d_A)$$
$$\pi_F = h_F - p_N \ell.$$

Then we can conclude from the above analysis that the monopolist will offer

- contract A if $\pi_A > \pi_F$,
- contract F if $\pi_F > \pi_A$

and be indifferent between the two contracts if $\pi_A = \pi_F$.

In the numerical example considered at the end of the previous section, the monopolist would opt for the full-insurance contract F, since $\pi_F = 30$ and $\pi_A = 2.31$ (as shown on page 353).

Now we give an example where the monopolist prefers to offer the partial-insurance contract A. Let us keep the same data as in the example considered at the end of the previous section, but change the value of p_E from $\frac{1}{20}$ to $\frac{1}{40}$. Thus we have that the vNM utility-of-money function is

$$\begin{cases} U_N(m) = \sqrt{m} & \text{if she chooses No-effort} \\ U_E(m) = \sqrt{m} - \frac{15}{16} & \text{if she chooses Effort} \end{cases}$$

$$\boxed{W_0 = 2,500 \qquad \ell = 1,600 \qquad p_E = \frac{1}{40} \qquad p_N = \frac{1}{10}}$$

Note that, if uninsured, the individual would choose Effort, since

$$\mathbb{E}[U_E(NI)] = \frac{1}{40}\sqrt{900} + \frac{39}{40}\sqrt{2,500} - \frac{15}{16} = 48.5625$$

and

$$\mathbb{E}[U_N(NI)] = \frac{1}{10}\sqrt{900} + \frac{9}{10}\sqrt{2,500} = 48.$$

Contract A is given by the solution to

$$\begin{cases} 48.5625 = \frac{1}{40}\sqrt{W_1^A} + \frac{39}{40}\sqrt{W_2^A} - \frac{15}{16} \\ \\ 48.5625 = \frac{1}{10}\sqrt{W_1^A} + \frac{9}{10}\sqrt{W_2^A} \end{cases}$$

The solution is $W_1^A = 1,392.22$ and $W_2^A = 2,481.29$, that is, $A = (1392.22, 2481.29)$. Thus $h_A = 2,500 - 2,481.29 = 18.71$ and $d_A = 2,481.29 - 1,392.22 = 1,089.07$.

Contract F is given by the solution to $\sqrt{W^F} = 48.5625$, which is $W^F = 2,358.32$ so that $F = (2358.32, 2358.32)$ and $h_F = 2,500 - 2,358.32 = 141.68$. Hence[8]

$$\pi_A = 18.71 - \frac{1}{40}(1,600 - 1,089.07) = \$5.94$$

$$\pi_F = 141.68 - \frac{1}{10}(1,600) = \$-18.32$$

so that the monopolist would offer contract A, thereby inducing the individual to reduce the probability of loss by choosing Effort.

What would the monopolist's profit be if it offered the full-insurance contract G which is given by the intersection of the 45° line and the indifference curve corresponding to Effort that goes through the NI point? In this example contract G is obtained by solving $\sqrt{W^F} - \frac{15}{16} = 48.5625$, that is, $G = (2450.25, 2450.25)$ with corresponding premium $h_G = 2,500 - 2450.25 = 49.75$. Thus one might be tempted to answer that the monopolist's profit would be $49.75 - \frac{1}{40}(1,600) = \$9.75$, but this answer is wrong! The individual would be very happy to purchase contract G because her best choice would then be No-effort, with an expected utility of $\sqrt{2,450.25} = 49.5$ (instead of 48.5625) and thus, as a matter of fact, the monopolist's profits would turn out to be $\pi_G = 49.75 - \frac{1}{10}(1,600) = \$-110.25$!

> Test your understanding of the concepts introduced in this section, by going through the exercises in Section 10.3.3 at the end of this chapter.

---

[8] Recall the assumption that, with contract A, the individual would choose Effort: see Footnote 6 on page 355.

10.3 Exercises

The solutions to the following exercises are given in Section 10.4 at the end of this chapter.

10.3.1 Exercises for Section 10.2.1: Two levels of unobserved effort

Exercise 10.1 Emily has an initial wealth of $80,000 and faces a potential loss of $36,000. The probability of loss depends on the amount of effort she puts into trying to avoid the loss. If she puts a high level of effort, then the probability is 5%, while if she exerts low effort the probability is 15%. Her vNM utility-of-money function is

$$U(m) = \begin{cases} \sqrt{m} & \text{if low effort} \\ \sqrt{m} - 1 & \text{if high effort.} \end{cases}$$

(a) If Emily remains uninsured, what level of effort will she choose?

(b) If Emily is offered a full insurance contract with premium $2,250 and she accepts it, what level of effort will she choose?

(c) If Emily is offered a full insurance contract with premium $2,250 will she accept it?

(d) What is the insurance company's expected profit from a full insurance contract with premium $2,250?

Exercise 10.2 Susan has an initial wealth of $10,000 and faces a potential loss of $1,900. The probability of loss depends on the amount of effort she puts into trying to avoid the loss. If she puts a high level of effort, then the probability is $\frac{1}{10}$, while if she exerts low effort the probability is $\frac{4}{10}$. Her vNM utility-of-money function is

$$U(m) = \begin{cases} \sqrt{m} & \text{if low effort} \\ \sqrt{m} - 2 & \text{if high effort} \end{cases}$$

(a) If Susan remains uninsured, what level of effort will she choose?

(b) If Susan is offered a partial insurance contract with premium $800 and deductible $200 and she accepts it, what level of effort will she choose?

(c) If Susan is offered the contract of Part (b) will she accept it?

Exercise 10.3 Bob owns a house near Lake Tahoe. The house is worth $949,000. He also has $1,000 in his bank account, so that his entire wealth is $950,000. The probability that there will be a forest fire next year is $\frac{1}{10}$. If a forest fire occurs then the house will incur damages equal to $400,000. However, by spending $x on protective measures Bob can reduce the probability that the fire will reach the house from $\frac{1}{10}$ to $\frac{1}{10} - \frac{x}{15,000}$. Thus the more he spends, the lower the probability. The most he can spend is $1,000. Bob's vNM utility of money function is $U(m) = 10 \ln(m)$.

(a) If Bob is not insured, which of the following four options will he choose (assuming that these are the only options)?

   (1) $x = 0$,

   (2) $x = \$400$,

   (3) $x = \$750$,

   (4) $x = \$1,000$.

(b) If Bob is offered a full-insurance contract with premium h, what value of x will he choose?

(c) Suppose that Bob is offered a full insurance contract with premium $h = \$40,000$. Will he purchase it?

Exercise 10.4 In this exercise we consider the case where the individual's effort has an effect not on the probability of loss but on the *size* of the loss.

Mike's initial wealth is $6,400 and he faces a potential loss with probability $\frac{1}{4}$. The size of the loss depends on his choice of effort: it he chooses Effort then the loss is $\ell_E = \$471$, while if he chooses No-effort then the loss is $\ell_N = \$1,216$. Mike's vNM utility-of-money function is

$$\begin{cases} U_N(m) = \sqrt{m} & \text{if he chooses No-effort} \\ U_E(m) = \sqrt{m} - 1 & \text{if he chooses Effort} \end{cases}$$

(a) If Mike is uninsured, will he choose Effort or No-effort?

(b) If Mike purchases a full-insurance contract with premium h, will he choose Effort or No-effort?

(c) Suppose that Mike is offered an insurance contract with premium $h = \$80$ and deductible $d = \$471$. Will he purchase it?

10.3.2 Exercises for Section 10.2.2: The reservation utility locus

Exercise 10.5 Consider again the information given in Exercise 10.2: Susan has an initial wealth of $10,000 and faces a potential loss of $1,900; the probability of loss depends on the amount of effort she puts into trying to avoid the loss; if she puts a high level of effort, then the probability is $\frac{1}{10}$, while if she exerts low effort the probability is $\frac{4}{10}$; her vNM utility-of-money function is

$$U(m) = \begin{cases} \sqrt{m} & \text{if low effort} \\ \sqrt{m} - 2 & \text{if high effort} \end{cases}$$

(a) What is Susan's reservation level of utility?

(b) Write two equations whose solution gives that point, call it A, on the indifference curve through NI that corresponds to high effort such that Susan's expected utility at A if she chooses low effort is equal to her reservation level of utility.

(c) Find a full-insurance contract, call it F, that yields Susan the same expected utility, when she chooses low effort, as contract A of Part (b). Calculate the premium of contract F

(d) Describe in words how you would draw the reservation utility locus for Susan.

Exercise 10.6 In this exercise we consider a slightly different type of vNM utility-of-money function, where instead of $U_E(m) = U_N(m) - c$ we have that $U_E(m) = \alpha U_N(m)$ with $0 < \alpha < 1$.

Tom has an initial wealth of $4,900 and faces a potential loss of $1,300; the probability of loss depends on the amount of effort he puts into trying to avoid the loss; if he puts a high level of effort, then the probability is $\frac{1}{8}$, while if he exerts low effort the probability is $\frac{3}{8}$; his vNM utility-of-money function is

$$U(m) = \begin{cases} \sqrt{m} & \text{if low effort} \\ \alpha\sqrt{m} & \text{if high effort} \end{cases} \text{ with } 0 < \alpha < 1.$$

(a) For what values of α would Tom choose high effort if uninsured?

(b) Let $\alpha = 0.9$. What is Tom's reservation level of utility?

(c) Let $\alpha = 0.98$. What is Tom's reservation level of utility?

(d) Assume that $\alpha = 0.98$. Write two equations whose solution gives that insurance contract, call it A, such that if Tom purchases this contract he gets his reservation level of utility, no matter whether he chooses low effort or high effort.

(e) Continue to assume that $\alpha = 0.98$. Find a full-insurance contract, call if F, such that Tom is indifferent between not insuring and purchasing contract F.

(f) Continue to assume that $\alpha = 0.98$. Describe in words how you would draw the reservation utility locus for Tom.

10.3.3 Exercises for Section 10.2.3: The profit-maximizing contract

Exercise 10.7 Carol has an initial wealth of $10,000 and faces a potential loss of $4,000; the probability of loss depends on the amount of effort she puts into trying to avoid the loss; if she puts a high level of effort, then the probability is $\frac{1}{10}$, while if she exerts low effort the probability is $\frac{1}{2}$; her vNM utility-of-money function is

$$U(m) = \begin{cases} 10\ln(\frac{m}{1{,}000}) & \text{if low effort} \\ 10\ln(\frac{m}{1{,}000}) - c & \text{if high effort} \end{cases} \quad \text{with } c > 0.$$

(a) For what values of c would Carol choose high effort if uninsured?

(b) Assume that $c = 1.8$. What insurance contract would a monopolist offer to Carol?

(c) Assume that $c = 1.5$. What insurance contract would a monopolist offer to Carol?

10.4 Solutions to Exercises

Solution to Exercise 10.1

(a) If Emily chooses low effort, her expected utility is
$$0.15\sqrt{80,000-36,000}+0.85\sqrt{80,000}=271.881$$
and if she chooses high effort, her expected utility is
$$0.05\left(\sqrt{80,000-36,000}-1\right)+0.95\left(\sqrt{80,000}-1\right)=278.189.$$
Thus she will choose high effort.

(b) Emily will choose low effort, because her utility will be $\sqrt{80,000-2,250}$ while with high effort it would be less, namely $\sqrt{80,000-2,250}-1$.

(c) She will accept the contract, because her utility if she accepts it is $\sqrt{80,000-2,250}=278.837$, while her best alternative would be to remain uninsured and choose high effort with an expected utility of 278.189.

(d) Since Emily will indeed buy insurance (and exert low effort), expected profits will be $2,250-0.15(36,000)=\$-3,150$, that is, a loss. Thus it would not be a good idea for the insurance company to offer this contract. □

Solution to Exercise 10.2

(a) If Susan is uninsured and chooses high effort, her expected utility is
$$0.1\left(\sqrt{10,000-1,900}-2\right)+0.9\left(\sqrt{10,000}-2\right)=97$$
while if she chooses low effort, her expected utility is
$$0.4\sqrt{10,000-1,900}+0.6\sqrt{10,000}=96.$$
Thus she will choose high effort.

(b) The contract under consideration (premium of \$800, deductible of \$200) corresponds to the following point in the wealth space: $C=(9000,9200)$. If Susan purchases this contract and chooses high effort, then her expected utility is
$$0.1\left(\sqrt{9,000}-2\right)+0.9\left(\sqrt{9,200}-2\right)=93.81$$
while if she chooses low effort, her expected utility is
$$0.4\sqrt{9,000}+0.6\sqrt{9,200}=95.5.$$
Thus, under this contract, she would choose low effort.

(c) She will **not** accept the contract, because her highest utility if she accepts it is 95.5, while her best alternative would be to remain uninsured and choose high effort with an expected utility of 97. □

Solution to Exercise 10.3

(a) If Bob chooses to spend $x on preventive measures his expected utility – when not insured – is

$$NI(x) = \left(\frac{1}{10} - \frac{x}{15,000}\right) 10 \ln(950,000 - 400,000 - x)$$
$$+ \left[1 - \left(\frac{1}{10} - \frac{x}{15,000}\right)\right] 10 \ln(950,000 - x).$$

Since $NI(0) = 137.096$, $NI(400) = 137.237$, $NI(750) = 137.361$ and $NI(1,000) = 137.449$, of the four options he will choose $x = \$1,000$.

(b) If he is fully insured at premium h then his utility, if he does not spend any money on preventive measures, is $10\ln(950,000 - h)$, while if he spends $x (with $x > 0$) then his utility is less, namely $10\ln(950,000 - h - x)$. Thus he will choose $x = 0$.

(c) As determined in Part (b), if he buys the full insurance contract with premium $40,000 then he will choose $x = 0$, so that his utility will be $10\ln(950,000 - 40,000) = 10\ln(910,000) = 137.21$. This is less than his expected utility if he remains uninsured and spends $1,000 on preventive measures, which is 137.449 as calculated in Part (a). Thus he will **not** accept the contract. □

Solution to Exercise 10.4

(a) If Mike is uninsured and chooses No-effort then his expected utility is

$$\mathbb{E}[U_N(NI)] = \frac{1}{4}\sqrt{6,400 - 1,216} + \frac{3}{4}\sqrt{6,400} = 78$$

while if he chooses Effort his expected utility is

$$\mathbb{E}[U_E(NI)] = \frac{1}{4}\sqrt{6,400 - 471} + \frac{3}{4}\sqrt{6,400} - 1 = 78.25.$$

Thus he will choose Effort, if not insured.

(b) With a full-insurance contract with premium h his utility if he chooses Effort is $\sqrt{6,400 - h} - 1$ while his utility if he chooses No-effort is higher, namely $\sqrt{6,400 - h}$. Thus he would choose No-effort (he does not care about the size of the loss, since he gets fully reimbursed by the insurance company if the loss occurs).

(c) When the deductible is $471 ($= \ell_E$, loss with Effort) it would not make sense for Mike to purchase the contract and choose Effort, because he would be better off by not insuring and choosing Effort (his wealth would be larger by an amount equal to the premium). Thus he would compare expected utility from no insurance with Effort (which was calculated to be 78.25 in Part (a)) with expected utility with the contract and No-effort which is (recall that the premium is $80)

$$\frac{1}{4}\sqrt{6,400 - 80 - 471} + \frac{3}{4}\sqrt{6,400 - 80} = 78.74.$$

Thus Mike would purchase the contract and choose No-effort. □

10.4 Solutions to Exercises

Solution to Exercise 10.5

(a) We saw in Part (a) of Exercise 10.2 that if Susan is uninsured and chooses low effort, her expected utility is 96 and if she chooses high effort her expected utility is 97. Thus her reservation level of utility is 97: she would not accept a contract that did not give her an expected utility of at least 97.

(b) Let $A = (W_1^A, W_2^A)$. The first equation says that A should lie on the indifference curve through NI corresponding to high effort. Since, as computed in Part (a) of Exercise 10.2, $\mathbb{E}[U_E(NI)] = 97$, the first equation is

$$0.1\left(\sqrt{W_1^A} - 2\right) + 0.9\left(\sqrt{W_2^A} - 2\right) = 97.$$

The second equation says that contract A gives the same expected utility whether Susan chooses high effort or low effort:

$$0.4\sqrt{W_1^A} + 0.6\sqrt{W_2^A} = 0.1\left(\sqrt{W_1^A} - 2\right) + 0.9\left(\sqrt{W_2^A} - 2\right).$$

The solution of these two equations is: $W_1^A = 8,649$ and $W_2^A = 9,933.44$. Thus A is the contract with premium $10,000 - 9,933.44 = \$66.56$ and deductible $9,933.44 - 8,649 = \$1,284.44$.

(c) We are looking for a level of wealth W such that

$$\sqrt{W} = 97.$$

The solution is $W = 9,409$. Thus $F = (9409, 9409)$, that is, a contract with premium $10,000 - 9,409 = \$591$ and zero deductible.

(d) The reservation utility locus for Susan is the union of the following two curves: (1) the portion of the indifference curve through NI corresponding to high effort from NI to point A, followed by (2) the portion of the indifference curve through A corresponding to low effort from point A to point F. □

Solution to Exercise 10.6

(a) When uninsured, Tom's expected utility is:

if low effort: $\quad \frac{3}{8}\sqrt{3,600} + \frac{5}{8}\sqrt{4900} = \frac{265}{4} = 66.25$

if high effort: $\quad \frac{1}{8}\alpha\sqrt{3,600} + \frac{7}{8}\alpha\sqrt{4900} = \frac{275}{4}\alpha = 68.75\alpha.$

Thus, when uninsured, Tom will choose high effort if $68.75\alpha > 66.25$, that is, if $\alpha > \frac{53}{55} = 0.9636$.

(b) The assumption is that $\alpha = 0.9$. Since in this case $\alpha < 0.9636$, Tom – when uninsured – will choose low effort. Thus his reservation level of utility is 66.25, as computed in Part (a).

(c) The assumption is that $\alpha = 0.98$. Since in this case $\alpha > 0.9636$, Tom – when uninsured – will choose high effort. Thus his reservation level of utility is $68.75(0.98) = 67.375$, as computed in Part (a).

(d) Let the contract be $A = \left(W_1^A, W_2^A\right)$. The equations are:

$$\frac{1}{8}(0.98)\sqrt{W_1^A} + \frac{7}{8}(0.98)\sqrt{W_2^A} = \frac{3}{8}\sqrt{W_1^A} + \frac{5}{8}\sqrt{W_2^A}$$

$$\frac{1}{8}(0.98)\sqrt{W_1^A} + \frac{7}{8}(0.98)\sqrt{W_2^A} = 67.375.$$

The solution is $W_1^A = 4{,}088$ and $W_2^A = 4{,}821.57$.

(e) The assumption is that $\alpha = 0.98$. Contract F is given by the solution to: $\sqrt{W} = 67.375$ which is $W = 4{,}539.39$. Thus $F = (4539.39, 4539.39)$.

(f) The reservation utility locus for Tom is the union of the following two curves: (1) the portion, from point NI to point A, of the indifference curve through NI corresponding to high effort followed by (2) the portion, from point A to point F, of the indifference curve through A corresponding to low effort. □

Solution to Exercise 10.7

(a) If Carol is uninsured and exerts low effort, her expected utility is:

$$\frac{1}{2}10\ln(6) + \frac{1}{2}10\ln(10) = 20.4717$$

while with high effort her expected utility is

$$\frac{1}{10}(10\ln(6) - c) + \frac{9}{10}(10\ln(10) - c) = 22.515 - c.$$

Thus she will choose high effort if $20.4717 < 22.515 - c$, that is, if $c < 2.0433$.

(b) The assumption is that $c = 1.8$, so that – if uninsured – Carol would choose high effort and her expected utility would be $22.515 - 1.8 = 20.715$. The monopolist would only consider two options:

- the partial-insurance contract A given by the intersection of the low-effort indifference curve corresponding to a utility of 20.715 and the high-effort indifference curve corresponding to a utility of 20.715, and
- the full-insurance contract F that makes Carol indifferent between (1) purchasing F and exerting low effort and (2) not insuring and exerting high effort.

Contract A is given by the solution to the following two equations:

$$\frac{1}{2}10\ln\left(\frac{W_1}{1{,}000}\right) + \frac{1}{2}10\ln\left(\frac{W_2}{1{,}000}\right) = \frac{1}{10}10\ln\left(\frac{W_1}{1{,}000}\right) + \frac{9}{10}10\ln\left(\frac{W_2}{1{,}000}\right) - 1.8$$

$$\frac{1}{2}10\ln\left(\frac{W_1}{1{,}000}\right) + \frac{1}{2}10\ln\left(\frac{W_2}{1{,}000}\right) = 20.715$$

10.4 Solutions to Exercises

which is $W_1 = 6,337.6$ and $W_2 = 9,939.33$, so that $A = (6337.6, 9939.33)$ with corresponding premium $h_A = 10,000 - 9,939.33 = \$60.67$ and deductible $d_A = 9,939.33 - 6,337.6 = 3,601.73$.

Contract F is given by the solution to $10\ln\left(\frac{W}{1,000}\right) = 20.715$, which is $W = 7,936.72$; thus $F = (7936.72, 7936.72)$ with corresponding premium $h_F = 10,000 - 7,936.72 = \$2,063.28$

Assuming that with contract A Carol would choose high effort, the expected profit with contract A is $h_A - \frac{1}{10}(\ell - d_A) = 60.67 - \frac{1}{10}(4,000 - 3,601.73) = \$20.84$. On the other hand, expected profit from Contract F is $h_F - \frac{1}{2}\ell = 2,063.28 - \frac{1}{2}(4,000) = \$63.28$. Thus the monopolist would offer the full-insurance contract F.

(c) The assumption is that $c = 1.5$, so that – if uninsured – Carol would choose high effort and her expected utility would be $22.515 - 1.5 = 21.015$. The monopolist would only consider two options:

- the partial-insurance contract A given by the intersection of the low-effort indifference curve corresponding to a utility of 21.015 and the high-effort indifference curve corresponding to a utility of 21.015, and

- the full-insurance contract F that makes Carol indifferent between (1) purchasing F and exerting low effort and (2) not insuring and exerting high effort.

Contract A is given by the solution to the following two equations:

$$\frac{1}{2}10\ln\left(\frac{W_1}{1,000}\right) + \frac{1}{2}10\ln\left(\frac{W_2}{1,000}\right) = \frac{1}{10}10\ln\left(\frac{W_1}{1,000}\right) + \frac{9}{10}10\ln\left(\frac{W_2}{1,000}\right) - 1.5$$

$$\frac{1}{2}10\ln\left(\frac{W_1}{1,000}\right) + \frac{1}{2}10\ln\left(\frac{W_2}{1,000}\right) = 21.015$$

which is $W_1 = 6,780.16$ and $W_2 = 9,865.07$, so that $A = (6780.16, 9865.07)$ with corresponding premium $h_A = 10,000 - 9,865.07 = \$134.93$ and deductible $d_A = 9,865.07 - 6,780.16 = 3,084.91$.

Contract F is given by the solution to $10\ln\left(\frac{W}{1,000}\right) = 21.015$, which is $W = 8,178.43$; thus $F = (8178.43, 8178.43)$ with corresponding premium $h_F = 10,000 - 8,178.43 = \$1,821.57$

Assuming that with contract A Carol would choose high effort, the expected profit with contract A is $h_A - \frac{1}{10}(\ell - d_A) = 134.93 - \frac{1}{10}(4,000 - 3,084.91) = \$43.42$. On the other hand, expected profit from Contract F is $h_F - \frac{1}{2}\ell = 1,821.57 - \frac{1}{2}(4,000) = \$-178.43$, a loss. Thus the monopolist would offer the partial-insurance contract A. □

11. Moral Hazard in Principal-Agent

11.1 Moral hazard in Principal-Agent relationships

In Chapter 6 we considered the case of a party, called the *Principal*, who intends to hire another party, called the *Agent*, to perform some activity, whose outcome is uncertain, because it is affected by external factors that cannot be controlled by either party. In that chapter we assumed that the uncertainty was completely exogenous, that is, not affected in any way by the parties involved, and we focused on the issue of efficient risk sharing.

In this chapter we want to extend the analysis by considering the possibility that the actions of the Agent might have some effect on the probabilistic outcomes. That is, we want to add moral hazard to that framework. Moral hazard is present whenever the Agent's behavior cannot be observed by the Principal.

The following table provides several examples of this situation.

Principal	Agent	Agent's unobserved action
Owner of the firm	Manager	Amount of time/effort spent running the firm
Client	Lawyer	Amount of time/care devoted to the case
Client	Doctor	Amount of time/care devoted to studying patient's symptoms
Insurance Company	Policyholder	Care to avoid theft/loss
Land owner	Farmer	Farming effort
Landlord	Tenant	Upkeep of building

Although, typically, the Agent cannot fully control the outcome, she can have some influence on it by exerting sufficient effort. For example, while a lawyer cannot guarantee that her client will win the lawsuit, she can make a victory more likely if she devotes a lot time and effort to preparing the case. The lawyer's behavior cannot be observed by the client, but the outcome of the lawsuit *is* observed and thus the client might want to make his payment to the lawyer dependent on the outcome, in order to provide the lawyer with the incentive to work hard. Examples of payments that are contingent on the observed outcome are: contingency fees for lawyers (if the client loses he owes nothing to the lawyer, if he wins he owes a percentage of what he has been awarded), stock options for managers (part of their salaries is in the form of a percentage of the profits of the firm), deductibles for policy-holders, etc.

11.2 Risk sharing under moral hazard

In this section we show that, in the presence of moral hazard, the principles of optimal risk sharing discussed in Chapter 6 no longer hold.

We shall use the notation shown in the following table:

Table 11.1: Notation

X_i $(i \in \{1,2,\ldots,n\})$ $X_1 < X_2 < \cdots < X_n$	Possible monetary outcomes
w_i $(i \in \{1,2,\ldots,n\})$	Payment to the Agent if X_i occurs
$U_P(m)$ $U_P'(m) > 0,\ U''(m) \leq 0$	Principal's vNM utility-of-money function
e	Agent's effort
$U_A(m,e)$ $\frac{\partial U_A(m,e)}{\partial m} > 0,\ \frac{\partial^2 U_A(m,e)}{\partial m^2} \leq 0,\ \frac{\partial U_A(m,e)}{\partial e} < 0$	Agent's vNM utility function
$\bar{u}$	Agent's reservation utility

The Agent's reservation level of utility $\bar{u}$ is that level of utility that the Agent can obtain with an "outside option", that is, by not signing a contract with the Principal. Thus any contract that is signed must give the Agent an expected utility of at least $\bar{u}$.

11.2 Risk sharing under moral hazard

We shall assume that the Agent's effort influences the outcome, in the sense that greater effort increases the probability of better outcomes. Consider first the case where there are only two outcomes: X_1 and X_2 (with $X_1 < X_2$), and two possible levels of effort: low-effort e_L and high effort e_H. Let p_1^L be the probability of the lower outcome (outcome X_1) when the Agent exerts *low* effort (so that the probability of the higher outcome is $(1-p_1^L)$) and p_1^H be the probability of the lower outcome (outcome X_1) when the Agent exerts *high* effort (so that the probability of the higher outcome is $(1-p_1^H)$). Then the assumption is that

$$p_1^L > p_1^H.$$

Let us begin with a simple example. The Principal is risk neutral:

$$U_P(m) = m,$$

while the Agent is risk averse, for any level of effort, and dislikes effort:

$$U_A(m,e) = \sqrt{m} - e.$$

There are two possible levels of effort for the Agent: $e_L = 10$ and $e_H = 12$. The Agent is currently employed elsewhere at a job that involves low effort e_L and pays a salary of \$169, so that her reservation level of utility is

$$\bar{u} = \sqrt{169} - e_L = 13 - 10 = 3. \qquad (11.1)$$

Let

$$X_1 = \$1,500 \quad \text{and} \quad X_2 = \$9,000$$

and suppose that, if a contract is signed and the Agent exerts low effort, then the probability of the lower outcome is 80%, while if the Agent exerts high effort then the probability of the lower outcome is 50%:

$$p_1^L = \frac{4}{5} \quad \text{and} \quad p_1^H = \frac{1}{2}.$$

We know from Chapter 6 that when one party is risk neutral and the other is risk averse, Pareto efficient risk sharing requires that all the risk be borne by the risk-neutral party; in other words, the risk-averse party (in this case the Agent) ought to be given a fixed income: $w_1 = w_2$. However, this principle clashes with the need to provide the Agent with an incentive to exert high effort: if the Agent is given a sure payment of \$w then her utility is $\sqrt{w} - 10$ is she choose e_L and $\sqrt{w} - 12$ is she choose e_H and therefore she will choose e_L. The Principal realizes this and figures out that the best (from his point of view) fixed-salary contract that he can offer the Agent is one that gives the Agent exactly her reservation utility, that is, contract $B = (w_1 = 169, w_2 = 169)$, in which case the Principal will face the money lottery

$$\begin{pmatrix} \$(1,500-169) & \$(9,000-169) \\ \frac{4}{5} & \frac{1}{5} \end{pmatrix}$$

whose expected utility for the Principal is

$$\mathbb{E}[U_P(B)] = \tfrac{4}{5}(1,500-169) + \tfrac{1}{5}(9,000-169) = 2,831. \tag{11.2}$$

Consider now the following alternative contract, which exposes the Agent to risk: $C = (w_1 = 100, w_2 = 484)$. Will the Agent accept this contract and, if she does, what level of effort will she exert? If the Agent exerts low effort, then she faces the money lottery

$$\begin{pmatrix} \$100 & \$484 \\ \tfrac{4}{5} & \tfrac{1}{5} \end{pmatrix}$$

whose expected utility for her is

$$\mathbb{E}[U_A(C,e_L)] = \tfrac{4}{5}\left(\sqrt{100}-10\right) + \tfrac{1}{5}\left(\sqrt{484}-10\right) = 2.4$$

which is below her reservation utility of 3.
If the Agent exerts high effort, then she faces the money lottery

$$\begin{pmatrix} \$100 & \$484 \\ \tfrac{1}{2} & \tfrac{1}{2} \end{pmatrix}$$

whose expected utility for her is

$$E[U_A(C,e_H)] = \tfrac{1}{2}\left(\sqrt{100}-12\right) + \tfrac{1}{2}\left(\sqrt{484}-12\right) = 4 \tag{11.3}$$

which exceeds her reservation utility. Hence the Agent will accept contract C and exert high effort.
Realizing this, the Principal knows that if he signs contract C then he will face the money lottery

$$\begin{pmatrix} \$(1,500-484) & \$(9,000-100) \\ \tfrac{1}{2} & \tfrac{1}{2} \end{pmatrix}$$

whose expected utility for him is

$$\mathbb{E}[U_P(C)] = \tfrac{1}{2}(9,000-484) + \tfrac{1}{2}(1,500-100) = 4,958. \tag{11.4}$$

By (11.3) the Agent prefers contract C to contract B and by (11.2) and (11.4) also the Principal prefers C to B, so that B is not **Pareto efficient**, despite the fact that it allocates risk optimally. Hence, when moral hazard is present, the principles of optimal risk sharing established in Chapter 6 no longer hold.

Let us now consider an example with three possible outcomes and three possible levels of effort. As before, the Principal is risk neutral and the Agent has the following utility

11.2 Risk sharing under moral hazard

function: $U_A(m,e) = \sqrt{m} - e$ with $e \in \{10, 12, 24\}$. The Agent's reservation utility is 3. The outcomes and corresponding probabilities are as follows:

outcome :	$196	$1,000	$5,000
probability if $e = 10$:	$\frac{1}{2}$	$\frac{1}{4}$	$\frac{1}{4}$
probability if $e = 12$:	$\frac{1}{4}$	$\frac{1}{4}$	$\frac{1}{2}$
probability if $e = 24$:	$\frac{1}{8}$	$\frac{1}{4}$	$\frac{5}{8}$

Consider the following contracts:
$$C = (w_1 = 196, w_2 = 196, w_3 = 196), \quad D = (w_1 = 0, w_2 = 200, w_3 = 1,680).$$

Under Contract C the Agent's utility is:
- if she chooses $e = 10$: $\sqrt{196} - 10 = 4$,
- if she chooses $e = 12$: $\sqrt{196} - 12 = 2$,
- if she chooses $e = 14$: $\sqrt{196} - 24 = -10$.

Thus she would choose $e = 10$.

Under Contract D the Agent's expected utility is:
- if she chooses $e = 10$:
$$\tfrac{1}{2}\left(\sqrt{0} - 10\right) + \tfrac{1}{4}\left(\sqrt{200} - 10\right) + \tfrac{1}{4}\left(\sqrt{1,680} - 10\right) = 3.78$$
- if she chooses $e = 12$:
$$\tfrac{1}{4}\left(\sqrt{0} - 12\right) + \tfrac{1}{4}\left(\sqrt{200} - 12\right) + \tfrac{1}{2}\left(\sqrt{1,680} - 12\right) = 4.03$$
- if she chooses $e = 24$:
$$\tfrac{1}{8}\left(\sqrt{0} - 24\right) + \tfrac{1}{4}\left(\sqrt{200} - 24\right) + \tfrac{5}{8}\left(\sqrt{1,680} - 24\right) = 5.15$$

Thus she would choose $e = 24$.

Hence the Principal's expected utility is:
- under contract C: $\left(\tfrac{1}{2}196 + \tfrac{1}{4}1,000 + \tfrac{1}{4}5,000\right) - 196 = 1,402$
- under contract D: $\tfrac{1}{8}(196 - 0) + \tfrac{1}{4}(1,000 - 200) + \tfrac{5}{8}(5,000 - 1,680) = 2,299.5$.

Thus both Principal and Agent prefer contract D to contract C so that the latter is not Pareto efficient, despite the fact that it allocates risk optimally, according to the principles established in Chapter 6.

What are the Pareto efficient contracts in a situation where there is moral hazard? We will approach this question in several steps.

> Test your understanding of the concepts introduced in this section, by going through the exercises in Section 11.5.1 at the end of this chapter.

11.3 The case with two outcomes and two levels of effort

In this section we assume that there are only two outcomes: X_1 and X_2 (with $X_1 < X_2$), and two possible levels of effort: low-effort e_L and high effort e_H. Let p_1^L be the probability of X_1 when the Agent exerts low effort and p_1^H the probability of X_1 when the Agent exerts high effort. We assume that

$$p_1^L > p_1^H. \tag{11.5}$$

We shall also assume that the Principal is risk neutral, so that his vNM utility-of-money function can be taken to be the identity function:

$$U_P(m) = m,$$

while the Agent is risk-averse and dislikes effort; in particular, we take her utility function to be[1]

$$U_A(m,e) = \begin{cases} U(m) & \text{if } e = e_L \\ U(m) - c & \text{if } e = e_H \end{cases} \quad c > 0, U'(m) > 0, U''(m) < 0. \tag{11.6}$$

The reader might have noticed the similarity between the situation under consideration and the insurance context analysed in Chapter 10 (compare (10.2) and (10.3) to (11.6)). Also in this case we can view a possible contract as a point in the positive quadrant of the (w_1, w_2) Cartesian plane and we can draw indifference curves for the Agent and the Principal.

Let us begin with the Agent. As in the context studied in Chapter 10, there are two indifference curves for the Agent that go through a point $(\hat{w}_1, \hat{w}_2)$:

- ◆ one - corresponding to high effort e_H - that joins all the contracts (w_1, w_2) that yield the same utility to the Agent as contract $(\hat{w}_1, \hat{w}_2)$ *if the Agent chooses e_H*, and

- ■ one - corresponding to low effort e_L - that joins all the contracts (w_1, w_2) that yield the same utility to the Agent as contract $(\hat{w}_1, \hat{w}_2)$ *if the Agent chooses e_L*.

We shall call the indifference curve corresponding to e_H the "H-indifference curve" and the indifference curve corresponding to e_L the "L-indifference curve". As explained in Chapter 10, at any point (w_1, w_2),

- ◆ the slope of the H-indifference curve is

$$-\frac{p_1^H}{1-p_1^H}\left(\frac{U'(w_1)}{U'(w_2)}\right) \tag{11.7}$$

- ■ the slope of the L-indifference curve is

$$-\frac{p_1^L}{1-p_1^L}\left(\frac{U'(w_1)}{U'(w_2)}\right) \tag{11.8}$$

---

[1] One can start with $U_A(m, e_L) = V(m) - e_L$ and $U_A(m, e_H) = V(m) - e_H$ and then define $U(m) = V(m) + e_L$ (recall from Chapter 3 that adding a constant is an "allowed transformation" of a vNM utility function) so that $U_A(m, e_L) = U(m)$ and $U_A(m, e_H) = V(m) - (e_H - e_L)$ and define $c = e_H - e_L$ and thus obtain (11.6).

11.3 The case with two outcomes and two levels of effort

It follows from (11.5) that (see Footnote 2 on page 345)

$$\frac{p_1^L}{1-p_1^L} > \frac{p_1^H}{1-p_1^H} \tag{11.9}$$

that is,

> the indifference curve through point (w_1, w_2) corresponding to **high effort** e_H is, at point (w_1, w_2), **less steep than**, the indifference curve through point (w_1, w_2) corresponding to **low effort** e_L.

This fact is illustrated in Figure 11.1.

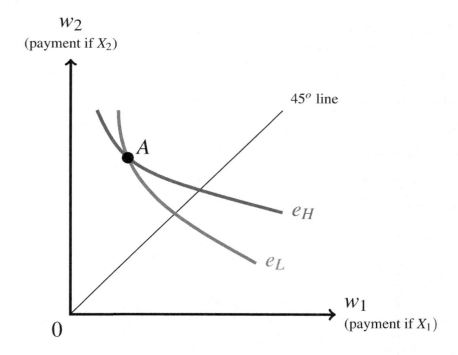

Figure 11.1: At point A, the indifference curve corresponding to high effort e_H is less steep than the indifference curve corresponding to low effort e_L.

The 45° line represents the fixed-wage contracts, that is, contracts (w_1, w_2) with $w_1 = w_2$.

Note that, in the case of insurance (Chapter 10), we restricted attention to contracts above the 45° line, because - in that context - a contract below the 45° line could not be interpreted as an insurance contract. On the other hand, in the Principal-Agent case, a contract below the 45° line *is* a meaningful contract and should not be ruled out in principle. However, by the following proposition, such contracts will not be observed in practice (if the parties are rational) since they are Pareto inefficient.

Proposition 11.3.1 Any contract (w_1, w_2) such that $w_1 > w_2$ is Pareto inefficient.

Proof. The proof of Proposition 11.3.1 is done in two steps.

Step 1. We first show that, *if offered a contract below the 45° line, the Agent will choose low effort e_L* (assuming that she finds the contract acceptable, that is, that the contract gives her at least her reservation utility). We can prove this either algebraically or graphically. The algebraic proof is as follows. Let $C = (w_1, w_2)$ be such that

$$w_1 > w_2. \qquad (11.10)$$

Then

$$\begin{aligned}
&\mathbb{E}[U_A(C, e_L)] - E[U_A(C, e_H)] \\
&= p_1^L U(w_1) + (1 - p_1^L) U(w_2) - \left[p_1^H U(w_1) + (1 - p_1^H) U(w_2) - c\right] \\
&= (p_1^L - p_1^H) U(w_1) - (p_1^L - p_1^H) U(w_2) + c \\
&= (p_1^L - p_1^H) [U(w_1) - U(w_2)] + c. \qquad (11.11)
\end{aligned}$$

By (11.5), $(p_1^L - p_1^H) > 0$; by assumption, $c > 0$; by (11.10) and the fact that $U(m)$ is increasing in m, $[U(w_1) - U(w_2)] > 0$. Thus (11.11) is positive, that is, $\mathbb{E}[U_A(C, e_L)] > E[U_A(C, e_H)]$.

Graphically, consider contract C in Figure 11.2.

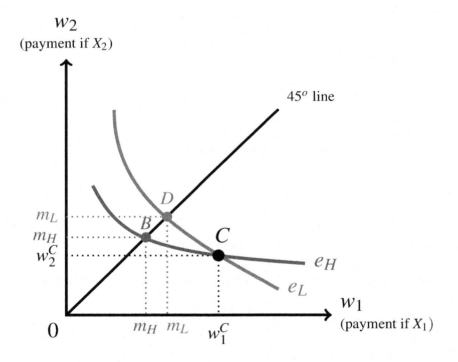

Figure 11.2: $\mathbb{E}[U_A(C, e_H)] = \mathbb{E}[U_A(B, e_H)] = U(m_H) - c$; $\mathbb{E}[U_A(C, e_L)] = \mathbb{E}[U_A(B, e_L)] = U(m_L)$.

By definition of indifference curve,

11.3 The case with two outcomes and two levels of effort

○ $\mathbb{E}[U_A(C, e_H)] = \mathbb{E}[U_A(B, e_H)] = U(m_H) - c$, and

○ $\mathbb{E}[U_A(C, e_L)] = \mathbb{E}[U_A(D, e_L)] = U(m_L)$.

Since $m_H < m_L$, $U(m_H) < U(m_L)$.

Thus $E[U_A(C, e_H)] < E[U_A(C, e_L)]$.

Step 2. Next we show that, for every contract C below the 45° line, there is a contract D on the 45° line such that: (1) the Agent is indifferent between C and D and (2) the Principal prefers D to C, so that C is not Pareto efficient. Figure 11.3 reproduces Figure 11.2 without the H-indifference curve, since in the previous step we showed that with contract C the Agent will choose low effort e_L. Let D be the contract at the intersection of the L-indifference curve through C and the 45° line and let m_L be the fixed wage of contract D.

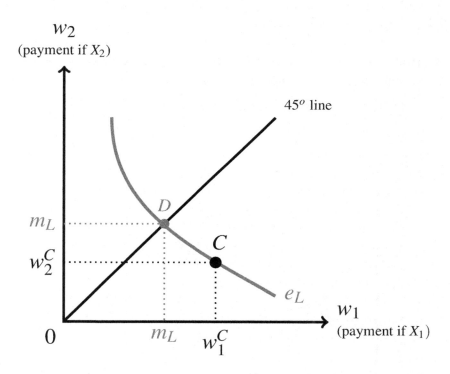

Figure 11.3: Contract D is Pareto superior to contract C.

For the Agent, contract C corresponds to the lottery $C = \begin{pmatrix} w_1^C & w_2^C \\ p_1^L & 1 - p_1^L \end{pmatrix}$ whose expected value is $\mathbb{E}[C] = p_1^L w_1^C + (1 - p_1^L) w_2^C$. By definition of risk-aversion, the Agent strictly prefers $\mathbb{E}[C]$ for sure to lottery C, that is, $U_A(\mathbb{E}[C], e_L) = U(\mathbb{E}[C]) > \mathbb{E}[U_A(C, e_L)]$ and, since D is on the same indifference curve as C, $\mathbb{E}[U_A(C, e_L)] = \mathbb{E}[U_A(D, e_L)] = U(m_L)$. Thus $U(\mathbb{E}[C]) > U(m_L)$, which implies, since $U(m)$ is increasing in m, that

$$\mathbb{E}[C] = p_1^L w_1^C + (1 - p_1^L) w_2^C > m_L. \tag{11.12}$$

For the Principal contract C corresponds to the lottery $\begin{pmatrix} X_1 - w_1^C & X_2 - w_2^C \\ p_1^L & 1 - p_1^L \end{pmatrix}$ whose expected value (and expected utility for the Principal, since he is risk neutral) is

$$p_1^L \left(X_1 - w_1^C \right) + \left(1 - p_1^L\right)\left(X_2 - w_2^C \right) = p_1^L X_1 + \left(1 - p_1^L\right) X_2 - \mathbb{E}[C] \quad (11.13)$$

On the other hand, for the Principal contract D corresponds to the lottery $\begin{pmatrix} X_1 - m_L & X_2 - m_L \\ p_1^L & 1 - p_1^L \end{pmatrix}$ whose expected value (and expected utility) is

$$p_1^L X_1 + \left(1 - p_1^L\right) X_2 - m_L. \quad (11.14)$$

It follows from (11.12), (11.13) and (11.14) that the Principal strictly prefers contract D to contract C. Thus contract C is Pareto inefficient. ∎

It follows from Proposition 11.3.1 that – if we are interested in Pareto efficiency – we can restrict attention to contracts on or above the 45° line.

We now want to determine which contracts on or above the 45° line are Pareto efficient. Consider contract C in Figure 11.4.

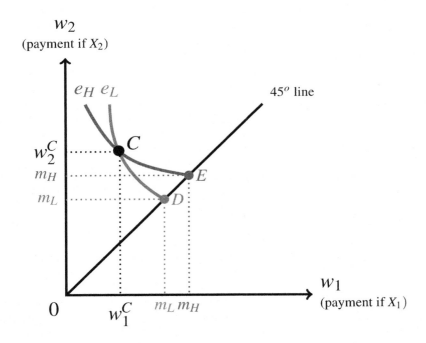

Figure 11.4: What level of effort will the Agent choose under contract C?

What level of effort will the Agent choose under contract C? The expected utility from contract C under low effort e_L is the same as with contract D under low effort and the latter is $U(m_L)$. The expected utility from contract C under high effort e_H is the same as with contract E under high effort and the latter is $U(m_H) - c$. Thus

11.3 The case with two outcomes and two levels of effort

- the Agent will choose e_L if $U(m_H) - U(m_L) < c$,
- the Agent will choose e_H if $U(m_H) - U(m_L) > c$,
- the Agent will be indifferent between e_L and e_H if $U(m_H) - U(m_L) = c$.

Now fix a level of utility $\hat{u}$ for the Agent, with $\hat{u} \geq \bar{u}$ (recall that $\bar{u}$ is the Agent's reservation utility: she will not accept a contract that gives her a utility below $\bar{u}$). We want to find the set of contracts on or above the 45° line that give the Agent utility $\hat{u}$ when she chooses the best level of effort for each of these contracts. Following the terminology of Chapter 10, we will call it the $\hat{u}$-*utility-locus*.

Let $\hat{m}$ be the solution to the equation $U(m) = \hat{u}$ (that is, $U(\hat{m}) = \hat{u}$). Then one contract on the $\hat{u}$-utility-locus is the fixed-wage contract $\hat{D} = (w_1 = \hat{m}, w_2 = \hat{m})$ and we know that under such contract the Agent will choose low effort e_L. Draw the two indifference curves through contract $\hat{D}$: see Figure 11.5.

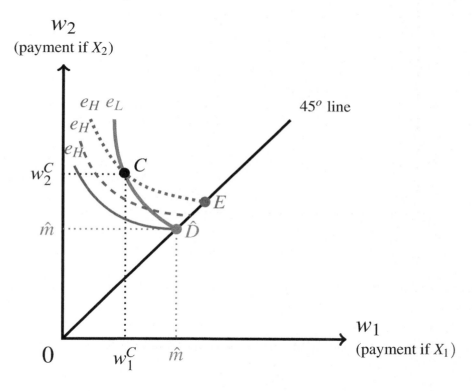

Figure 11.5: The two indifference curves through point $\hat{D}$ and two more H-indifference curves.

The H-indifference curve that goes through point $\hat{D}$ (the continuous less steep curve) corresponds to a level of utility *less than* $\hat{u}$ (namely $U(\hat{m}) - c = \hat{u} - c < \hat{u}$). Consider now the dashed H-indifference curve: it is above the one that goes through $\hat{D}$ and thus corresponds to higher utility. As we consider higher and higher H-indifference curves the level utility keeps increasing. At some stage we must reach an H-indifference curve that corresponds to utility $\hat{u}$. Suppose it is the dotted curve in Figure 11.5. Let $C = (w_1^C, w_2^C)$ be the point of intersection between this H-indifference curve and the L-indifference curve that goes through $\hat{D}$. Then it must be that $\mathbb{E}[U_A(C, e_H)] = \mathbb{E}[U_A(C, e_L)] = \hat{u}$, that is,

$$p_1^H U(w_1^C) + (1 - p_1^H) U(w_2^C) - c = p_1^L U(w_1^C) + (1 - p_1^L) U(w_2^C) = \hat{u}.$$

Once we reach point C, in order to keep utility constant at the value $\hat{u}$ we need to stop traveling along the L-indifference curve and switch to the dotted H-indifference curve. Thus the $\hat{u}$-utility-locus if given by the union of two segments of two indifference curves, just like in the case of insurance.

Figure 11.6 shows the $\hat{u}$-utility-locus, where $\hat{u} = U_A(\hat{m}, e_L) = U(\hat{m})$, as the union of the two thick curves.

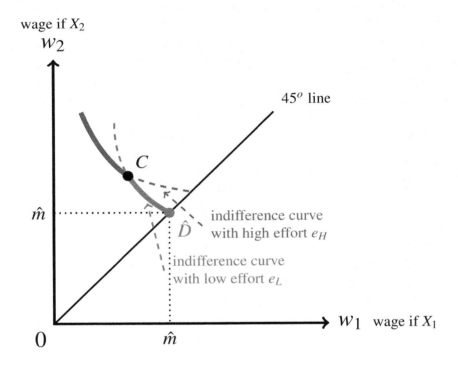

Figure 11.6: The $\hat{u}$-utility-locus (where $\hat{u} = U_A(\hat{m}, e_L) = U(\hat{m})$) is the union of the two thick curves.

What contracts on the $\hat{u}$-utility-locus are Pareto efficient? We will show that the only candidates are contracts C and $\hat{D}$ in Figure 11.6.

So far we have focused on the indifference curves of the Agent. Now we turn to the Principal, whom we have assumed to be risk neutral. Recall from Chapter 5 (Section 5.1.1) that the indifference curves of a risk-neutral individual are downward-sloping straight lines with slope $-\frac{p}{1-p}$, where p is the probability of the outcome measured on the horizontal axis. In the present context, there are two possible values of p: p_L, if the Agent chooses low effort e_L, and p_H, if the Agent chooses high effort e_H, with $p_L > p_H$. Thus through any contract C on or above the 45° line we can draw two straight-line indifference curves for the Principal:

- a steeper one with slope $-\frac{p_L}{1-p_L}$, connecting all the contracts that give the same utility to the Principal, conditional on the Agent choosing e_L, and
- a less steep one with slope $-\frac{p_H}{1-p_H}$, connecting all the contracts that give the same utility to the Principal, conditional on the Agent choosing e_H.

11.3 The case with two outcomes and two levels of effort

Which indifference curve for the Principal is relevant at contract C depends on the choice of effort of the Agent under contract C. Figure 11.7 shows the two indifference curves of the Principal through a point C.

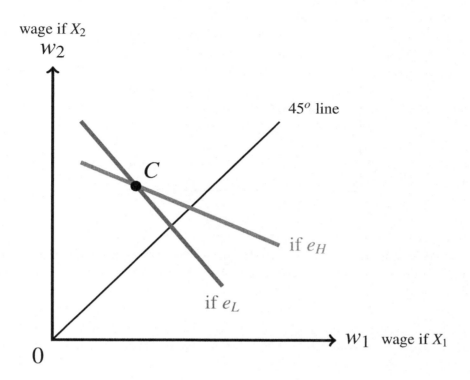

Figure 11.7: The two possible indifference curves of the Principal through contract C.

With an argument similar to the one used in Chapter 2 (Section 2.5), one can show that

1. given two contracts A and B, both of which would induce the Agent to choose high effort e_H, if B lies below the Principal's indifference curve through A then the Principal gets higher utility from B than from A, that is, he prefers B to A,

2. given two contracts D and E, both of which would induce the Agent to choose low effort e_L, if E lies below the Principal's indifference curve through D then the Principal gets higher utility from E than from D, that is, he prefers E to D.

The reader is asked to prove Point 1 in Exercise 11.6 and Point 2 in Exercise 11.7. The above two claims are illustrated in Figures 11.8 and 11.9.

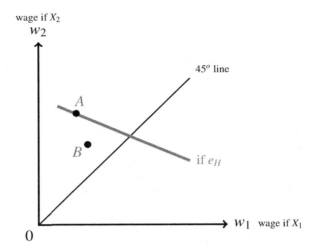

Figure 11.8: Assuming that the Agent would choose e_H under both contract A and contract B, the Principal prefers contract B to contract A.

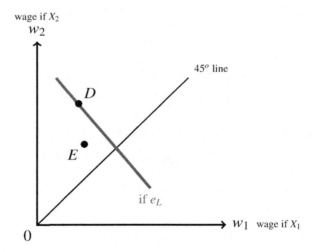

Figure 11.9: Assuming that the Agent would choose e_L under both contract D and contract E, the Principal prefers contract E to contract D.

11.3 The case with two outcomes and two levels of effort

Let us focus on an L-indifference curve *for the Agent* and consider two points: point $F = (w^F, w^F)$ lying *on* the 45° line and point $D = (w_1^D, w_2^D)$ lying *above* the 45° line (so that $w_1^D < w_2^D$), and *assume that, under contract D, the Agent would choose low effort e_L*. By (11.8) (page 374), the slope of the Agent's indifference curve at point F is

$$-\frac{p_1^L}{1-p_1^L} \frac{U'(w^F)}{U'(w^F)} = -\frac{p_1^L}{1-p_1^L};$$

thus, at point F, the Principal's L-indifference curve (which is the relevant one, since we know that at a point on the 45° line the Agent chooses low effort e_L) is *tangent* to the Agent's L-indifference curve. On the other hand, the slope of the Agent's indifference at point D is

$$-\frac{p_1^L}{1-p_1^L} \frac{U'(w_1^D)}{U'(w_2^D)}.$$

Since $w_1^D < w_2^D$ and $U'(m)$ is decreasing in m (because $U''(m) < 0$, by risk aversion), $\frac{U'(w_1^D)}{U'(w_2^D)} > 1$ and thus

$$\frac{p_1^L}{1-p_1^L} \frac{U'(w_1^D)}{U'(w_2^D)} > \frac{p_1^L}{1-p_1^L}$$

so that the Principal's indifference curve through point D is less steep than the Agent's indifference curve through D (recall the assumption that, under contract D, the Agent would choose e_L).

Figure 11.10 shows the relative slopes of the indifference curves of Principal and Agent at a point above the 45° line (point D) and at a point on the 45° line (point F).

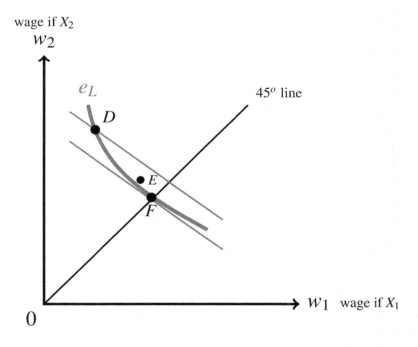

Figure 11.10: The relative slopes of the indifference curves of Agent and Principal for the case where the Agent chooses low effort e_L.

It follows from the above that a contract on an *L*-indifference curve of the Agent which is *above* the $45°$ line (such as point *D* in Figure 11.10) is not Pareto efficient (as long it yields higher utility to the Agent under low effort than under high effort): there are contracts in the region between the two curves - such as contract *E* in Figure 11.10 - that are better for both the Agent and the Principal. On the other hand, a contract at the intersection of an *L*-indifference of the Agent and the $45°$ line (such as point *F* in Figure 11.10) is a *candidate* for Pareto efficiency.

Next we use a similar argument for contracts that are on an *H*-indifference curve of the Agent and above the $45°$ line. Fix such a contract, call it *A*, and *assume that under contract A the Agent is better off with high effort e_H than with low effort e_L*. Figure 11.11 shows the relative slopes of the indifference curves of Principal and Agent at a point above the $45°$ line (point *A*) for a contract that induces the Agent to choose high effort e_H. Since the *H*-indifference curve of the Principal through point *A* is less steep than the *H*-indifference curve of the Agent at point *A*, there are contracts between the two (such as point *B* in Figure 11.11) that are better for both. Thus points such as point *A* in Figure 11.11 are not **Pareto efficient** (given the hypothesis that under contract *A* the Agent would choose high effort e_H).

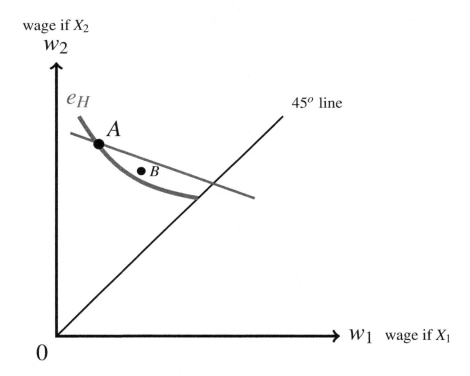

Figure 11.11: The relative slopes of the indifference curves of Principal and Agent at a point above the $45°$ line (point *A*) for a contract that induces the Agent to choose high effort e_H.

11.3 The case with two outcomes and two levels of effort

We can now put together Figures 11.6 (reproduced below as Figure 11.12), 11.10 and 11.11 to complete the argument that, for any level of utility $\hat{u}$ of the Agent, there are only two contracts on the $\hat{u}$-utility-locus that are candidates for Pareto efficiency.

The top-left shaded area in Figure 11.12 consists of contracts that would induce the Agent to choose high effort e_H (since they are above the H-indifference curve for level of utility $\hat{u}$ and to the left of the L-indifference curve for level of utility $\hat{u}$), while the bottom-right shaded area consists of contracts that would induce the Agent to choose low effort e_L (these contracts are above the L-indifference curve for level of utility $\hat{u}$ and below the H-indifference curve for level of utility $\hat{u}$). Thus the argument illustrated in Figure 11.11 rules out all the contracts on the H-indifference curve (for level of utility $\hat{u}$) to the left of point C (**the first segment of the $\hat{u}$-utility-locus**) and the argument illustrated in Figure 11.10 rules out all the contracts on the L-indifference curve (for level of utility $\hat{u}$) to the right of point C (**the second segment of the $\hat{u}$-utility-locus**) except for point $\hat{D}$ on the 45° line.

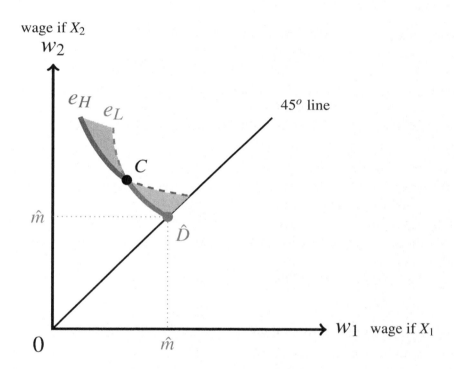

Figure 11.12: Copy of the $\hat{u}$-utility-locus of Figure 11.6. The top-left shaded area consists of contracts that would induce the Agent to choose high effort e_H, while the bottom-right shaded area consists of contracts that would induce the Agent to choose low effort e_L.

> **R** Recall that, at any contract F on the 45° line, the (straight-line) L-indifference curve of the Principal is tangent to the (convex) L-indifference curve of the Agent (see Figure 11.10). Hence any contract E that induces the Agent to choose low effort e_L and gives the Agent higher utility than F must lie above the Agent's L-indifference curve through F and thus must be worse for the Principal than F.

From now on we will *assume that, given a contract under which the Agent is indifferent between choosing low effort e_L and choosing high effort e_H, the Agent will choose high effort e_H.*[2]

Lemma 11.1 Let $\hat{D} = (\hat{m}, \hat{m})$ be a contract on the 45° line and let $\hat{u}$ be the utility of the Agent under contract $\hat{D}$ (the Agent will choose e_L under this contract and thus $\hat{u} = U(\hat{m})$). Let $C = (w_1^C, w_2^C)$ be a contract that gives utility $\hat{u}$ to the Agent no matter whether she chooses e_L or e_H. Then

1. if $\hat{D} \succ_P C$ (that is, the Principal prefers contract $\hat{D}$ to contract C), then $\hat{D} \succ_P E$ (the Principal prefers $\hat{D}$ to E) for every contract $E \neq \hat{D}$ on the $\hat{u}$-utility-locus of the Agent,

2. if $C \succ_P \hat{D}$ (that is, the Principal prefers contract C to contract $\hat{D}$), then $C \succ_P E$ (the Principal prefers C to E) for every contract $E \neq C$ on the $\hat{u}$-utility-locus of the Agent.

Proof.

1. Assume that $\hat{D} \succ_P C$. Pick an arbitrary contract E above the 45° line and on the $\hat{u}$-utility-locus of the Agent. By the Remark on page 385, if E induces the Agent to choose e_L then $\hat{D} \succ_P E$. Suppose, therefore, that E induces the Agent to choose high effort e_H. Then either $E = C$, and thus $\hat{D} \succ_P E$ by hypothesis, or $E \neq C$, in which case E lies on the first segment of the $\hat{u}$-utility-locus of the Agent, to the left of point C. Then, by the argument illustrated in Figure 11.11, $C \succ_P E$ and thus, by transitivity (since $\hat{D} \succ_P C$), $\hat{D} \succ_P E$.

2. Assume that $C \succ_P \hat{D}$. Pick an arbitrary contract $E \neq C$ above the 45° line and on the $\hat{u}$-utility-locus of the Agent. If E induces the Agent to choose high effort e_H then E lies on the first segment of the $\hat{u}$-utility-locus of the Agent, to the left of point C; then, by the argument illustrated in Figure 11.11, $C \succ_P E$. Suppose, therefore, that E induces the Agent to choose low effort e_L. Then E lies on the second segment of the $\hat{u}$-utility-locus of the Agent, to the left of point $\hat{D}$. Then, by the argument illustrated in Figure 11.10, $\hat{D} \succ_P E$ and thus, by transitivity (since $C \succ_P \hat{D}$), $C \succ_P E$. ∎

Proposition 11.3.2 Let $\hat{D} = (\hat{m}, \hat{m})$, $\hat{u}$ and C be as in Lemma 11.1. Then

1. if $\hat{D} \succ_P C$ then $\hat{D}$ is the only Pareto efficient contract on the $\hat{u}$-utility-locus of the Agent,

2. if $C \succ_P \hat{D}$ then C is the only Pareto efficient contract on the $\hat{u}$-utility-locus of the Agent,

3. if $C \sim_P \hat{D}$ (that is, the Principal is indifferent between C and $\hat{D}$) then C and $\hat{D}$ are the only Pareto efficient contracts on the $\hat{u}$-utility-locus for the Agent.

Proof. We already proved that, among the contracts on the $\hat{u}$-utility-locus of the Agent, C and $\hat{D}$ are the only candidates for Pareto efficiency. It is clear that if the Principal prefers $\hat{D}$ to C then $\hat{D}$ Pareto dominates C and thus C is not Pareto efficient, so that $\hat{D}$ is the only candidate for Pareto efficiency; similarly, if the Principal prefers C to $\hat{D}$ then C Pareto dominates $\hat{D}$ and thus $\hat{D}$ is not Pareto efficient, so that C is the only candidate for Pareto

---

[2]We made the same assumption in Chapter 10. See the remarks in that section about this assumption: the same considerations apply here.

11.3 The case with two outcomes and two levels of effort

efficiency.

Next we prove that if $\hat{D} \succ_P C$ (the Principal prefers $\hat{D}$ to C) then $\hat{D}$ is Pareto efficient. Suppose, by contradiction, that $\hat{D}$ is not Pareto efficient. Then there exists a contract $F \neq \hat{D}$ that is better than $\hat{D}$ for one of the parties and at least as good as $\hat{D}$ for the other party. It cannot be that $F \sim_A \hat{D}$ (the Agent is indifferent between F and $\hat{D}$) because then it must be that F lies on the $\hat{u}$-utility-locus of the Agent and $F \succ_P \hat{D}$ (the Principal prefers F to $\hat{D}$), which contradicts Point 1 of Lemma 11.1. Thus it must be that $F \succ_A \hat{D}$ (the Agent prefers F to $\hat{D}$) and

$$F \succsim_P \hat{D} \quad \text{(the Principal considers } F \text{ to be at least as good as } \hat{D}\text{).} \tag{11.15}$$

By (11.15) and the Remark on page 385, it must be that F induces the Agent to choose high effort e_H. Let E be the point at the intersection of the H-indifference curve of the Agent corresponding to utility $\hat{u}$ and the H-indifference curve of the Principal through point F (the straight line with slope $-\frac{p_1^H}{1-p_1^H}$). Then $E \sim_P F$ (the Principal is indifferent between E and F) and, by Point 1 of Lemma 11.1, $\hat{D} \succ_P E$ so that, by transitivity, $\hat{D} \succ_P F$, contradicting (11.15).

Next we prove that if $C \succ_P \hat{D}$ then C is Pareto efficient. Suppose, by contradiction, that C is not Pareto efficient. Then there exists a contract $F \neq C$ that is better than C for one of the parties and at least as good as C for the other party. It cannot be that $F \sim_A C$ because then it must be that F lies on the $\hat{u}$-utility-locus of the Agent and $F \succ_P C$, which contradicts Point 2 of Lemma 11.1. Thus it must be that $F \succ_A C$ and

$$F \succsim_P C. \tag{11.16}$$

Suppose first that contract F induces the Agent to choose low effort e_L. Let E be the point at the intersection of the L-indifference curve of the Agent corresponding to utility $\hat{u}$ and the L-indifference curve of the Principal through point F (the straight line with slope $-\frac{p_1^L}{1-p_1^L}$). Then $E \sim_P F$ and, by Point 2 of Lemma 11.1, $C \succ_P E$ so that, by transitivity, $C \succ_P F$, contradicting (11.16). Suppose, therefore, that contract F induces the Agent to choose high effort e_H. Let G be the point at the intersection of the H-indifference curve of the Agent corresponding to utility $\hat{u}$ and the H-indifference curve of the Principal through point F (the straight line with slope $-\frac{p_1^H}{1-p_1^H}$). Then $G \sim_P F$ and, by Point 2 of Lemma 11.1, $C \succ_P G$ so that, by transitivity, $C \succ_P F$, contradicting (11.16).

The proof of Point 3 is along the same lines and we will omit it. ∎

In Exercises 11.10-11.12 the reader is asked to characterize and draw (1) the set of contracts that make the Principal indifferent between the Agent exerting low effort and the Agent exerting high effort and (2) the set of contracts that make the Agent indifferent between low effort and high effort.

We conclude this section with two observations.

(R) First of all, it follows from Proposition 11.3.2 that, if a contract is Pareto efficient and is not a fixed-salary contract, then it is characterized by a larger payment to the Agent if the outcome is the better outcome X_2 and a smaller payment if the outcome is the worse outcome X_1. Such contracts are called *incentive contracts* because their role is to provide an incentive to the Agent to exert high effort (thereby increasing the probability of the better outcome X_2).

Secondly, if the Principal has all the bargaining power (because, for example, there is "perfect competition" among possible Agents) and thus the Principal is able to offer a contract that keeps the Agent at her reservation level of utility, call it $\bar{u}$, then the Principal will offer to the Agent that contract on the $\bar{u}$-utility-locus of the Agent that maximizes his own expected utility. By Lemma 11.1, such a contract is either a fixed-wage contract or that incentive contract that makes the Agent indifferent between choosing low effort and choosing high effort (see Exercise 11.13).

> Test your understanding of the concepts introduced in this section, by going through the exercises in Section 11.5.2 at the end of this chapter.

11.4 The case with more than two outcomes

So far we have restricted attention to the case where there are only two outcomes and two levels of effort. The logic of the Principal-Agent problem remains the same if there are three or more outcomes and possibly more than two levels of effort. However, the conclusion highlighted in the above Remark, namely that an incentive contract is characterized by payments that are an increasing function of the outcome, does not generalize to the case of more than two outcomes. For example, suppose that there are three possible outcomes X_1, X_2 and X_3 with $X_1 < X_2 < X_3$. As usual, a contract can be written as a triple (w_1, w_2, w_3), where w_i is the payment to the Agent if the outcome is X_i ($i \in \{1, 2, 3\}$). Then it is not necessarily the case that a Pareto efficient incentive contract $C = (w_1, w_2, w_3)$ is such that $w_1 < w_2 < w_3$. We will give an example of this below.

In the case of two outcomes, X_1 and X_2 with $X_1 < X_2$, we could express that fact that high effort e_H makes better outcomes more likely by postulating that $p_1^L > p_1^H$, where p_1^L is the probability of the worse outcome X_1 when the Agent chooses low effort e_L and p_1^H is the probability of the worse outcome X_1 when the Agent chooses high effort e_H. When there are more than two outcomes (and possibly more than two levels of effort), then the fact that higher effort makes better outcomes more likely can be expressed using the notion

11.4 The case with more than two outcomes

of *first-order stochastic dominance* introduced in Chapter 4 (Definition 4.4.1). Thus the general setting is as follows:

possible outcomes: $X_1, X_2, \ldots, X_n$ $(n \geq 2)$

levels of effort: $e_1, e_2, \ldots, e_m$ $(m \geq 2)$

probability distribution
over $\{X_1, \ldots, X_n\}$ given e_i: P_i

assumptions:
$$\begin{cases} X_1 < X_2 < \cdots < X_n \\ e_1 < e_2 < \cdots < e_m \\ P_m >_{FOC} P_{m-1} >_{FOC} \cdots >_{FOC} P_2 >_{FOC} P_1 \end{cases}$$

where $P_i >_{FOC} P_j$ means that the probability distribution P_i dominates the probability distribution P_j in the sense of first-order stochastic dominance (Chapter 4, Definition 4.4.1).

We will not characterize the solution to the general problem, since it is rather complex and requires more advanced mathematical tools than we have employed so far (in particular, the notion of constrained optimization).

We conclude this section with an example that shows that, when there are more than two outcomes, a Pareto efficient incentive contract does not necessarily involve payments that are an increasing function of the outcomes. Suppose that the Agent can choose between a low level of effort e_L and a high level of effort e_H and, as usual, the Principal cannot monitor the Agent's effort. The Agent's reservation utility is 10 and thus she will not accept any contract that (with the optimal choice of effort) will give her a utility of less than 10. The Principal is risk neutral while the Agent's utility function is given by:

$$U_A(m, e) = \begin{cases} \sqrt{m} & \text{if } e_L \\ \sqrt{m} - 1 & \text{if } e_H \end{cases}$$

There are three possible outcomes with the probabilities listed in the following table:[3]

outcome:	$X_1 = \$100$	$X_2 = \$120$	$X_3 = \$200$
probability if e_L:	$\frac{1}{2}$	$\frac{1}{2}$	0
probability if e_H:	$\frac{2}{5}$	$\frac{1}{10}$	$\frac{1}{2}$

Suppose that the Principal has all the bargaining power, so that he will only offer contracts that give the Agent her reservation utility of 10. Among such contract that, furthermore, induce the Agent to choose low effort e_L the one that gives the Principal the largest expected utility is the fixed-wage contract $F = (w_1 = 100, w_2 = 100, w_3 = 100)$ in which case the Principal's expected utility is $\frac{1}{2}(100 - 100) + \frac{1}{2}(120 - 100) + 0(200 - 100) = 10$. Consider

---

[3] Note that the probability distribution associated with e_H dominates that associated with e_L in the sense of first-order stochastic dominance.

now the following incentive contract $C = (w_1 = 81, w_2 = 100, w_3 = 163.84)$. Under this contract the Agent's expected utility is:

if she chooses e_L: $\quad \frac{1}{2}\sqrt{81} + \frac{1}{2}\sqrt{100} = 9.5$

if she chooses e_H: $\quad \frac{2}{5}\sqrt{81} + \frac{1}{10}\sqrt{100} + \frac{1}{2}\sqrt{163.84} - 1 = 10.$

Thus the Agent would accept contract C and exert high effort e_H. With contract C the Principal's expected utility is $\frac{2}{5}(100-81) + \frac{1}{10}(120-100) + \frac{1}{2}(200-163.84) = 27.68$. Thus the Agent is indifferent between F and C, while the Principal prefers C to F; hence C Pareto dominates F.

Next we show that contract C is not the contract that maximizes the Principal's expected utility among the contracts that induce the Agent to choose e_H and give her an expected utility of 10. To find such a contract, we need to solve the following constrained maximization problem:

choose w_1, w_2, w_3 to maximize $\quad \frac{2}{5}(100-w_1) + \frac{1}{10}(120-w_2) + \frac{1}{2}(200-w_3)$
$$= 152 - \tfrac{2}{5}w_1 - \tfrac{1}{10}w_2 - \tfrac{1}{2}w_3$$

subject to

$$\tfrac{2}{5}\sqrt{w_1} + \tfrac{1}{10}\sqrt{w_2} + \tfrac{1}{2}\sqrt{w_3} - 1 \geq 10 \qquad (IR)$$

$$\tfrac{2}{5}\sqrt{w_1} + \tfrac{1}{10}\sqrt{w_2} + \tfrac{1}{2}\sqrt{w_3} - 1 \geq \tfrac{1}{2}\sqrt{w_1} + \tfrac{1}{2}\sqrt{w_2}. \qquad (IC)$$

(*IR*) is the *individual rationality* constraint for the Agent: it says that the proposed contract must give the Agent an expected utility of at least 10 if she chooses high effort e_H and (*IC*) is the *incentive compatibility* constraint for the Agent: it says that, under the proposed contract, the Agent cannot get higher expected utility by choosing low effort e_L. We now show that, at a solution to the above maximization problem, both constraints must be satisfied as equalities. We will do so without explicitly employing the tools of constrained maximization (the Kuhn-Tucker conditions).

First we argue that, at a solution of the maximization problem, the (*IR*) constraint must be satisfied as an equality. Pick an arbitrary triple (w_1, w_2, w_3) at which the (*IR*) constraint is satisfied as a strict inequality and the (*IC*) constraint is also satisfied (possibly as an equality). Now *decrease* the value of w_2 by a small amount, so that the (*IR*) constraint is still satisfied. Then, since the maximand, that is the function $152 - \frac{2}{5}w_1 - \frac{1}{10}w_2 - \frac{1}{2}w_3$, is decreasing in w_2, its value will increase. The only concern is that decreasing w_2 might lead to a violation of the (*IC*) constraint; however, if w_2 is decreased, the left-hand-side (LHS) of the (*IC*) constraint decreases less than the right-hand-side (RHS) of it and thus the constraint will be preserved.[4] Since we were able to increase the value of the maximand without violating the constraints, the triple we started with could not have been a solution to the maximization problem. Thus the (*IR*) constraint must be satisfied as an equality.

---

[4] The derivative, with respect to w_2, of the LHS of (*IC*) is $\frac{1}{10}\left(\frac{1}{2\sqrt{w_2}}\right)$ which is less than the derivative, with respect to w_2, of the RHS of (*IC*) which is $\frac{1}{2}\left(\frac{1}{2\sqrt{w_2}}\right)$.

11.4 The case with more than two outcomes

From the (IR) constraint satisfied as an equality, namely

$$\tfrac{2}{5}\sqrt{w_1} + \tfrac{1}{10}\sqrt{w_2} + \tfrac{1}{2}\sqrt{w_3} - 1 = 10$$

we can solve for $\sqrt{w_3}$ to obtain

$$\sqrt{w_3} = 22 - \tfrac{4}{5}\sqrt{w_1} - \tfrac{1}{5}\sqrt{w_2}. \tag{11.17}$$

Defining new variables $y_i = \sqrt{w_i}$ ($i = 1, 2, 3$) (so that (11.17) can be written as $y_3 = 22 - \tfrac{4}{5}y_1 - \tfrac{1}{5}y_2$), we can rewrite the maximization problem as follows:

choose y_1, y_2 to maximize $= 152 - \tfrac{2}{5}(y_1)^2 - \tfrac{1}{10}(y_2)^2 - \tfrac{1}{2}\left(22 - \tfrac{4}{5}y_1 - \tfrac{1}{5}y_2\right)^2$
subject to

$$\tfrac{2}{5}y_1 + \tfrac{1}{10}y_2 + \tfrac{1}{2}\left(22 - \tfrac{4}{5}y_1 - \tfrac{1}{5}y_2\right) - 1 \geq \tfrac{1}{2}y_1 + \tfrac{1}{2}y_2 \tag{IC}$$

The next step in the argument is to show that if the (IC) constraint is satisfied as a strict inequality then the function $152 - \tfrac{2}{5}(y_1)^2 - \tfrac{1}{10}(y_2)^2 - \tfrac{1}{2}\left(22 - \tfrac{4}{5}y_1 - \tfrac{1}{5}y_2\right)^2$ is not maximized. This part of the proof is developed in Exercise 11.15.

Thus the (IC) constraint must be satisfied as an equality, that is, it must be that

$$\tfrac{2}{5}y_1 + \tfrac{1}{10}y_2 + \tfrac{1}{2}\left(22 - \tfrac{4}{5}y_1 - \tfrac{1}{5}y_2\right) - 1 = \tfrac{1}{2}y_1 + \tfrac{1}{2}y_2$$

which simplifies to

$$y_2 = 20 - y_1 \tag{11.18}$$

Using (11.18) we can reduce the maximization problem to the following unconstrained one:

choose y_1 to maximize

$$152 - \tfrac{2}{5}(y_1)^2 - \tfrac{1}{10}(20-y_1)^2 - \tfrac{1}{2}\left[22 - \tfrac{4}{5}y_1 - \tfrac{1}{5}(20-y_1)\right]^2$$
$$= \tfrac{74}{5}y_1 - \tfrac{17}{25}y_1^2 - 50.$$

Let $f(y_1) = \tfrac{74}{5}y_1 - \tfrac{17}{25}y_1^2 - 50$; then $f'(y_1) = \tfrac{74}{5} - \tfrac{34}{25}y_1$ and setting this equal to zero and solving we obtain $y_1 = \tfrac{185}{17}$; from this and (11.18) we get that $y_2 = 20 - \tfrac{185}{17} = \tfrac{155}{17}$; finally, replacing these two values into $y_3 = 22 - \tfrac{4}{5}y_1 - \tfrac{1}{5}y_2$ we get that $y_3 = \tfrac{195}{17}$. Thus, since $y_i = \sqrt{w_i}$ we get the following solution to the original maximization problem:

$$w_1 = \left(\tfrac{185}{17}\right)^2 = 118.43, \quad w_2 = \left(\tfrac{155}{17}\right)^2 = 83.13, \quad w_3 = \left(\tfrac{195}{17}\right)^2 = 131.57.$$

Let D be the corresponding contract: $D = (w_1 = 118.43, w_2 = 83.13, w_3 = 131.57)$. The Agent's expected utility from this contract is

$$\mathbb{E}[U_A(D)] = \tfrac{2}{5}\sqrt{118.43} + \tfrac{1}{10}\sqrt{83.13} + \tfrac{1}{2}\sqrt{131.57} - 1 = 10$$

and the Principal's expected utility is

$$\mathbb{E}[U_P(D)] = \tfrac{2}{5}(100 - 118.43) + \tfrac{1}{10}(120 - 82.13) + \tfrac{1}{2}(200 - 131.57) - 1 = 30.53$$

Under contract D the Agent is paid the least if the intermediate outcome ($120) obtains. If the outcome turns out to be $120 then she is paid approximately $83, while if the outcome turns out to be lower ($100) then she is paid more: approximately $118! The reason is that from a low outcome of $100 one cannot infer that the Agent did not work hard: it is almost as likely that she exerted high effort as it is that she exerted low effort. On the other hand, the intermediate outcome ($120) is much more likely if the Agent chooses low effort than if she chooses high effort, hence it makes sense to associate a relatively low payment to that outcome.

> Test your understanding of the concepts introduced in this section, by going through the exercises in Section 11.5.3 at the end of this chapter.

11.5 Exercises

The solutions to the following exercises are given in Section 11.6 at the end of this chapter.

11.5.1 Exercises for Section 11.2: Risk sharing under moral hazard

Exercise 11.1 A risk-neutral Principal wants to hire an Agent to run her firm. The Agent's utility depends on two things: money and effort. Denote effort by e and assume that it can take on only two values: e_L (for low) and e_H (for high). Let the Agent's utility function be given as follows (where m denotes money)

$$U_A(m,e) = \begin{cases} \sqrt{90+m} - 9 & \text{if } e = e_L \\ \sqrt{90+m} - 10 & \text{if } e = e_H. \end{cases}$$

Assume that if they don't sign a contract they both get a utility of zero. The Agent's effort cannot be observed by the Principal and thus cannot be made part of the contract. There are only three possible outcomes (profit levels): $\$-100$, $\$100$, $\$500$. If the Agent works hard, better outcomes are more likely than if the Agent does not work hard:

outcome (profits):	$\$-100$	$\$100$	$\$500$
probability if $e = e_L$:	$\frac{1}{2}$	$\frac{1}{4}$	$\frac{1}{4}$
probability if $e = e_H$:	$\frac{1}{4}$	$\frac{1}{4}$	$\frac{1}{2}$

Show that, of the following contracts, C is Pareto superior to B.
CONTRACT B (fixed wage): the Agent will be paid $w = 10$, no matter what the profits of the firm.
CONTRACT C (contingent wage): the Agent will get nothing ($w = 0$) if the profit of the firm is either -100 or 100, while she will get $w = 100$ if the profit of the firm is 500.

Exercise 11.2 Mr. O owns a firm. He can either run the firm himself or hire Ms. M to run it for him. If he runs the firm himself he gets a utility of 0. If he hires Ms. M, he will not be able to check whether she works hard or not. Under the management of Ms. M, the firm's profit levels and corresponding probabilities would be as follows (e denotes effort, e_L is low effort and e_H is high effort):

profit:	$0	$100	$800
probability if $e = e_L$:	$\frac{1}{2}$	$\frac{1}{4}$	$\frac{1}{4}$
probability if $e = e_H$:	$\frac{1}{4}$	$\frac{1}{4}$	$\frac{1}{2}$

Mr. O is risk neutral. Ms. M is currently unemployed and her current utility is 0; her utility function is as follows (m denotes money and e denotes effort):

$$U_A(m,e) = \begin{cases} m - 8 & \text{if } e = e_L \\ m - 10 & \text{if } e = e_H \end{cases}$$

Consider the following contracts.
CONTRACT A: Mr. O hires Ms. M and pays her a fixed wage of $10 (i.e. Ms. O's wage will be $10 no matter what the profits of the firm).
CONTRACT B: Mr. O hires Ms. M on the following terms: if the profit of the firm is less than $800, Ms. M will get nothing; if the profit is $800 Ms. M will get $24.
  (a) Which of the two contracts would Ms. M find acceptable?
  (b) How does Ms M rank the three options: (1) sign contract A, (2) sign contract B, (3) remain unemployed.
  (c) How does Mr O rank the two contracts?

11.5.2 Exercises for Section 11.3: Two outcomes and two levels of effort

Exercise 11.3 Suppose that there are only two outcomes, $X_1 = \$2,000$ and $X_2 = \$5,000$, and two levels of effort: low effort e_L and high effort e_H. The Principal is risk neutral, while the Agent's utility function is given by

$$U_A(m,e) = \begin{cases} \sqrt{m} & \text{if } e = e_L \\ \sqrt{m} - 4 & \text{if } e = e_H. \end{cases}$$

The probability of X_1 is $\frac{1}{4}$ if the Agent chooses e_L and $\frac{1}{10}$ if the Agent chooses e_H. Consider contract $C = (w_1 = 1,600, w_2 = 2,500)$.
  (a) Calculate the slope, at point C, of the Agent's indifference curve corresponding to low effort e_L that goes through contract C.
  (b) Calculate the slope, at point C, of the Agent's indifference curve corresponding to high effort e_H that goes through contract C.
  (c) Calculate the Agent's expected utility from contract C.
  (d) Calculate the Principal's expected utility from contract C.

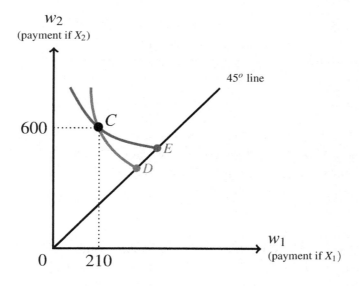

Figure 11.13: The figure for Exercise 11.4.

Exercise 11.4 Suppose that there are only two outcomes, X_1 and X_2 (with $X_1 < X_2$), and two levels of effort: low effort e_L and high effort e_H. The Principal is risk neutral, while the Agent's utility function is given by

$$U_A(m,e) = \begin{cases} \ln(m) & \text{if } e = e_L \\ \ln(m) - 1 & \text{if } e = e_H. \end{cases}$$

The probability of X_1 is $\frac{2}{5}$ if the Agent chooses e_L and $\frac{1}{5}$ if the Agent chooses e_H.

(a) Under contract C in Figure 11.13, would the Agent choose e_L or e_H?
(b) Calculate the coordinates of contract D in Figure 11.13.
(c) Calculate the coordinates of contract E in Figure 11.13.

Exercise 11.5 Suppose that there are only two outcomes, $X_1 = \$1,000$ and $X_2 = \$1,500$, and two levels of effort: low effort e_L and high effort e_H. The Principal is risk neutral, while the Agent's utility function is given by (with $a > 0$)

$$U_A(m,e) = \begin{cases} \sqrt{m} & \text{if } e = e_L \\ \sqrt{m} - a & \text{if } e = e_H. \end{cases}$$

The probability of X_1 is $\frac{1}{2}$ if the Agent chooses e_L and $\frac{1}{5}$ if the Agent chooses e_H. Consider contract $C = (w_1 = 625, w_2 = 900)$.

(a) For what values of a would the Agent choose e_H under contract C?
(b) Let $a = 1$. Find a fixed-wage contract D such that the Agent is indifferent between C and D.

Exercise 11.6 Let A and B be two contracts above the 45° line such that the Agent would choose high effort e_H under either contract. Prove that, if B lies below the Principal's indifference curve through A, then the Principal gets higher utility from B than from A, that is, he prefers B to A. ■

Exercise 11.7 Let D and E be two contracts above the 45° line such that the Agent would choose low effort e_L under either contract. Prove that, if E lies below the Principal's indifference curve through D, then the Principal gets higher utility from E than from D, that is, he prefers E to D. ■

Exercise 11.8 Suppose that there are only two outcomes, $X_1 = \$1,000$ and $X_2 = \$1,500$, and two levels of effort: low effort e_L and high effort e_H. The Principal is risk neutral, while the Agent's utility function is given by

$$U_A(m,e) = \begin{cases} \sqrt{m} & \text{if } e = e_L \\ \sqrt{m} - 1 & \text{if } e = e_H. \end{cases}$$

The probability of X_1 is $\frac{1}{2}$ if the Agent chooses e_L and $\frac{2}{5}$ if the Agent chooses e_H. Assume that, if a contract makes the Agent indifferent between choosing e_L and choosing e_H, then the Agent chooses e_H.

(a) Find the fixed-wage contract, call it D, that gives the Agent a utility equal to 24.
(b) Find the contract, call it C, that (1) makes the Agent is indifferent between choosing e_L and choosing e_H and (2) gives the Agent an expected utility of 24.
(c) Is contract D Pareto efficient?
(d) Is contract C Pareto efficient?

■

Exercise 11.9 Repeat Exercise 11.8 with the same data with one exception: the probability of X_1 is $\frac{1}{3}$ if the Agent chooses e_H. ■

Exercise 11.10
(a) What properties must contract $C = (w_1, w_2)$ satisfy in order for the Principal to be indifferent between the Agent exerting low effort e_L and the Agent exerting high effort e_H?
(b) For every $w_1 \geq 0$, let $w_2 = f(w_1)$ be such that the contract $(w_1, f(w_1))$ makes the the Principal indifferent between the Agent exerting low effort e_L and the Agent exerting high effort e_H. Find the expression for the function $f(w_1)$.
(c) Draw the graph of the function $w_2 = f(w_1)$ in the (w_1, w_2) plane and identify two regions: (1) the region where the Principal prefers e_L, (2) the region where the Principal prefers e_H.

■

11.5 Exercises

Exercise 11.11 Suppose that there are only two outcomes: X_1 and X_2, with $X_1 < X_2$, and two levels of effort: low effort e_L and high effort e_H. The Agent's utility function is given by (where m denotes money, e denotes effort and $c \geq 1$ is a constant)

$$U_A(m,e) = \begin{cases} \ln(m) & \text{if } e = e_L \\ \ln(m) - c & \text{if } e = e_H. \end{cases}$$

The probability of X_1 is p_1^L if the Agent chooses e_L and p_1^H if the Agent chooses e_H, with $p_1^L > p_1^H$.

Let the function $w_2 = g(w_1)$ be such that, for every $w_1 \geq 0$, the contract $(w_1, g(w_1))$ has the property that the Agent is indifferent between choosing e_L and choosing e_H.

(a) Find the expression for the function $w_2 = g(w_1)$.

(b) Draw the graph of the function $w_2 = g(w_1)$ and identify two regions:

(1) the region where the Agent prefers e_L,

(2) the region where the Agent prefers e_H.

∎

Exercise 11.12 Suppose that there are only two outcomes: X_1 and X_2, with $X_1 < X_2$, and two levels of effort: low effort e_L and high effort e_H. The Agent's utility function is given by (where m denotes money, e denotes effort, c is a positive constant, $U'(m) > 0$, $U''(m) < 0$)

$$U_A(m,e) = \begin{cases} U(m) & \text{if } e = e_L \\ U(m) - c & \text{if } e = e_H \end{cases}$$

The probability of X_1 is p_1^L if the Agent chooses e_L and p_1^H if the Agent chooses e_H, with $p_1^L > p_1^H$.

Let the function $w_2 = g(w_1)$ be such that, for every $w_1 \geq 0$, the contract $(w_1, g(w_1))$ has the property that the Agent is indifferent between choosing e_L and choosing e_H.

Let $A = (w_1^A, w_2^A)$ be a point (above the 45° line) at which the Agent is indifferent between e_L and e_H; thus $w_2^A = g(w_1^A)$. Find the slope of the function $g(\cdot)$ at point A.

[Hint: use the method employed in Chapter 5 (Section 5.1.4) to determine the slope of an indifference curve (or, if you are familiar with it, use the implicit function theorem).]

∎

Exercise 11.13 Ann's current fixed salary is $16,900. She is bored with her job and she will accept any new employment that does not make her worse off relative to her current situation. Peter is thinking of starting a business and hiring an agent to run it for him. Peter will not be able to monitor the agent, but knows that the agent can either be lazy or work hard. There are two possible levels of income from the business: $22,000 and $36,000. If the agent is lazy the probability of the income being $22,000 is 50% while if the agent works hard it is 40%. Peter likes money (prefers to have more rather than less) and is risk neutral. Ann also likes money, but she is risk averse; furthermore, she dislikes effort. Her vNM utility function is as follows (where m denotes money and e effort: e_L means that she is lazy and e_H means that she works hard): $U_A(m,e) = \begin{cases} \sqrt{m} & \text{if } e = e_L \\ \sqrt{m} - 3 & \text{if } e = e_H \end{cases}$. What contract will Peter offer to Ann?

11.5.3 Exercises for Section 11.4: The case with more than two outcomes

Exercise 11.14 A Principal is considering hiring an Agent to run his firm. The Principal will not be able to monitor the Agent's effort, which can be either low e_L or high e_H. There are three possible outcomes with probabilities that are affected by the Agent's level of effort, as shown in the following table:

outcome:	$X_1 = \$1,000$	$X_2 = \$2,000$	$X_3 = \$3,000$
probability if e_L :	$\frac{1}{2}$	$\frac{1}{4}$	$\frac{1}{4}$
probability if e_H :	$\frac{1}{2}$	0	$\frac{1}{2}$

The Agent's utility function is

$$U_A(m,e) = \begin{cases} \sqrt{m} & \text{if } e = e_L \\ \sqrt{m} - 1 & \text{if } e = e_H \end{cases}$$

and her reservation utility is 20. Consider the following contract (where w_i is the payment to the Agent if the outcome is X_i) $C = (w_1 = \$484, w_2 = \$900, w_3 = \$961)$.

(a) If offered contract C, will the Agent accept it?

(b) What level of effort will the Agent choose if offered contract C?

(c) Show that contract C is not Pareto efficient, by constructing an alternative contract D that Pareto dominates C. [Hint: outcome X_2 is evidence that the Agent chose low effort, thus the value of w_2 can be used to induce the Agent to choose high effort.]

11.5 Exercises

Exercise 11.15 Consider the maximization problem given on page 391, namely

$$\text{choose } y_1, y_2 \text{ to maximize}$$

$$f(y_1, y_2) = 152 - \tfrac{2}{5}(y_1)^2 - \tfrac{1}{10}(y_2)^2 - \tfrac{1}{2}\left(22 - \tfrac{4}{5}y_1 - \tfrac{1}{5}y_2\right)^2$$

subject to

$$\tfrac{2}{5}y_1 + \tfrac{1}{10}y_2 + \tfrac{1}{2}\left(22 - \tfrac{4}{5}y_1 - \tfrac{1}{5}y_2\right) - 1 \geq \tfrac{1}{2}y_1 + \tfrac{1}{2}y_2 \qquad (IC)$$

The objective of this exercise is to show that, if the (IC) constraint is satisfied as a strict inequality, then the function $f(y_1, y_2)$ is not maximized. This can be done by showing that at every point (y_1, y_2) such that $y_1 \geq 0$, $y_2 \geq 0$ and $y_1 + y_2 < 20$ (the shaded area in Figure 11.14) either $\frac{\partial}{\partial y_1} f(y_1, y_2) > 0$ or $\frac{\partial}{\partial y_2} f(y_1, y_2) > 0$ (or both), so that the value of the function can be increased by increasing either y_1 or y_2, until the (IC) constraint becomes an equality.

(a) Calculate the partial derivative $\frac{\partial}{\partial y_1} f(y_1, y_2)$ and show in the (y_1, y_2) plane the region where $\frac{\partial}{\partial y_1} f(y_1, y_2) > 0$.

(b) Calculate the partial derivative $\frac{\partial}{\partial y_2} f(y_1, y_2)$ and show in the (y_1, y_2) plane the region where $\frac{\partial}{\partial y_2} f(y_1, y_2) > 0$.

(c) Verify that the shaded area shown in Figure 11.14 is entirely contained in the union of the two regions identified in Parts (a) and (b).

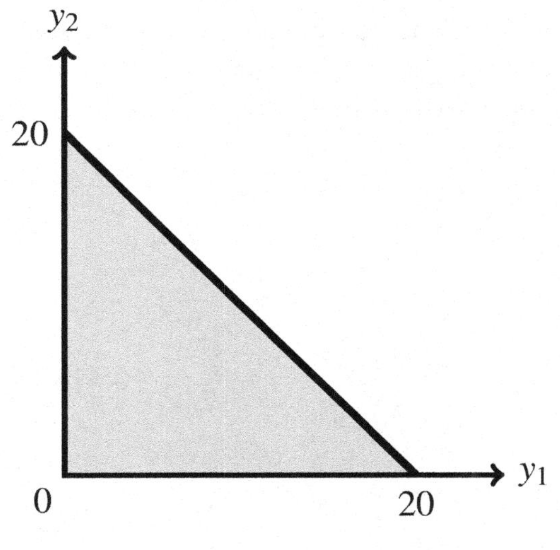

Figure 11.14: The shaded area is the set of points (y_1, y_2) such that $y_1 \geq 0$, $y_2 \geq 0$ and $y_1 + y_2 < 20$.

11.6 Solutions to Exercises

Solution to Exercise 11.1

CONTRACT B. If the Agent works hard, she will get a utility of $U_A(10, e_H) = \sqrt{90+10} - 10 = 0$; if she does not work hard, her utility will be: $U_A(10, e_L) = \sqrt{90+10} - 9 = 1$. Hence she will choose $e = e_L$, that is, she will not work hard. The Principal can figure this out and will realize that his expected utility from this contract is:
$\frac{1}{2}(-100 - 10) + \frac{1}{4}(100 - 10) + \frac{1}{4}(500 - 10) = 90$.

CONTRACT C. If the Agent works hard, her expected utility will be: $\frac{1}{4}(\sqrt{90} - 10) + \frac{1}{4}(\sqrt{90} - 10) + \frac{1}{2}(\sqrt{90+100} - 10) = 1.635$. If she does not work hard, her expected utility will be: $\frac{1}{2}(\sqrt{90} - 9) + \frac{1}{4}(\sqrt{90} - 9) + \frac{1}{4}(\sqrt{90+100} - 9) = 1.561$. Hence she will choose e_H, that is, she will work hard. The Principal can figure this out and will realize that his expected utility from this contract is: $\frac{1}{4}(-100) + \frac{1}{4}(100) + \frac{1}{2}(500 - 100) = 200$.

Thus contract C is Pareto superior to contract B, despite the fact that it does not allocate risk optimally. □

Solution to Exercise 11.2

Let us first see what wold happen under each contract.

CONTRACT A. If Ms. M chooses $e = e_L$ her utility is $10 - 8 = 2$, if she chooses $e = e_H$ her utility is $10 - 10 = 0$. Hence she will choose $e = e_L$. Hence Mr. O's expected utility is $\frac{1}{2}(-10) + \frac{1}{4}(100 - 10) + \frac{1}{4}(800 - 10) = 210$.

CONTRACT B. If Ms. M chooses $e = e_L$ her expected utility is $\frac{1}{2}(-8) + \frac{1}{4}(-8) + \frac{1}{4}(24 - 8) = -2$. If she chooses $e = e_H$ her expected utility is $\frac{1}{4}(-10) + \frac{1}{4}(-10) + \frac{1}{2}(24 - 10) = 2$. Thus she will choose $e = e_H$. Hence Mr. O's expected utility is $\frac{1}{4}(0) + \frac{1}{4}(100) + \frac{1}{2}(800 - 24) = 413$.

(a) Ms. M would find both contracts acceptable, since they give her (with the appropriate choice of effort) higher utility than her current level of utility.
(b) Ms. M is indifferent between the two contracts and prefers either of them to remaining unemployed.
(c) Mr. O prefers contract B to contract A. □

Solution to Exercise 11.3

(a) The slope is

$$-\frac{\frac{1}{4} \frac{1}{2\sqrt{1,600}}}{\frac{3}{4} \frac{1}{2\sqrt{2,500}}} = -\frac{5}{12} = -0.4167.$$

(b) The slope is

$$-\frac{1}{9} \frac{\sqrt{2,500}}{\sqrt{1,600}} = -\frac{5}{36} = -0.1389.$$

(c) First we have to figure out whether the Agent will choose e_L or e_H under contract C.
- $\mathbb{E}[U_A(C, e_L)] = \frac{1}{4}\sqrt{1,600} + \frac{3}{4}\sqrt{2,500} = 47.5$.
- $\mathbb{E}[U_A(C, e_H)] = \frac{1}{10}\sqrt{1,600} + \frac{9}{10}\sqrt{2,500} - 4 = 45$.

11.6 Solutions to Exercises

Thus the Agent will choose e_L and her expected utility is 47.5.

(d) $\mathbb{E}[U_P(C)] = \frac{1}{4}(2{,}000 - 1{,}600) + \frac{3}{4}(5{,}000 - 2{,}500) = 1{,}975.$ □

Solution to Exercise 11.4

First of all, note that the steeper indifference curve corresponds to e_L and the less steep one to e_H.

(a) The Agent's expected utility from contract C is:

(1) if she chooses e_L: $\frac{2}{5}\ln(210) + \frac{3}{5}\ln(600) = 5.977$,

(2) if she chooses e_H: $\frac{1}{5}\ln(210) + \frac{4}{5}\ln(600) - 1 = 5.187$.

Thus the Agent would choose e_L.

(b) $D = (m_D, m_D)$ where m_D is the solution to $\ln(m) = \frac{2}{5}\ln(210) + \frac{3}{5}\ln(600) = 5.977$. Thus $m_D = 394.26$.

(c) $E = (m_E, m_E)$ where m_E is the solution to $\ln(m) - 1 = \frac{1}{5}\ln(210) + \frac{4}{5}\ln(600) - 1 = 5.187$. Thus $m_E = 486.38$. □

Solution to Exercise 11.5

(a) The Agent's expected utility from contract C is:

(1) if she chooses e_L: $\frac{1}{2}\sqrt{625} + \frac{1}{2}\sqrt{900} = 27.5$,

(2) if she chooses e_H: $\frac{1}{5}\sqrt{625} + \frac{4}{5}\sqrt{900} - a = 29 - a$.

Thus the Agent will choose e_H if $a < 1.5$ (and will be indifferent if $a = 1.5$).

(b) When $a = 1$ under contract C the Agent chooses e_H and gets a utility of 28. Thus $D = (m, m)$ where m is the solution to $\sqrt{m} = 28$, that is, $m = 784$ (under a fixed-wage contract the Agent chooses e_L). □

Solution to Exercise 11.6

This is a repetition of the argument used in Chapter 2 (Section 2.5). Let A' be the point at the intersection of the 45° line and the Principal's (straight-line) H-indifference curve through point $A = (w_1^A, w_2^A)$ and let B' be the point at the intersection of the 45° line and the Principal's (straight-line) H-indifference curve through point $B = (w_1^B, w_2^B)$. Then $A' = (m_{A'}, m_{A'})$, where $m_{A'} = p_1^H w_1^A + (1 - p_1^H) w_2^A$, and $B' = (m_{B'}, m_{B'})$, where $m_{B'} = p_1^H w_1^B + (1 - p_1^H) w_2^B$. Since point B lies below the Principal's indifference curve through A,

$$m_{B'} < m_{A'}. \tag{11.19}$$

For the Principal, the expected utility of A is the same as the expected utility of A' (since they belong to the same indifference curve) and the latter is equal to $\mathbb{E}^H[X] - m_{A'}$, where $\mathbb{E}^H[X] = p_1^H X_1 + (1 - p_1^H) X_2$; similarly, the expected utility of B is the same as the expected utility of B' (since they belong to the same indifference curve) and the latter is equal to $\mathbb{E}^H[X] - m_{B'}$. Thus, by (11.19), the expected utility of B' is greater than the expected utility of A'; therefore, the expected utility of B is greater than the expected utility of A. □

Solution to Exercise 11.7

This is a repetition of the argument used in Exercise 11.6. Let D' be the point at the intersection of the $45°$ line and the Principal's (straight-line) L-indifference curve through point $D = (w_1^D, w_2^D)$ and E' be the point at the intersection of the $45°$ line and the Principal's (straight-line) L-indifference curve through point $E = (w_1^E, w_2^E)$. Then $D' = (m_{D'}, m_{D'})$, where $m_{D'} = p_1^L w_1^D + (1-p_1^L) w_2^D$, and $E' = (m_{E'}, m_{E'})$, where $m_{E'} = p_1^L w_1^E + (1-p_1^L) w_2^E$. Since point E lies below the Principal's indifference curve through D,

$$m_{E'} < m_{D'}. \tag{11.20}$$

For the Principal, the expected utility of D is the same as the expected utility of D' (since they belong to the same indifference curve) and the latter is equal to $\mathbb{E}^L[X] - m_{D'}$, where $\mathbb{E}^L[X] = p_1^L X_1 + (1-p_1^L) X_2$; similarly, the expected utility of E is the same as the expected utility of E' (since they belong to the same indifference curve) and the latter is equal to $\mathbb{E}^L[X] - m_{E'}$. Thus, by (11.20), the expected utility of E' is greater than the expected utility of D'; therefore, the expected utility of E is greater than the expected utility of D. □

Solution to Exercise 11.8

(a) Since it is a fixed-wage contract, the Agent will choose e_L. Thus $D = (m,m)$ where m is the solution to $\sqrt{m} = 24$, that is, $m = 576$.

(b) Contract $C = (w_1, w_2)$ is given by the solution to the following equations:

$$\tfrac{2}{5}(\sqrt{w_1} - 1) + \tfrac{3}{5}(\sqrt{w_2} - 1) = \tfrac{1}{2}\sqrt{w_1} + \tfrac{1}{2}\sqrt{w_2}$$

$$\tfrac{2}{5}(\sqrt{w_1} - 1) + \tfrac{3}{5}(\sqrt{w_2} - 1) = 24$$

The solution is $w_1 = 361$ and $w_2 = 841$. Thus $C = (361, 841)$.

In order to answer Parts (c) and (d) let us see how the Principal ranks the two contracts C and D. $\mathbb{E}[U_P(D)] = \tfrac{1}{2}(1,000 - 576) + \tfrac{1}{2}(1,500 - 576) = 674$, while

$$\mathbb{E}[U_P(C)] = \tfrac{2}{5}(1,000 - 361) + \tfrac{3}{5}(1,500 - 841) = 651.$$

Thus $D \succ_P C$. Hence, by Proposition 11.3.2, D is the only Pareto efficient contract on the utility locus of the Agent corresponding to a utility of 24. Thus

(c) Yes, contract D is Pareto efficient.

(d) No, contract C is not Pareto efficient. □

Solution to Exercise 11.9

(a) The answer to this question remains the same: $D = (576, 576)$.

(b) Contract $C = (w_1, w_2)$ is given by the solution to the following equations:

$$\tfrac{1}{3}(\sqrt{w_1} - 1) + \tfrac{2}{3}(\sqrt{w_2} - 1) = \tfrac{1}{2}\sqrt{w_1} + \tfrac{1}{2}\sqrt{w_2}$$

$$\tfrac{1}{3}(\sqrt{w_1} - 1) + \tfrac{2}{3}(\sqrt{w_2} - 1) = 24$$

The solution is $w_1 = 441$ and $w_2 = 729$. Thus $C = (441, 729)$.

11.6 Solutions to Exercises

In order to answer Parts (c) and (d) let us see how the Principal ranks the two contracts C and D. As calculated in the previous exercise, $\mathbb{E}[U_P(D)] = 674$, while

$$\mathbb{E}[U_P(C)] = \tfrac{1}{3}(1{,}000 - 441) + \tfrac{2}{3}(1{,}500 - 729) = 700.33.$$

Thus $C \succ_P D$. Hence, by Proposition 11.3.2, C is the only Pareto efficient contract on the utility locus of the Agent corresponding to a utility of 24. Thus

(c) No, contract D is not Pareto efficient.

(d) Yes, contract C is Pareto efficient. □

Solution to Exercise 11.10

(a) It must be that

$$p_1^L(X_1 - w_1) + (1 - p_1^L)(X_2 - w_2) = p_1^H(X_1 - w_1) + (1 - p_1^H)(X_2 - w_2)$$

that is (rearranging the terms), $(p_1^L - p_1^H)(X_1 - w_1) = (p_1^L - p_1^H)(X_2 - w_2)$ and, dividing both sides by $(p_1^L - p_1^H)$,

$$X_1 - w_1 = X_2 - w_2. \tag{11.21}$$

(b) It follows from (11.21) that

$$w_2 = X_2 - X_1 + w_1$$

which is the equation of a straight line with slope 1.

(c) See Figure 11.15. □

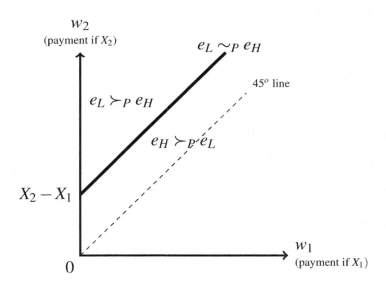

Figure 11.15: The straight line is the set of contracts that make the Principal indifferent between the Agent choosing low effort e_L and the Agent choosing high effort e_H. For contracts above the line the Principal is better off if the Agent chooses low effort and for contracts below the line the Principal is better off if the Agent chooses high effort.

Solution to Exercise 11.11

(a) A contract (w_1, w_2) makes the Agent indifferent between e_L and e_H if and only if

$$p_1^L \ln(w_1) + (1 - p_1^L) \ln(w_2) = p_1^H \ln(w_1) + (1 - p_1^H) \ln(w_2) - c.$$

Rearranging the terms in the above equation we get

$$\ln(w_2) - \ln(w_1) = \frac{c}{p_1^L - p_1^H}.$$

Note that, since $c \geq 1$ and $0 < p_1^L - p_1^H < 1$, $\frac{c}{p_1^L - p_1^H} > 1$. From the above equation we get that (e denotes the irrational number 2.71828...)

$$e^{\ln(w_2) - \ln(w_1)} = e^{\frac{c}{p_1^L - p_1^H}} \quad \text{that is} \quad \frac{w_2}{w_1} = e^{\frac{c}{p_1^L - p_1^H}}.$$

Thus $g(w_1) = e^{\frac{c}{p_1^L - p_1^H}} w_1$.

(b) See Figure 11.16. □

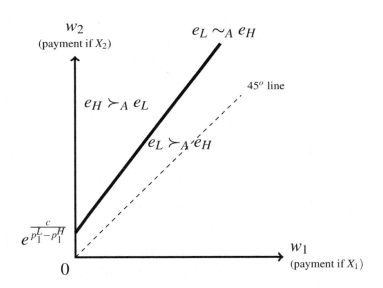

Figure 11.16: The straight line is the set of contracts that make the Agent indifferent between choosing low effort e_L and choosing high effort e_H. For contracts above the line the Agent is better off choosing high effort and for contracts below the line the Agent is better off choosing low effort.

11.6 Solutions to Exercises

Solution to Exercise 11.12

Let $A = \left(w_1^A, w_2^A\right)$ be a contract (above the 45° line) that makes the Agent indifferent between choosing e_L and choosing e_H. Then

$$p_1^L U(w_1^A) + \left(1 - p_1^L\right) U(w_2^A) = p_1^H U(w_1^A) + \left(1 - p_1^H\right) U(w_2^A) - c,$$

that is,

$$U(w_2^A) - U(w_1^A) = \frac{c}{p_1^L - p_1^H}. \tag{11.22}$$

Let $B = \left(w_1^B, w_2^B\right)$ be a contract close to A that also makes the Agent indifferent between choosing e_L and choosing e_H. Then

$$U(w_2^B) - U(w_1^B) = \frac{c}{p_1^L - p_1^H}. \tag{11.23}$$

We want to calculate the slope of the segment that joins A and B. Since B is close to A,

$$U(w_1^B) \simeq U(w_1^A) + U'(w_1^A)\left(w_1^B - w_1^A\right), \tag{11.24}$$

$$U(w_2^B) \simeq U(w_2^A) + U'(w_2^A)\left(w_2^B - w_2^A\right). \tag{11.25}$$

Replacing (11.24) and (11.25) in (11.23) we get

$$\underbrace{U(w_2^A) - U(w_1^A)}_{=\frac{c}{p_1^L - p_1^H} \text{ by (11.22)}} + U'(w_2^A)\left(w_2^B - w_2^A\right) - U'(w_1^A)\left(w_1^B - w_1^A\right) = \frac{c}{p_1^L - p_1^H}$$

from which it follows that

$$U'(w_2^A)\left(w_2^B - w_2^A\right) - U'(w_1^A)\left(w_1^B - w_1^A\right) = 0,$$

that is,

$$\frac{\overbrace{w_2^B - w_2^A}^{rise}}{\underbrace{w_1^B - w_1^A}_{run}} = \frac{U'(w_1^A)}{U'(w_2^A)},$$

that is, the slope of the curve $w_2 = g(w_1)$ at point A is $\frac{U'(w_1^A)}{U'(w_2^A)}$. Since point A is above the 45° line, $w_1^A < w_2^A$ and thus (since $U'(m)$ is decreasing because $U''(m) < 0$), $U'(w_1^A) > U'(w_2^A)$ so that $\frac{U'(w_1^A)}{U'(w_2^A)} > 1$. Hence the curve is increasing with a slope greater than 1 everywhere. □

Solution to Exercise 11.13

Since Ann is currently on a fixed salary, her current choice of effort is e_L and thus her current utility is $\sqrt{16,900} = 130$; call this value her *reservation utility*. Peter will thus make sure that he offers Ann a contract that gives her exactly her reservation utility, not more. Thus Peter will offer that contract on the 130-utility-locus of Ann that maximizes Peter's own utility. By Lemma 11.1 we know that this contract is either the fixed-wage contract $D = (16900, 16900)$ or that contract, call it $C = (w_1, w_2)$, that makes Ann indifferent between choosing e_L and choosing e_H (and gives her an expected utility equal to 130). To find contract C we must solve the following system of two equations:

$$\tfrac{2}{5}(\sqrt{w_1} - 3) + \tfrac{3}{5}(\sqrt{w_2} - 3) = \tfrac{1}{2}\sqrt{w_1} + \tfrac{1}{2}\sqrt{w_2}$$

$$\tfrac{2}{5}(\sqrt{w_1} - 3) + \tfrac{3}{5}(\sqrt{w_2} - 3) = 130.$$

The solution is $w_1 = 13,225$ and $w_2 = 21,025$. Thus $C = (13225, 21025)$. It only remains to check which of C and D gives higher utility to Peter.

Peter's expected utility from D is: $\tfrac{1}{2} 22000 + \tfrac{1}{2} 36000 - 16900 = 12,100$.

Peter's expected utility from C is: $\tfrac{2}{5}(22000 - 13225) + \tfrac{3}{5}(36000 - 21025) = 12,495$.

Thus Peter will offer Ann the contingent contract $C = (13225, 21025)$. □

Solution to Exercise 11.14

The Agent's expected utility under contract C is:

if low effort e_L: $\quad \tfrac{1}{2}\sqrt{484} + \tfrac{1}{4}\sqrt{900} + \tfrac{1}{4}\sqrt{961} = 26.25$

if high effort e_H: $\quad \tfrac{1}{2}\sqrt{484} + \tfrac{1}{2}\sqrt{961} - 1 = 25.5$.

(a) Since the Agent can achieve a utility of at least 25.5 and her reservation utility is 20, she will accept contract C.

(b) Under contract C the Agent will choose low effort, since it gives her higher utility than high effort.

(c) Since the middle outcome X_2 can only occur if the Agent chooses low effort, the Principal can provide an incentive to the Agent to choose high effort by setting $w_2 = 0$. Let us keep the value $w_1 = 484$ and find a contract with $w_2 = 0$ that gives the Agent a utility of 26.25 if she chooses high effort, by solving the equation $\tfrac{1}{2}\sqrt{484} + \tfrac{1}{2}\sqrt{w_3} - 1 = 26.25$. The solution is $w_3 = 1,056.25$. Now consider contract $D = (w_1 = 484, w_2 = 0, w_3 = 1056.25)$. The Agent's expected utility under contract D is:

if low effort e_L: $\quad \tfrac{1}{2}\sqrt{484} + \tfrac{1}{4}\sqrt{1,056.25} = 19.125$

if high effort e_H: $\quad \tfrac{1}{2}\sqrt{484} + \tfrac{1}{2}\sqrt{1,056.25} - 1 = 26.25$.

Thus the Agent chooses high effort e_H. The Principal's expected utility is:

with C: $\quad \tfrac{1}{2}(1000 - 484) + \tfrac{1}{4}(2000 - 900) + \tfrac{1}{4}(3000 - 961) = 1,042.75$

with D: $\quad \tfrac{1}{2}(1000 - 484) + \tfrac{1}{2}(3000 - 1056.25) = 1,229.875$.

Thus contract D Pareto dominates contract C. □

11.6 Solutions to Exercises

Solution to Exercise 11.15

(a) The partial derivative of f with respect to y_1 is

$$\frac{\partial}{\partial y_1} f(y_1, y_2) = \tfrac{1}{25}(440 - 36y_1 - 4y_2).$$

Thus $\frac{\partial}{\partial y_1} f(y_1, y_2) > 0$ if and only if $y_2 < 110 - 9y_1$. The set of points (y_1, y_2) such that $\frac{\partial}{\partial y_1} f(y_1, y_2) > 0$ is shown as the shaded area in Figure 11.17.

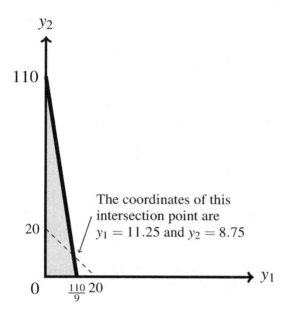

Figure 11.17: The shaded area is the set of points (y_1, y_2) such that $y_2 < 110 - 9y_1$ (equivalently, such that $\frac{\partial}{\partial y_1} f(y_1, y_2) > 0$). (The drawing is not accurate in terms of scale, because we wanted the coordinates to be spaced sufficiently apart to be readable.)

(b) The partial derivative of f with respect to y_2 is

$$\frac{\partial}{\partial y_2} f(y_1, y_2) = \tfrac{1}{25}(110 - 4y_1 - 6y_2).$$

Thus $\frac{\partial}{\partial y_2} f(y_1, y_2) > 0$ if and only if $y_2 < \tfrac{55}{3} - \tfrac{2}{3}y_1$. The set of points (y_1, y_2) such that $\frac{\partial}{\partial y_2} f(y_1, y_2) > 0$ is shown as the shaded area in Figure 11.18.

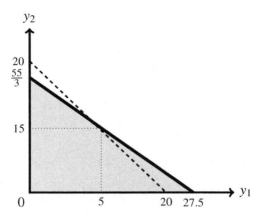

Figure 11.18: The shaded area is the set of points (y_1, y_2) such that $y_2 < \frac{55}{3} - \frac{2}{3}y_1$ (equivalently, such that $\frac{\partial}{\partial y_2}f(y_1, y_2) > 0$). (The drawing is not accurate in terms of scale, because we wanted the coordinates to be spaced sufficiently apart to be readable.)

(c) The shaded area in Figure 11.19 shows the union of the two shaded areas of Figures 11.17 and 11.18 which contains the set of points below the line of equation $y_2 = 20 - y_1$. Algebraically, this can be seen as follows. The point of intersection between the line of equation $y_2 = 110 - 9y_1$ and the line of equation $y_2 = 20 - y_1$ has coordinates $(y_1 = 11.25, y_2 = 8.75)$; from $y_1 = 0$ to $y_1 = 11.25$ the area under the line of equation $y_2 = 20 - y_1$ is entirely contained within the area under the line of equation $y_2 = 110 - 9y_1$ (that is, for $y_1 \leq 11.25$, if $y_2 < 20 - y_1$ then $y_2 < 110 - 9y_1$). The point of intersection between the line of equation $y_2 = \frac{55}{3} - \frac{2}{3}y_1$ and the line of equation $y_2 = 20 - y_1$ has coordinates $(y_1 = 5, y_2 = 15)$; from $y_1 = 5$ to $y_1 = 20$ the area under the line of equation $y_2 = 20 - y_1$ is entirely contained within the area under the line of equation $y_2 = \frac{55}{3} - \frac{2}{3}y_1$ (that is, for $y_1 \geq 5$, if $y_2 < 20 - y_1$ then $y_2 < \frac{55}{3} - \frac{2}{3}y_1$). □

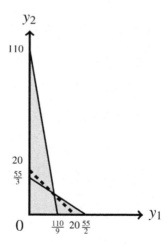

Figure 11.19: The shaded area shows the union of the two shaded areas of Figures 11.17 and 11.18 which contains the set of points below the line of equation $y_2 = 20 - y_1$.

12. Glossary

Adverse selection or hidden type
    A situation of asymmetric information where the uninformed party realizes that the terms of a proposed contract determine the composition of the pool of individuals who will find that contract acceptable; contractual terms that would be beneficial to the uninformed party, if everybody found the contract acceptable, might have undesirable consequences because of an adverse effect on the proportion of "bad types" within the pool of applicants.

Asymmetric information
    A situation where one of the two parties to a potential transaction has valuable information that is not available to the other party.

Deductible
    The amount, specified in an insurance contract, for which the insured is liable on each loss (so that, in case of loss, the insurance provider will reimburse only an amount equal to the difference between the loss and the deductible).

Expected value of a money lottery
    A number associated with money lotteries, obtained by multiplying each monetary prize by its probability and adding up all the corresponding numbers.

Full insurance
    An insurance contract with zero deductible.

Incentive contract
    A contractual arrangement according to which payments to one of the parties are based, at least in part, on the observed outcome (taken as an indicator of performance).

Index
An observable characteristic (such as race or gender) that cannot be changed.

Indifference curve
A graphical representation of the set of alternatives (e.g. contracts) that an individual considers to be just as good as some specified alternative (thus the individual is indifferent among all of them).

Lottery
A list of possible outcomes with corresponding probabilities.

Money lottery
A lottery where the possible outcomes are sums of money.

Monopoly
A industry consisting of only one firm.

Moral hazard or hidden action
A situation where the behavior of one of the parties to a contract cannot be monitored by the other party. Such behavior is relevant in that it affects the probabilities associated with the various outcomes. The un-monitored party behaves differently when fully shielded from risk as compared to the case where he/she is partly or fully exposed to the risk.

Pareto efficiency
A situation X is Pareto efficient if there is no other feasible situation Y such that everybody considers Y to be at least as good as X and at least one person strictly prefers Y to X.

Partial insurance
An insurance contract with positive deductible.

Premium
The amount paid by the holder of an insurance policy for coverage under the contract.

Principal-Agent relationship
A contractual relationship where one party (the Principal) hires another party (the Agent) to perform a task whose outcome is typically affected by external factors that are not under the control of either party.

Risk aversion
One of the possible attitudes to risk, where the individual considers a money lottery to be worse than the expected value of the lottery for sure.

Risk neutrality
One of the possible attitudes to risk, where the individual considers a money lottery to be just as good as the expected value of the lottery for sure.

Risk love
> One of the possible attitudes to risk, where the individual considers a money lottery to be better than the expected value of the lottery for sure.

Risk sharing
> The distribution of risk between the parties to a contract (typically a Principal-Agent relationship) by means of a payment scheme.

Separating equilibrium
> A situation where individuals are presented with a menu of choices and different types of individuals make different choices, thereby separating themselves from the other types.

Signal
> An observable characteristic (such as an educational certificate) which is available to, and can be chosen by, everybody.

Signaling
> The phenomenon by which some types of individuals expend resources on a signal in order to credibly convey information about themselves, since other types find it too costly to imitate the signaling activity.

Index

A

adverse selection 227, 322
affine transformation 61
Allais paradox 68
Arrow-Pratt measure 89
asymmetric information 227, 299
attitude to risk
    risk aversion 17
    risk love 17
    risk neutrality 17

B

basic outcome 55
belief 229
    revision 231
    updating 229

C

CARA 93
certainty equivalent 19
concavity 82
conditional probability 229
convexity 83
credit rationing 242
CRRA 93

D

dominance
    first-order stochastic 94, 389
    second-order stochastic 95

E

Edgeworth box 167
Ellsberg paradox 70
expected utility 57
expected value 17

F

fair odds line 28

H

hidden
    action 343, 344
    features 236
    type 227

I

incentive compatibility constraint 264
index 305
indifference curve 114

reservation 122
slope 118
individual rationality 189
individual rationality constraint 264
information 231
insurance
    budget line 128
    contract 21
    mutual 138
insurance contract
    deductible 21
    mutually beneficial 122
    premium 21
isoprofit line 25
    average 260

L

lottery
    compound 63
    money 16
    non-degenerate 17
    simple 55

M

mean preserving spread 95
menu of contracts
    finite 127
    infinite 128
monopoly 32, 124, 256, 257, 354
moral hazard 322, 343, 344, 369
multiplicity of equilibria 304
mutual insurance 138

N

normalized utility function 60

P

Pareto
    dominance 167
    efficiency 167, 236
    improvement 236, 301
    inefficiency 301, 304
    ranking 304
perfect competition 34, 125, 276

Petrakis, Emmanuel 97
Pratt, John 90
preferences
    completeness 19, 63
    continuity 31
    indifference 19
    strict preference 19
    transitivity 19, 63
Principal-Agent 165, 369

R

Rasmusen, Eric 97
rationality
    individual 189
reservation
    indifference curve 122, 189
    level of utility 349
    utility 189
    utility locus 348
revision 231
risk
    allocation 165
    sharing 165
risk premium 20
Rothschild, Michael 97

S

self-confirming beliefs 298
separating equilibrium 302, 303
signal 302
signaling equilibrium 298, 301, 303
Stiglitz, Joseph 97
stochastic dominance
    first-order 94, 389
    second-order 95, 98

T

type 254

U

updating 229
utility-of-money function 79

V

von Neumann-Morgenstern
    ranking 57
    utility function 57

W

warranty 322
wealth diagram 22

Made in the USA
Middletown, DE
07 July 2020